Inquiring after God

Blackwell Readings in Modern Theology

General Editors: L. Gregory Jones and James J. Buckley
Duke University, North Carolina; Loyola College, Maryland

Blackwell Readings in Modern Theology is a series of constructive anthologies on important topics in modern theology. Each volume brings together both classic and newly commissioned essays on a particular theme. These essays will provide students and teachers in colleges, universities, and seminaries with a critical entry to key debates. For a full contents listing or for more information visit our website at http://www.blackwellpublishers.co.uk/religion

Published works
The Theological Interpretation of Scripture
Classic and Contemporary Readings
Edited by Stephen E. Fowl

The Postmodern God
A Theological Reader
Edited by Graham Ward

Inquiring after God
Classic and Contemporary Readings
Edited by Ellen T. Charry

Forthcoming
Theology after Liberalism
Classic and Contemporary Readings
Edited by John Webster and George Schner

Inquiring after God

Classic and Contemporary Readings

Edited by

Ellen T. Charry

Copyright © Blackwell Publishers Ltd 2000
Editorial matter and arrangement copyright © Ellen T. Charry 2000

First published 2000

2 4 6 8 10 9 7 5 3 1

Blackwell Publishers Ltd
108 Cowley Road
Oxford OX4 1JF
UK

Blackwell Publishers Inc.
350 Main Street
Malden, Massachusetts 02148
USA

British Library Cataloguing in Publication Data

A CIP catalogue record for this book is available from the British Library.

Library of Congress Cataloging-in-Publication Data

Inquiring after God: classic and contemporary readings / edited by
Ellen T. Charry.
    p.   cm. — (Blackwell readings in modern theology)
Includes bibliographical references and index.
ISBN 0–631–20543–8 (alk. paper)
ISBN 0–631–20544–6 (pbk. : alk. paper)
1. Christian life. 2. Theology, Doctrinal Introductions.
I. Charry, Ellen T. II. Series.
BV4511.I53 1999
230—dc21
                                            99-32755
                                             CIP

Typeset in 10½ on 12 pt Ehrhardt
by Ace Filmsetting Ltd, Frome, Somerset
Printed in Great Britain by T. J. International, Padstow, Cornwall

This book is printed on acid-free paper.

To
DANA
who lives a godly, righteous, and sober life

Contents

Notes on Contributors — ix

Acknowledgments — xi

Time Line — xv

Introduction — xvi

1 Inquiring after God through Theological Study — 1
   Classic Texts: St. Anselm of Canterbury, St. Bonaventure — 4
   Contemporary Reflection: Diogenes Allen — 16

2 Inquiring after God by Means of Scientific Study — 29
   Sacred Texts: Psalm 8:3–4, Isaiah 45:18 — 31
   Classic Text: St. Thomas Aquinas — 31
   Contemporary Reflection: Nancey Murphy — 34

3 Inquiring after God through Discernment — 53
   Classic Text: Julian of Norwich — 55
   Contemporary Reflection: Elisabeth K. J. Koenig — 62

4 Inquiring after God when Working — 81
   Classic Texts: John Calvin, John Paul II — 83
   Contemporary Reflection: Edward Collins Vacek, SJ — 89

5 Inquiring after God through Friendship — 108
   Classic Text: Aelred of Rievaulx — 111
   Contemporary Reflection: Caroline J. Simon — 121

6 Inquiring after God in Marriage 133
Classic Text: St. Augustine of Hippo 136
Contemporary Reflection: Richard J. Foster 145

7 Inquiring after God when Afflicted 156
Classic Text: St. John Chrysostom 159
Contemporary Reflection: Simone Weil 170

8 Inquiring after God by Repentance and Forgiveness 179
Classic Text: St. Catherine of Siena 182
Contemporary Reflection: L. Gregory Jones 191

9 Inquiring after God when Meditating on Scripture 207
Sacred Text: 1 John 2:18–25, 4:1–21 210
Classic Text: St. Augustine of Hippo 211
Contemporary Reflection: C. Clifton Black 221

10 Inquiring after God when Preaching 232
Sacred Texts: Psalm 14:1–2, 2 Corinthians 4:1–7 234
Classic Texts: St. Augustine of Hippo, John Calvin 235
Contemporary Reflection: Cornelius Plantinga, Jr. 244

11 Inquiring after God around the Lord's Table 257
Classic Text: Martin Luther 260
Contemporary Reflection: Raymond Moloney, SJ 270

12 Inquiring after God through Art 278
Classic Texts: Icon Painting, Architecture, Poetry 282
Contemporary Reflection: Nicholas Wolterstorff 295

13 Inquiring after God when at Prayer 306
Sacred Text: The Lord's Prayer 309
Classic Text: St. Maximus Confessor 309
Contemporary Reflection: Bishop Kallistos Ware 322

Index 337

Notes on Contributors

Diogenes Allen is the Stuart Professor of Philosophy at Princeton Theological Seminary, Princeton, NJ. He is an ordained minister in the Presbyterian Church (USA). His most recent book is *Spiritual Theology* (1997).

C. Clifton Black is Otto A. Piper Professor of Biblical Theology at Princeton Theological Seminary and an ordained elder in the United Methodist Church. His most recent work is the *Introduction, Commentary, and Reflections on the Letters of John* in *The New Interpreter's Bible* (1998).

Ellen T. Charry is the Margaret W. Harmon Associate Professor of Systematic Theology at Princeton Theological Seminary. Her most recent book is *By the Renewing of Your Minds* (1997).

Richard J. Foster is the founder of Renovaré, an infrachurch movement committed to the renewal of the Church in all its multifaceted expressions. His most recent book is *Streams of Living Water* (1998).

L. Gregory Jones is Dean and Professor of Theology, Duke University Divinity School, Durham, NC. He is an ordained elder in the United Methodist Church. His most recent book is *Embodying Forgiveness* (1995).

Elisabeth K. J. Koenig is Professor of Ascetical Theology at the General Theological Seminary, New York, NY. Her essays have appeared in several journals including *Anglican Theological Review*, *Sewanee Theological Review*, and *Horizons*.

Raymond Moloney, SJ, is Professor of Systematic Theology and Liturgy at the Milltown Institute, Dublin. His most recent book is *The Eucharist* (1995).

Nancey Murphy is Professor of Christian Philosophy at Fuller Theological Seminary, Pasadena, CA. Her most recent book is *Anglo-American Postmodernity: Philosophical Reflections on Science, Religion, and Ethics* (1997).

Cornelius Plantinga, Jr. is Dean of the Chapel at Calvin College, Grand Rapids, MI, and an ordained minister of the Christian Reformed Church in North America. His most recent book is *Not the Way It's Supposed to Be: A Breviary of Sin* (1995).

Caroline J. Simon is Associate Professor of Philosophy at Hope College, Holland, MI. She is the author of *The Disciplined Heart: Love, Destiny and Imagination* (1997).

Edward Collins Vacek, SJ, is Professor of Christian Ethics at Weston Jesuit School of Theology, Cambridge, MA. He is the author of *Love, Human and Divine* (1994).

Bishop Kallistos of Diokleia (Timothy Ware) is Spalding Lecturer in Eastern Orthodox Studies at Oxford and a Fellow of Pembroke College. His most recent work is *The Orthodox Way* (1995).

Simone Weil (1909–43) was a French philosopher, educator, political theorist, and religious mystic. Her primary theological work was *Gravity and Grace* (1952).

Nicholas Wolterstorff is the Noah Porter Professor of Philosophical Theology at Yale Divinity School, New Haven, CT. His most recent book is *Divine Discourse: Philosophical Reflections on the Claim that God Speaks* (1995).

Acknowledgments

I am indebted to many people beginning with the series editors, James J. Buckley and L. Gregory Jones, for inviting me to prepare this volume and supporting its construction. I wish to thank Princeton Theological Seminary for defraying costs of manuscript typing and editorial assistance. It might not have come to fruition without the extensive and indefatigable editorial care of James Mead to whom I am utterly grateful.

The editor and publishers are grateful to the following holders of copyrights for their permission to reprint material included in this book:

Abbot Suger, "On What was Done under His Administration," in Abbot Suger, *On the Church of St. Denis and its Art Treasures*, ed. and trans. Erwin Panofsky (Princeton University Press, 1946); copyright © 1946, renewed © 1973 Princeton University Press. Reprinted by permission of Princeton University Press and Dr Gerda Panofsky.

Aelred of Rievaulx, *Spiritual Friendship*, trans. Mary Eugenia Laker (Cistercian Publications Consortium Press, 1974).

Diogenes Allen, "Intellectual Inquiry and Spiritual Formation," in *Essentials of Christian Community: Essays for Daniel W. Hardy*, ed. David F. Ford and Dennis L. Stamps (Edinburgh: T. & T. Clark, 1996).

Thomas Aquinas, "Whether There is a God, Article 3: Is There a God?," from *Summa Theologiae* (London: Blackfriars in conjunction with Eyre & Spottiswoode, 1964), part I, Q.2, article 3.

Bishop Kallistos Ware, "God as Prayer," in *The Orthodox Way* (Crestwood, NY: St Vladimir's Seminary Press, 1995).

John Calvin, *The Institutes of the Christian Religion*, ed. John T. McNeill, trans. F. L. Battles (Library of Christian Classics, vols XX and XXI). Used by permission of Westminster/John Knox Press (1960) and SCM Press, London (1961).

John Calvin, "Social Ethics: The Use of God's Gifts," from *Calvin: Commentaries*, ed. Joseph Haroutunian and Louise Pettibone Smith (Library of Christian Classics, vol. XXIII). Used by permission of Westminster/John Knox Press (1958) and SCM Press, London (1958).

Catherine of Siena, *The Dialogues*, from *Catherine of Siena*, trans. Suzanne Noffke, OP; © 1980 by the Society of St Paul the Apostle in the State of New York. Used by permission of the Paulist Press.

Donald Davie, "Old Dissent, 1700–1740," from *A Gathered Church* (New York: Oxford University Press, 1978). Reprinted by permission of Oxford University Press.

Stephen Gero, "The Definition of the Iconoclast Council of 754," from *Byzantine Iconoclasm during the Reign of Constantine V* (Louvain: Corpussco, 1977); reprinted by permission of Peeters, Leuven.

John of Damascus, *On the Divine Images*, trans. David Anderson (Crestwood, NY: St Vladimir's Seminary Press, 1980).

Julian of Norwich, *Showings*, from *Julian of Norwich*, trans. Edmund Colledge, OSA.; © 1978 by the Missionary Society of St. Paul the Apostle in the State of New York. Used by permission of the Paulist Press.

Martin Luther, "The Blessed Sacrament of the Holy and True Body of Christ," from *Luther's Works*, ed. E. Theodore Bachman, vol 35; copyright © 1960 Fortress Press. Used by permission of Augsburg Fortress.

Martin Luther, "Exposition of Psalm 127, for the Christians at Riga in Livonia," from *Luther's Works*, ed. Walther L. Brandt, vol. 45; copyright © 1962 Muhlenberg Press. Used by permission of Augsburg Fortress.

Raymond Moloney, SJ, "Sharing," from *The Eucharist* (Collegeville, MN: The Liturgical Press); copyright © 1995 by the Order of St. Benedict, Inc. Used with permission.

Pope John Paul II, "Laborem Exercens," from *On Human Work* (Washington, DC: United States Catholic Conference, 1981); reprinted with permission of Libreria Editrice Vaticana.

St. Anselm, "Proslogion: Preface, Chapter One," from *The Prayers and Meditations of St. Anselm*, trans. Sister Benedicta Ward (Harmondsworth: Penguin Books, 1973).

St. Augustine, *Confessions*, trans. Henry Chadwick (Oxford: Oxford University Press, 1991).

St. Augustine, "Homilies 7 and 8 on 1 John," from *Augustine: Later Works*, ed. John Burnaby (Library of Christian Classics, vol. VIII). Used by permission of Westminster/John Knox Press (1980) and SCM Press (1955).

St. Bonaventure, "On Contemplating the Most Blessed Trinity in its Name which is the Good," from *St. Bonaventure, The Soul's Journey into God – The Tree of Life: The Life of Saint Francis* (trans., Ewert Counsins; © 1978 by the Missionary Society of St. Paul the Apostle in the State of New York. Used by permission of the Paulist Press).

St. John Chrysostom, "A Treatise to Prove that No One Can Harm the Man who does not Injure Himself," from *Nicene and Post-Nicene Fathers*, ed. P. Schaff (Peabody, MA: Hendricksen, 1994), vol. 9, first series.

St. Maximus the "Confessor," "Commentary on Our Father," from *Maximus Confessor: Selected Writings*, trans. George C. Berthold; © 1985 by George Berthold. Used by permission of the Paulist Press.

St. Theodore of Studios, *On the Holy Icons*, trans. Catharine P. Roth (Crestwood, NY: St. Vladimir's Seminary Press, 1981).

Caroline J. Simon, *The Disciplined Heart: Love, Destiny and Imagination* (Grand Rapids, MI: Wm B. Eerdmans, 1997). William Kennedy, extracts from *Ironweed* (New York: Penguin Books); copyright © 1979, 1981, 1983 by William Kennedy. Used by permission of Viking Penguin, a division of Penguin Books, USA, Inc.

Simone Weil, "The Love of God and Affliction," from *Waiting for God* by Simone Weil; copyright © 1951 by G. P. Putnam's Sons; renewed © 1979 by G. P. Putnam's Sons). Reprinted by permission of The Putnam Publishing Group.

Nicholas Wolterstorff, *Art in Action: Toward a Christian Aesthetic* (Grand Rapids, MI: Eerdmans, 1980). Reprinted by permission of Eerdmans Publishing Company.

Due to the wide range of sources from which the materials have come some discrepancies of style are inevitable, although we have tried to minimize variation.

Time Line

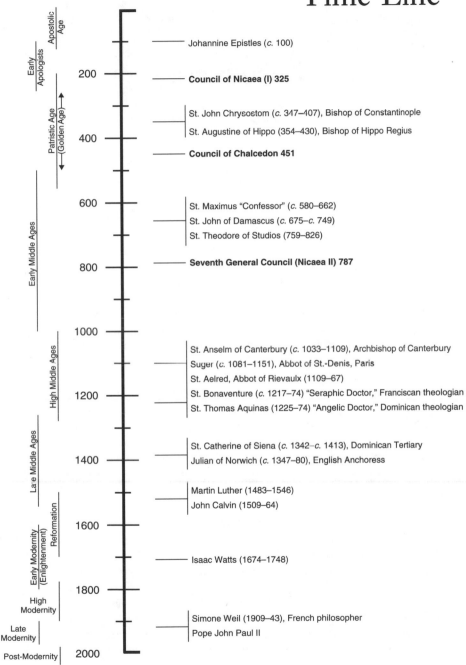

Apostolic Age

Early Apologists

Patristic Age —(Golden Age)—

Johannine Epistles (*c.* 100)

200 **Council of Nicaea (I) 325**

St. John Chrysostom (*c.* 347–407), Bishop of Constantinople

St. Augustine of Hippo (354–430), Bishop of Hippo Regius

400 **Council of Chalcedon 451**

Early Middle Ages

600 St. Maximus "Confessor" (*c.* 580–662)

St. John of Damascus (*c.* 675–*c.* 749)

St. Theodore of Studios (759–826)

800 **Seventh General Council (Nicaea II) 787**

1000

High Middle Ages

St. Anselm of Canterbury (*c.* 1033–1109), Archbishop of Canterbury

Suger (*c.* 1081–1151), Abbot of St.-Denis, Paris

St. Aelred, Abbot of Rievaulx (1109–67)

1200 St. Bonaventure (*c.* 1217–74) "Seraphic Doctor," Franciscan theologian

St. Thomas Aquinas (1225–74) "Angelic Doctor," Dominican theologian

Late Middle Ages

St. Catherine of Siena (*c.* 1342–*c.* 1413), Dominican Tertiary

1400 Julian of Norwich (*c.* 1347–80), English Anchoress

Reformation

Martin Luther (1483–1546)

John Calvin (1509–64)

1600

Early Modernity (Enlightenment)

Isaac Watts (1674–1748)

1800

High Modernity

Simone Weil (1909–43), French philosopher

Late Modernity

Pope John Paul II

Post-Modernity **2000**

◆ XV

Introduction

Ellen T. Charry

Applied Theological Inquiry

This is a work in applied Christian theology for beginning theologians. It offers an opportunity to learn from more than thirty Christians throughout history who have inquired after God in order to understand themselves and the world better. The purpose of bringing them together is to help readers think after them and so practice inquiring after God themselves.

By Christian theology we mean sustained reflection on God and the things of God. It is a group project that is taken up in every generation so that each can benefit from its predecessors. Theology is a living conversation. As in any conversation, some of the partners will disagree from time to time, sometimes passing their disagreements on to their heirs. Yet listening to earlier debates gives later interlocutors the advantage of listening to other Christians at some emotional distance so that they can avoid repeating earlier errors on one hand, and benefit from accumulated wisdom on the other.

Because Christian theology is extended conversation important themes look different from age to age. What is clear in one century may become cloudy in another and vice versa. This book exemplifies the conversational conception of theology by concatenating inquirers separated by hundreds of years.

Theological inquiry is sparked when questions arise about God and the things of God. Because Christianity was birthed by Judaism it has always interfaced with Jews, even though this has been an unusually painful and arduous conversation. Moreover, since early Christians came from the pagan world, Christian theology has continuously been in conversation with philosophical and spiritual traditions, like Stoicism and Neoplatonism. In the past three centuries Christian theology has been challenged by new ideas. This is another way of saying that Christian theology engages the conceptions of truth that surround it. Sometimes it drinks deeply of them, for better and for worse.

Since most people do not have the leisure to sit quietly and think through the beliefs of the faith, most Christians have relied on those who have been fortunate enough to do so. The church's theologians worked out the basic doctrines of God, Christ and the Holy Spirit over a period of about five hundred years and regularly revisit them. They work through the heritage of the church when addressing problems and challenges. In doing so they inevitably interact with extra-Christian frames of reference as noted above.

Theology is always written for an intended audience in a given set of circumstances: potential believers or skeptics, confused or reticent Christians, opponents of the faith. The tone and style of theology will vary with the circumstance: narrowly or broadly focused, pugnacious or irenic in tone, and so forth. Theology is written in many genres also. There are doctrinal treatises, treatises for instruction, letters, sermons, dialogues, polemics, poetry and stories, debates, and scriptural exegesis. Finally there are large-scale comprehensive and critical presentations of the entire faith, dogmatic and systematic treatments in which all the doctrines and practices are interpreted through a single theme to secure the consistency of every point of faith and practice. In this book we will consider several different theological genres.

By now it should be evident that a lot is going on in theology. How it understands its tasks varies slightly from age to age. Yet theology is properly speaking a religious undertaking that seeks to draw readers into understanding God and interpreting themselves and reality on that basis. Christian theology, then, is a conceptual framework for inquiring after the nature of reality, including oneself. This means that it is difficult to remain detached from it. People are emotionally invested in how the inquiry goes, for they themselves are at stake.

As already noted, Christian theology is entwined with Jewish theology. The Bible of the Jews became the scriptures of the Christians because Christians worship the God of the Jews. Jewish scripture interprets the world and the life of the Jewish people from the assumption that God is the center of it all. Christians interpreted the events surrounding Jesus of Nazareth in Jewish terms – the Law of Moses and the prophets and the psalms. Roman religion and pagan moral philosophy also helped them to understand him. The resulting documents became the earliest guidance for followers of Jesus. The New Testament in turn became the basis for specifying the beliefs and practices that became normative Christian faith.

Belief that God is the center of reality, the creator of heaven and earth, liberator of Israel, and the one who raised Jesus from the dead lends an understandable urgency to the theological task. For in studying God, the world and oneself are seen as part of a great divine drama of creation, suffering, and redemption. From a theological perspective articulation of this framework is necessary for properly understanding, well, just about everything. To put it directly, Christianly speaking there is no such thing as self-understanding except (*coram Deo*) as standing before God.

The religious purpose of theology, then, is to help people understand God so that they visualize and articulate themselves and reality in terms of him whom they believe to be the center of things. For example, imagine being in a group of strangers with a designated facilitator who invites each person to introduce him or herself. A Christian theological introduction would be: "I am a member of the body of Christ and my name is Sarah Comstock." Or, "I am a forgiven sinner and my name is Robert Winton." A nontheological introduction would be: "My name is Sarah Comstock and I am a teacher." Or, "My name is Robert Winton and I am from Kentucky." Of course, many Christians would introduce themselves nontheologically. This is understandable because it requires a good deal of training and effort to think Christianly, even for believers. Those who have not thought through their "Christianness" may have it jumbled up with other identities and experience conflict or confusion about it. Yet in order to know whether one is willing to stand under the authority of God one should first be clear about what is being asked, since Christian confession carries consequences and obligations.

This book is an attempt to help readers learn to think better theologically so that they may see what Christian claims (or any set of claims, for that matter) actually entail. So it applies Christianity to various aspects of life. This way one can decide whether or not one wishes to accept Christian beliefs (or another set of beliefs) with integrity. Gaining the skill to think through oneself and the world on the basis of any organized outlook puts a foundation under one's life so that it can be lived more responsibly. Learning to think and speak "Christian", then, is but one example of an intentional life. It is a good framework to practice with, since so many have undertaken it before.

Theology in Postmodernity

Beginning in the seventeenth century modernity challenged the religious foundation of western civilization. Philosophers, historians, and text critics, some of whom we will hear about in due course, found Christian beliefs unintelligible and backward. They set themselves to criticizing them on the grounds of modern reason. The doctrine of the Trinity, long-pondered and struggled with, became an embarrassment. The doctrine of Christ and the claim of his resurrection likewise did not readily pass the test of modern credibility. Christian theologians responded by reinterpreting their doctrines in terms other than divine revelation. This back and forth continued for three centuries. Many theologians agreed that Christianity had to change or die an anachronistic death.

Along with the apologetic attempt to defend religious claims, in the last 150 years an army of scholars has grown up who study Christian texts and ideas with purely historical interests. They set aside religious interests for the academic task of describing the beliefs and practices of the Christian faith, not to discern and assess what they disclose of God. Modern historical scholarship and critical analysis examine how Christian texts and doctrines came to be as they are without asking religious questions. This nonreligious enterprise was located in the university. It was a new turn for theology that had been done in universities since their inception in the twelfth century. On this view, theology as a religious undertaking is academically inappropriate. Christian communities have to fend for themselves. But this is difficult, since the leadership and the membership of the churches are all educated in the nonreligious academy where theological nurture is excluded.

All this may be beginning to change, however. Oddly enough, despite the fact that many predicted the end of religion with the rise of modernity, it seems that the turn of the millennium coincides with the end of modernism itself. The modern distinction between faith and reason, belief and objective knowledge, on which the division between history and theology depended since the seventeenth century, is no longer clear. A serious criticism of modernity (known as postmodernism) is that what once appeared to be rigorous standards of reason and logic that produced objective truth are now recognized to carry within them the particular questions, attitudes, judgments, and values of the thinker.[1] Objectivity and subjectivity can no longer be as clearly distinguished as high modernism claimed. All claims to truth carry a perspective on the issue being examined, the data evaluated, and the results offered. What Immanuel Kant thought was "pure" reason turns out to be located reason.

This does not mean, however, that getting distance on what is being examined is not possible or important – only that it is not utterly possible. Working at gaining distance on oneself as an inquirer is essential to prevent distortion and manipulation of the subject matter at hand. Self-examination becomes important for any inquiry.

Postmodernism, at least in its stronger and popularized form, takes the doubt about pure reason to an extreme and uses it as an ideology, a set of principles. Rather than encourage a self-critical located reason, that would temper manipulation of knowledge, it insists that knowledge is simply a function of power.[2] Society has been led to think some things to be true, good, and real because powerful people, who are interested only in protecting their privilege, have constructed knowledge a certain way. And since extreme postmoderns assume that people in power are malevolent, everyone else is considered to be victims. Law, government, medicine, education, art, marriage, work are all interpreted as the malevolent imposition of the interests of the few on the many. While there is truth to the claim that knowledge carries power with it, the embrace of raw power is ominous. Arguing on principle that there is only power is fundamentally nihilistic and potentially anarchist. Yet this is not the whole postmodern story.

What is being proposed is not that there is no knowledge, truth, and goodness, only that there is no broadly accepted standard for discerning these because all judgments are at least partially shaped by circumstance, training, and experience. Pure reason may be an illusion, but that does not mean that reason is a false notion. What is recognized by postmodernism is that various interpretations, ways of reasoning, frameworks of meaning are interested, not disinterested. Some interests function in a principled way to interpret reality, like Marxism, feminism, and rigorous postmodernism itself. Religious traditions may function similarly for they too interpret the world based on a clear set of principles. Race can also function as a pervasive interpretation of reality. Because reason no longer stands above all of these interests it is tempting to say that all lay equal claim to the truth. Each is no more than a rhetorical or linguistic myth, equally unprovable and undeniable.

While it is not necessarily the case that all interests are equally valid or good frameworks for interpreting reality it has become unclear how to adjudicate their claims. While appeal to shared values and authority seems impossible across competing myths this does not mean that they are arbitrary. It is not that they do not appeal to authorities but that they appeal to *different* authorities because they cling to different values. The question remains whether their appeal is to worthy authorities and what the implications of adopting any of these values would look like when applied pervasively. Judgments of this sort are crucial. Leaving the outcome to raw power politics is a less than inviting prospect.

The nihilist postmodern outlook argues that the virtues and values of western civilization are harmful: humility and self-sacrifice come in for special criticism, along with the Christian notion of sin. Freedom is offered as the highest good. Taken to its end, if freedom is the highest good, there should be no laws identifying crimes and misdemeanors, or marriage to control sexual activity. So the claim that morality is simply the imposition of the interests of power elites is an expression of the conflict among competing values – order vs. freedom, for example. Christianity too is based on a set of values, not ones that it claims people choose for themselves, however, but those given by God. Still it must argue for the goodness of its values, only now there are many competing alternatives.

What irritates rigorous postmodernism about Christianity is that it claims not to be a secular myth alongside others but the truth of God who transcends the very history that other frameworks limit themselves to. What is new is the recognition that none of these frameworks is simply the objective truth as Christianity was once thought to be, and then modernity was thought to be, and now postmodernity is reported to be. All are interpretations based on certain sets of values (goodness, power, freedom, and so on). The postmodern argument against Christianity is, then, not that it is not true but that its values are bad.

Ironically, as long as postmodernism distrusts reason it cannot disqualify a religious outlook. The modern arguments against the classic proofs for the existence of God were only valid when readers trusted reason. Once it is seen that reason itself interprets and does not simply report what is the case, arguments against the existence of God fail. The most that postmodernity can say is that it does not like interpreting reality religiously. For if all truth claims are at least in part interpretations there is no way to disqualify religious interpretations. Continuing to object to making religious claims is a holdover from modernity. It is no use objecting that Christians are victims of a false consciousness. On the terms of postmodernism everyone lives and moves in a consciousness. It depends which one one finds most adequate. Perhaps it is easiest to support the one one knows best. Yet to be sure, one should inquire further.

Recognizing that the modern division between objectivity and subjectivity no longer holds, this volume presents Christian theology as a religious activity. It works through a set of beliefs and practices that carry with them an interpretation of self and reality and commends a way of life based on them. It is hoped that the reader will consider this possibility at least as charitably as any other, say, inquiry as political activity.

Reclaiming Theological Nurture

One of the benefits of the loss of modernity is the possibility of again taking seriously a religious vision of truth that is wider than facts and the agreement of ideas alone. Throughout modernity critics of religion suspected miracles, revelation, heaven and hell. Even more seriously, however, the modern view eliminated the possibility that truth is linked to goodness. But as modern sensibilities themselves crumble it becomes evident that knowledge *is* value-linked. In this climate, while arguments must be brought for the virtue of one value system over another, and recognizing that this must be done self-critically, and very cautiously, goodness and wisdom may again become intelligible constituents of truth. All this is to suggest that the present intellectual climate ought to be more sympathetic to a religious outlook than has been the case for the past 350 years when truth and knowledge seemed to rule God out.

In addition to this postmodern turn in the intellectual climate there is the fact that Christian theology has not stood still over the past 300 years. Modernity has enabled Christians to understand their own claims more clearly, or more deeply, and to apply them better. Believers now generally realize that if creation is very good they are bound to attend to human well-being in this world and to good stewardship of the earth's resources as well. Additionally, the modern insistence on fairness and human and civil rights has enabled Christians to see more clearly that being created in the image of God requires that people be treated well even when one disagrees with them, even when they are weak or bad, and even when one believes that they misunderstand God or lead people astray. In other words, it enables Christians to apply the dominical command to love one's enemies. All of this is to the good, and Christians owe a deep vote of thanks to the criticisms of Christianity that modernity has spawned. These have made Christian theology more truly Christian in some cases.

Still, the fact that theology has survived modernity, and that the latter is now questioned, is causing some rethinking. Perhaps recognizing that human longing and need cannot be satisfied in purely material or concrete terms (at least not for long) but require spiritual and moral guidance and aid may reopen the possibility of theology as a religious practice. This volume is offered as a contribution to that task by asking how Christian beliefs and practices can nurture people intellectually, morally, and psychologically in the course of everyday life and work.

Classic Christian theology holds that the popular understanding of strength and weakness is the reverse of what is the case. Acknowledging that one needs help, that one fails, is a sign of spiritual strength, not weakness. Those who, by the grace of God, recognize that they need to be taught by, or perhaps more pointedly, healed by God, in order to begin again, are spiritually strong, while those who exert power over others to increase their own fortunes or to build up their sense of self are weak. This book then, is written for the spiritually strong who want divine guidance and for those willing to consider that possibility.

In this spirit, although we will read classic philosophical arguments for the existence of God that seek to persuade readers that it is rational to believe in God so that they accept certain Christian propositions to win eternal life, that will not be the goal of our inquiry. Rather, the classic arguments are enlisted in the service of religious thinking along a broad front. The hope is that life with God may commend itself as a true and honorable way of understanding oneself and the world. This approach, in short, does not seek to argue for the existence of God but for the truth of life with God.

Preparing for Theological Inquiry

Because ours is an age in which admitting failure and the need for help in controlling oneself, especially from God, is viewed as weakness, while toughness, even violent toughness and bravado and the ability to gain power over others is seen as strength, it will be helpful at the outset to explain theological nurture, so that the reader will be prepared for the several inquiries contained herein. Within this it will be necessary to explain what is meant by theological knowledge, as well as how it may be acquired, for the approach to these questions will be different from other areas of study, as well as from other approaches to theological study.

Learning to think theologically requires getting inside other people's minds and thinking with and behind them. Since communication between two minds is always difficult, it will require imagination and certain virtues to enter into theological ways of seeing and thinking about things. The virtues include, but are not limited to humility, patience, modesty, faith, hope, and love. Humility is the ability to let go of one's surefootedness enough to attend to other ways of seeing, hearing, and thinking. Patience, both with oneself and with the material at hand, is necessary for this and all learning. A third virtue is intellectual modesty, for without the recognition that one lacks something, learning is not possible. The theological virtues of faith (trust that the effort is worthwhile), hope (expectation that God will make it possible), and love (devotion to the goal), are also requisite.

Now, introducing a book by telling readers that they must be virtuous in order to undertake the task is probably discouraging to most readers, and a poor strategy on the part of the author. Who would pursue such a project? Who can do it? Who would claim to be so mature? The point of bringing this up is not to establish entrance requirements for reading this book, but to point to the challenge that theological inquiry presents. For theological study is a religious practice in which God's grace may reshape the seeker. Studying theology is riskier than studying chemistry because its goal is the nourishment and transformation of the soul. Although one need not be a believer – indeed a pinch of skepticism may be healthy – one must at some point be tempted by God, in order to understand theological knowledge religiously. In a word, engaged theological study itself renders one vulnerable to God. It is already a religious activity. At this point it is appropriate to be a bit nervous.

We have now arrived at the paradoxical place where one needs to have a certain disposition of mind and heart. Yet how can this be forced? How can we possess that which we seek? The Christian answer is that one must rely on God's grace to give one the heart and mind to know "him." There seems to be no way one can beat down the door.

On the other hand, experiencing this problem itself is proper preparation for theological study. It suggests that the goal of applied theology is spiritual maturity. To press the point, it is to apprise readers that grace may intervene to turn information into wisdom. This is why theological inquiry is so risky. Other disciplines seek to impart information that may be interesting, helpful, or necessary to proceed smoothly through the world. Genuine theological knowledge, by contrast, ought to transform as it informs. That is, applied theology forms the seeker. In this regard, while God is the one sought, he is also seeking the seeker, granting grace to some to know him in this richer sense in the process. Growing in humility, patience, and modesty is already a gift of healing, for it is not something that one can do for oneself. For as soon as one says, I am or have become humble, modest, and ready to learn God, one is utterly defeated. From this perspective the proper way to prepare for theological study is to pray for God's grace. It is also the responsibility of Christians to aid one another's theological formation. So we have collected the testimony of practiced guides. Each will work a bit differently because each has a different angle of vision.

Models of Theology

Theological nurture is not something that can be talked about apart from everyday life. It must be done *in media res*, in the midst of things. This perspective appeals to a broad sense of understanding that cannot separate thinking from other psychological and emotional faculties of the soul. Appeal to this fuller understanding is now made possible by the critique of reason as pure. It is distinguishable from, yet not discontinuous with, other types pursued by the west.

One type of western theology that was mentioned earlier seeks to synthesize the doctrines of the faith. It treats all the doctrines and practices of the Christian faith to demonstrate their intellectual and theological integrity. It has two subtypes. Dogmatic theology selects a single doctrine as the most important and interprets all the doctrines around it. For example, Reformed dogmatics interprets Christian doctrines through the doctrine of the sovereignty of God. Lutheran dogmatics interprets them through the doctrine of justification by faith. Karl Barth sought to explain all the doctrines through Jesus Christ. Systematic theology selects a principle rather than a doctrine of the faith. Immanuel Kant sought to demonstrate that all the doctrines are rational.

Friedrich Schleiermacher sought to demonstrate that all the doctrines promote piety. The common interest of systematic and dogmatic theology is to show the tidiness of all the teachings of the faith.

Another theological task is apologetics. It offers a defense of the faith when it is challenged, as it has been since birth. The assumption here is that Christians must be able to give good reasons for believing as they do, especially when their claims appear absurd or malevolent to others or perhaps even to themselves. Apologetics takes various forms.

In the ancient church Christians had to defend themselves against pagans who believed that the death of Christ could not be about God because it shows weakness, not power (at least in the pagan understanding of power and weakness). They also had to defend themselves against Jews who thought that God's becoming human was impossible. Subsequently and regularly Christians have had to defend the doctrine of the Trinity against Jews and Muslims who hold to a strict monotheism and find the Christian teaching that God is Father, Son, and Holy Spirit offensive.

A polemical form of apologetics argues that intellectual objections to Christianity are ill-founded and offers a rationale for Christian belief. Or, it argues that the criticisms of Christianity are themselves false. G. K. Chesterton's famous book *Orthodoxy*, written at the beginning of the twentieth century, is a defense of Christianity against secularism and is a good example of this type of theology.

Sometimes apologetics follows a different path. Here the approach is sympathetic to a system of truth external to Christian doctrine. It seeks to reinterpret the content of the faith so that it makes sense in terms of this other sensibility. This has sometimes taken the form of rendering Christian claims lucid in terms of an external system of thought. Platonism, Aristotelianism, Kantianism, Hegelianism, Marxism, the existentialism of Martin Heidegger, and feminism have all been adopted as suggestions for understanding Christianity better. These suggestions have often served to address intellectual and moral criticisms of the faith at a time when these systems of thought appear at least as true or even truer than Christianity. Inevitably other theologians will see problems with these suggestions and offer correctives of the correctives. And so the conversation continues.

A third theological task, sometimes closely linked with systematics and apologetics and sometimes standing independently, is the modern discussion of theological method. Theological method was especially important through-out modernity, because a simple appeal to scripture and miracles was no longer intellectually respectable. It became critical when revelation could no longer support Christian beliefs and practices. Theology had to worry about the authority for its claims.

This was not new. It began in the Middle Ages when the recovery of Aristotle challenged Christian truth. Modern science created a similar crisis. Method points out where to look for the truth of God. Traditionally the sources for theology were some combination of scripture, philosophy, and the teaching of the church. Other authorities (locations for truth) are also proposed from time to time. Based on the authority of these sources, a consistent method of argument is presented, for example, the application of a fundamental doctrine or principle as with dogmatic or systematic theology. Lengthy discussion of the rationale and the procedure to be followed explain the project to the reader. This introduction functions in this capacity, wending its way through modernism and postmodernism to a vision of theology after postmodernism.

Theologians are not only the attorneys for the Christian tradition, they are also its physicians. Theology is needed to correct erroneous understandings of God and the things of God when these arise from time to time, for Christians are as likely to misunderstand their own faith as are others. For example, Christians believe that God is both just and merciful, holding human beings to standards of righteousness and yet filled with compassion at their sinfulness. Understanding how God balances these two is not easy. In some periods of Christian history one of these has been stressed to the exclusion of the other. When this happens Christians experience either despair in the face of God's wrath and the demands of righteousness, or such unrealistic support from God that they cease to hold themselves and one another accountable. Theologians assume responsibility for pointing out these weaknesses in the way the faith is being understood and offer suggestions for correcting it by reinterpreting doctrines so that they reflect the truth of God better than previously. So, if God is both just and merciful Christians must be both loved and chastised by God simultaneously. And if God is the source of goodness and wisdom – that is, the truth – his ways of being both just and merciful have implications for individual behavior as well.

All of these theological models are important and overlap one another at many points. Nevertheless, none directly seeks to disclose the theological nurture that Christian doctrines and practices may offer. Systematic and dogmatic theology address the coherence and intelligibility of the doctrines of the faith. Apologetics defends or corrects specific Christian doctrines in the face of intellectual and moral objections. People who stand outside the faith and those who maintain a degree of skepticism within the Church provide a great service to other Christians by critically examining theological claims. Discussion of method has been central throughout modernity once revelation was sliced out from under theology.

Theology as Religious Activity

As noted above, theology has different tasks to pursue. Various critics and advocates of the tradition have different concerns. Not all of them can be handled at one time. And certainly not everyone should attend to the same issue, or see an issue from the same vantage point, since that would surely lead to yet another distortion of the faith, since one is always too close to one's own concerns to see its pitfalls.

Let us review the rationale we have presented for theology as religious activity. The modern standard set by reason was that one should become or remain a Christian only if persuaded that the claims Christian belief entails are logically demonstrable. Two observations suggest that this concern no longer controls the discussion.

First, appeal to reason is not how the vast majority of Christians have either become or remained so. Few have had the skill or leisure to participate in such a refined process. This is not because individuals are not capable of grasping cognitive claims, although the number of such capacitated persons is probably far smaller than academic theologians have often imagined. Rather, it is because rational criteria alone do not account for how people live. Temperament and socialization have a lot to do with people's attitudes, expectations, and behavior. It ought to be at least as reasonable to be Christian because Christianity nurtures the soul well as it is to be Christian because Christian claims are intelligible and consistent.

Second, theology that nurtures the mind and spirit should be particularly helpful because the postmodern landscape is spiritually and morally bleak. Perhaps it is only in such a state of despair that the authority of God will appear inviting rather than oppressive. If science and technology are unable to save, perhaps salvation by God will again be seen as a "good reason" for turning to God. It will undoubtedly take a long time for this to happen, and the process will be very painful. But there is no reason for theology not to prepare itself in the meantime. As Roman civilization decayed, the Christian Church prepared to step into the breach. If history is now repeating itself, Christians would do well to learn from their own history.

Perhaps inadvertently, feminism has been most helpful in legitimating theological nurture, for it recognizes dependency and care-giving as healthy and admirable aspects of human nature. Even though it is, in many ways, an expression of the modern insistence on individual rights, feminism has paved the way for the reclamation of a broader and more realistic understanding of human nature. It balances modernity's heavy reliance on deductive reasoning, individuation, and stress on detachment with concern for attachment and mutual encouragement that are central to appreciating God's care of the soul.

The postmodern recognition of the value-ladenness of knowledge also invites the reclamation of religious thinking about areas of life that have been distanced from God during modernity. Here we look at study, science, reflective discernment, work, friendship, marriage, affliction, and art. We will also consider specifically Christian practices as religious rather than cultural practices. This is tantamount to trying on a pair of shoes before purchasing them.

To explain this attempt at religious thinking fully a few more comments are in order. Since there are potential misunderstandings in every approach to the issue at hand, three important ones must be noted here. First, the approach taken here is not an invitation to anti-intellectualism. The distinction between reflection and action is very ancient, and it is easy to let go of one side of the tension. This approach is predicated on the assumption that separating thought from action is dangerous. They are interdependent, each one necessary to enrich and correct the other. Separated, thought withers and action decays. Thought without action becomes inaccessible or, worse, divorced from life. Action without continuous reevaluation is easily corrupted. It does not matter where one begins. It has often been the practice of theology to remain within the realm of thought alone.

Here we seek to integrate thought and action, recognizing that religious inquiry shapes action. Two steps have been taken in this volume to avoid having either thought or action bolt from the other. To keep reflection rooted in action, we have organized the theological inquiries around everyday life. And to keep action from going off on its own we have rooted each consideration of everyday life in the doctrinal heritage of the church.

Second, some will object that the main form of applied theology today is liberation theology, and so this book should be written in this vein. The theory-praxis emphasis here is often interpreted politically. In the process the spiritually nourishing link between reflection and action may become obscured. Theological nurture may be thought to be apolitical, quietistic, or mystical.

One of the hopes of this volume is to dispel this impression. It is precisely to show that thoughtful theological practice rooted in Christian doctrine entails social and public responsibility. In several chapters the interpersonal and social implications of the inquiry are explicit. What is not part of its purview is a particular program of political action and critical recommendations for bringing Christianity in line with it.

A Word to Beginning Theologians

Theologizing from the midst of life is like entering a roller-skating rink in full swing. One is dropped into the middle and must begin skating. The chapters span a number of activities of life. Not everyone will experience all of them in the course of a lifetime. Although the experience of affliction is included here, some will be fortunate enough to be spared. Some will be sought, like friendship and perhaps marriage. And some may be unavoidable, like the need for forgiveness and repentance. Some will come only to those moved in a certain direction, like the practices of art and science. Some are available primarily in the church, like preaching and the sacrament of the altar. Others will be available to all, like study, scripture meditation, work, prayer, and discernment.

A word must be said about the selection of included themes and texts. While the themes were chosen to represent various aspects of life and Christian practice, there has been no attempt to be comprehensive, only suggestive. Each theme is treated diachronically, with premodern and contemporary texts, some of which have been especially commissioned for this volume, set in conversation with one another. This gives the student a long perspective on each theme. In some cases, like marriage, the ancient piece has been exceedingly influential, and contemporary reflection on the topic must come to terms with it whether directly or indirectly. In other cases, like affliction, the ancient text did not become influential, but is included because it provides a stimulating counterpoint to thinking of our own day. Theological conversation takes place across the ages, in which the latest generation is ever beholden to its predecessors who provide the foundation from which continuous rethinking draws its strength and integrity.

A reasonable, vaguely intuitive order has been imposed on the themes, beginning with the notion of theological study itself and the virtues and attitudes necessary for undertaking it. Sometimes chapters have been roughly paired, as with friendship and marriage, and preaching and sacrament. The order is not decisive, however. Because inquiring after God is done in the midst of things, and things are untidy, it would be misleading to identify a starting point. The procedure here is more like standing on the surface of a sphere and looking toward the center than reading a page beginning at the top and working toward the bottom.

It might have helped beginning students to have ordered the material chronologically, so that the student gains a feel for the development of Christian thought. But since some chapters include texts from more than one period, such ordering is not possible. A time line of the figures included herein is at the beginning of the volume. The editor's chapter introductions provide background on theological doctrines. Annotations will help orient theological beginners. Various readers and teachers may wish to begin at some point other than the first chapter and proceed in what seems an appropriate manner.

A second point about the ordering of the material may be helpful. The chapters have not been structured so as to distinguish Christian practices like preaching, prayer, and eucharist from general activities and circumstances of daily life that apply to Christian and non-Christian alike, like work, friendship, marriage, affliction, and repentance and forgiveness. The separation of what could be two categories has been avoided partly because the division is not as easy to make as may at first appear. Topics like marriage, discernment, repentance, and affliction, while they have a distinctive history in the Christian heritage, are also experiences of non-Christians. But there is also a principle at stake here. A theological outlook is comprehensive not fragmented. Given the Christian understanding that God is the center of reality and all that is belongs to "him," it makes no sense to think that one stands before God at the altar but not at the office. Every location falls under a theological purview.

The Christian view that everyone – even those who deny or are unaware of the fact – stands before God follows from the doctrine of creation. Those who take this condition seriously must theologize, that is, struggle with who they are as standers-before-God and what they are to do and refrain from doing. The theological task falls on everyone, whether they realize it or not, and whether they exercise it or not. The difference between the great theologians of history, some of whom we will encounter here, and people in the street is that the former have been more deliberate in exercising their theological responsibilities than the latter. This book is designed to help its readers become more deliberate and sophisticated theologians.

To do this we have drawn from various Christian resources: Greek-speaking Christianity and Latin-speaking Christianity, women and men, Orthodox, Catholics and Protestants, ancient, medieval, modern, and contemporary. Of course, the Christian tradition is too vast to have every instructive perspective included here. While their location shaped what these writers thought about and how they thought, they were all pondering God and inviting readers into life with him.

Notes

1   Hans-Georg Gadamer, *Truth and Method* (New York: Crossroad, 1988).
2   Michel Foucault, *The History of Sexuality*, vol. 1, trans. R. Hurley (New York: Vintage, 1978); *Discipline and Punish: The Birth of the Prison*, trans. A. Sheridan (New York: Vintage 1977); *Power/Knowledge: Selected Interviews and Other Writings*, ed. Colin Gordon (New York: Pantheon, 1980).

Inquiring after God through Theological Study

Throughout most of Christian history, theology was a spiritual undertaking. In fact, it was only with the creation of a naturalistic perspective that the idea arose that one could stand outside the spiritual realm to think about Christian claims as a set of ideas among other ideas, or as a cultural artifact among other artifacts. Interest was not in the origin of Christian beliefs and practices or how they were to be organized, but in how they could help us know and love God better and be transformed thereby. Such reflection was itself an act of obedience and service in proclaiming the truth of God.

One example of this type of theology is offered in the work of St. Anselm of Canterbury (1033–1109). Anselm was born in Italy, but spent most of his life as a monk in France. He was the abbot of a large monastery where he was responsible for the spiritual and intellectual development not only of his monks but also of the children who studied in the monastery school. He was renowned as a compassionate and wise pedagogue, a brilliant philosopher, and an advocate of the monastic life, that is, the life of prayer. In his person he embodied the unity of the spiritual and the intellectual life. He is famous for his letters encouraging friends to take up or in other ways support the monastic life, as well as for his long and eloquent prayers. Perhaps he is most well known for his logical arguments in support of contended Christian claims. The *Proslogion*, his treatise on the existence of God, known as the ontological argument, argues from the nature of existence itself. He assumes that we can conceptualize God who is perfect, but the question remains whether that reality really exists. He argues that logically it must exist. Otherwise, we could think of something greater than that which nothing greater can be thought – and that is absurd.

Although this argument has been severely criticized since the eighteenth century, it has been pivotal in the shift from reason as a means of discerning the wisdom of

◆ 1

God to reason as producing precise factual data about the way things are. This is not at all what Anselm intended, however. His goal was to enhance his spiritual life by humbling himself before God, and setting aside the distractions that kept him from enjoying the presence of God above all else. The *Proslogion* is set in a long prayer for grace in understanding God, suggesting that belief precedes understanding. This is suggested by Anselm's famous phrase, *"credo ut intelligam,"* "I believe so that I may understand." He is using rational argument to deepen or clarify beliefs he already holds. Of course, nonbelievers may also find his arguments helpful.

The second selection comes from St. Bonaventure (1217–74), an Italian who studied in Paris. He was a member of the Franciscan Order, monks who followed the mendicant way of life of St. Francis of Assisi (1181–1226). Bonaventure was dubbed the Seraphic doctor because in his writing he employed the symbol of the six-winged seraph of Isaiah's vision in the Temple (Isa. 6), that St. Francis testified appeared to him in a vision at Mt. Alverna in the form of a crucified man. In that vision the five wounds of Christ were imprinted on St. Francis. Bonaventure uses the six wings to symbolize the three stages of the spiritual journey described in his most important spiritual work, *The Soul's Journey into God*. Here is another example of the intellect seeking spiritually nourishing knowledge of God. Bonaventure wanted intimacy with God through his intellectual journey. Understanding in this sense is another word for contemplation.

Bonaventure begins where Anselm left off in the *Proslogion*. Building upon the notion that God is a logical necessity, *The Soul's Journey into God* seeks to better understand God's triunity. It invites intellectual participation in God. The journey into God is an inquiry into the doctrine of the Trinity set forth symbolically. God is seen and known through and in reflection upon things that we know or that Christians accept on faith. The sixth chapter reflects on God's goodness. Bonaventure inquires through the symbol of the seraph. Each of two paired chapters proceeds through one of the three pairs of the seraph's wings. The last pair that covers the seraph's face symbolizes the Trinity. Chapter 5 on the being of God emphasizes the unity, while chapter 6 on the goodness of God emphasizes the threeness, representing the being of God and the goodness of God, respectively. Each of the wings is in turn represented through the symbolism of one of the cherubim that face each other on the sacred ark of ancient Israel (Exod. 25).

That God is both simple and undifferentiated goodness, yet at the same time distinguishable as three "Identities" or "Persons" (*hypostases* in Greek) – Father, Son, and Holy Spirit – is a central mystery of the faith. It constitutes the distinctive Christian doctrine of God, the Trinity. Specific language developed to describe how the Father, Son, and Holy Spirit are differentiated from one another yet are one God. Although Bonaventure speaks of emanation, the preferred way of articulating the individuation and unity of the three-personed God worked out in the fourth century is to refer to the Father as ungenerated and to the Son as generated by the Father. The Spirit is spoken of as breathed, spirated, or proceeding from the Father (in the west, from the Father and the Son). To be sure that this does not imply the inferiority or subordination of the Son (Jesus Christ) and the Holy Spirit to the Father (suggesting that they are somehow less God or lesser gods), the other two are said to be of one being, or consubstantial, or co-equal with the Father. Thus, in knowing Jesus Christ and the Holy Spirit one grasps the goodness and love of God himself. God both self-communicates and reveals goodness and love in the *hypostases*, the Holy Trinity of Christian praise and worship. All three divine Identities are fully God, co-equal, co-eternal, and mutually intimate, so that through the Son and Holy Spirit, Christians may be assured that they truly know God.

By attending carefully to the divine love and goodness communicated by the Son and Holy Spirit, Bonaventure argues, the Christian becomes intimate with God, and experiences the love and goodness that are God. The great mystery to be celebrated is that the infinite goodness, power, wisdom, and love that are God become human in the Incarnation.

From this spiritual/intellectual journey Bonaventure arrives at awe and wonder at the beauty of the very being of God that embraces him. The result of this knowledge is joyous illumination. The delight is in being able to imagine one's way to the being of God, and to be spiritually nourished both by getting there and by abiding there.

Professor Diogenes Allen, the contemporary interlocutor with these classic texts, argues that the spiritual perspective that enabled these and other earlier writers to enjoy God intellectually should still be part of the theological task. Today it might be more difficult to do that because we are no longer primed for intellectual enjoyment, perhaps especially enjoyment of God. In essence – and this recapitulates the ancient Christian observation that we are hindered from knowing God by our sins – the difficulty in knowing and loving God lies in the orientation of our desires. It is difficult for moderns and postmoderns to desire God, and so it is difficult to enjoy understanding him. We tend to define happiness materially rather than spiritually, and so we may fail to enjoy the beauty of divine goodness.

In essence, Professor Allen's essay argues that if we are unable to inquire after God in order to be spiritually nourished by the intellectual journey itself, we are deprived of an important use of the mind, and so our souls atrophy. It should be no hindrance to theology to say that it requires a particular intellectual and spiritual formation made possible only by God himself. So, it is sound to argue that savoring God requires longing for God. Just as those who study painting see more and better at an exhibition than the untrained eye, those whose prayer life is lively and whose spiritual "eyes" and "ears" are well developed will more readily enjoy God. But it is not to be assumed that such training itself attunes one to God. The yearning for God and the spiritual life itself must be awakened by God's grace. Wanting God cannot be forced; it is a gift.

CLASSIC TEXTS

St. Anselm of Canterbury, *Proslogion*

Preface

At the pressing entreaties of some of my brethren I published a short work as an example of meditation on the meaning of faith, from the point of view of someone who, by silent reasoning in his own mind, inquires into things about which he is ignorant. When I reflected that this consisted in a connected chain of many arguments, I began to ask myself if it would be possible to find one single argument, needing no other proof than itself, to prove that God really exists, that he is the highest good, needing nothing, that it is he whom all things need for their being and well-being, and to prove whatever else we believe about the nature of God. I turned this over in my mind often and carefully; sometimes it seemed to me that what I was seeking was almost within my grasp; sometimes it eluded the keenness of my thought completely; so at last in desperation I was going to give up looking for something that it was impossible to find. But when I wanted to put the idea entirely out of my mind, lest it occupy me in vain and so keep out other ideas in which I could make some progress, then it began to force itself upon me with increasing urgency, however much I refused and resisted it. So one day, when I was tired out with resisting its importunity, that which I had despaired of finding came to me, in the conflict of my thoughts, and I welcomed eagerly the very thought which I had been so anxious to reject.

It seemed to me that this thing which had given me such joy to discover would, if it were written down, give pleasure to any who might read it. So I have written the following short work, dealing with this matter and with several others, from the point of view of someone trying to raise his mind to the contemplation of God, and seeking to understand what he believes. It does not seem to me that either this work or the one I mentioned before deserves to be called a book or to bear the name of its author; but I do not think they should be distributed without some sort of title, which might make those into whose hands they come read them, so I have given them these titles: the first, "An example of Meditation on the Meaning of Faith"; and the second, "Faith in Search of Understanding".

Under these titles they have both already been transcribed by several people, and many of them (above all the reverend archbishop of Lyons, Hugh, apostolic delegate in Gaul, who has commanded this by his apostolic authority) have urged me to put my name on them. For the sake of greater convenience I have called the first book Monologion, that is, a soliloquy; and the other Proslogion, that is, a colloquy.

Chapter 1: In which the mind is aroused to the contemplation of God

Come now, little man,
turn aside for a while from your daily employment,
escape for a moment from the tumult of your thoughts.
Put aside your weighty cares,
let your burdensome distractions wait,
free yourself awhile for God
and rest awhile in him.
Enter the inner chamber of your soul,
shut out everything except God
and that which can help you in seeking him,
and when you have shut the door, seek him.
Now, my whole heart, say to God,
"I seek your face,
Lord, it is your face I seek."

O Lord my God,
teach my heart where and how to seek you,
where and how to find you.
Lord, if you are not here but absent,
where shall I seek you?
But you are everywhere, so you must be here,
why then do I not seek you?
Surely you dwell in light inaccessible –
where is it? and how can I
have access to light which is inaccessible?
Who will lead me and take me into it
so that I may see you there?
By what signs, under what forms, shall I seek you?
I have never seen you, O Lord my God,
I have never seen your face.
Most High Lord,
what shall an exile do
who is as far away from you as this?
What shall your servant do,
eager for your love, cast off far from your face?

He longs to see you,
but your countenance is too far away.
He wants to have access to you,
but your dwelling is inaccessible.
He longs to find you,
but he does not know where you are.
He loves to seek you,
but he does not know your face.
Lord, you are my Lord and my God,
and I have never seen you.
You have created and re-created me,
all the good I have comes from you,
and still I do not know you.
I was created to see you,
and I have not yet accomplished that for which I was made.
How wretched is the fate of man
when he has lost that for which he was created.
How hard and cruel was the Fall.
What has man lost, and what has he found?
What has he left, and what is left to him?
He has lost blessedness for which he was made
and he has found wretchedness for which he was not made.
He had left that without which there is no happiness,
and he has got that which is nothing but misery.
Once man did eat angels' food,
and now he hungers for it;
now he eats the bread of sorrow,
which then he knew nothing of.
Ah, grief common to all men,
lamentation of all the sons of Adam.
Adam was so full he belched, we are so hungry we sigh;
he had abundance, and we go begging.
He held what he had in happiness and left it in misery;
we are unhappy in our wants and miserable in our desires,
and ah, how empty we remain.
Why did he not keep for us that which he possessed so easily,
and we lack despite such labour?
Why did he shut out our light
and surround us with darkness?
Why did he take away our life and give us the hurt of death?
From whence have we wretched men been pushed down,
to what place are we being pushed on?
From what position have we been cast down,
where are we being buried?
From our homeland into exile,
from the vision of God into our own blindness,

from the deathless state in which we rejoiced
into the bitterness of a death to be shuddered at.
Wretched exchange, so great a good for so much evil.
A grievous loss, a grievous sorrow,
the whole thing is grievous.

Alas, I am indeed wretched,
one of those wretched sons of Eve,
separated from God!
What have I begun, and what accomplished?
Where was I going and where have I got to?
To what did I reach out, for what do I long?
I sought after goodness, and lo, here is turmoil;
I was going towards God, and I was my own impediment.
I sought for peace within myself,
and in the depths of my heart I found trouble and sorrow.
I wanted to laugh for the joy of my heart,
and the pain of my heart made me groan.
It was gladness I was hoping for,
but sighs came thick and fast.

O Lord, how long?
How long, Lord, will you turn your face from us?
When will you look upon us and hear us?
When will you enlighten our eyes and show us your face?
When will you give yourself to us again?
Look upon us, Lord, and hear us,
enlighten us and show yourself to us.
Give yourself to us again that it may be well with us,
for without you it is ill with us.
Have mercy on us,
as we strive and labour to come to you,
for without you we can do nothing well.
You have invited us to cry out, "Help us":
I pray you, Lord, let me not sigh without hope,
but hope and breathe again.
Let not my heart become bitter because of its desolation,
but sweeten it with your consolation.
When I was hungry I began to seek you, Lord;
do not let me go hungry away.
I came to you famished;
do not let me go from you unfed.
Poor, I have come to one who is rich,
miserable, I have come to one who is merciful;
do not let me return empty and despised.
If before I eat I sigh,

after my sighs give me to eat.
Lord, I am so bent I can only look downwards,
raise me, that I may look upwards.
My iniquities have gone over my head,
they cover me and weigh me down like a heavy burden.
Take this weight, this covering, from me,
lest the pit close its mouth over me.
Let me discern your light,
whether from afar or from the depths.
Teach me to seek you,
and as I seek you, show yourself to me,
for I cannot seek you unless you show me how,
and I will never find you
unless you show yourself to me.
Let me seek you by desiring you,
and desire you by seeking you;
let me find you by loving you,
and love you in finding you.

I confess, Lord, with thanksgiving,
that you have made me in your image,
so that I can remember you, think of you, and love you.
But that image is so worn and blotted out by faults,
so darkened by the smoke of sin,
that it cannot do that for which it was made,
unless you renew and refashion it.
Lord, I am not trying to make my way to your height,
for my understanding is in no way equal to that,
but I do desire to understand a little of your truth
which my heart already believes and loves.
I do not seek to understand so that I may believe,
but I believe so that I may understand;
and what is more,
I believe that unless I do believe I shall not understand.

Chapter 2: That God really exists

Now, Lord, since it is you who gives understanding to faith, grant me to
understand as well as you think fit, that you exist as we believe, and that you
are what we believe you to be. We believe that you are that thing than which
nothing greater can be thought. Or is there nothing of that kind in existence,
since "the fool has said in his heart, there is no God" [Ps. 14:1]? But when
the fool hears me use this phrase, "something than which nothing greater
can be thought," he understands what he hears; and what he understands

is in his understanding, even if he does not understand that it exists. For it is one thing to have something in the understanding, but quite another to understand that it actually exists. It is like a painter who, when he thinks out beforehand what he is going to create, has it in his understanding, but he does not yet understand it as actually existing because he has not yet painted it. But when he has painted it, he both has it in his understanding and actually has it, because he has created it. So the fool has to agree that the concept of something than which nothing greater can be thought exists in his understanding, since he understood what he heard and whatever is understood is in the understanding. And certainly that than which nothing greater can be thought cannot exist only in the understanding. For if it exists only in the understanding, it is possible to think of it existing also in reality, and that is greater. If that than which nothing greater can be thought exists in the understanding alone, then this thing than which nothing greater can be thought is something than which a greater can be thought. And this is clearly impossible. Therefore there can be no doubt at all that something than which a greater cannot be thought exists both in the understanding and in reality.

Chapter 3: That which it is not possible to think of as not existing

This *is* so truly, that it is not possible to think of it not existing. For it is possible to think of something existing which it is not possible to think of as not existing, and that is greater than something that can be thought not to exist. If that than which nothing greater can be thought, can be thought of as not existing, then that than which nothing greater can be thought is not the same as that than which nothing greater can be thought. And that simply will not do. Something than which nothing greater can be thought so truly exists that it is not possible to think of it as not existing.

This being is yourself, our Lord and God. Lord my God, you so truly are, that it is not possible to think of you as not existing. And rightly so. For if someone's mind could think of something better than you, the creature would rise higher than its creator and would judge its creator; which is clearly absurd. For whatever exists except you alone can be thought of as not existing. Therefore you alone of all most truly are, and you exist most fully of all things. For nothing else is as true as that, and therefore it has *less* existence. So why does the fool say in his heart, "there is no God" [Ps. 14:1], when it is perfectly clear to the reasoning mind that you exist most fully of all? Why, except that he is indeed stupid and a fool?

Chapter 4: That what the fool said in his heart is something that it is not possible to think

Now how has he "said in his heart" what it is not possible to think; for how could he avoid thinking that which he "said in his heart," for to say in one's heart is to think? But if he really did, or rather because he really did, both think, because he said in his heart, and not say in his heart, because he was not able to think, then there is not only one way of saying in one's heart and thinking. For in a way one thinks a thing when one thinks the word that signifies the thing; but one thinks it in another way when the thing itself is understood. So in one way it is possible to entertain the concept that God does not exist, but not in the other way. For no one who truly understands that which God is, can think that God does not exist, though he may say those words in his heart, either without any, or with a special, meaning. For God is that than which nothing greater can be thought. Whoever truly understands this, understands that [God] is of such a kind of existence that he cannot be thought not to exist. So whoever understands this to be the nature of God, cannot think of him as not existing.

Thank you, good Lord, thank you, for it was by your gift that I first believed, and now by your illumination I understand; if I did not want to believe that you existed, still I should not be able not to understand it.

Chapter 5: God is whatever it is better to be than not to be; he exists in himself alone; and he creates everything else out of nothing

What are you, then, Lord God, you than whom nothing greater can be thought? What are you but that which exists alone over all things, and has made everything else out of nothing? For whatever is not that, is something less than can be thought; but this cannot be thought about you. Then what good can be lacking to the highest good, through whom all other good exists? So you are just, true, blessed, and whatever it is better to be than not to be. For it is better to be just than unjust, blessed than not blessed.

St. Bonaventure, *The Soul's Journey into God*

Chapter Six: On contemplating the most blessed trinity in its name which is good

1. After considering the essential attributes of God,
the eye of our intelligence
should be raised to look upon
the most blessed Trinity,
so that the second Cherub
may be placed alongside the first.
Now just as being itself is
the root principle
of viewing the essential attributes,
and the name
through which the others become known,
so the good itself is
the principal foundation
for contemplating the emanations.

2. See, then, and observe
that the highest good is without qualification
that than which no greater can be thought.
And it is such
that it cannot rightly be thought
not to be,
since to be is in all ways better than not to be;
it is such
that it cannot rightly be thought of unless it be thought of
as three and one.
For good is said to be
self-diffusive;
therefore the highest good must be
most self-diffusive.
But the greatest self-diffusion cannot exist unless it is
actual and intrinsic,
substantial and hypostatic [universal and identifiable],
natural and voluntary,
free and necessary,
lacking nothing and perfect.
Therefore, unless there were eternally in the highest good

a production which is actual and consubstantial [with the Father],
and a hypostasis [identity] as noble as the producer,
as in the case in a producing by way of generation [i.e. Christ] and
aspiration [i.e. Holy Spirit],
so that it is from an eternal principle eternally coproducing
so that there would be a beloved [Christ]
and a cobeloved [Holy Spirit],
the one generated and the other spirated,
and this is
the Father and the Son and the Holy Spirit –
unless these were present,
it would by no means be the highest good
because it would not diffuse itself in the highest degree.
For the diffusion in time in creation
is no more than a center
or point
in relation to the immensity of the divine goodness.
Hence another diffusion can be conceived
greater than this,
namely, one in which
the one diffusing [Father] communicates to the other
his entire substance and nature.
Therefore it would not be the highest good
if it could lack this,
either in reality or in thought.
If, therefore, you can behold with your mind's eye
the purity of goodness,
which is the pure act
of a principle loving in charity
with a love
that is both free and due and a mixture of both,
which is the fullest diffusion
by way of nature and will,
which is a diffusion by way of the Word [Logos, pre-existent Christ],
in which all things are said,
and by way of the Gift, in which other gifts are given,
then you can see
that through the highest communicability of the good,
there must be
a Trinity of the Father and the Son and the Holy Spirit.
From supreme goodness,
it is necessary that there be in the Persons
supreme communicability;
from supreme communicability, supreme consubstantiality;
from supreme consubstantiality, supreme configurability;
and from these supreme coequality

and hence supreme coeternity;
finally, from all of the above, supreme mutual intimacy,
by which one is necessarily in the other
by supreme interpenetration
and one acts with the other
in absolute lack of division
of the substance, power and operation
of the most blessed Trinity itself.

3. But when you contemplate these things,
do not think
that you comprehend the incomprehensible.
For you still have something else to consider
in these six properties
which strongly leads our mind's eye
to amazement and admiration.
For here is
supreme communicability with individuality of persons,
supreme consubstantiality with plurality of hypostases,
supreme configurability with distinct personality,
supreme coequality with degree
supreme coeternity with emanation,
supreme mutual intimacy with mission.
Who would not be lifted up in admiration
at the sight of such marvels?
But we understand with complete certitude
that all these things are in the most blessed Trinity
if we lift up our eyes
to the superexcellent goodness.
For if there is here
supreme communication and true diffusion,
there is also here
true origin and true distinction;
and because the whole is communicated and not merely part,
whatever is possessed is given,
and given completely.
Therefore, the one emanating and the one producing
are distinguished by their properties
and are one in essence.
Since, then, they are distinguished by their properties,
they have
personal properties and plurality of hypostases
and emanation of origin
and order, not of posteriority but of origin,
and a sending forth,
not involving a change of place but free inspiration

by reason of the producer's authority
which the sender has in relation to the one sent.
Moreover, because they are one in substance,
there must be unity
in essence, form, dignity, eternity, existence and unlimitedness.
Therefore, when you consider these in themselves one by one,
you have matter for contemplating the truth;
when you compare them with one another,
you have reason to be lifted up to the highest wonder.
Therefore, that your mind may ascend
through wonder to wondering contemplation,
these should be considered together.

4. For the Cherubim who faced each other
also signify this.
The fact that they faced each other,
"with their faces turned toward the Mercy Seat" [Exod. 25:17-22],
is not without a mystical meaning,
so that what Our Lord said in John
might be verified:
"This is eternal life
that they may know you, the only true God,
and Jesus Christ, whom you have sent" [John 17:3].
For we should wonder
not only at the essential and personal properties of God
in themselves
but also in comparison with
the superwonderful union of God and man
in the unity of the Person of Christ.

5. For if you are the Cherub
contemplating God's essential attributes,
and if you are amazed
because the divine Being is both
first and last,
eternal and most present,
utterly simple and the greatest or boundless,
totally present everywhere and nowhere contained,
most actual and never moved,
most perfect and having nothing superfluous or lacking,
and yet immense and infinite without bounds,
supremely one and yet all-inclusive,
containing all things in himself,
being all power, all truth, all goodness –
if you are this Cherub,
look at the Mercy Seat and wonder

that in him there is joined
the First Principle with the last,
God with man, who was formed on the sixth day;
the eternal is joined with temporal man,
born of the Virgin in the fulness of time,
the most simple with the most composite,
the most actual with the one who suffered supremely and died,
the most perfect and immense with the lowly,
the supreme and all-inclusive one
with a composite individual distinct from others,
that is, the man Jesus Christ.

6. But if you are the other Cherub
contemplating the properties of the Persons,
and you are amazed
that communicability exists with individuality,
consubstantiality with plurality,
configurability with personality,
coequality with order,
coeternity with production,
mutual intimacy with sending forth,
because the Son is sent by the Father
and the Holy Spirit by both,
who nevertheless is with them and never departs from them
if you are this Cherub,
look at the Mercy Seat and wonder
that in Christ
personal union exists
with a trinity of substances and a duality of natures;
that complete agreement exists
with a plurality of wills;
that mutual predication of God and man exists
with a plurality of properties;
that coadoration exists
with a plurality of excellence,
that coexaltation above all things exists
with a plurality of dignity;
that codomination exists
with a plurality of powers.

7. In this consideration is the perfection of the mind's illumination
when, as if on the sixth day of creation,
it sees man made to the image of God.
For if an image is an expressed likeness,
when our mind contemplates
in Christ the Son of God,

who is the image of the invisible God by nature,
our humanity
so wonderfully exalted, so ineffably united,
when at the same time it sees united
the first and the last,
the highest and the lowest,
the circumference and the center,
"the Alpha and the Omega" [Rev. 1:8, 21:6, 22:13],
the caused and the cause,
the Creator and the creature,
that is, "the book written within and without" [Ezek. 2:9; Rev. 5:1],
it now reaches something perfect.
It reaches the perfection of its illuminations
on the sixth stage,
as if with God on the sixth day of creation;
nor does anything more remain
except the day of rest on which
through mystical ecstasy
the mind's discernment comes to rest
"from all the work which" it "has done" [Gen. 2:2].

CONTEMPORARY REFLECTION

Intellectual Inquiry and Spiritual Formation

Diogenes Allen

There is a noticeable gap between academic theology and the practice of Christian devotion. Consider, for example, the following statement of the agenda for theologians by James McClendon that opened his review of Geoffrey Wainwright's *Doxology*, an approach to systematic theology from the standpoint of the praise of God.

The major problems facing Christian theology in the western world at the present time – problems neither new [n]or transient but persistent since the Enlightenment or earlier – may be summarized under the headings of

RELEVANCE (the gap between modes of thought available to theology and those prevailing in the wider society), PLURALISM (the conscious plurality of the world religions, but also the ongoing plurality within Christianity itself), and (inclusive of these two) TRUTH or TRUTHFULNESS (the question, whether any existing theology may be judged true by the standards of truth acceptable in general, or even in the Christian community). . . . Theology has . . . proved to be a frustrating discipline to many intelligent Christians, who perceive its standing problems and deplore its lack of headway despite its many changes of method and angles of approach.[1]

Although McClendon himself does not approach theology as he has described it, he has described the approach that is typical of a large part of academic theology today. For example, in the widely used textbook, *Christian Theology*, edited by Peter Hodgson and Robert H. King, each chapter summarizes traditional Christian doctrines around one of the classical loci, examines the challenges posed to the traditional doctrines in modern times, and then gives a constructive response in terms set by the Enlightenment challenges. It is this last feature – a reconstruction in terms set by the Enlightenment challenges – to which I object. It is to approach theology from issues that are primarily *extrinsic* to the nature of God, and not from issues that arise *in the first instance* from the nature of God and ourselves in relation to God. The latter problems are primarily *intrinsic* to theology, and for that reason arise in every age and culture. They do not have to be characterized by such qualifications as "the western world," and "since the Enlightenment."

I do not mean to imply that extrinsic issues are irrelevant to theology. Quite the contrary, they are integral to the theological task of relating all things to God. But when theologians have not worked through problems intrinsic to theology for themselves, they miss the spiritual formation that can result from this engagement, with the result that extrinsic problems lead them to regard theology as a "frustrating discipline" and to "deplore its lack of headway." The treatment of extrinsic problems, while neglecting those that are intrinsic, also greatly contributes to the gap between intellectual inquiry and devotion.

The Role of Spiritual Formation in Intellectual Inquiry

Intrinsic to theology is the nature of the reality to be known and our human capacity to know that reality. God's essence far surpasses the power of our senses and intellect to know it. This is suggested by the absence of any representation of God in the Holy of Holies in the Temple of ancient Israel. It underlies Thomas Aquinas's claim that God is not a member of any genus, and the stress in neo–orthodoxy that God is not a being among beings, but wholly other. The only way God can be known is by self-revelation. God has done so in many ways, but has most clearly revealed God's intentions to the people of ancient Israel and above all in Jesus Christ. In addition to our inability fully to comprehend God intellectually, even with revelation, our hearts and minds have been perverted by disobedience or sin. The reception of divine revelation requires repentance; an increase in our understanding of revelation requires continuing spiritual growth. As it is expressed by Ludwig Wittgenstein: "In religion every level of devoutness must have its appropriate form of expression which has no sense at a lower level. This doctrine, which means something at a higher level, is null and void for someone who is still at the lower level; he *can* only understand it *wrongly* and so these words are *not* valid for such a person."[2] An increase in our understanding of God leads in turn to an increase in our love for God and our love for neighbor.

The difficulty of knowing God because of his nature and our condition clearly implies that in theology intellectual inquiry cannot properly be detached inquiry. For example, Julian of Norwich compares knowledge of God to wounds. She specifies three wounds: the wound of contrition (repentance and continuing repentance for one's disobedience); the wound of compassion (love of neighbor); and the wound of longing (love for God).[3]

People can of course be taught theology and, given intelligence and diligence, even perform well as theologians, but this may be no more than a knowledge *about* God. Richard of St. Victor stresses that it is useless for us to know about God unless we long for God. "[I]t is vain that we grow in riches of divine knowledge unless by them the fire of love is increased in us. For love arising from knowledge and knowledge coming from love must always grow in us, each ministering to the increase of the other by mutual growth, and love and knowledge developing in turn."[4] Both Julian and Richard understand the Christian life as involving an ascent toward God or becoming closer to God. This understanding is common to all Christian spirituality. A divorce between intellectual inquiry and spiritual formation occurs when intellectual inquiry is not concerned with ascent toward God. This happens quite easily because spiritual ascent is not required for discussing doctrines. Doctrines themselves do not include our response, whereas our response is the focus of devotion. The crucial question for ascent to God is how we may find, or be present to him, who is beyond the capacity of our senses and intellect. As we have said, the answer is only by divine revelation. But in order for us to know God not only must he reveal Godself, we must also respond by receiving that self-revelation. It is only by spiritual formation that we can respond, and thus begin our journey into God. Our lives must increasingly be formed by God. We rise to God through an increase in knowledge and love of God, and the goal of our ascent is to culminate in some form of union with God. There is no detached knowing of God any more than there is a detached love of neighbor or a detached attitude toward one's failure to obey God.

Where there is academic inquiry concerning what people with a commitment to God have said, thought, and done, we have the study of religion, not theology. The Bible and theology are approached historically, sociologically, psychologically, and politically. Now that the study of religion is accepted in most academic centers, intellectual inquiry has increasingly become identified with these approaches. Theologians find themselves required to justify their work in terms of extrinsic standards, such as McClendon mentions. This is not wholly illegitimate, and it can be valuable. But a preoccupation with extrinsic issues has caused many theologians to neglect the intellectual inquiry that is intrinsic to theology, an inquiry which requires personal involvement and an aspiration to know and love God.

For most of Christian history, intellectual inquiry and spiritual aspiration toward God went hand in hand. For example, Anselm in his *Proslogion* begins, as he always does when he engages in intellectual inquiry, with meditations intended to awaken the mind from its torpor.

> Come now, little man,
> turn aside for a while from your daily employment,
> escape for a moment from the tumult of your thoughts.
> Put aside your weighty cares,
> let your burdensome distractions wait,
> free yourself awhile for God
> and rest awhile in him.
> Enter the inner chamber of your soul,
> shut out everything except God
> and that which can help you in seeking him,
> and when you have shut the door, seek him.
> Now, my whole heart, say to God,
> "I seek your face,
> Lord, it is your face I seek."   (ch. 1)

Anselm believes that to increase our knowledge of God through intellectual inquiry we must on *each occasion* of inquiry begin by seeking to free ourselves from all distractions so that we may desire him with our whole heart. Rather than having our mind and heart filled with a multitude of desires, pulling us in different directions, we must focus on God, whom we do not see, but whom we hope to come to know face to face by increasing our understanding of God. The mind is to be aroused from its torpor "to the contemplation of God" (ch. 1) by being reminded that God is not a member of the created order, but dwells "in light inaccessible" (ch. 1). Accordingly, Anselm confesses, "I cannot seek you unless you show me how, and I will never find you unless you show yourself to me" (ch. 1). These remarks – as well as lamentation over the effects of our disobedience which hinders our search and a fervent expression of hope because of our redemption by Christ – fill about nine times as much space as the above quoted passage. Anselm concludes this meditation with the remark that in our intellectual inquiry we are not to expect fully to understand God. "I am not trying to make my way to your height, for my understanding is in no way equal to that, but I do desire to understand a little of your truth which my heart already believes and loves" (ch. 1).

This heartfelt meditation occurs *before* Anselm presents his ontological proof. In this reflection on God's existence, Anselm comes to understand that God's existence is not like the existence of everything that does or might exist. God's existence is a necessary existence. Through this intellectual inquiry, Anselm has come to understand something he had not understood before, but which he had believed and loved. He has found a precise way to distinguish God and the world, and thereby to prevent the mind from confusing God with what is not God.[5] With this understanding, he has now drawn closer to God whom he has been seeking.

Robert Sokolowski has argued convincingly in *The God of Faith and Reason* that Anselm's preparation for intellectual inquiry is intrinsic to the task itself and, more generally, that without spiritual formation there is no discernment of God in theological study.[6] We cannot here reproduce Sokolowski's argument, but it is clear that Anselm's inquiry is motivated by a love for God, and that he believes that his reflection has resulted in an increased understanding of God. His intellectual quest is to understand matters intrinsic to theology, namely the nature of God and our human condition. They are transcultural matters. They should be present, affecting theological study in any culture and at any period of time, because God's nature does not change and all human beings are limited in their capacity to know God and suffer from the effects of sin.

Anselm is convinced that theological inquiry is possible only for someone who has become converted to a spiritual perspective. His inquiry, like that of his master, Augustine, is based on belief. He writes, "I do not seek to understand so that I may believe, but I believe so that I may understand; and what is more, I believe that unless I do believe I shall not understand" (ch. 1).

Anselm does not seek to *arrive* at belief by a study of the world and the views of the world prevalent in the various fields of inquiry. Nor does he think that he has to solve various problems extrinsic to theology *before* he can believe and, that unless he does so, he cannot engage in theological inquiry. Rather, Anselm, as a practicing Christian, has been engaged with the reality of God and, because of that engagement, believes and loves, and seeks *more* understanding in order to know and love God better. His frustrations spring from God's hiddenness, our human limitations, and our disobedience.

I submit that one who has wrestled with these intrinsic matters, as has Anselm, regards the problems extrinsic to theology differently from those who have not been shaped or formed by wrestling with the problems intrinsic to theology. One does not think that one must deal with various extrinsic problems, such as McClendon has described, *before* one can do theology. Above all, one does not think that one may somehow *arrive* at a spiritual perspective by approaching God from a naturalistic perspective. It should be no surprise that theologians who neglect the study of questions that are intrinsic to theology, and who do not become formed by this study, should find theology a frustrating discipline and deplore lack of progress with solving problems extrinsic to theology.

If one has spent, as I have, most of one's academic life wrestling with problems extrinsic to theology, such as those posed by Logical Positivism, and by the modes of thought prevalent since the Enlightenment, and by the recent concern with pluralism, one is indeed pleased and even relieved when one believes one has found a way to deal with these and other extrinsic problems. But one's engagement with them is not marked with the kind of anxiety that fears that, unless one finds a way to deal with them, theology and the faith upon which theology is based cannot be held with intellectual integrity. If one's need for redemption and one's aspirations are operative, and if one has wrestled with the spiritual ascent toward God found in all major theologians prior to the Enlightenment, and in some of them since, one's concern with extrinsic matters is serious but not decisive for one's theological study. This is one of the great benefits of studying those theologians who wrestle with questions intrinsic to theology, for those whose task is also to be primarily concerned with intellectual inquiry. To be unengaged and to be spiritually unformed or even malformed does indeed open a theologian of today to the frustrations and despondency that McClendon so frankly states.

The Role of Intellectual Inquiry in Spiritual Formation

Not all forms of spiritual formation are concerned with intellectual inquiry. For example, Bernard of Clairvaux* focuses much of his attention on the earthly life of Jesus, especially on his crucifixion, and seeks to be emotionally

---

* St. Bernard of Clairvaux (1090–1153), builder of the Cistercian Order and spiritual theologian.

affected by gazing on them lovingly. By virtue of an increasingly purified love, he hopes to achieve a closer and closer unity with God. Bernard is not concerned with intellectual inquiry, as were the academic theologians of the universities. He is quite content with the doctrinal orthodoxy he inherited.

Ignatius Loyola* owes a great deal to the affective spirituality of Bernard. In his *Spiritual Exercises* he relies heavily on the use of the imagination. We are to bring before our mind's eye various events of the life of Jesus as vividly as possible, so that we may be affected by them. As we increasingly commit ourselves to Christ's kingdom, we are to seek to discern God's intention for us that we might do God's will. Thus Loyola's use of contemplation differs from the use of contemplation in speculative spirituality. There contemplation is to increase our understanding and love of God until it culminates in knowledge of God face to face. Loyola's spirituality is explicitly *practical*. Contemplation is used to form one to be better able to discern and do God's will in daily life.

Not all speculative spirituality is concerned with intellectual inquiry. For example, Evagrius of Pontus,† who is quite important for the ascetic theology of the Eastern church and, through John Cassian,‡ a major influence on the Western church, focused almost exclusively on pure prayer as the means to knowledge of created beings and to a knowledge of God face to face. Continuing intellectual inquiry into the meaning of Christian doctrines by him or others seemed to have no role in his understanding of our spiritual ascent.

There are, however, some types of speculative spirituality in which intellectual inquiry is integral to the spirituality. We can see this clearly in Bonaventure. In *Disputed Questions on the Mystery of the Trinity*, Bonaventure studies the movement within the life of God. Subsequently, in his spiritual classic, *The Soul's Journey into God*, his earlier intellectual inquiry forms the rungs of a ladder, so to speak, for our ascent into the life of God. Bonaventure's inquiry into the dynamic inner life of God is guided by what God has revealed Godself to be, Father, Son, and Holy Spirit. From this, he tries to understand the reasons or the principles of the divine movement in God. Although Bonaventure is deeply influenced by Augustine in other works, his reflections on the Trinity are based on an analysis of goodness, not human cognitive experience as in Augustine. He fuses important elements from Denis the Areopagite,§ Anselm, and Aristotle into an original synthesis.

---

* St. Ignatius Loyola (*c.*1491–1556), founder of the Society of Jesus (Jesuits) during the Catholic Reformation and author of *Spiritual Exercises*.
† Evagrius Pontus, a fourth-century monk and mystical theologian at Constantinople.
‡ John Cassian, a fourth-century monastic teacher who bought Eastern monasticism to Europe.
§ A mystical theologian of the sixth century who set the tone for much Christian spirituality.

According to Denis and Plotinus,* good is by its nature self-diffusive. By this principle, God is necessarily self-communicative. But this neoplatonic principle of the self-diffusion of the good is not sufficient for Bonaventure. God is not only diffusive by nature but also by will. In addition, he argues, following Anselm, that God is such that none greater can be conceived. Accordingly, the goodness of God is such that none greater can be conceived, and the highest good must be the most self-diffusive. Thus, in *The Soul's Journey into God*, Bonaventure states,

> . . . the greatest self-diffusion cannot exist unless it is
> actual and intrinsic,
> substantial and hypostatic,
> natural and voluntary,
> free and necessary,
> lacking nothing and perfect.   (6.2)

The created universe is not sufficient to be considered the self-diffusion of God's substance and nature. The only possible self-diffusion of God is God. So, the primary diffusion of goodness is the Son and the Spirit. God's diffusion of Godself by nature is the Son who, as the perfect diffusion of the Father, is himself God. Divine self-diffusion by nature is the Son who, as the perfect diffusion of the Father, is himself God. Divine self-diffusion by will is God the Holy Spirit who, as the perfect diffusion of God the Father and Son, is also God. Since one diffusion is by nature and the other by will, the Son and the Spirit are distinct.

Bonaventure argues that there are and can be only two such diffusions of God. According to Aristotle, the only ways something can happen is by accident, by nature, or by will. God does not act by accident. God acts by nature, and since this act is perfect, there can be only one Son. God acts freely, and since this act is perfect, there can be only one Holy Spirit. God can thus be seen to be three and only three Persons. Although Bonaventure has much more to say about the interrelations in the life of God, this is all we need for our purposes. For we can see that, by using the principles that good is self-diffusive, that God is perfect, and that God acts by nature and by will, Bonaventure has made the movement of the Trinity accessible to thought, and thereby to devotion. Even though he relies on Denis's principle that goodness is self-diffusive and, as in Denis, the ascent of the soul culminates in ecstasy, in this part of his work, Bonaventure does not use the *via negativa*, which is so associated with Denis's account of the

---

* A third-century neoplatonist philosopher and mystic whose work strongly influenced the formation of the doctrine of the Trinity.

ascent. In Bonaventure it is what can be put before the mind that is vital for the ascent.

In the *The Soul's Journey into God*, Bonaventure seeks to specify various features of nature, human nature, and God for the mind to contemplate. In the Prologue he stresses, as do Julian, Richard, and Anselm, that one needs to be involved with God in order to know God. Although Bonaventure is writing for believing and practicing Christians, he emphasizes that the readers must prepare themselves with an earnest intent of ascending into the life of God. Otherwise, the knowledge he imparts will be useless.

The organization of *The Soul's Journey into God* is modeled on the vision of the six-winged seraph that appeared to St. Francis. Two parts of the book direct one to contemplate the vestiges of God in the universe; two parts focus on the image of God in human nature, especially as restored by Jesus; and two parts direct us to contemplate the Trinity. The mind is thus to look outward, inward, and upward in its journey into God. In the fifth and sixth meditations the mind is instructed to look upward by reflecting on two names of God, "being" and "goodness", respectively. The name of God as "being" enables Bonaventure to understand the unity of God, and the name of "goodness" enables him to understand the movement in God's life. Our concern is with the movement in God's life.

In the sixth meditation, Bonaventure draws on his earlier work, *Disputed Questions on the Mystery of the Trinity*, in order to provide rungs for our ascent. In other words, he tells us which things to think about as we contemplate God's inner life as Father, Son, and Spirit and how, by thinking about them, to move more fully into the life of God. Inquiry into the Trinity, which is often an occasion for bafflement for many Christians, and sometimes even an embarrassment, in Bonaventure's hands becomes a part of our spiritual formation. His intellectual work on the Trinity, presented in meditative form, gives a conceptual structure to divine self-love. This conceptual structure enables us to see, on the one hand, the inadequacy of the universe as the highest or best reality, because it is not great enough or good enough to be the perfect diffusion of God's goodness. On the other hand, it enables us to recognize God's generosity in creating a glorious universe when God did not need to make a universe at all, since he is already fully and perfectly self-expressive in his own inner life as Trinity. This generosity includes God's intent for human beings to share as fully as possible in the divine life which, because of our sin, is achievable only through the Holy Spirit's bringing us into full unity with the crucified, incarnate Son. By tracing (or 'reducing,' as he would say) the biblical account of creation and redemption into the movement in the divine life itself, Bonaventure has immensely heightened our understanding of God's transcendence and generosity. Contemplating what Bonaventure's intellectual work has made accessible to us should ignite an ardor for God. By contemplating God's life, one may have one's love for him so purified and heightened that one may, even in this life, experience the presence of God face to face in a moment of ecstasy. Thus, Bonaventure demonstrates that the Trinity is a most promising place to begin one's journey to God.

It is worth noting that Bonaventure's work shows the inadequacy of Plotinus, Hegel,* and process theologians. Good is indeed self-diffusive in Plotinus, but the diffusions are not perfect or full, and all the diffusions are necessary, including those that give us the universe, since the One or the Good is impersonal, without will. Hegel's divine movement is the movement of the universe itself. For Bonaventure the universe is too small and not good enough to be God's self-diffusion. It is in no way coequal to that than which none greater or better can be conceived. The panentheism of process theology is distinct from Hegel's pantheism, but it has similar inadequacies. In process theology, not only does God need a universe in order to increase in value, God is a being among others. In all three views it is not possible to characterize a divine generosity that is comparable to the immense generosity Bonaventure is able to characterize through his understanding of the movement in the divine life. He enables one to see the immense importance of the notion commonly expressed in theology and spirituality, which at first sight seems peculiar and even repulsive, that God can love only himself. That is, nothing can be as full a diffusion of God as the movement of God in the divine life itself.

Questions Extrinsic to Theology

Anselm and Bonaventure considered questions extrinsic to theology, as have theologians before and after them. This is because the consideration of questions that are extrinsic to theology nonetheless is integral to the task of theology. We can compare theology's task to that of a flashlight or torch: it casts light enabling us to see. In theology we seek to see all things in the light of God, but if we have not wrestled with questions intrinsic to God's nature and our condition in relation to God, then our batteries will be weak and the bulb will cast only a dim light.[7]

However, it has been difficult for some theologians in the modern period, as they wrestle with extrinsic problems, to cast light on them. At various times in the modern period the prospects for theology, because of developments in science and philosophy, have looked dire. This certainly

---

* Georg Wilhelm Friedrich Hegel, a nineteenth-century German Idealist philosopher who worked out the modern notion of the dialectical movement of history.

was the case when I was a student in the 1950s. But today the situation in both areas has been transformed, as an atheistic point of view, even if dominant, is no longer considered to be indisputably normative. But whether the situation is favorable or unfavorable at any particular time, Christian thinkers who study questions intrinsic to theology and whose intellectual work is integral to their spiritual formation do not take their bearings solely, or even predominantly, from the state of the discussion of extrinsic problems. Such thinkers can live with temporary frustrations and lack of headway because they have wrestled with questions intrinsic to God's nature and our condition, and they have found both illumination and nourishment. Let me illustrate the current struggle with extrinsic questions by considering the issue of foundationalism.

Foundationalism in philosophy was an attempt to find foundations for our claims to knowledge. Although particular truths are discovered at different times and are rooted in various historical and cultural circumstances, it was once believed that, if our claims could be shown to be necessary or incorrigible, they had universal validity. René Descartes* thought the mind had the power to find incorrigible principles to serve as the foundations of knowledge. John Locke† tried to find foundations in sense-experiences that are incorrigible. Immanuel Kant‡ based necessity and universality on the synthetic activity of reason. The overthrow of all these attempts, and the claim that there are no foundations, makes it appear as if there is nothing upon which to rest our truth-claims. They are all a matter of historical and cultural circumstances, and therefore lack universal validity. All claims, including theological ones, are social constructions.

It is widely assumed today that foundationalism and antifoundationalism are the only alternatives. Perhaps an analogy may help loosen the grip of the assumption and enable us to see that there is another alternative. Some people were once troubled about what the earth rests on. Things fall unless they rest on the earth, but what does the earth rest on? What keeps it from falling down? Locke mentions the Indian story that the earth rests on the back of a giant elephant. But that is only a temporary expedient, since we must now find out what the elephant rests on. As he pointed out, to say it rests on the back of a giant turtle does not get us out of the difficulty. The turtle must rest on something or it will fall.

So too it seems with truth-claims. Without a foundation for our claims

---

* René Descartes, seventeenth-century French philosopher, often called the Father of Modernity, who based truth on self-sufficient reason and philosophical method.
† John Locke, seventeenth-century English philosopher, who developed modern empiricism.
‡ Immanuel Kant, eighteenth-century German philosopher, who established the modern philosophical foundation for science, ethics, aesthetics, and judgment, and rational religion.

that transcends our culture or subculture, we are left with relativism. It seems that the only thing to stop our free-fall from relativism into nihilism is some sort of "legitimate" or warranted social consensus. In America the best known attempts to provide such a consensus are Richard Rorty's work in philosophy[8] and George Lindbeck's in theology.[9] But both eschew universal claims and provide no warrant for universal truth-claims or claims that transcend a culture or subculture.

However, Christian teachings concerning our knowledge of God transform the situation. The entire framework of foundationalism and antifoundationalism is transcended by the conviction that God must manifest Godself and that we must become spiritually formed in order to respond to God's manifestations. Such a view did not arise because of a lack of confidence in our ability to gain knowledge as such. Nor did it arise because of the failure of attempts to know God. It arose after our reception of God's self-manifestation. From God's self-manifestation, theological reflection led to the realization that we can know God only insofar as God makes Godself known. This was learned from wrestling with questions intrinsic to God's nature and our condition. The transcultural status of theological claims that arise from questions intrinsic to theology is not based on the possibility of an incorrigible foundation, nor is it threatened by the absence of such a foundation.

Warrant for Christian claims can be found because all claims about God are *suspended*, so to speak, from that which is not a member of the universe. Just as the earth without anything to rest on is not in danger of falling, because it is suspended in space by forces between various bodies, so too are theologians able to practice their vocation without an incorrigible foundation on which to rest their inquiries, and without fear that the lack of such a foundation renders their claims mere social constructions. God's self-revelation provides the light by which theologians practice their calling to seek to understand God and all things in relation to God. Of course such understanding as theologians are able to gain is deeply affected culturally. But because God, who is related to history and society, also transcends all history and culture, what is understood is not necessarily culture bound. A theologian who has wrestled with questions intrinsic to theology, questions that are not culture bound, knows this, and should not be intimidated by the extrinsic claim that because there are no foundations to knowledge to give our claims universality, all claims must be culture bound.[10]

Most of a theologian's work in the western world today will probably be directed toward extrinsic matters because there are so many new intellectual, technical, and cultural developments which need to be understood in the light of God. But that work is likely to be more intellectually fruitful, and will be more relevant to spiritual formation, if it is deeply informed by

◆ 27

questions that are transcultural, not in the sense of developing a 'global theology,' but in the sense of a theology that is suspended from God who is not a member of the universe.

Notes

1 In *Faith and Philosophy*, 3:2 (April 1986), pp. 222–3.
2 *Culture and Value*, trans. Peter Winch (Oxford: Basil Blackwell, 2nd edn, 1980), p. 32e.
3 *Showings*, trans. Edmund Colledge and James Walsh (New York: Paulist Press, 1978), p. 127.
4 *Selections from Contemplation*, trans. Clare Kirchberger (London: Faber & Faber, 1957), p. 161.
5 We will see how useful this is to Bonaventure.
6 *The God of Faith and Reason* (Notre Dame: University of Notre Dame Press, 1982).
7 This is fully argued in my article "Manifestations of the Supernatural According to Simone Weil," *Cahiers Simone Weil*, 17 (September 1994), pp. 290–307.
8 *Objectivity, Relativism, and Truth* (Cambridge: Cambridge University Press, 1991).
9 *The Nature of Doctrine: Religion and Theology in a Postliberal Age* (Philadelphia: Westminster Press, 1984).
10 See previous note.

Inquiring after God by Means of Scientific Study

Since the rise of modern science in the seventeenth century there has been much conflict between religion and science because religion rests on the doctrines of creation and providence – that the world was created by God and is sustained by "his" goodness – while science rests on the idea that the world is the result of random forces. On the scientific view, religion's assumption that God is the creator and sustainer of the world is unnecessary and impedes human inquiry into the workings of nature that enable us to gain better control over it.

Awareness of this tension is not limited to modernity, however. The great scholastic theologian of the twelfth century, St. Thomas Aquinas, recognized the importance of scientific claims made ever since Aristotle. He wrote his monumental work, the *Summa Theologiae*, to synthesize all learning, both sacred and secular, into a great unified, architectonic whole within a Christian theological framework, hoping to head off precisely the conflict between science and religion that has raged throughout modernity. Of course, St. Thomas lived centuries before modern experimental science. In his day modern science was primarily Aristotelian metaphysics. But it presented itself as an extra-Christian truth that had to be recognized, just as modern empirical science later would be.

As one might expect from one of history's greatest theologians, although he realized that there is "no need to suppose that a God exists" he did not come to this skeptical conclusion. This was because Christian scriptures and the theological tradition of the Church constituted a revealed and revered body of literature. His solution to the problem was to integrate these two truthful traditions, Christianizing Aristotle in some cases and using Aristotle's insights to understand Christianity better. With this method he posed his famous "five ways," five philosophical arguments to demonstrate the existence of God.

Skepticism – now atheism – is more widespread now than when Thomas first acknowledged its possibility. Yet today people on both sides of the argument are more cautious than their predecessors in argument between science and religion. While still holding to the idea that science can explain the world without referring to God, and deriding the Genesis creation story as unscientific, a few contemporary scientific cosmologists are more sober about the extent of their knowledge and the prospects for more and better knowledge than ever before, admitting that all their research and study yield limited knowledge of the origin of the cosmos. All the information science has garnered about the earth, its solar system, its galaxy, and beyond, is but a tiny bit of knowledge. Scientists are beginning to acknowledge the awesomeness of reality, both on a macro and a micro level, as putting them in touch with (something like) God, even if their meaning is not a reference to the God of the Bible.

For their part theologians and philosophers are also more cautious. Professor Nancey Murphy, our contemporary interpreter, is not as confident as Thomas was with his five ways. She is well aware that the classic arguments for the existence of God, beginning with Anselm's and including Thomas's, have been seriously criticized by modern philosophers, notably David Hume and Immanuel Kant in the eighteenth century, as well as by later scientists. Philosophy of religion has been unable to refute skepticism about the existence of God definitively. But it can do something else.

Professor Murphy points to features of reality that arouse a sense of awe and wonder about the created order that may drive one to look toward the majesty, power, and goodness of God as depicted in Christian scripture and tradition. This development constitutes an about face for the conversation between religion and science in which both sides have often seen the other as an opponent to be bested in the argument. Perhaps the most famous case of this relationship between science and religion was the heresy trial of Galileo in the seventeenth century, when he was forced by the Church to recant his commitment to Copernican theory. Here, on the contrary, after centuries of acrimonious debate, scientists and theologians may again begin to talk with one another as St. Thomas had hoped.

Thus, spiritual understanding may be aided by scientific study, now that Christians have accepted the good uses to which modern science is put. For its part, scientific understanding may again be brought under the canopy of a theological framework that could actually help guide it in salutary ways. For today many acknowledge that scientific "advances" may themselves be morally and socially ambiguous as we see with issues like cloning and the ability to sustain life in precarious circumstances at both ends of the lifecycle.

SACRED TEXTS

Psalm 8:3–4

When I look at your heavens, the work of your fingers,
the moon and the stars that you have established;
what are human beings that you are mindful of them,
mortals that you care for them?

Isaiah 45:18 (REB)

Thus says the LORD, the creator of the heavens, he who is God, who made
the earth and fashioned it and by himself fixed it firmly, who created it
not as a formless waste but as a place to be lived in: I am the LORD, and
there is none other.

CLASSIC TEXT

St. Thomas Aquinas, *Summa Theologiae* (Part I, Q.2)

Whether there is a God: Article 3. Is there a God?

THE THIRD POINT: 1. It seems that there is no God. For if, of two mutually
exclusive things, one were to exist without limit, the other would cease to
exist. But by the word "God" is implied some limitless good. If God then
existed, nobody would ever encounter evil. But evil is encountered in the
world. God therefore does not exist.

2. Moreover, if a few causes fully account for some effect, one does not
seek more. Now it seems that everything we observe in this world can be
fully accounted for by other causes, without assuming a God. Thus natural

31

effects are explained by natural causes, and contrived effects by human reasoning and will. There is therefore no need to suppose that a God exists. ON THE OTHER HAND, the book of *Exodus* represents God as saying, "I am who I am" [Ex. 3:14].

REPLY: There are five ways in which one can prove that there is a God.

The first and most obvious way is based on change. Some things in the world are certainly in process of change: this we plainly see. Now anything in process of change is being changed by something else. This is so because it is characteristic of things in process of change that they do not yet have the perfection towards which they move, though able to have it; whereas it is characteristic of something causing change to have that perfection already. For to cause change is to bring into being what was previously only able to be, and this can only be done by something that already is: thus fire, which is actually hot, causes wood, which is able to be hot, to become actually hot, and in this way causes change in the wood. Now the same thing cannot at the same time be both actually *x* and potentially *x*, though it can be actually *x* and potentially *y*: the actually hot cannot at the same time be potentially hot, though it can be potentially cold. Consequently, a thing in process of change cannot itself cause that same change; it cannot change itself. Of necessity[,] therefore[,] anything in process of change is being changed by something else. Moreover, this something else, if in process of change, is itself being changed by yet another thing; and this last by another. Now we must stop somewhere, otherwise there will be no first cause of the change, and, as a result, no subsequent causes. For it is only when acted upon by the first cause that the intermediate causes will produce the change: if the hand does not move the stick, the stick will not move anything else. Hence one is bound to arrive at some first cause of change not itself being changed by anything, and this is what everybody understands by God.

The second way is based on the nature of causation. In the observable world causes are found to be ordered in series; we never observe, nor ever could, something causing itself, for this would mean it preceded itself, and this is not possible. Such a series of causes must however stop somewhere; for in it an earlier member causes an intermediate and the intermediate a last (whether the intermediate be one or many). Now if you eliminate a cause you also eliminate its effects, so that you cannot have a last cause, nor an intermediate one, unless you have a first. Given therefore no stop in the series of causes, and hence no first cause, there would be no intermediate causes either, and no last effect, and this would be an open mistake. One is therefore forced to suppose some first cause, to which everyone gives the name "God."

The third way is based on what need not be and on what must be, and runs as follows. Some of the things we come across can be but need not be, for we find them springing up and dying away, thus sometimes in being and sometimes not. Now everything cannot be like this, for a thing that need not be, once was not; and if everything need not be, once upon a time there was nothing. But if that were true there would be nothing even now, because something that does not exist can only be brought into being by something already existing. So that if nothing was in being nothing could be brought into being, and nothing would be in being now, which contradicts observation. Not everything therefore is the sort of thing that need not be; there has got to be something that must be. Now a thing that must be, may or may not owe this necessity to something else. But just as we must stop somewhere in a series of causes, so also [must we stop] in the series of things which must be[,] and [we] owe this to other things. One is forced therefore to suppose something which must be, and owes this to no other thing than itself; indeed it itself is the cause that other things must be.

The fourth way is based on the gradation observed in things. Some things are found to be more good, more true, more noble, and so on, and other things less. But such comparative terms describe varying degrees of approximation to a superlative; for example, things are hotter and hotter the nearer they approach what is hottest. Something therefore is the truest and best and most noble of things, and hence the most fully in being; for Aristotle says that the truest things are the things most fully in being. Now "when many things possess some property in common, the one most fully possessing it causes it in the others: fire," to use Aristotle's example, "the hottest of all things, causes all other things to be hot" [*Metaphysics* II, I.993b25]. There is something therefore which causes in all other things their being, their goodness, and whatever other perfection they have. And this we call "God."

The fifth way is based on the guidedness of nature. An orderedness of actions to an end is observed in all bodies obeying natural laws, even when they lack awareness. For their behavior hardly ever varies, and will practically always turn out well; which shows that they truly tend to a goal, and do not merely hit it by accident. Nothing however that lacks awareness tends to a goal, except under the direction of someone with awareness and with understanding; the arrow, for example, requires an archer. Everything in nature, therefore, is directed to its goal by someone with understanding, and this we call "God."

Hence: 1. As Augustine says, "Since God is supremely good, he would not permit any evil at all in his works, unless he were sufficiently almighty and good to bring good even from evil" [*Enchiridion* 11]. It is therefore a mark of the limitless goodness of God that he permits evils to exist, and draws from them good.

2. Natural causes act for definite purposes under the direction of some

higher cause, so that their effects must also be referred to God as the first of all causes. In the same manner contrived effects must likewise be referred back to a higher cause than human reasoning and will, for these are changeable and can cease to be, and, as we have seen, all changeable things and things that can cease to be require some first cause which cannot change and of itself must be.

HAVING RECOGNIZED that a certain thing exists, we have still to investigate the way in which it exists, that we may come to understand what it is that exists. Now we cannot know what God is, but only what he is not; we must therefore consider the ways in which God does not exist, rather than the ways in which he does. We treat then

> first, of the ways in which God does not exist,
> secondly, of the ways in which we know him,
> thirdly, of the ways in which we describe him.

The ways in which God does not exist will become apparent if we rule out from him everything inappropriate, such as compositeness, change and the like. Let us inquire then

> First, about God's simpleness, thus ruling out compositeness.
> And then, because in the material world simpleness implies imperfection and incompleteness, let us ask
> secondly, about God's perfection,
> thirdly, about his limitlessness,
> fourthly, about his unchangeableness,
> fifthly, about his oneness.

CONTEMPORARY REFLECTION

Inquiring after God through Creation

Nancey Murphy

The passage from the *Summa Theologiae* of Thomas Aquinas is one of the most famous instances of "proofs for the existence of God" based on characteristics of the universe. The question of whether proofs of this sort (or of any other sort) are, in fact, possible has been a major topic of debate in philosophy of religion for centuries. One purpose of this essay will be to consider the value of such intellectual exercises. I shall conclude that they do not work, *purely* as intellectual exercises, to convince the skeptic of God's existence, but they do offer a model for knowing God nonetheless. Reflection on certain features of the universe (its order, for instance) serves to raise intellectual questions and instill a sense of wonder that together can lead one to inquire about God.

We shall look at some findings in contemporary cosmology that raise issues today that are comparable to those raised by Thomas's "five ways." In an era when many suppose that science has displaced theology as a source of answers to life's basic questions, it is interesting to note that science itself seems inevitably to raise the sort of questions that many have taken, throughout western history, to be questions ultimately about God. Finally, we shall ask, how is the inquirer changed by reflecting upon the cosmos as *creation*?

Proofs for the Existence of God?

It is customary in discussing arguments for the existence of God to classify them into three types. (i) Ontological arguments are those that are based on the concept or idea of God, and claim that a being of this sort could not fail to exist. The most famous of such arguments was constructed by Anselm of Canterbury. (ii) Cosmological arguments are based upon some general feature of the universe (the cosmos). One example is Thomas's third way, based on the *contingency* of the universe; this is said to require that there be a *necessary* being, which is God. (iii) Teleological arguments are those based on evidence of intelligent design or purpose in the universe. Thomas's fifth way is an instance of this sort of argument. He argues that in nature we find inorganic objects operating in such a way that they achieve an end or purpose. But inorganic objects are without knowledge; how then can they direct themselves toward an end? Since they cannot, we presume that they are directed by another, by an intelligent being, and this we call God.

Thomas had a similar argument in his major apologetic work, the *Summa contra Gentiles*, which Frederick Copleston describes as follows:

> . . . [w]hen many things with different and even contrary qualities co-operate towards the realisation of one order, this must proceed from an intelligent Cause or Providence; *et hoc dicimus Deum* [and this we call God]. If the proof as given in the *Summa Theologiae* emphasises the internal finality of the

inorganic object, that given in the *Summa contra Gentiles* emphasises rather the co-operation of many objects in the realisation of the one world order or harmony.[1]

The best known teleological or design argument from the modern period was William Paley's (1743–1805). Paley concentrated on examples from anatomy, stressing the ways in which various parts of the eye, for instance, cooperate in complex ways to produce sight. He argued that we can explain the adaptation of means to ends only if we postulate a supernatural designer. Paley was affected by his context in the industrial age: his argument relies on an analogy between the order of a biological organism and a human artifact such as a watch.[2]

However, the analogy between natural teleology (that is, natural ordering that achieves some end) and human design had already been called into question by David Hume* before Paley's book was published. In his *Dialogues concerning Natural Religion*, Hume presents a classic example of the argument from design:

> CLEANTHES: . . . Look round the world: contemplate the whole and every part of it: You will find it to be nothing but one great machine, subdivided into an infinite number of lesser machines, and even their most minute parts, are adjusted to each other with an accuracy, which ravishes into admiration all men, who have ever contemplated them. The curious adapting of means to ends, throughout all nature, resembles exactly, though it much exceeds, the productions of human contrivance; of human designs, thought, wisdom, and intelligence. Since therefore the effects resemble each other, we are led to infer, by all the rules of analogy, that the causes also resemble; and that the Author of Nature is somewhat similar to the mind of man; though possessed of much larger faculties, proportioned to the grandeur of the work, which he has executed. By this argument *a posteriori*, and by this argument alone, do we prove at once the existence of a Deity, and its similarity to human mind and intelligence.[3]

However, Hume argued, the hypothesis of an intelligent designer is only one possible explanation of the world and depends very much on the analogy between organic order and intentional design. Why not take biological order itself as basic instead and explain the existence of the world by means of biological propagation? Furthermore, while the universe does exhibit a great deal of order and purpose, there is disorder and evil as well. So how can we know that it was created by one, all good God? Perhaps it was produced by

---

* David Hume, a seventeenth-century Scottish philosopher, who criticized both reason and revelation as inadequate grounds for belief in God.

a team of imperfect deities working together? Or, perhaps it is merely a fortuitous arrangement of atoms. This last suggestion is the one contemporary skeptics are most likely to find persuasive.

Despite Paley's failure to answer Hume's prior challenges, his argument was a favorite among Christian apologists in the nineteenth century. This is a major reason why many Christians found Charles Darwin's (1809–82) evolutionary theory so troubling. Darwin argued that both the fitness of organs to fulfill their functions and the fitness of organisms to their environments could be explained purely in terms of natural processes: a combination of variation and natural selection.

Hume and Darwin notwithstanding, it is Immanuel Kant's critiques of all three types of argument for the existence of God that has had the most powerful impact on Christianity – so much so that to this day many Protestants reject all attempts at natural theology and steer clear of philosophy.

Kant began his philosophical career as a rationalist metaphysician but was "awakened from [his] dogmatic slumbers" by reading Hume's skeptical arguments. Kant's later work can be summed up as the attempt to achieve three goals: (i) to save Newtonian science from Hume's skepticism; (ii) to save human freedom from (deterministic) Newtonian science; and (iii) to save religion from both Newtonian determinism and Humean skepticism.

To accomplish the first of these goals, Kant distinguished between the *content* of our experience (colors, noises, and so on) and the *form* of that experience. Its form consists in the fact that the sensations are perceived as belonging to individual objects, extended in space and time, and as causally related to one another. The forms of experience, he argued, are imposed on it by the human mind. Arithmetic, geometry, and Newtonian science are about the forms of experience only, not the content.

An analogy may help to clarify Kant's insights. Consider the experience of watching television. There are certain characteristics of the experience that result from the properties of television technology (the analogy with the mind), for example, the images will always be composed of small colored (or black and white) dots on a flat surface within a rectangular frame. These features are part of the *form* of the experience. The *content* of the programs is analogous to the content of sensory experience. We know that (apart from a change in television technology) the form of television experience will always be constant, regardless of changes in content. Similarly, so long as the structures of the mind are unchanging (and Kant never imagined otherwise), these three branches of knowledge were safe from revision or refutation.

However, this assurance came at a cost: things-as-they-appear-to-us, that is, the world of "en-formed" experience, he called "phenomena." Things-as-they-are-in-themselves he called "noumena." We can only know phenomena – things that appear to us in time and space – never noumena. We cannot even say that there are noumenal objects that cause our phenomenal experiences, since object-hood (substance) and causality are phenomenal categories only and cannot legitimately be applied to noumena or to relations between noumena and phenomena.

Kant produced a revolution in philosophy by applying this theory of knowledge to metaphysical speculation and argument. We can see the consequences by returning to our pursuit of the various arguments for the existence of God. Kant's critique of the teleological arguments goes as follows: God, if there is one, must be a noumenon, since God is not a possible object of human sensory experience. And thus any argument for God's existence based on a supposed *causal* relation between God and the phenomenal world is invalid, for reasons just explained. We violate the limits of human knowledge by attempting to extend the causal relation beyond experience. Kant writes:

> Now I maintain that all attempts to employ reason in theology in any merely speculative manner are altogether fruitless and by their very nature null and void, and that the principles of its employment in the study of nature do not lead to any theology whatsoever. . . . All synthetic principles of reason allow only of an immanent employment; and in order to have knowledge of a supreme being we should have to put them to a transcendent use, for which our understanding is in no way fitted. If the empirically valid law of causality is to lead to the original being, the latter must belong to the chain of objects of experience, and in that case it would, like all appearances, be itself again conditioned.[4]

Kant claimed that the cosmological argument – an argument based on some feature of the universe, such as its contingency – depends implicitly on an ontological argument, that is, on an argument based on the definition of God. His reasoning here is obscure, but I believe his point can be made as follows. Suppose we can argue to the necessary existence of some x by showing that its existence is a *necessary condition* for the existence of all that we know to exist. How, then, to identify this x with the highest reality, namely God? Only by means of a concept that characterizes God as the one and only necessary being. But if we can make this step we could just as well have begun with the concept of God as necessarily existing, as does the ontological argument.

Kant then criticized the ontological argument – a criticism taken by most to be devastating. All such arguments treat existence as a *predicate* – that is, as a characteristic or quality of God. But to say that God exists does not add information about God (it does not predicate existence of the subject, God, who might otherwise have lacked it); rather it says that the concept *God* (however defined) has an instance – it is *instantiated*. And so the argument is simply confused.

Kant's critiques of the theistic proofs are dependent in some instances upon acceptance of a number of the details of his own philosophy. Since Kant's day a number of philosophers have attacked specific historical arguments, pointing out that they rest on what we today would see as simple linguistic or logical errors. For example, in Thomas's third way, the sentence "Necessarily something exists" is *not* equivalent to "There exists a necessary being." That is, "necessarily" is properly a qualifier for a statement, not a predicate or characteristic of a being.

The final blow to this whole enterprise comes from more restricted views of the role of *proof* itself. Most contemporary philosophers now recognize that proof, strictly speaking, is only possible within a formal system such as geometry, since it always depends on the truth and cogency of a set of premises. However, in an argument for the existence of God, the premises themselves can always be called into question.

What, then, is the value of looking at nature for inquiring after God? We can certainly say that for those who already believe in God and believe that the universe is God's creation, there is something to be learned about God's ways by examining the divine handiwork in nature. But can we say more? Can inquiry begin with nature and move toward God, or must God's existence and character always be known or assumed in advance? I hope to show, using current examples from scientific cosmology, that it is possible to begin with the order of nature and move from there to a consideration of God.

Current Cosmology and Creation

Cosmology is the science that studies the physical structure of the universe. Building on the results of other sciences such as physics and astrophysics, it has made great progress in describing the composition of the physical universe, its origin and development, and in projecting what will happen in the distant future. Findings regarding the physical conditions in the universe that make life possible here on earth are the most interesting of all. Perhaps there is no other science that raises so many questions that verge on the theological. We consider here two issues: the origin of the universe and its characteristic of being "finely tuned" for life.[5]

Big-Bang Cosmology

In 1917 Albert Einstein put forward the view that the universe was static, that is, completely unchanging over time when viewed on the largest scales. Since then, however, evidence has been accumulating in support of a model of the universe as expanding. The first piece of evidence was the fact that light received from other parts of the universe is "red-shifted." That is, just as the sound of a truck moving away at high speed is distorted – the sound waves are "stretched out" – so too, the light from distant galaxies is distorted by the fact that the light waves are "stretched out."

If the universe is expanding, we can project back in time to a point from which the expansion must have begun; the universe must have originated in a singular state of extremely high density. Thus, the implication of the current expansion of the universe is that it had a beginning a finite time ago. Estimates of the age of the universe range from 10 to 18 billion years. Because matter gets hotter as we go back in time toward this initial state, cosmologists speak of the origin of the universe as the Hot Big Bang.

This set of discoveries leading to the conclusion that the universe had a beginning has been taken to have religious implications, by believers and atheists alike. The cosmologist Frederick Hoyle worked on an alternative "steady-state" model of the universe precisely because he saw the Big-Bang model to be too closely associated with "theological biases." Pope Pius XII welcomed the Big-Bang theory as evidence for creation of the universe by God.

In contrast, many theologians since Friedrich Schleiermacher* have claimed that the doctrine of creation is not about the temporal origin of the universe, but rather about the dependence of everything that exists upon God. On this view, an eternal, static universe would be no less dependent on God than one developing temporally. In general it has been common among those indebted to the liberal theological tradition of the nineteenth century, as well as to the neo-orthodox movement of the mid-twentieth, to understand the nature of religious faith and theology in such a way that scientific findings are almost by definition irrelevant to theology. These understandings can be traced ultimately to Kant's distinction between the phenomenal sense world and the noumenal world of things-in-themselves. Science pertains to the phenomenal; God, human morality, and immortality pertain to the noumenal world. Schleiermacher distinguished three spheres of human life: knowing, doing, and feeling. Science pertains to knowing and religion to feeling. More recent versions distinguish, for instance, between scientific facts and religious values or meanings.

So the question of what a Christian ought to make of Big-Bang theory is a difficult one. My approach here will not be to argue for any direct theological implications (far less that it serves as proof of divine activity), but

---

* Friedrich Schleiermacher (1772–1829), known as the father of modern theology, based belief in God on an aspect of human experience, once reason and revelation were no longer thought to be viable foundations.

rather to reflect on the *questions* that this scientific development raises. We may note in passing the similarities between these questions and some of the issues lying behind Thomas's five ways. My claim will be that science raises questions at its boundaries to which Christian theology may provide plausible answers.

The first question Big-Bang theory raises has to do with the issue of time. If the universe began some finite amount of time in the past, then what preceded its appearance? Nothing? It is more difficult to imagine this "nothing" than one might think, as Marguerite Shuster points out. Start backwards. Throw out people and everything they feel and everything they make. Throw out plants and animals. Throw out water and earth. Throw out planets and stars. Throw out gases and solids, particles and waves. Throw out time and space. When you are left with absolute emptiness, throw out even that. Now, maybe, you are getting close to talking about *nothing*.[6] And now, she says, maybe, you are ready to ask why *something* should ever appear.

At this point we may recall Thomas's argument: "[I]f everything need not be, once upon a time there was nothing. But if that were true there would be nothing even now, because something that does not exist can only be brought into being by something already existing. So that if nothing was in being nothing could be brought into being, and nothing would be in being now."

I claimed above that theistic "proofs" cannot truly function as proofs because, outside of a formal system, one can always call into question either the truth or the cogency of one or more of the premises. Contemporary cosmologists would, in fact, question the cogency of Thomas's phrase "at one time there was nothing in existence." That is, measures of time in science all depend in one way or another on physical changes. If there is nothing physical, then there can be no measure of time. An even more telling objection comes from the fact that contemporary physicists operate with a concept of space-time, a four-dimensional manifold that interacts with the stuff of the universe. And, strange as it may sound, space-time originated at the Big Bang along with the material constituents of the universe. So, from the perspective of contemporary physics and cosmology, time before the Big Bang is not merely unmeasurable, the very concept of time is undefined.

The question of "the time before the beginning," like the question of existence out of nothing, has a long theological history. Augustine replied to an inquiry about what God might have been doing before creation by pointing out that the question itself involves a false assumption. God did not create the world in time; rather time itself is one of God's creatures.[7]

Another question that emerges from reflection on the Big Bang is: what caused it? This is a difficult question for science and, some would say, a question necessarily beyond the bounds of science. Science formulates theories about causes in nature by recognizing regularities. Once formulated, these laws of nature can be used to make predictions about the future or to project backwards in time to the beginning. There are two reasons why science, then, cannot tell us about the cause of the Big Bang. First, the Big Bang is a "singularity," a unique event. Therefore, we can have no knowledge of regular sequences involving Big Bangs.[8] Second, and more subtle, the laws of nature, like time itself, seem to come with the universe, not to precede it.[9] If the laws arise along with the entities they regulate (or to put it more simply, if the laws merely reflect the regular behavior of entities in the universe), then they cannot govern the original emergence of the universe itself. In this case, we have no way of speaking scientifically of the *cause* of the universe.[10]

Again, we are considering issues similar to those addressed in Thomas's "five ways." Both the first and second proof concern causation. The question in the second proof about the first efficient cause is most relevant today, since this comes closest to our contemporary understanding of causation. A contemporary translation of the *Summa* makes the point well: "The second way is based on the very notion of cause. In the observable world causes derive their causality from other causes; we never observe, nor ever could we, something causing itself."[11] This way of putting it suggests that we are looking not merely for a first event in a temporal causal series, but for the very ground of causal efficacy. This is close to the question of the origin of the laws of nature themselves, which we take up in the following subsection.

First, however, it is necessary to look at competing answers to the questions already raised. The issues raised so far have to do with time and causation. (i) What preceded the Big Bang temporally, and does the very notion of time before the Big Bang make sense? (ii) What caused the Big Bang?

Christians (and readers within other religious traditions as well) may be thinking that there is only one answer: "In the beginning God created the heavens and the earth" (Gen. 1:1). However, we cannot jump so quickly to this answer. The questions raised by Big-Bang cosmology certainly fall at the boundaries of science, as I have stressed above. However, some cosmologists have taken this as a stimulus to attempt to push the boundaries of science itself. Most notable here is the work of Stephen Hawking and James Hartle.

Hawking and Hartle have developed a model of the evolution of the universe that represents it as temporally finite as we look back toward the past, yet without a beginning. Their model is based on the factor mentioned above, that since the work of Einstein we cannot think of space and time as separable. By adding considerations from quantum physics, they speculate that prior to the universe's reaching a certain (very small!) size – 10^{-33} cm in diameter – time is so thoroughly merged with space that it loses its directionality. Thus, we cannot trace the history of the universe back "in a straight line" to a beginning point. So, as a result of these quantum effects, the most probable structure for space-time under some circumstances may actually be four-dimensional space. Hartle and Hawking argue that precisely those circumstances prevailed in the very early universe. That is, if we imagine going backward in time toward the Big Bang, then, when we reach about one Planck time (i.e. 10^{-43} seconds) after what we thought was the initial singularity, something peculiar starts to happen. Time begins to "turn into" space. Rather than having to deal with the origin of space-time, therefore, we now have to contend with four-dimensional space. As a consequence, there may be no origin of the universe. Nevertheless, that does not mean that the universe is infinitely old. Time is limited in the past, but has no boundary as such.[12]

So this is a treatment of the question of time. Hartle's and Hawking's model also provides for treatment of the question of causation. Here, again, quantum theory is crucial: the universe came into existence spontaneously as a quantum fluctuation. Quantum physics is the branch of science that applies primarily to atoms and molecules, to the smallest things. The universe is a big thing, the biggest thing we can imagine. But if it has in fact expanded from a very small size, then there must have been a time sufficiently early on when quantum effects would have been important. Physicist Paul Davies says:

> Now, the essence of quantum physics is something called Heisenberg's Uncertainty Principle. This, roughly speaking, says that everything that can be observed or measured is subject to unpredictable fluctuations, to uncertainty. In the laboratory, this leads to circumstances where events can occur without well-defined prior causes. That is to say, in the words of Tommy Cooper, they happen "just like that"! We see, for example, the nuclei of radioactive atoms decaying "just like that." If you ask, "Why did it decay at that moment, rather than some other?" there is no answer. It is a genuinely spontaneous event. . . . Of course, it's a huge extrapolation to say that, given this spontaneity, we can explain how the Universe as a whole can come into being "just like that" – through a spontaneous quantum event.[13]

Davies endorses Hawking's conclusion that this model has theological implications. As Hawking himself remarks, "So long as the universe had a beginning, we could suppose it had a creator. But if the universe is completely self-contained, having no boundary or edge, it would have neither beginning nor end: it would simply be. What place, then, for a creator?"[14]

Davies is not so quick as Hawking to conclude that a theological answer to the existence of the universe can be avoided:

> So does this mean that the existence of the universe can be "explained" scientifically without the need for God? Can we regard the universe as forming a closed system, containing the reason for its existence entirely within itself? The answer depends on the meaning to be attached to the word "explanation." Given the laws of physics, the universe can, so to speak, take care of itself, including its own creation. But where do these laws come from? Must we, in turn, find an explanation for *them*?[15]

Hawking's cosmological model is regarded as *highly* speculative. However, it is important to consider it for two reasons. First, it shows the difficulty of making good on any claim that the boundary of scientific knowledge lies *here* and therefore that any further explanation must be theological. However, second, it shows the near inevitability with which such cosmological speculations open the door to inquiring after God. Davies is explicit about this. In the Preface to *God and the New Physics* he says, "It may seem bizarre, but in my opinion science offers a surer path to God than religion. Right or wrong, the fact that science has actually advanced to the point where what were formerly religious questions can be seriously tackled, itself indicates the far-reaching consequences of the new physics."[16]

Cosmological Fine-Tuning

Since the 1950s cosmologists and other scientists have been amassing measurements and calculations suggesting that the universe is "anthropic" [human oriented], that is, it appears to be "fine-tuned" to support intelligent life. There is a small set of basic numbers that accounts for the general features of the universe such as its rate of expansion, temperature, degree of homogeneity, and chemical composition. These numbers include the strengths of the four basic forces (gravity, electromagnetism, and the strong and weak nuclear forces), its mass (i.e. the total amount of "stuff" in it), and a few others. Calculations show that if any of these numbers had been much different from what it is, the general features of the universe would be vastly different – different in ways that would make any imaginable form of life impossible. In most cases, the universe would have been, in Isaiah's words, a "formless waste."

All of these calculations assume the general outlines of the Big-Bang theory described above. Working our way forward from the earliest phase, the universe would first have been composed of a "matter-energy soup" since matter, as we know it, could not have formed under the earliest conditions.

The first matter to form would have been particles of the lightest gases: hydrogen and helium. Stars would have formed when gravitational attraction condensed clouds of gas with enough centripetal force to produce nuclear burning.

As stars go through their lifespan, heavier elements are "cooked" in their nuclear furnaces. At a particular point in the life of a star it explodes, distributing the heavier elements as dust in the surrounding region. Our planet, and indeed our bodies, are composed of this dust. Current estimates suggest that this process takes about ten billion years.

Thus, for life to exist in the universe, the universe must be at least ten billion years old. Here we can see one of the needs for fine-tuning. The mass of the universe and the strength of the gravitational constant need to be carefully balanced. Two forces are operating on the expansion speed of the universe – the outward force of the initial explosion and the gravitational force that tends to pull it all back together. Gravitational pull is related to the amount of matter in the universe. If the universe were more massive than it is, or if the force of gravity itself were stronger, the universe would have first slowed its expansion and then collapsed in on itself before life had a chance to develop. Alternatively, if the universe had been smaller or the force of gravity weaker, it would have spread out and cooled off too quickly for stars to form and, again, it would have remained lifeless.

In some cases, numerical estimates of requirements such as these have been made. Carbon is one of the basic elements needed for life, and many of the calculations have to do with necessary conditions for its formation and distribution. If the nuclear strong force were 1 percent weaker or stronger, carbon would not form within the stellar ovens. In fact, it has been calculated that the strong force had to be within 0.8–1.2 times its actual strength for there to be any elements at all with atomic weights greater than 4. Also, if electromagnetism had been stronger, stars would not explode and the heavier elements needed for life would not be available.

The nuclear weak force's very weakness makes our sun burn gently for billions of years instead of blowing up like a bomb. Had this force been appreciably stronger, stars of this sort would be impossible. But if it were much weaker, the universe would be composed entirely of helium.

Here are some remarkable numbers. Electrons and protons have equal but opposite charges. It has been estimated that a charge difference of more than one part in 10 billion would mean that there could be no macroscopic objects; that is, there could be no solid bodies weighing more than about a gram. The ratio of the strengths of electromagnetism to gravity appears to be crucial. Changes in either force by one part in 10^{40} (ten followed by forty zeros) would spell catastrophe for stars like our sun. The ratio between gravity and the nuclear weak force may have to be adjusted as accurately as one part in 10^{100}

power to avoid either a swift collapse of the universe or an explosion.

Cosmologists began noting these remarkable coincidences in the 1950s. By now several books have appeared with page after page of such conclusions.[17] What are we to make of these results? Again we come to a point where established results of science raise a question that many take to call for a theological answer. Russell Stannard asks: "What are we to make of it? Are [these conditions] just coincidences? If so, we're talking of odds far in excess of winning first prize in the national lottery. Or are we to conclude that physics has found God?"[18]

We can notice here, as in the case of the questions raised by Big-Bang cosmology, similarities with issues raised in earlier design arguments. Thomas's two teleological arguments, one in the *Summa Theologiae* and the other in the *Summa contra Gentiles*, together form a close parallel. In the *Summa contra Gentiles* Thomas emphasizes the cooperation of many objects in the realization of the one world order. Recognition of the fine-tuning involves us in reflecting on the cooperation of many factors (laws and constants) in the realization of this one of many possible universes. In the *Summa Theologiae* Thomas emphasizes the goal-directedness of natural processes. The fine-tuning argument stresses the extent to which these many laws and constants seem to be directed toward the goal of making life possible.

There is a lovely bit of irony in the way the fine-tuning raises the question of design. It was Darwin's evolutionary theory that put a definitive end to design arguments such as Paley's, based on the fitness of biological organisms to their environments. Yet evidence for the fine-tuning itself appears only when we ask: what conditions are necessary to make possible the *evolution* of life in the universe?

As I have throughout, I emphasize that the fine-tuning provides no theistic proof.[19] Again, as in the case of the questions arising from Big-Bang cosmology, there are other possible responses. One suggestion is that, while it is amazing that the universe should have turned out to be life-supporting, this is just a matter of chance and there is nothing more to be said. Paul Davies responds to this suggestion as follows:

> . . . whereas many of my colleagues may feel comfortable with this astonish-ingly felicitous set of laws as just something that has no reason, it seems to me that the essence of the scientific method is to regard the Universe as having a rational basis, and arbitrary or absurd features are not really allowed. To stop the line of questioning at this stage seems to be far too premature. Our existence as sentient beings in the Universe links in to the basic laws of the Universe in a very meaningful way. And I think that provides human beings, in a modest but nevertheless important way, with some sort of deeper significance to their lives.[20]

A natural move to explain (explain away?) the wonder at finding the universe finely tuned for life is to propose that it is but one of vastly many universes – all different – and that we naturally find ourselves in the one (or one of the ones) that, by random variation, happened to be suitable for life. This involves postulations, perhaps, trillions and trillions of universes, all with a different mix of fundamental constants. Some believe that this is a simpler way to account for the fine-tuning of the universe than to invoke the concept of the creator.[21]

Yet another suggestion is that it will someday be shown that there is only one set of numbers that can be used to solve the equations comprising the basic laws of nature. If so, this would, in a sense, provide a scientific explanation for the fine-tuning of the individual constants, masses, and other quantities. It provides no ultimate explanation, however, because we still can wonder at the coincidence that the only possible universe is also life-supporting, and at the fact that this one-and-only possibility is instantiated. This returns us to the question of why there is something rather than nothing.

So, while the anthropic issue seems inevitably to raise the question of design and thus of God, it certainly does not settle it. It also raises in a more profound way the question of the status of the laws of nature. It may be possible to say that the universe is self-explanatory *given* the laws of physics. But then one has to ask about the source or status of those laws themselves. When early modern scientists spoke of "the laws of nature" they no doubt understood the term as a metaphorical extension of the notion of divine law from the realm of theological ethics. The ontological status of the laws of nature was unproblematic: they were ideas in the mind of God (a move for which the way had already been paved by Christian Platonists who "located" Plato's realm of the forms in the mind of God).

What status have the laws of nature in contemporary thought? Paul Davies notes that:

> As long as the laws of nature were rooted in God, their existence was no more remarkable than that of matter, which God also created. But if the divine underpinning of the laws is removed, their existence becomes a profound mystery. Where do they come from? Who "sent the message"? Who devised the code? Are the laws simply *there* – free floating, so to speak – or should we abandon the very notion of laws of nature as an unnecessary hangover from a religious past?[22]

Davies, along with a number of other scientists, opts for what I shall call a Plato*istic* account of the laws of nature, meaning that, like Plato's eternal forms, the laws have an existence independent of the entities they govern. However, no one, to my knowledge, has provided a suitable account of how (or where) the laws might "exist" and how they affect physical reality: the same problems that have led most philosophers to abandon Platonic metaphysics. Furthermore, William Stoeger has argued persuasively that no such account of the laws of nature is necessary. All one needs to recognize is that there are objective regularities and relationships in nature, which scientists describe in human language and with the aid of mathematics.[23]

Stoeger's view appears the most credible account of the status of the laws of nature, but even if his arguments were not persuasive, this would still be the most viable option, since there seems to be no intelligible answer to the question of *how* the laws of nature could "exist" independently of either the mind of God or of the reality that instantiates them. Still, Stoeger's account leaves unanswered the question of what accounts for the objective regularities and relations in nature *if not* pre-existing laws.

Theological Perspectives

I have just argued that the examination of the cosmos in the light of current science raises the question of God, even though none of these results strictly requires a theistic answer. I have also suggested that this is an important development in a secularized world where the point of inquiring about God seems to have been forgotten. However, an equally important influence to be expected from cosmology, at least for believers, is a deeper insight into the purposes of God and God's relationship with us, on the one hand, and into our intrinsic relatedness to the rest of the cosmos, on the other.

God's Purposes

The Psalmist writes:

> When I look at your heavens, the work of your fingers,
> the moon and the stars that you have established;
> What are human beings that you are mindful of them,
> mortals that you care for them?   (8:3–4)

How much more than the Psalmist are we able to appreciate the wonder of the cosmos itself and, with these recent discoveries, to appreciate the fact that, in a certain sense, it all appears to have been created with us in mind.

Since the Copernican revolution humans have been removed from the center of the universe. We have also discovered how small our planet is in comparison to the vastness of the universe, and how short is our history in comparison to its age. Our view of the natural world has been "deanthropocentrized." But the present cosmological results show that if God were to have creatures such as ourselves, then the whole universe had to be created pretty much as it is in order for that to be possible. It had to have about as much matter in it – as many stars, galaxies, planets – and it had to be about as old as it is. We are not now at the center of the universe, but for believers it is certainly possible to see ourselves as the point or end of it all. We can say, literally, that all the stars in the heavens, even the billions we cannot see, were created for our sake.

I am not arguing that we could draw these "anthropocentric" conclusions from cosmology alone. Rather, I am saying that for those whose views of the place of humankind in God's universe are shaped by the biblical creation stories, *we* find our theological perspective confirmed by the cosmologist's results in a rather striking manner.

In speaking of a biblical view of humankind's place in the cosmos, however, I need to be specific about my interpretation of the *point* of the creation stories (Gen. 1:1–2:4a and 2:4b-24). I am assuming, with the majority of contemporary scholars, that the point of the stories is not to provide a chronology of events (as creationists assume) but rather to speak of the character of the created order and of God's relation to it: of God's sovereignty and freedom with respect to the cosmos; of the goodness and order of the cosmos. Most important for our purposes is the position humans are assigned in these stories. In the Yahwist's account (Gen. 2:4bff.) the special relation of the earth creature (*'adam*) to God is symbolized in its animation by the divine breath and its naming of the animals. In the Priestly account (Gen. 1:1ff.) the creation of humans is the climax of the creative drama, and their special relation to God is expressed in the divine decision to make them "in our image, after our likeness." In light of both of these stories, it makes sense to look at the results from cosmology and say – not how odd, how surprising that the universe happened to be suited for intelligent life – but rather, how wonderfully it suits God's purposes.

Environmental Ethics

For many years Christians have thought of the natural world as a stage for human life and history. As such it was seen to have little intrinsic value to God. There was no strong theological tendency to counter those who took biblical language about dominion (cf. Ps. 8:5–8) as a license to exploit and destroy the environment.

The cosmology we have just examined, however, highlights the interconnectedness of human life with its natural environment. We are the result of an unimaginably complex, finely tuned, multi-billion-year process. A better analogy than that of actors on a stage to represent our relation to the natural world is to think of ourselves as fruit on a tree. Without the tree, without a healthy tree, we could not be here. Carl Sagan, for all his limitations as a theologian, makes the point nicely in saying that we are made of star dust. Immersion in the world of science, especially contemporary cosmology and astronomy, produces a sense of reverence for the natural world that may be a more effective deterrent to exploitation than any calculations of dire future consequences.

However, there is a second motive for environmental consciousness built into a theistic interpretation of contemporary cosmology. Let us think what the process of creation tells us about the character of the Creator. The immense time span speaks of the Creator's patience. True, a thousand years is as a day for God, but we still have to recognize a vast difference between the instantaneous creation that Christians assumed for many years and the slow, painstaking process that current cosmology suggests.

The point I wish to emphasize here is the great respect God seems to show for the integrity of the entities and processes that have been created. Diogenes Allen emphasizes that creation involves God's self-limitation – a withholding of divine power so that other things, things genuinely distinct from God, can exist.

> When God creates, it means that he allows something to exist which is not himself. This requires an act of profound renunciation. He chooses out of love to permit something else to exist, something created to be itself and to exist by virtue of its own interest and value. God renounces his status as the only existent – he pulls himself back, so to speak, in order to give his creation room to exist for its own sake.[24]

This voluntary restraint, exercised for the sake of people *and things* out of respect for their reality, is grace. "The very creation of the world is an act of such grace."[25]

The view that God withholds power to allow for free *human* actions is commonplace. It has long been recognized that God wants no coerced responses to divine initiatives. But the Christian tradition itself suggests that we must extend this view of divine self-limitation, speaking not only of free *will* but of free *processes*, going right back to the very beginning of creation. God brings the universe into being with its in-built laws, initial conditions, and potentialities, and allows the entities and processes as they unfold to become "created co-creators."[26] God values and respects the integrity of each new order of being as it emerges. There are obvious implications for our attitudes toward the natural world: a corresponding respect for nature with its intricate patterns and balances.

Conclusion

One of the most surprising developments in the contemporary intellectual world is an outpouring of interest in theological questions among astronomers, physicists, and cosmologists. These scholars reach a wide variety of conclusions, and theologians will find some of their reflections philosophically and theologically naive. Yet those theologians cannot but celebrate the ways in which the pursuit of fundamental scientific answers has raised, in the heart of secular academia, the same questions that have encouraged religious pursuits in the west for over two millennia.

I have been careful not to claim that these recent scientific advances can be used to prove God's existence to the skeptic. I do claim that they serve as a starting point for cooperative inquiry involving believers and nonbelievers alike. I have also emphasized that the position one takes in answer to these questions is self-involving. One cannot see the universe as designed without proper response to the Designer. When we look at the heavens, the work of God's fingers, the moon and the stars that God has established, we cannot but conclude, with the Psalmist:

> Oh Lord, our Sovereign, how majestic is your name in all the earth! (Ps. 8:9, NRSV)

Notes

1 F. Copleston, *A History of Philosophy*, vol. 2 (New York: Image/Doubleday, 1993), p. 344.

2 W. Paley, *Natural Theology; or Evidences of the Existence and Attributes of the Deity, Collected from the Appearances of Nature* (London, 1802).

3 D. Hume, *Dialogues concerning Natural Religion*, in Richard Wollheim (ed.), *Hume on Religion* (Cleveland and New York: Meridian Books, 1963), pp. 115–16.

4 I. Kant, *Critique of Pure Reason*, 3.7.

5 For more detailed accounts of current cosmology and the questions raised for theologians, see Ian Barbour, *Religion in an Age of Science: The Gifford Lectures, Volume One* (San Francisco: Harper and Row, 1990); Nancey Murphy and George F. R. Ellis, *On the Moral Nature of the Universe: Theology, Cosmology, and Ethics* (Minneapolis: Fortress, 1996).

6 From a sermon preached at Knox Presbyterian Church, Pasadena, Calif., 10 January 1978; published in Paul K. Jewett, *God, Creation, and Revelation: A Neo-Evangelical Theology* (Grand Rapids: Eerdmans, 1991), p. 506.

7 St. Augustine, *Confessions*, trans. Henry Chadwick (Oxford: Oxford University Press, 1991), pp. 229–30, XI.xii(14)–xiii(15).

8   This is parallel to one of Hume's criticisms of the design argument.

9   This is a contested point, however. Some scientists seem to hold a view of natural laws similar to Plato's concept of the Forms or Ideas: they are eternal and precede the material entities that they determine. But this position raises its own sort of questions. See the section, "Cosmological Fine-Tuning" below.

10 See Paul Davies, *The Mind of God: The Scientific Basis for a Rational World* (New York: Simon and Schuster, 1992), ch. 2.

11 *Summa Theologiae: A Concise Translation*, ed. Timothy McDermott (Westminster, MD: Christian Classics, 1989), p. 12.

12 Davies, *The Mind of God*, pp. 63, 67.

13 Interview with Russell Stannard, published in Stannard, *Science and Wonders: Conversations about Science and Belief* (London and Boston: Faber and Faber, 1996), p. 14.

14 Davies, *The Mind of God*, p. 68, quoting Stephen Hawking, *A Brief History of Time* (London and New York: Bantam, 1988), p. 141.

15 Davies, *The Mind of God*, p. 68.

16 Paul Davies, *God and the New Physics* (New York: Simon and Schuster, 1983), p. ix.

17 Two prominent books are J. Barrow and F. Tipler, *The Anthropic Cosmological Principle* (Oxford: Oxford University Press, 1986) and John Leslie, *Universes* (London and New York: Routledge, 1989). The figures above are from Leslie.

18 Stannard, *Science and Wonders*, p. 23.

19 The fine-tuning can, however, be used as corroborative evidence for theological research programs. See my "Evidence of Design in the Fine-Tuning of the Universe," in *Quantum Cosmology and the Laws of Nature: Scientific Perspectives on Divine Action*, ed. Robert J. Russell, Nancey Murphy, and C. J. Isham (Vatican City State and Berkeley, CA: Vatican Observatory and Center for Theology and the Natural Sciences, 1993), pp. 407–35

20 Quoted by Stannard, *Science and Wonders*, p. 24.

21 See Stannard, *Science and Wonders*, pp. 24–5.

22 Davies, *The Mind of God*, p. 81.

23 W. Stoeger, "Contemporary Physics and the Ontological Status of the Laws of Nature," in *Quantum Cosmology and the Laws of Nature*, pp. 209–34.

24 Diogenes Allen, *The Traces of God in a Frequently Hostile World* (Cambridge, MA: Cowley, 1981), p. 35. Allen is much influenced here by the writings of Simone Weil.

25 Allen, *Traces of God*, p. 36.

26 This is Philip Hefner's term. See *The Human Factory: Evolution, Culture, and Religion* (Minneapolis: Fortress Press, 1993).

3

Inquiring after God through Discernment

Theology is, perhaps above all, a discipline of discernment. Whether one begins by examining the doctrinal tradition, a personal encounter with God, a sobering personal experience, or the culture in which one is located, theology is thinking through and beyond these points of entry until deeper realizations about God's truth emerge. Discernment is not one's first thoughts about God, but one's considered and reconsidered thought.

In this chapter we meet a theologian who spent many years considering the relationship between the faith of the Church that she received and accepted and her experience of God the Holy Trinity. Her work was prompted by an intense vision of the crucified Christ that she had on 13 May 1373, when she was delirious and near death with fever at the age of thirty. Julian of Norwich was an anchoress, a recluse who lived in a small set of rooms attached to the town church. Even though her whole book is about her vision of the cross of Christ, a very personal experience, she tells us little about herself beyond what has been said above. We do not even know her name. Julian of Norwich is taken from St. Julian's Church in Norwich, in the eastern part of England where she lived.

Julian claimed theological authority from neither herself nor her education, but solely from this revelation from God, which took her twenty years to understand and write down. Her theological concern, like many before her, is with the struggle between divine judgment and divine mercy. The Church teaches that although God is good, some people go to hell. In Julian's day people were often terrified instead of attached to God because divine wrath was more vivid to them than was God's mercy. To help people overcome their fear of punishment Julian focused her theology on God's love, the power of Christ to effect it, and the salvation of the believer through the union of the soul with God. The pathway into spiritual comfort is prayer that enables one to join one's soul to the Lord's will, despite the weight of sin that drags one down to nought.

Julian was a bold theologian. She was well aware of and accepts the Church's teaching that we are judged because of our sins, but she also knew that becoming preoccupied with one's fallenness can be psychologically corrosive. Reflecting on her vision of Christ's passion she discerned that it is God's love for the good that we want to do, not what we actually are and do that is most important to God. And it is clinging to that graciousness that strengthens us and prevents us from being psychologically separated from God on account of his displeasure. Becoming one with God psychologically is true happiness; being separated from God is true despair.

In explaining the close relationship between God and the soul that she envisioned, Julian used the analogy of the relationship between a lord and a servant. While it is an unequal relationship, it is filled with love and trust, not hostility and anxiety. This image reflects a positive view of the feudal culture of Julian's day. Feudalism was an intricate set of hierarchical contractual arrangements in which a wealthy and powerful nobleman or landlord provided land and military protection to an inferior in return for use of the land and service. Loyalty, integrity, and trust on both sides were essential to the success of such arrangements. The agreement was concluded with a kiss, pledges of loyalty, and sometimes the exchange of tokens. Although feudalism deteriorated into exploitative relationships, Julian took the model at its best as a symbol of the loving care that God offers to his servants on earth whose duty it is to love and serve him in return.

In her interpretive essay on Julian, Professor Elisabeth Koenig details the process of discernment that Julian outlines as a path of spiritual and psychological growth through increased clarity of vision and growth in compassion. To that end, she enters into a contemporary debate about "mysticism." While modern writers of the nineteenth and twentieth centuries have often depicted mysticism as a purely subjective experience of eternity that is universal and transcends all cultures and religious traditions, Professor Koenig argues that the spiritual path is a process of discernment that is both subjective and objective, cognitive and affective, that both undoes and transforms the self for spiritual wholeness. Contrary to the older reading of mysticism, union with God does not entail transcending the historic tradition to reach an ethereal and formally empty experience of eternity that some religious traditions of India and China seek. Rather, becoming one with God means delving more deeply into the texts, events, and personages who populate the historic tradition to work through them and be undone and transformed by them.

Julian of Norwich, *Showings*

The First Chapter

This is a revelation of love which Jesus Christ, our endless bliss, made in sixteen showings, of which the first is about his precious crowning of thorns; and in this was contained and specified the blessed Trinity, with the Incarnation and the union between God and man's soul, with many fair revelations and teachings of endless wisdom and love, in which all the revelations which follow are founded and connected. . . .

The Second Chapter

This revelation was made to a simple, unlettered creature, living in this mortal flesh, the year of our Lord one thousand, three hundred and seventy-three, on the thirteenth day of May; and before this the creature had desired three graces by the gift of God. The first was recollection of the Passion. The second was bodily sickness. The third was to have, of God's gift, three wounds. As to the first, it seemed to me that I had some feeling for the Passion of Christ, but still I desired to have more by the grace of God. I thought that I wished that I had been at that time with Magdalen and with the others who were Christ's lovers, so that I might have seen with my own eyes the Passion which our Lord suffered for me, so that I might have suffered with him as others did who loved him. Therefore I desired a bodily sight, in which I might have more knowledge of our saviour's bodily pains, and of the compassion of our Lady and of all his true lovers who were living at that time and saw his pains, for I would have been one of them and have suffered with them. I never desired any other sight of God or revelation, until my soul would be separated from the body, for I believed that I should be saved by the mercy of God. This was my intention, because I wished afterwards, because of that revelation, to have truer recollection of Christ's Passion. . . .

The Third Chapter

And when I was thirty and a half years old, God sent me a bodily sickness in which I lay for three days and three nights, and on the third night I received all the rites of Holy Church, and did not expect to live until day. And after this I lay for two days and two nights, and on the third night I often thought that I was on the point of death, and those who were with me often thought so. And yet in this I felt a great reluctance to die, not that there was anything on earth which it pleased me to live for, or any pain of which I was afraid, for I trusted in the mercy of God. But it was because I wanted to live to love God better and longer, so that I might through the grace of that living have more knowledge and love of God in the bliss of heaven. Because it seemed to me that all the time that I had lived here was very little and short in comparison with the bliss which is everlasting, I thought: Good Lord, can my living no longer be to your glory? And I understood by my reason and the sensation of my pains that I should die; and with all the will of my heart I assented to be wholly as was God's will.

So I lasted until day, and by then my body was dead from the middle downwards, as it felt to me. Then I was helped to sit upright and supported, so that my heart might be more free to be at God's will, and so that I could think of him whilst my life would last. My curate was sent for to be present at my end; and before he came my eyes were fixed upwards, and I could not speak. He set the cross before my face, and said: I have brought the image of your saviour; look at it and take comfort from it. It seemed to me that I was well, for my eyes were set upwards towards heaven, where I trusted that I by God's mercy was going; but nevertheless I agreed to fix my eyes on the face of the crucifix if I could, and so I did, for it seemed to me that I would hold out longer with my eyes set in front of me rather than upwards. After this my sight began to fail. It grew as dark around me in the room as if it had been night, except that there was ordinary light trained upon the image of the cross, I did not know how. Everything around the cross was ugly and terrifying to me, as if it were occupied by a great crowd of devils.

After this the upper part of my body began to die, until I could scarcely feel anything. My greatest pain was my shortness of breath and the ebbing of my life. Then truly I believed that I was at the point of death. And suddenly at that moment all my pain was taken from me, and I was as sound, particularly in the upper part of my body, as ever I was before. I was astonished by this sudden change, for it seemed to me that it was by God's secret doing and not natural; and even so, in this ease which I felt, I had no more confidence that I should live, nor was the ease I felt complete for me, for I thought that I would rather have been delivered of this world, because that was what my heart longed for. . . .

The Fourth Chapter

And at this, suddenly I saw the red blood running down from under the crown, hot and flowing freely and copiously, a living stream, just as it was at the time when the crown of thorns was pressed on his blessed head. I perceived, truly and powerfully, that it was he who just so, both God and man, himself suffered for me, who showed it to me without any intermediary.

And in the same revelation, suddenly the Trinity filled my heart full of the greatest joy, and I understood that it will be so in heaven without end to all who will come there. For the Trinity is God, God is the Trinity. The Trinity is our maker, the Trinity is our protector, the Trinity is our everlasting lover, the Trinity is our endless joy and our bliss, by our Lord Jesus Christ and in our Lord Jesus Christ. And this was revealed in the first vision and in them all, for where Jesus appears the Blessed Trinity is understood, as I see it. . . .

The Forty-First Chapter

After this our Lord revealed about prayer, in which revelation I saw two conditions in our Lord's intention. One is rightful prayer; the other is confident trust. But still all our trust is often not complete, because we are not sure that God hears us, as we think, because of our unworthiness and because we are feeling nothing at all; for often we are as barren and dry after our prayers as we were before. And thus when we feel so, it is our folly which is the cause of our weakness, for I have experienced this in myself. And our Lord brought all this suddenly to my mind, and revealed these words and said: I am the ground of your beseeching. First, it is my will that you should have it, and then I make you to wish it, and then I make you to beseech it. If you beseech it, how could it be that you would not have what you beseech? And so in the first reason and in the three that follow, our Lord reveals a great strengthening, as can be seen in the same words.

And in the first reason, where he says: if you beseech, he shows his great delight, and the everlasting reward that he will give us for our beseeching. And in the second reason, where he says: How could it be? this was said as an impossibility; for it is the most impossible that that may be that we should seek mercy and grace and not have it. For everything which our good Lord makes us to beseech he himself has ordained for us from all eternity. So here we may see that our beseeching is not the cause of the goodness and grace which he gives us, but his own goodness. And that he truly revealed in all these sweet words, where he says: I am the foundation. And our good Lord wants this to be known by his lovers on earth. And the more that we know this, the more shall we beseech, if it be wisely accepted, and this is our Lord's intention.

Beseeching is a true and gracious, enduring will of the soul, united and joined to our Lord's will by the sweet, secret operation of the Holy Spirit. Our Lord himself is the first receiver of our prayer, as I see it, and he accepts it most thankfully, and greatly rejoicing he sends it up above, and puts it in a treasure-house where it will never perish. It is there before God with all his holy saints, continually received, always furthering our needs. And when we shall receive our bliss, it will be given to us as a measure of joy, with endless, honourable thanks from him.

Our Lord is most glad and joyful because of our prayer; and he expects it, and he wants to have it, for with his grace it makes us like to himself in condition as we are in nature, and such is his blessed will. For he says: Pray wholeheartedly, though it seems to you that this has no savour for you; still it is profitable enough, though you may not feel that. Pray wholeheartedly, though you may feel nothing, though you may see nothing, yes, though you think that you could not, for in dryness and in barrenness, in sickness and in weakness, then is your prayer most pleasing to me, though you think it almost tasteless to you. And so is all your living prayer in my sight.

Because of the reward and the endless thanks that he will give us there, because he covets to have us praying continually in his sight, God accepts the good will and the labour of his servants, however we may feel, and therefore it pleases him that we work in prayer and in good living by his help and his grace, reasonably and with discretion, preserving our powers for him until we have in the fulness of joy him whom we seek, who is Jesus. . . .

Thanksgiving also belongs to prayer. Thanksgiving is a true inward acknowledgment, we applying ourselves with great reverence and loving fear and with all our powers to the work that our Lord moved us to, rejoicing and giving thanks inwardly. And sometimes the soul is so full of this that it breaks out in words and says: Good Lord, great thanks, blessed may you be. And sometimes the heart is dry and feels nothing, or else, by the temptation of our enemy, reason and grace drive the soul to implore our Lord with words, recounting his blessed Passion and his great goodness. And so the power of our Lord's word enters the soul and enlivens the heart and it begins by his grace faithful exercise, and makes the soul to pray most blessedly, and truly to rejoice in our Lord. This is a most loving thanksgiving in his sight. . . .

The Forty-Third Chapter

Prayer unites the soul to God, for though the soul may be always like God in nature and in substance restored by grace, it is often unlike him in condition, through sin on man's part. Then prayer is a witness that the soul wills as God wills, and it eases the conscience and fits man for grace. And so he teaches us to pray and to have firm trust that we shall have it; for he beholds us in love, and wants to make us partners in his good will and work. And so he moves us to pray for what it pleases him to do, and for this prayer and good desire which come to us by his gift he will repay us, and give us eternal reward. . . .

The Fiftieth Chapter

. . . Good Lord, I see in you that you are very truth, and I know truly that we sin grievously all day and are very blameworthy; and I can neither reject my knowledge of this truth, nor see that any kind of blame is shown to us. How can this be? For I know by the ordinary teaching of Holy Church and by my own feeling that the blame of our sins continually hangs upon us, from the first man until the time that we come up into heaven. This, then, was my astonishment, that I saw our Lord God showing no more blame to us than if we were as pure and as holy as the angels are in heaven. And between these two oppositions my reason was greatly afflicted by my blindness, and I could have no rest for fear that his blessed presence would pass from my sight, and I should be left in ignorance of how he may look on us in our sin. For either I ought to see in God that sin was all done away with, or else I ought to see in God how he sees it, by which I might truly know how it is fitting for me to see sin and the way in which we have blame. . . .

The Fifty-First Chapter

And then our courteous Lord answered very mysteriously, by revealing a wonderful example of a lord who has a servant, and gave me sight for the understanding of them both. The vision was shown doubly with respect to the lord, and the vision was shown doubly with respect to the servant. One part was shown spiritually, in a bodily likeness. The other part was shown more spiritually, without bodily likeness. So, for the first, I saw two persons in bodily likeness, that is to say a lord and a servant; and with that God gave me spiritual understanding. The lord sits in state, in rest and in peace. The servant stands before his lord, respectfully, ready to do his lord's will. The lord looks on his servant very lovingly and sweetly and mildly. He sends him to a certain place to do his will. Not only does the servant go, but he dashes off and runs at great speed, loving to do his lord's will. And soon he falls into a dell and is greatly injured; and then he groans and moans and tosses about and writhes, but he cannot rise or help himself in any way. And of all this, the greatest hurt which I saw him in was lack of consolation, for he could not turn his face to look on his loving lord, who was very close to him, in whom is all consolation; but like a man who was for the time extremely feeble and foolish, he paid heed to his feelings and his continuing distress, in which distress he suffered . . . great pains. . . .

The Eighty-Second Chapter

But here our courteous Lord revealed the moaning and the mourning of our soul, with this meaning: I know well that you wish to live for my love, joyfully and gladly suffering all the penance which may come to you; but since you do not live without sin, you are depressed and sorrowful, and if you could live without sin, you would suffer for my love all the woe which might come to you, and it is true. But do not be too much aggrieved by the sin which comes to you against your will.

And here I understood that the lord looked on the servant with pity and not with blame; for this passing life does not require us to live wholly without sin. He loves us endlessly, and we sin customarily, and he reveals it to us most gently. And then we sorrow and moan discreetly, turning to contemplate his mercy, cleaving to his love and to his goodness, seeing that his is our medicine, knowing that we only sin.

And so by the meekness which we obtain in seeing our sin, faithfully recognizing his everlasting love, thanking him and praising him, we please him. I love you and you love me, and our love will never be divided in two; and it is for your profit that I suffer. And all this was revealed in spiritual understanding, he saying these blessed words: I protect you very safely.

And by the great desire which I saw in our blessed Lord that we shall live in this way, that is to say in longing and rejoicing, as all this lesson of love shows, I understood that all which is opposed to this is not from him, but it is from enmity. And he wants us to know it by the sweet light of grace of his substantial and natural love.

If there be any such l[o]ver on earth, who is continually protected from falling, I do not know, for it was not revealed to me. But this was revealed, that in falling and in rising we are always preciously protected in one love. For we do not fall in the sight of God, and we do not stand in our own sight; and both these are true, as I see it, but the contemplating of our Lord God is the higher truth. So we are much indebted to him, that he will in this way of life reveal to us this high truth, and I understood that while we are in this way, it is most profitable to us that we see these both together. For the higher contemplation keeps us in spiritual joy and true delight in God; the other, which is the lower contemplation, keeps us in fear, and makes us ashamed of ourselves.

But our good Lord always wants us to remain much more in the contemplation of the higher, and not to forsake the knowledge of the lower, until the time that we are brought up above, where we shall have our Lord Jesus for our reward, and be filled full of joy and bliss without end.

The Eighty-Third Chapter

In this matter I had touching, sight and feeling of three properties of God, in which consist the strength and the effect of all the revelation. . . . The properties are these: life, love and light. In life is wonderful familiarity, in love is gentle courtesy, and in light is endless nature. . . .

Our faith is a light, coming in nature from our endless day, which is our Father, God; in which light our Mother, Christ, and our good Lord the Holy Spirit lead us in this passing life. This light is measured with discretion, and it is present to us in our need in the night. The light is the cause of our life, the night is the cause of our pain and all our woe, in which woe we deserve endless reward and thanks from God; for we by his mercy and grace willingly know and believe our light, walking therein wisely and mightily. And at the end of woe, suddenly our eyes will be opened, and in the clearness of our sight our light will be full, which light is God, our Creator, Father, and the Holy Spirit, in Christ Jesus our saviour.

So I saw and understood that our faith is our light in our night, which light is God, our endless day.

The Eighty-Fourth Chapter

This light is charity, and the measuring of this light is performed for us to our profit by the wisdom of God; for the light is not so generous that we can see clearly our blessed day, nor is it all shut off from us, but it is such a light as we can live in meritoriously, with labour deserving the honourable thanks of God. And this was seen in the sixth revelation, where he says: I thank you for your service and your labour. So charity keeps us in faith and in hope. And faith and hope lead us in charity, and in the end everything will be charity. . . .

The Eighty-Sixth Chapter

This book is begun by God's gift and his grace, but it is not yet performed as I see it. . . . And from the time that it was revealed, I desired many times to know in what was our Lord's meaning. And fifteen years after and more, I was answered in spiritual understanding, and it was said: What, do you wish to know your Lord's meaning in this thing? Know it well, love was his meaning. Who reveals it to you? Love. What did he reveal to you? Love. Why does he reveal it to you? For love. Remain in this, and you will know more of the same. But you will never know different, without end. . . .

CONTEMPORARY REFLECTION

Julian of Norwich and the Drama of Christian Discernment

Elisabeth K. J. Koenig

So I saw and understood that our faith is our light in our night, which light is God, our endless day.   (Julian of Norwich, *Showings*[1])

Marye [Magdalene] . . . is a lyghtar, for . . . she toke the lyght [wythinforth], wyth which afterward she enlumyned other.   (*The Golden Legende*[2])

When Rachel Hosmer, OSH, my first spiritual director, would speak to me about what happened to her when she prayed, it was as though I were seeing flares launched onto the dark side of the moon. In the temporary radiance, a new country appeared. I caught glimpses there of what God's love is like; I began to desire it and believe that it was offered to me, even when my own vision was occluded by the darkness of intellectual uncertainty and emotional angst.

During this same period, I was engaged in graduate work at Columbia University and Union Theological Seminary in New York City. Professors and students at both institutions presented myriad and complex reasons why talk about experience of God is very often specious. Generally, I saw their points and even tossed a few logs of my own onto the fire. Objections came from every field of inquiry:

- *Theological* – Is God an object among objects to be discerned through the senses as other objects are? Or: how would one distinguish an experience of God from one that was humanly generated?
- *Philosophical* – Can anything coming from the realm of subjectivity in fact be communicated or publicly examined?
- *Sociological or ideological* – Inadvertently, but inevitably, people use religious language to mask issues of power. For example: "From where I stand in society, my experience of God is more criterial than yours is; therefore, you should submit to my demands."
- *Political* – "I wish I had an experience of God, but the Church has oppressed so many people for so long [especially women], and I personally have been hurt so much, that I am prevented from using its theological language. Therefore, I am left without the means to talk about God either to myself or to anyone else and wouldn't recognize an experience of God even if I had one."
- *Moral* – Talk about God is only a projection of your own powerfulness and an unconscionable failure to use your might effectively for moral purposes.
- *Psychological* – What people deem experience of God is nothing more than repressed sexuality, or else it is the super-ego writ large.
- *Spiritual* – An angel of darkness often comes disguised as an angel of light.
- *Apophatic* – God is hidden; therefore, so-called "mystical" language does not concern experience of God so much as it points to the fact of God's hiddenness.

Today in my classroom, my students and I continue to reflect on and respond to issues such as these. Indeed, twentieth-century people from many walks of life can point to situations where failure to discern the potential duplicity of religious language has had destructive consequences for our humanity. Conscionable theology, it seems clear, must engage in this realm of discourse, often termed the hermeneutics of suspicion. However, theology needs also to be able to set its own reasonable limits on these efforts at deconstruction.[3]

I was already becoming convinced that this was so as, throughout my graduate years, Rachel continued to impress me with her integrity. A highly intelligent, well-educated elderly nun and priest, regarded by some as very dear and by others as overbearing and quite fierce, she knew many of the reasons why you could not talk about God and yet continued to do so in such a way that dismissing her words became impossible for me. Neither her friends nor her enemies would label Rachel's way private, sweet, or sentimental; instead, this doggedly determined sister traveled a road of political engagement. She had helped to rescue a young Jewish girl from Nazi Germany, had worked as a missionary in West Africa, and throughout her whole life continually had spoken in favor of simplicity and voluntary poverty, and against injustice, violence, and oppression.[4]

Thus my friendship with Rachel during the last ten years of her life forever cast a different sort of light on the question of inquiring after God through experience. She had challenged me to develop and live out a credible spirituality; therefore, although my profession still concerns theology and the life of the mind, discussions that are purely academic never again will fully satisfy me. How would you finally prove anything, anyway? I now think it more profitable for one seeking God to ask what is shown in the lives of people who claim that their sacrifice of self stems from an experience of a God who is, at once, attractive and beautiful, loving, challenging, and truthful.

That said, wanting to know what makes the life of faith visible should not require a fanatical, bit-in-the-teeth flight from problematic issues like those stated above. In particular, it demands both philosophical and theological grappling with the question of the relationship between inner reality and outer reality, a question that involves, but is not exhausted by, that of how subjective experience can be communicated. These are not easy questions to answer, and I would not for a moment wish to suggest that they are; but they are good questions – fruitful questions that can, if pursued, shed light on the relationships between theology and art, theology and psychology, theology and the social sciences, and what might constitute truthful discourse in any of these areas. In what follows, I hope to show that there are resources in the work of the fourteenth-century English anchoress, theologian, and visionary, Julian of Norwich, for clarifying some of Christianity's most profound responses to questions like these. But first, a few words about Julian and her writing.

On Mysticism

There is no evidence that Julian's *Book of Showings* was well known among her contemporaries, a fact that makes all the more remarkable her ongoing popularity among twentieth-century people.[5] Although the works of other fourteenth-century spiritual authors like Richard Rolle and Walter Hilton were widely circulated among theologically interested lay people, Julian, perhaps due to the complexity and difficulty of her work, is remembered only in four wills and mentioned in one literary work, the *Book of Margery*

Kempe. The odd and flamboyant Margery from the nearby town of King's Lynn describes several days she spent in spiritual consultation with Julian, who apparently was a fairly well-known spiritual guide. However, Margery never mentions Julian's writing.[6] In 1670, the English Benedictine Serenus Cressy published his modernized version of Julian's long text[7] but, again, there was very little response to it. By contrast, in our century three editions of her original Middle English have appeared, along with at least seven modernizations, and many, many collections of excerpts.[8]

Julian was among those late medieval theologians and lay people who, in reaction to the excesses of scholasticism, had come to believe that human affect can yield genuine theological understanding.[9] From the eleventh through the fifteenth centuries, piety focused more and more on the emotional richness of Jesus' earthly humanity. Even learned people believed that they could be educated theologically through feeling. Julian's writing belongs within this tradition, for she states quite clearly at the beginning of her *Book* that her understanding of God's love will come through feeling what Christ felt during his passion (286). Thus, her bodily experience of dying, the accompanying sixteen visions, and her emotional reactions to both were worthy of Julian's subsequent twenty years' contemplation. Indeed, she considered all three to be direct communications of God's love. Like many of her contemporaries, Richard Rolle in particular, Julian focuses on the details of Jesus' crucifixion, the blood gushing out from under the crown of thorns, the scourging and spitting, the wound to his side, the deep drying-out of the body. Her writing is distinctive, however, because she evidences no particular fascination with suffering itself ("If I had known the pain for what it was I should have been loath to pray for it" – p. 212); instead, her goal in describing the passion is to make God's love visible to her readers. Julian is uncommon also because, in contrast to the other fourteenth-century English mystics, who are mainly concerned to describe prayer or stages of spiritual growth, Julian actually attempts to recreate for herself and for her readers the visionary experience she had on 13 May 1373. Most remarkable was the fact that, by virtue of these revelations, Julian felt herself to be united or "oned" to God in love, even while she believed herself to be fallen and therefore blameworthy. It is this experience in particular, that is, the existential, felt experience of being united to God through loving prayer, that Julian effectively recreates through visual imagery and theological assertion in her *Book of Showings*.

The plan of my argument is as follows. First, I intend to show that Julian's category of "one-ing" is correlated with her understanding of a cross-centered process of Christian discernment, which, in turn, has everything to do with how she understands faith. Our only access to the Trinity being, for Julian, Jesus' blood-streaked face, we shall see how her description of the flow of his blood signals a union of inner and outer reality culminating in our being drawn up, in Christ's body, into the very life of the Trinity.

Next, I propose to explore the significance of her *Book*'s chiaroscuro effect. By this I mean that visually and spatially, light and dark enhance each other, and that Julian (certainly influenced by Johannine themes) plays throughout on this effect to lead her readers through a discernment process like the one which had become familiar to her after twenty years spent in contemplative prayer. We shall see also how it is significant that, with regard to two themes, that of light and darkness and that of the contribution of inner contemplative experience to the life of the Christian community, Julian represents herself in a role almost identical to that of Mary Magdalene, the "lighter," as the latter was known through the *Golden Legend* and in the drama of Julian's time. Consequently, exploration of Magdalene-associated themes in her text will facilitate our understanding of how Julian regards discernment. Moreover, drama seems to be a genre not unfamiliar, at least in spirit, to Julian. Several commentators have referred to her visions as being like "allegorical drama," or to the whole progression of her text as depicting a cosmic drama.[10]

I explore this issue in some depth for one important reason: growth in the process of Christian discernment seems to involve a particular kind of dialogical drama between the soul and God, a drama defined by Julian's use of Mary Magdalene imagery, and enlarged by her own maturation in faithful seeing. This last element, maturation, leads to a discussion of the relationship between Julian's experience and church doctrine, which will be the natural place to focus theologically on the issue I mentioned above. That is, how can we speak authentically about the relationship between inner reality and outer reality? Alternatively, to give the problem a more concrete application, and one that Julian makes herself,[11] what does it mean for limited, fallen people to perform in the world that which has been discerned of Christian truth?

A focus on the correlative processes of "one-ing" and discernment in Julian of Norwich may have an additional benefit: it may furnish a fresh perspective on the problems associated with the modern search for a universal "mystical" experience. F. C. Bauerschmidt, in his article entitled "Julian of Norwich – Incorporated," offers a comprehensive and useful rehearsal of the issue. He begins by questioning "modernity's construction of the category 'mysticism' and Julian's location under that rubric."[12] As an example of this popular but not very helpful approach to texts, Bauerschmidt quotes Arthur Edward Waite, "doyen of the Hermetic Society of the Golden Dawn," who wrote in 1906, "I have no personal doubt that true mystics of every age and country constitute an unincorporated fellowship communicating continually together in the higher consciousness." Rejecting this, Bauerschmidt proposes "to reconstrue Julian's work, not as an instance of a putatively universal and ahistorical 'mysticism,' but as a particular reading of the Christian tradition that seeks to imagine and commend a specific form of social existence, characterized by a compassion that mirrors in history the divine sociality of Father, Son and Spirit."[13]

In other words, the attempt to demonstrate "the almost uncanny universality of the religious experience"[14] is not very fruitful; it does not add much to our understanding either of religious texts or of religious experience. More profitable, as I (with some qualification) think Bauerschmidt successfully demonstrates, is to insist on the impossibility of dividing "human existence into the inner mystical sphere and the external political sphere and [declaring] a truce or division of labor between them." Bauerschmidt goes on to show that "Julian of Norwich offers a specific, though not necessarily detailed, vision of the common life, one grounded in the Gospel narratives of Jesus (particularly the passion narrative)."[15] Although a contemplative, ultimately enclosed as an anchoress in a cell, Julian always manifests a social concern; she writes for the sake of her "even Christians" and in order to build up the Body of Christ.

I heartily agree with most of Bauerschmidt's analysis and his conclusions. However, I also think that it is important to press his argument further in order to respond to a question, often unexpressed, but intensely felt and not wholly unreasonable, in the approach of people who are searching for a "universal" experience. That question is: given where I stand in history and society, what must I do, or how must I comport myself, in order to experience divine reality in a way that is, if not the same, at least analogous to the one the "mystics" claim to have had?[16] Or, to emphasize the Christian's social responsibility, one might ask: how do I, with the help of God's grace, make concrete and real in my own relations with others the compassion that "mirrors in history the divine sociality of Father, Son, and Spirit"? In other words, I do not think Bauerschmidt goes far enough in describing how Julian actually shows, in the dynamic movement of her text, the process of becoming "one-d" or united to God[17] or, especially, what the accompanying awareness might be like. Such awareness has to be a recognizable component of the process of discernment. I suspect that Bauerschmidt's neglect of this process may be due to a less than full appreciation of inner reality and how growth occurs in this sphere of human experience.

Discernment for Julian

We have documentation from the New Testament up to the present time that there is an identifiable process of Christian discernment, that it involves inwardness, a state, or states of awareness and cognition, that individuals mature in, the result of which (frequently) is the strengthening of the community of faith.[18] From St. Paul to twentieth-century liberation theology's appropriation of Ignatius Loyola's "Rules for the Discernment of Spirits," we find theologians who suggest that discernment is not confined to the cognitive or intellectual dimensions of human experience, although it most certainly includes those. Maturation in Christian discernment also contains affective and even physical dimensions which can be felt.

Extrapolating a bit from Julian's description, I think we could claim that the person who has been united to God and who, as a result, has been made whole in herself, eventually begins to feel emotionally more balanced and stable, intellectually more nimble, clear, and creative, and spiritually more patient, loving, connected to other people and to God, and, possibly, more playful and humorous, as Julian apparently did herself. The omnipresence of the cross, however, means that the process is never simple, clear-cut, or finalized. To express this somewhat differently, a person's thoughts and feelings that may have been obsessive, distorted, or "stuck," may through all the Christian disciplines, especially contemplative prayer, begin to be released and to flow into important new channels that come from and lead to God's Word. Only then will he or she have something substantial to offer the community of faith.

It would seem, therefore, that the arduous process of contemplative prayer, which incorporates Julian's concept of "noughting" (being "brought low," "despised," or even "annihilated") in the form of the wrenching away of objects of desire, as well as attempts to manipulate both social situations and one's relationship with God, may be worth the trouble, after all! Indeed, I am convinced that this path of prayer is the chief concern of Julian's whole *Book*. Accordingly, I will be suggesting throughout this article that both one-ing and discernment involve a painful process of being undone which imitates God as God is known in Jesus' passion ("For he who is highest and most honourable was most foully brought low, most utterly despised; for the most important point to apprehend in his Passion is to meditate and come to see that he who suffered is God . . ." – p. 213). Furthermore, while the result seems to be a relatively ego-less, unified, and loving state of mind, perhaps even an "altered state of consciousness" (that suspicious phrase!), it is perhaps better to bracket questions about the universal nature of that subjective, inner experience in order to ask instead what results from the accompanying process of discernment.

I think that discernment merits attention within the context of contemporary debates over religious experience because it embraces dimensions of the Christian witness that are, at once, personal, interior, and subjective and communal, historical, doctrinal, moral, political, and aesthetic. In sum, its results can be made visible, communicable, and shareable. In this, the discernment process mirrors Julian's overall project, which is to make apparent and accessible not only the subjective experience of being beloved of God, but, more importantly, the consequences of that experience for the community of faith.

For Julian, "one-ing" and growth in what I am calling discernment, but which she terms increased clarity of vision, are deepening and expansive movements that transform the self that has been undone by imitating Christ on the cross. She depicts this interpenetration of inner and outer reality and experience in at least four ways: (i) by means of imagery associated with Christ's blood; (ii) through a play on themes of darkness and light; (iii) through identifying herself with the Magdalene and employing imagery associated with her; and (iv) by the specific way she uses her "schewinges" or visions in the text. Each of these themes serves a particular function in taking her readers through the transformative process she believes she experienced herself at God's behest. Julian is highly conscious that prayer is like being led or drawn by God, delicately but insistently, and with a particular quality of attention and vigilance, through the inner and outer events of one's life: "He showed himself in another way on earth [different from 'Incarnation' and 'his blessed passion'] as if it were on pilgrimage, that is to say that he is here with us, leading us, and will be until he has brought us all to his bliss in heaven" (p. 337). There are essentially two results: union with God and clarity of vision (which is also equivalent to faith, for Julian).

1. Christ's Blood

The image of flowing blood, which dominates Julian's visions is, for her, the sign of God's radical dispossession and self-donation in Jesus. In addition, it initiates a remarkable process in Julian's text, a process through which both inner and outer experience are united by means of a procession through abandonment, humiliation, and mourning.[19] I intend to show that, like the reciprocal movements through darkness and light, like the progression of her "schewinges," and like the trajectory defined by Magdalene imagery, the image of flowing blood speaks of a change brought about in Julian through contemplative prayer. But it is a change that may also be effected in her readers, if they can follow an itinerary in their own experience and in their own praying analogous to the one defined by these images.[20] The change essentially has to do with detachment and a consequent enhanced capacity for compassion.

Julian saw "the red blood running down from under the crown [of Jesus], hot and flowing freely and copiously, a living stream, just as it was at the time when the crown of thorns was pressed on his blessed head" (p. 181). She says further that the "bleeding continued until many things were seen and understood" (p. 188). All sixteen of her visions and their associated imagery and teaching were "contained and specified" in the one image of Christ's head crowned with thorns and the blood flowing down. After enumerating them all, she emphasizes the fact that her Lord gave her "space and time to behold it" (p. 199). Julian remarks that there was so much blood that if it had been other than a spiritual vision "the bed and everything all around it would have been soaked in blood" (p. 200). She likens it to the waters of the earth which, while plenteous, are nevertheless precious because they sustain life.

Most important, Julian sees that the blood that for love flowed from Jesus' wounds is somehow the same as the blood of every woman and man: "it is our own nature" (the Middle English word is "kynde"). Here, I think, Julian invites her readers to be more than mere observers, for if one follows her reflection on the blood, one is overtaken by and drawn into a reality whose locus appears at first to be only on the outside. Julian realizes that the blood Christ shed is the same blood that sustains her own life, a very subjective experience. In fact, a more intimate image of God's love could hardly be found; it is the foundation of what she calls God's "wonderful courtesy and familiarity" (p. 189). But if God's intimacy to our own subjectivity is beyond understanding,[21] Julian's experience of the objectivity of its powerfulness also transports her beyond an exclusive preoccupation with her own experience. The blood that she sees begins to flow as pellet-like drops falling from under the crown of thorns and descending down to hell where it "breaks its bonds, and delivered all that were there which belong to the court of heaven" (p. 200). Following this mighty descent, Christ's blood mounts up to heaven where it continues to flow everywhere.

2. Darkness and Light

This upward and expansive movement is paradigmatic of the general direction and movement of the whole text of the *Book of Showings*. However, the flow is far from a triumphalism, because its trajectory is always, as here, against the background of Christ's blood shed on the cross, and it is always accompanied by a deeper penetration into an inwardness colored by "noughting," or the experience of being brought low. A concomitant image of space, whether dark or lighted, is associated with this movement. Thus, the first space Julian shows us is the small, dark, contracted one surrounding her deathbed. But in her later chapters, where she has awakened into an image of her own soul in the midst of her heart ("I saw the soul so large as if it were an endless citadel and also as though it were a blessed kingdom"), space has opened up into enormous and luminous proportions. The fate of the image of space in *Showings* makes clear that this huge and light-filled sense of soul is not a form of narcissism, exclusively focused on self or inner experience. Instead, the movement has advanced from Julian's own particular concerns to those that are universal. Now a social image describes her soul: it is a fine city where Jesus, representing the unity of humanity and divinity, sits in peace and rest. The pilgrimage to this "high mountain citadel" is, however, never untroubled. Fortunately, other spiritual pilgrims – notably, Mary Magdalene – have charted the course.

3. Mary Magdalene

More than any other image or literary device in the *Book of Showings*, Julian's use of Mary Magdalene reveals the process whereby inner and outer experience and reality are united through a modification of sensibility that results from the prayerful working through of loss. Her *Book* has often been recognized as a long teaching on prayer and, for medieval people, Mary Magdalene was the model par excellence of one who prays through all the vicissitudes of life. Moreover, Julian specifically identifies herself with the Magdalene in two respects: affectively, she wants to experience Jesus' passion as intensely as Mary Magdalene did and, morally, she wants her own past history of sin to be turned into honor, as she believes the Magdalene's was (pp. 177–8 and 242–3). Thus, Julian artfully employs images derived from the Mary Magdalene tradition to show her readers that prayer is a dynamic process of seeking, finding, and losing God, indeed, a drama involving episodes of profound humiliation, abandonment, loss, and deepest mourning.

The idea of drama depicts as well Julian's one-ing and discernment process whose affective, dialogical style of praying leads to spiritual maturation. By dialogical, I mean a back-and-forth exchange between the soul and God whose inspiration in ancient and medieval times was often the biblical book, the Song of Songs. A sea-change in the emotional dimensions of one's personality is the result of such an exchange between God and the human being. Inordinate desire and controlling behavior atrophy, with the result that peacefulness and compassion can now body forth a fresh, new effective life. Echoing the Magdalene of medieval drama, Julian sums up her own search this way: "I saw him and sought him, and I had him and I lacked him" (p. 193). We could say that Julian's whole effort in prayer and writing stems from a catastrophic experience of loss which she shares with the Magdalene: Julian's visions of Jesus vanish and never reappear in all her twenty years of contemplation: "This kind of vision of him cannot persist in this life" (p. 261); "The vision would pass, and it is faith which preserves the blessed revelation . . . for he left with me neither sign nor token whereby I could know it" (p. 317). In a sense, the creation of her *Book* fills the vacuum.

Psychoanalytically, the affective and moral transformation Julian undergoes resembles a typical trajectory of mourning and individuation described brilliantly by Peter Homans and which he will go on to argue is the condition for uniting inner and outer reality:

> individuation is . . . the fruit of mourning. Somehow, in a way that is not really understood, the experience of loss can stimulate the desire "to become who one is." That in turn can throw into motion a third process, that should be called "the creation of meaning." This action is at once a work of personal growth and a work of culture.[22]

Thus, in mourning and the consequent creation of meaning, inner and outer experience are united. To understand how such a thing could happen, I think we need not only to value the inward dimensions of prayer (as Julian most certainly does) but also to become familiar with the internal process of spiritual growth as Julian explicates it. The organizing principle is "noughting."

For Julian, "we are all in part troubled, and we shall be troubled, following our master Jesus until we are fully purged of our mortal flesh and all our inward affections which are not very good" (p. 225). In other words, Christians will inevitably suffer in this world, but their suffering (which always, in some sense, concerns the undoing of desire and attachment), Julian thinks, participates in Christ's atoning work. Here Julian follows St. Paul: our suffering contributes vitally to the "sacrament of restored human unity."[23] As she puts it, "[Jesus] sits in our soul working us all into him. In this working he wants us to be his helpers, giving all our intention to him, learning his laws, observing his teaching, desiring everything to be done which he does, truly trusting in him . . ." (p. 292). This theme of Jesus working on the soul is a very prominent and serious one for Julian. Clearly, it denotes some kind of process, and to that issue I now turn.

In her parable of the lord and his servant, the servant is a symbolic, allegorical figure who conflates Adam, Christ, and every human being. He is sent by the lord to perform a task that, somehow, the lord is unable to accomplish himself. The task has to do with procuring a food from the earth and it entails arduous labor on the servant's part:

> And then I understood that he was to do the greatest labour and the hardest work there is. He was to be a gardener, digging and ditching and sweating and turning the soil over and over, and to dig deep down, and to water the plants at the proper time. And he was to persevere in his work, and make sweet streams to run, and fine and plenteous fruit to grow, which he was to bring before the lord and serve him with to his liking. And he was never to come back again until he had made all this food ready as he knew was pleasing to the lord . . . (p. 274)

The chapters that follow, which reflect an extended theological interpretation of the parable, continue this theme of working. But this time the laborer is Christ our Mother: "And so our Mother is working on us in various ways, in whom our parts are kept undivided; . . . in mercy he reforms and restores us, and by the power of his Passion, his death and his Resurrection he unites us to our substance"[24] (p. 294). It is clear from Julian's words that this "work" has to do with "one-ing", which is our spiritual bringing to birth: "Our true Mother Jesus, he alone bears us for joy and for endless life, blessed may he be. So he carries us within him in love and travail, until the full time when he wanted to suffer the sharpest thorns and cruel pains that ever were or will be, and at the last he died. . . . [H]e did not want to cease working . . ." (p. 298).

Why is this "work" so arduous, in Julian's view? I think it is difficult because it is essentially the work of "noughting," of having undone in us and in our deepest interiority all that resists God. Existentially, Julian is describing the inner experience of human beings when they do not get what they want; when, for example, they lose their health, are abandoned by loved ones, humiliated by others, and wounded by any of the various limit-situations of life. In Chapter Sixty-One, Julian declares how "it is profitable to us to mourn and to weep," for she understands that mourning for our grasping, sinful responses to these painful experiences is essential to the life of faith. At the same time, she recognizes also that everything within us resists such mourning because, in our hurt, we panic and do not know which way to turn. We resemble Julian's servant in the parable who, when fallen into a ditch and greatly injured,

> groans and moans and tosses about and writhes . . . the greatest hurt was . . . lack of consolation for he could not turn his face to look on his loving lord, who was very close to him . . . but like a man who was for the time extremely feeble and foolish, he paid heed to his feelings and his continuing distress, in which distress he suffered seven great pains . . . severe bruising . . . clumsiness of his body . . . weakness . . . that he was blinded in his reason and perplexed in his mind . . . that he could not rise . . . that he lay alone . . . that the place in which he lay was narrow and comfortless and distressful. (p. 268)

When, as Julian observes, we are "feeble and foolish," "distressed," and "blinded" in our reason and "perplexed" in our minds, our tendency is to deny the reality of pain if we can, averting it by hurling ourselves into involvement with external things. But Julian says, "we need to see [our fall]; and if we do not see it, though we fell, that would not profit us" (p. 300). What is the profit Christians will gain from seeing their fallenness? It is the recognition that there are no longer grounds for imagining that, in any sense, they acquire God's love by their own merits, and precisely that truth releases them from the twin cycles of exercising virtue in order to harness God's power, or of trying to construct their own identities. Thus, it is very precisely "by the experience of this falling [that] we shall have a great and marvellous [*sic*] knowledge of love in God without end; for enduring and marvellous [*sic*] is that love which cannot and will not be broken because of offences" (p. 300). In addition, when we mourn for our fallenness "our beloved Mother [Jesus]" "will sprinkle us all with his precious blood, and make our soul most pliable and most mild, and heal us most gently in the course of time" (p. 304). With a variety of metaphors, images, and theological speculations, Julian depicts how this process of healing goes on in the person who is disposed toward God.

Again, that does not mean that the process is easy. To the proud self dominated by ego concerns (but, in fact, lacking real ego strength), the full recognition of one's personal involvement with sin and of one's utter dependence on God's grace can be a hard pill to swallow. Yet, it is the only medicine which can bring about that quality of integration which Julian depicts as "one-ing." Therefore, to help her "even Christians" in their spiritual growth, Julian gives them guidance about how to proceed and how not to proceed.

For example, when, during her suffering as she is watching Jesus' agony on the cross, she hears a tempter say, "Look up to heaven to his Father," she rejects this with all her might saying, "No, I cannot, for you [the crucified Jesus] are my heaven" (p. 211). It would be hard to overemphasize the importance of this passage, for it epitomizes Julian's whole approach to God: her only access to the Trinity is through Jesus on the Cross.

4. Discernment and Julian's Schewinges

We have already learned that for Julian "prayer leads us in the right way and unites us to God"; thus it ought not to be altogether surprising to discover that, in Julian's Middle English, "schewinges," the word she uses for her visions, also has the connotation of "leading." "Sheuen," for example, meant "to point out," and the index finger was the "sheuinge finger." Thus "sheuen" was the equivalent of "indicate" or "lead to a place or event."[25] Julian is not the only author to have described prayer as a process of being led by God, or Jesus, or the Holy Spirit. For example, Gregory of Nyssa makes God's leading a central issue in his *Life of Moses*, and Ignatius of Loyola remarked that prayer felt to him as though he were a small boy being led by his Teacher.[26] Significantly, Julian uses her art in the literary construction of her text so that her "schewinges" lead in a particular way. For her, prayer includes the pursuit of certain visual signs in her awareness. The goal of this pursuit is not only to derive from the showings their spiritual and theological meaning, but, more importantly, to be drawn through them into deeper relation and union with God ("one-ing").

Her account of her sixteenth vision is instructive in this regard. This "schewying" begins with a description of Julian's own moment of doubt: "Then a man of religion came to me and asked me how I did, and I said that during that day I had been raving" (p. 310). When Julian tells this cleric about her visions, he becomes very serious, and she is ashamed for having doubted their validity: "And when I saw that he treated it so seriously and so respectfully, I was greatly ashamed, and wanted to make my confession" (p. 311).

In the rest of this revelation, Julian says a great deal about the nature of "schewying." First, she makes clear that it is not only inner, visionary experience that is her concern. People can also be shown who God is through creation, outer reality: "Everything which God has made shows [shewyth] his dominion" (p. 313).

However, there are destructive, disintegrating forces that block one's perception of God's goodness within and without. Julian describes these throughout her *Book* and in a variety of ways. Here, in revelation 16, it is actually the devil who thwarts her contemplative efforts. After the cleric leaves, Julian falls asleep and dreams that the devil is at her throat, his face right next to hers: "I never saw anything like him; his colour was red, like a newly baked tile, with black spots like freckles, uglier than a tile" (p. 311).

Julian instantly counters the devil's attack with a return to her "schewynge": "And at once I had recourse to what our Lord had revealed to me on that same day, and to all the faith of Holy Church, for I regarded them both as one, and I fled to them as to my source of strength" (p. 312). The result is that the devil and all his ugly revelation "vanished" and Julian is restored to "great rest and peace, without wickedness of body or fear of conscience" (p. 312).

Immediately thereafter the Lord shows Julian a vision that apparently confers on her a high degree of integration and peace:

And then our Good Lord opened my spiritual eye, and showed me my soul in the midst of my heart. I saw the soul as wide as if it were an endless citadel, and also as if it were a blessed kingdom, and from the state which I saw in it, I understood that it is a fine city. In the midst of that city sits our Lord Jesus, true God and true man, a handsome person and tall, highest bishop, most awesome king, most honourable Lord. And I saw him splendidly clad in honours. He sits erect there in the soul, in peace and rest, and he rules and guards heaven and earth and everything that is. (p. 313)

This "schewynge" manifests the delight God has in the creation of the human being. Julian's artful way of asserting the power of this delight over every other feeling of doubt or fear draws her readers toward the possibility she has discovered for herself the prospect of restoration to wholeness in God in spite of sin.

For Julian, this is a truth that must be seen: "And what can make us to rejoice more in God than to see in him that in us, of all his greatest works, he has joy?" Those who see this will find their wholeness in God, regardless of how other "men" may blame or condemn. "This was a delectable sight and a restful showing, which is without end, and to contemplate it while we are here is most pleasing to God and very great profit to us. And this makes the soul which so contemplates like to him who is contemplated, and unites it in rest and peace" (p. 314). Believers become like the God they contemplate. At the same time, they receive, by God's gracious act, an integrity accompanied by peace.

After this, the devil came to trouble Julian again, and he occupied her "all that night and into the morning, until it was a little after sunrise" (p. 316). What she learns from this affliction is that the "schewynges" and their message of God's love will pass. In fact, they may be replaced by demonic upheavals; but she is to keep her awareness focused on the possibility of love and wholeness nevertheless. This in fact is the same lesson she had learned earlier from the Lord's own strategy with her.

Here is the essence of discernment. Although many other authors, beginning with St. Paul, testify to this mode of experiencing God through distinguishing influences that are conducive to the individual's spiritual wholeness and to the upbuilding of the community from ones that are disintegrative, I know of no other place in literature where the inquiry after God through experience is given so focused and detailed a representation. A close reading of revelation 16 describes the culmination of this process. Julian has been taught one singular way of adhering to wholeness and love in God, no matter what may assail her in this life. Whether she experiences well-being or woe, judgment, blame, impatience, sloth, anger, fear, or "doubtful dread," she must fasten herself to the "schewynges" themselves. The Lord says to her: "But accept it and believe it and hold firmly to it, and comfort yourself with it and trust in it, and you will not be overcome" (p. 317).

For Julian, spiritual discipline means that the Gospel-based "schewynges" are to be aggressively appropriated, learned by heart, fastened on with all one's might, invested with absolute trust, and used for strength and comfort against whatever may threaten disintegration of the soul. Moreover, and most significantly, this process constitutes the heart of Christian discernment, as many people have affirmed from the New Testament period, through the Desert Fathers, the Patristic era, the Middle Ages, and up to our own time.

Conclusion

Implicit in all areas of my discussion has been one fundamental point: we do not need to choose between subjective and objective interpretations of religious experience because both are true. Perhaps western people are prone to think that they must choose between individualism and collectivism, or between the prophetic and the institutional. Julian's ample reflections on the relationship between inner and outer experience suggest otherwise. A contemplative through and through, she is completely sensitive to the dynamism of internal processes, so much so that at times she seems to value the inner life over the outer: "And so I hope that by his grace he lifts up and will draw our outer disposition to the inward, and will make us all at unity with him . . ." (p. 318). In truth, however, Julian's understanding is much more expansive than her valuation of the inner life would seem to indicate. Always, she will insist that "our precious lover helps us with spiritual light and true teaching . . . from within and from without . . ." (p. 318). Coming from without, moreover, are "Holy Mother Church" and its doctrines. Both are objective, social, and historical realities. That interpretation of doctrine is a central concern of Julian's visions is clear from the first page of her "long text" where she says, "in this [showing] was contained and specified the blessed Trinity, with the Incarnation and the union between God and man's soul" (p. 175).[27]

However, if Julian's visions serve to interpret doctrine, they do so for pastoral reasons. Above all, she wants her readers to relish the experience she had of being beloved of God. Furthermore, such acts of interpretation have an existential effect on the interpreter that is, at once, historical, communal, and social, as well as personal, particular, and perspectival.[28] The interpreter both appropriates to herself and becomes part of the historical reality she interprets. But if she accomplishes this we must say, finally, that she does so for the sake of her community. The person who has, in the presence of God, remained faithful and attentive to inner process, the person who has journeyed unflinchingly through experiences of noughting and mourning, in the end possesses an integrity and a maturity of vision that is lacking in those who blame other people or external agents for such painful, infuriating, or frustrating experiences. On the other hand, the Christian tradition of discernment will never argue that people arrive at a state where their understanding is infallible; sin and the cross preclude that. Julian's solution is to insist that we are given just the amount of light that we need:

> This light is measured with discretion, and it is present to us in our need in the night. . . . The measuring of this light is performed for us to our profit

by the wisdom of God; for the light is not so generous that we can see clearly our blessed day, nor is it all shut off from us, but it is such a light as we can live in meritoriously, with labour deserving the honourable thanks of God.   (p. 340)

Notes

1   Julian of Norwich, *Showings* (New York: Paulist Press, 1978), p. 340.

2   David A. Mycoff, *A Critical Edition of the Legend of Mary Magdalena from Caxton's Golden Legende of 1483* (Salzburg: Institut für Anglistik und Amerikanistik, 1985), pp. 117–18.

3   For a provocative reflection on this matter, see Rowan Williams, "The Suspicion of Suspicion: Wittgenstein and Bonhoeffer," in Richard H. Bell (ed.), *The Grammar of the Heart: New Essays in Moral Philosophy and Theology* (San Francisco: Harper & Row, 1988), pp. 36–53.

4   To learn more about this pioneering woman, see her autobiography: Rachel Hosmer, *My Life Remembered: Nun, Priest, Feminist* (Cambridge, MA: Cowley, 1988).

5   Julian, apparently, did not give a title to her work. I refer to it as *Showings* or *The Book of Showings*, because that is the most frequent name Julian gave her visions throughout her text, as Edmund Colledge, OSA, and James Walsh, SJ, point out. Their modernization, from which my citations are taken, and which was the inaugural volume in the Paulist Press series "Classics in Western Spirituality," is the translation of their critical edition (*A Book of Showings to the Anchoress Julian of Norwich* [Toronto: Pontifical Institute of Mediaeval Studies, 1978]).

6   *The Book of Margery Kempe*, trans. B. A. Windeatt (London: Penguin Books, 1985), pp. 77–8. Margery's *Book* was lost for centuries until, in 1934, a fifteenth-century manuscript was rediscovered in the Butler-Bowdon county manor.

7   Her *Book* has come down to us in two versions, the "short text," and the much more complex and theologically more sophisticated "long text." Nicholas Watson has explored the relationship between these two texts, and their dating, in "The Composition of Julian of Norwich's *Revelation of Love*," *Speculum*, vol. 68 (July 1993), pp. 637–83.

8   Christina von Nolcken's *Middle English Prose: A Critical Guide to Major Authors and Genres*, ed. A. S. G. Edwards (New Brunswick, NJ: Rutgers University Press, 1984) has a bibliography of editions and translations of Julian of Norwich up to the year 1984. In addition, the Consortium for the Teaching of the Middle Ages has published a students' text: *The Shewings of Julian of Norwich*, ed. Georgia Ronan Crampton (Kalamazoo, MI: Medieval Institute Publications, 1993). There also have been two recent modernizations: M. L. Del Mastro, *The Revelation of Divine Love in Sixteen Showings: Made to Dame Julian of Norwich* (Tarrytown, NY: Triumph Books, 1994) and Father John-Julian, OJN, *A Lesson of Love: The Revelations of Julian of Norwich* (New York: Walker, 1988).

9   For elucidation of this affective trend in theology, see Caroline Walker Bynum, *Jesus*

as Mother: Studies in the Spirituality of the High Middle Ages (Berkeley: University of California Press, 1982), pp. 129–30. See also V. A. Kolve, *The Play Called Corpus Christi* (Stanford, CA: Stanford University Press, 1966), p. 4; and Denise Despres, *Ghostly Sights: Visual Meditation in Late-Medieval Literature* (Norman, OK: Pilgrim, 1989). Another altogether fascinating work which treats this development in piety within the context of drama is Gail McMurray Gibson's *The Theater of Devotion: East Anglian Drama and Society in the Late Middle Ages* (Chicago: University of Chicago Press, 1989).

10 See Elizabeth Alvida Petroff, *Medieval Women's Visionary Literature* (New York: Oxford University Press, 1986), p. 300. Petroff's introduction contains a very interesting and helpful typology of medieval women's visionary experience. See also F. C. Bauerschmidt, "Julian of Norwich – Incorporated," *Modern Theology*, vol. 13 (1997), pp. 75–100.

11 "This book is begun by God's gift and his grace, but it is not yet performed, as I see it" (p. 324).

12 Bauerschmidt, "Julian of Norwich – Incorporated," p. 76.

13 Ibid.

14 Karen Armstrong, *Visions of God: Four Medieval Mystics and Their Writings* (New York: Bantam Books, 1994), p. viii.

15 Bauerschmidt, "Julian of Norwich – Incorporated," p. 82.

16 David Tracy's suggestion that there is an analogical religious imagination and that it involves a "journey of intensification into one's own particularity" could take this discussion a long way, I think, were there space to develop his argument here. See his *The Analogical Imagination* (New York: Crossroad, 1981), especially ch. 10.

17 The classical term is *theosis*, or divinization. For a full discussion of this important topic, see Rowan Williams, "Deification," in Gordon S. Wakefield (ed.), *The Westminster Dictionary of Christian Spirituality* (Philadelphia: Westminster Press, 1983), pp. 106–8.

18 For very full descriptions of the classical tradition of Christian discernment, see Joseph T. Lienhard, SJ, "On 'Discernment of Spirits' in the Early Church," *Theological Studies*, vol. 41 (1980), pp. 505–29; and Richard Joseph Sweeney, *Christian Discernment and Jungian Psychology: Toward a Jungian Revision of the Doctrine of Discernment of Spirits* (Ann Arbor, MI: University Microfilms International, 1985).

19 The most profound treatment of the utmost significance of mourning to the process of uniting inner reality and outer reality that I have come upon is Peter Homans's *The Ability to Mourn: Disillusionment and the Social Origins of Psychoanalysis* (Chicago: University of Chicago Press, 1989).

20 For a modern description of an apparently universal process similar to this, see Stephen Crites, "The Narrative Quality of Experience," *Journal of the American Academy of Religion*, vol. 29 (September 1971), pp. 291–311.

21 Augustine's theme developed especially in the *De Trinitate*.

22 Homans, *The Ability to Mourn*, p. 9.

23 Bauerschmidt, "Julian of Norwich – Incorporated," p. 95.

24 For more extensive treatments of the important relationship between "substance" and "sensuality" in Julian than I have space for here, see Grace Jantzen, *Julian of*

◆ 79

Norwich: Mystic and Theologian (New York: Paulist Press, 1988), pp. 137–149; and Bauerschmidt, "Julian of Norwich – Incorporated," pp. 87–8.

25 *Middle English Dictionary* (Ann Arbor: University of Michigan, 1954), part S.6, pp. 686–7.

26 Ignatius of Loyola, "The Autobiography," *The Spiritual Exercises and Selected Works*, ed. George E. Ganss, SJ (New York: Paulist Press, 1991), p. 79.

27 Elizabeth Alvilda Petroff discusses the import of doctrinal visions in her very wonderful Introduction to *Medieval Women's Visionary Literature* (Oxford: Oxford University Press, 1986), p. 9.

28 See Erich Auerbach's essay "Figura," in *Scenes from the Drama of European Literature* (Gloucester, MA: Peter Smith, 1973), pp. 54–60.

Inquiring after God when Working

Throughout most of Christian history, when Christians sought to know God better they turned from their labor (usually manual) to the study of Christian texts, prayer, or silence. Rarely did they think to learn of God in their work or think about work theologically. This is now changing. We have in this chapter three selections representing both Protestant and Catholic perspectives on work.

The Protestant view is represented by the magisterial sixteenth-century reformer, John Calvin (1509–64). As became customary for Protestants, he approached the question at hand through scripture. In this selection, Calvin is commenting on the beginning of Psalm 127 that reads, "Unless the Lord builds the house, those who build it labor in vain. Unless the Lord keeps the city, the watchman guards in vain. It is vain that you rise up early, sit up late, and eat the bread of sorrow; for to him who enjoys his favor, he gives while he sleeps." Calvin's comments reflect the view that the benefits of wealth and comfort that accrue through it pose a danger to Christians' spiritual well-being even as they improve physical well-being. He has taken care to point to the distance between God and us because he recognizes that when one is successful in work and gains wealth or renown one may be tempted to glory in the triumph and forget the true source of one's success: God.

Calvin also seeks to "repulse foolish self-confidence" and encourage trust in God's provident care. He does not, however, want to discourage human endeavor and so is careful to encourage productive work in a spirit of devotion to and trust of God. This support for human effort and activity, guided by prayer and with the hope of God's blessing, contributed mightily to the energetic building of the modern world with its emphasis on industry, creativity, and development of the resources given in creation and in human ingenuity.

The two other pieces are from a Roman Catholic perspective and both come from the twentieth century. One is from Pope John Paul II's encyclical *On Human Work*, published in 1981. Pope John Paul is among the first to create a spirituality of work that not only warns against the dangers of taking our work too seriously, and thereby distracting us from honoring God, but sees human beings as cooperating with God in the work of creation and redemption through the dignity of human labor and creativity. Not surprisingly, then, the Pope begins his reflection with the creation story in Genesis and interprets human work as an extension of God's own work that thereby honors him.

The contemporary reflection in this collection, written by Fr. Edward Vacek, develops Pope John Paul's theology of work, arguing that human dignity is part and parcel of the goodness of God's creation. Human work honors God by co-operating with his work, and that work develops us in godly ways. It enhances our social skills, enables us to participate in the production of goods and services that benefit others, develops our talents and abilities, teaches us virtues, and provides us with a constructive and healthy identity. In all of these ways, therefore, a theological understanding of work develops our life as God's own.

Work as a proper means of human dignity and the development of technical, social, and emotional skills and virtues is an important model to be held up for those created in the divine dignity. And Christian entrepreneurs may well be guided and even chided by these religious norms. Far too often dehumanizing and deforming work has been the only experience of work many people have ever known. The testimony of Simone Weil on the destructive effects of automotive workers in France in the 1930s, included later in this volume, is eloquent testimony to just how fresh and how needed the more enlightened Christian perspectives are. Slave labor, child labor, sweatshop labor, migrant labor, forced prostitution, and so forth are not things of the past. Wherever unequal power relationships pertain there is the danger of the exploitation of the weaker by the stronger.

Vacek notes that even where exploitation is not obvious, not all labor is dignifying and uplifting in and of itself. Repetitive, boring work dulls rather than hones the mind and senses and can breed health hazards. Additionally, many people are locked into work for which they are not temperamentally suited and may lack the skills or financial means to free themselves. Poor working conditions are equally demoralizing and depress productivity and personal satisfaction from work. Still others, unappreciated or underpaid for the work they do, may become ashamed of their work rather than being ennobled by it. In all of these situations women have long borne the brunt of the underside of work. That has changed drastically in the post-industrial west since the Second World War. Government regulation has improved the lot of workers in industrialized nations. Now post-industrial economics carry other strengths and weaknesses. A "knowledge" economy overlaid on a service economy tends to work against those who cannot benefit from education.

Business has not generally looked to theology for guidance. Governmental regulation of labor, production, and commerce is essential to protect workers, consumers, and the environment. Yet Christian theological reflection on work has its own word to contribute. Godly stewardship of the earth and its resources, godly treatment of workers by management, and godly attention to work itself by workers and management are part of Christian responsibility.

CLASSIC TEXTS

John Calvin, *Commentaries on the Psalms*

"Song of Ascents of Solomon. Except the Lord build the house, they labor in vain that build it. Except the Lord keep the city, the watchman watcheth but in vain."

"It is vain for you to rise up early, to sit up late, to eat the bread of sorrow: for so he giveth his beloved sleep." Ps. 127:1–2.

. . . [Solomon] emphasizes for a double reason that both the world and the lives of men are divinely governed. First, whenever men succeed in something, their ingratitude leads them to credit it solely to themselves, and God is not given his due honor. To correct this flagrant wrong, Solomon declares that nothing goes well for us except so far as God prospers our actions. Secondly, he intends to repulse the foolish self-confidence of men who, ignoring God and relying only on their own wisdom or strength, dare to start anything that comes to their heads. Therefore, he sweeps away everything which they rashly claim for their own and calls them to humility and prayer to God.

But he does not disparage man's labor or his effort and planning. For any virtue of ours is worthy of praise if we employ it in our zeal for the fulfillment of duty. The Lord does not want us to be like logs of wood, or to sit idle; he expects us to put to use whatever abilities we may have. It is of course true that the heaviest part of our labors comes from God's curse. But even if man's original state of integrity had remained, God would still have desired us to keep busy. Adam was put in a garden to cultivate it. Solomon does not condemn what God approves, and certainly not the labor men undertake gladly at God's command and offer to him as an acceptable sacrifice. But to keep men from being blinded by pride and from grasping at what belongs to God, he warns them that hard work wins success only so far as God blesses our labor.

By "house" he does not mean just the wooden or stone building. He includes in it the whole family economy, as a little farther on by the word "city" he does not mean merely the buildings and the surrounding walls but the common welfare of the whole state. He also is using the part for the whole (synecdoche) when he speaks of "building" and "guarding". He is making the general statement that whatever effort, wisdom, or industry men expend in looking after a family or in protecting a city will be ineffectual unless God from heaven orders a prosperous outcome. We need to remember often what has just been said. For since blind pride almost fills the minds of men and leads them in contempt of God to an immoderate exercise of their own abilities, nothing is more salutary for them than to be called to order and reminded that whatever they attempt will quickly come to nothing, unless the grace of God alone sustains it and makes it to prosper.

When philosophers dispute about the political state, they cleverly put together everything which seems to apply to the subject. They show acutely the reasons for and the means of establishing a state; and again they describe the faults by which a good state is frequently corrupted. In fact they search out with the greatest skill all that is needed to understand the matter. But they leave out the main point: that however much men excel in wisdom and ability, they cannot accomplish what they undertake unless God takes it in his hand and uses it as his instrument. Who of the philosophers has ever recognized that human politics are only a tool directed by the hand of God? They have made human virtue the prime cause of good fortune.

When men in sacrilegious boldness rush off to found cities and to regulate the state of the whole world, the Holy Spirit rightly exposes such insanity. So let each one of us work as he can in the line of his duty, giving to God the praise for every success we have. For it is altogether wrong to divide the credit as many try to do, giving half to God and claiming the other half for themselves because they have worked so hard. We must prize the blessing of God alone and live under its reign.

But if even our earthly welfare depends wholly on God's good pleasure, with what wings shall we fly to heaven? A man may establish a decent household with a way of life that suits him; men may make good laws and practice justice – but all such achievements are but a crawling on the ground, and the Holy Spirit pronounces them all transitory. Still less to be tolerated is the madness of those who strive to penetrate heaven by their own strength.

From this doctrine we may gather that it is not strange if world affairs are turbulent and confused, if in cities the rule of law is overthrown; if husbands and wives bring bitter and groundless accusations against each other, parents complain of their children, and all men bewail their lot. How many today devote themselves to the service of God in the practice of their own proper calling? How many, puffed up with pride, are not trying constantly to exalt themselves? God justly pays today's sad wage to unthankful men who defraud him of his honor. But if all should humbly submit themselves to God's providence, the blessing which Solomon celebrates would certainly shine bright in every aspect of our life, both public and private. . . .

"In vain." Solomon now explains more fully that it is useless for men to wear themselves out with hard work and grow weak with fasting in order to acquire wealth, since wealth also is the gift of God alone. In order to impress them more effectively, he speaks to each man individually: "For you [he says] it is vain." He mentions specifically the two means which are commonly reckoned to contribute most to amassing wealth. For when men do not spare their labor, but consume night and day in business and spend little of what they gain from their labor on their living, it is not surprising that they accumulate riches in a short space of time. But Solomon declares that there is nothing gained by poor living and perpetual labor.

Not that he forbids living economically or getting up early in the morning to work; but he does urge us to prayer, to the invocation of God. And in order to inspire us to gratitude, he says that anything which obscures God's goodness is vanity. For we prosper only when our hope rests wholly upon God; and moreover the outcome of our work will depend on how we pray. But if anyone pushes God into the background and hastens eagerly ahead, his hurried rush will surely end in a fall. The prophet is not advising men to succumb to indolence and to make no plans in all their lives, merely to doze and indulge their inertia; on the contrary, his point is that, when they pursue the tasks divinely imposed upon them, they ought always to begin with prayer and invocation to God, and offer their labors for his blessing. . . .

"Surely he will give to his beloved sleep." This describes exactly the way in which God's blessing on his sons and servants is manifested. For acceptance of the futility of mere human striving would not be enough; the addition of a promise is needed if men are to perform their duties with a sure hope. . . . [Solomon] speaks as if God in his indulgence, were encouraging his servants to be idle. But since we know from the law that men were created to work and since in the next psalm we shall see that farmers are regarded as blessed of God when they eat what their own hands have produced, it is certain that "sleep" does not mean doing nothing but rather the tranquil labor to which men of faith apply themselves in obedient trust. . . .

If anyone objects that the faithful often stew in bitter cares and worry about the future when they are hard pressed by the want of everything they need and destitute of all means of support, I answer: If the faith and devotion of the servants of God were perfect, the blessing of God which the prophet here describes would be plainly visible. And as for those who worry too much

– that is due to their own sin in not resting firmly upon God's providence. I even add that they are punished more severely than unbelievers, because it is good for them to suffer anxiety for a time, so that they may attain the quiet of this sleep. But meantime God's kindness [to his servants] persists, and shines always in the midst of the shadows [of this world]; for the Lord supports his sons as with sleep.

PAPAL ENCYCLICAL

John Paul II, *Laborem Exercens*: Elements for a Spirituality of Work

(Chapter 5)

A Particular Task for the Church

... The church considers it her duty to speak out on work from the viewpoint of its human value and of the moral order to which it belongs, and she sees this as one of her important tasks within the service that she renders to the evangelical message as a whole.

At the same time she sees it as her particular duty to form a spirituality of work which will help all people to come closer, through work, to God, the creator and redeemer, to participate in his salvific plan for man and the world and to deepen their friendship with Christ in their lives by accepting, through faith, a living participation in his threefold mission as priest, prophet and king, as the Second Vatican Council so eloquently teaches.

Work as a Sharing in the Activity of the Creator

... The word of God's revelation is profoundly marked by the fundamental truth that man, created in the image of God, shares by his work in the activity of the creator and that, within the limits of his own human capabilities, man in a sense continues to develop that activity, and perfects it as he advances further and further in the discovery of the resources and values contained in the whole of creation. ...

This description of creation, which we find in the very first chapter of the Book of Genesis, is also in a sense the first "gospel of work." For it shows what the dignity of work consists of: It teaches that man ought to imitate

God, his creator, in working, because man alone has the unique characteristic of likeness to God. Man ought to imitate God both in working and also in resting, since God himself wished to present his own creative activity under the form of work and rest. . . .

Awareness that man's work is a participation in God's activity ought to permeate, as the council teaches, even "the most ordinary everyday activities. For, while providing the substance of life for themselves and their families, men and women are performing their activities in a way which appropriately benefits society. They can justly consider that by their labor they are unfolding the creator's work, consulting the advantages of their brothers and sisters, and contributing by their personal industry to the realization in history of the divine plan."* . . .

"Far from thinking that works produced by man's own talent and energy are in opposition to God's power, and that the rational creature exists as a kind of rival to the creator, Christians are convinced that the triumphs of the human race are a sign of God's greatness and the flowering of his own mysterious design. For the greater man's power becomes, the farther his individual and community responsibility extends. . . . People are not deterred by the Christian message from building up the world, or impelled to neglect the welfare of their fellows. They are, rather, more stringently bound to do these very things."† . . .

In this way the world will be permeated by the spirit of Christ and more effectively achieve its purpose in justice, charity and peace. . . . Therefore, by their competence in secular fields and by their personal activity, elevated from within by the grace of Christ, let them work vigorously so that by human labor, technical skill, and civil culture, created goods may be perfected according to the design of the creator and the light of his word.‡

Christ, The Man of Work

. . . [Jesus] belongs to the "working world," he has appreciation and respect for human work. It can indeed be said that he looks with love upon human work and the different forms that it takes, seeing in each one of these forms a particular facet of man's likeness with God, the creator and father. . . .

. . . the church has always proclaimed what we find expressed in modern

* Second Vatican Ecumenical Council, Pastoral Constitution on the Church in the Modern World, "Gaudium et Spes," 34: AAS 58 (1966), 1052–3.
† Ibid.
‡ Second Vatican Ecumenical Council, Dogmatic Constitution on the Church, "Lumen Gentium," 36: AAS 57 (1965), 41.

terms in the teaching of the Second Vatican Council: "Just as human activity proceeds from man, so it is ordered toward man. For when a man works he not only alters things and society, he develops himself as well. He learns much, he cultivates his resources, he goes outside of himself and beyond himself. Rightly understood, this kind of growth is of greater value than any external riches which can be garnered. . . . Hence, the norm of human activity is this: that in accord with the divine plan and will, it should harmonize with the genuine good of the human race, and allow people as individuals and as members of society to pursue their total vocation and fulfill it."*

Such a vision of the values of human work, or in other words such a spirituality of work, fully explains what we read in the same section of the council's pastoral constitution with regard to the right meaning of progress: "A person is more precious for what he is than for what he has. Similarly, all that people do to obtain greater justice, wider brotherhood, and a more humane ordering of social relationships has greater worth than technical advances. For these advances can supply the material for human progress, but of themselves alone they can never actually bring it about."† . . .

Human Work in the Light of the Cross and the Resurrection of Christ

. . . Sweat and toil, which work necessarily involves in the present condition of the human race, present the Christian and everyone who is called to follow Christ with the possibility of sharing lovingly in the work that Christ came to do.‡ This work of salvation came about through suffering and death on a cross. By enduring the toil of work in union with Christ crucified for us, man in a way collaborates with the son of God for the redemption of humanity. He shows himself a true disciple of Christ by carrying the cross in his turn every day§ in the activity that he is called upon to perform. . . .

If it is true that the many forms of toil that go with man's work are a small part of the cross of Christ, what is the relationship of this new good to the resurrection of Christ? The council seeks to reply to this question also, drawing light from the very sources of the revealed word: "Therefore, while we are warned that it profits a man nothing if he gains the whole world and

---

* Second Vatican Ecumenical Council, Pastoral Constitution on the Church in the Modern World, "Gaudium et Spes," 35: AAS 58 (1966), 1053.
† Ibid.
‡ See John 17:4.
§ See Luke 9:23.

loses himself" (cf. Lk. 9:25), the expectation of a new earth must not weaken but rather stimulate our concern for cultivating this one. For here grows the body of a new human family, a body which even now is able to give some kind of foreshadowing of the new age. Earthly progress must be carefully distinguished from the growth of Christ's kingdom. Nevertheless, to the extent that the former can contribute to the better ordering of human society, it is of vital concern to the kingdom of God.*

. . . it is through man's labor that not only "the fruits of our activity" but also "human dignity, brotherhood and freedom" must increase on earth.† Let the Christian who listens to the word of the living God, uniting work with prayer, know the place that his work has not only in earthly progress but also in the development of the kingdom of God, to which we are all called through the power of the Holy Spirit and through the word of the Gospel. . . .

CONTEMPORARY REFLECTION

Inquiring after God in our Work

Edward Collins Vacek, SJ

Why should we Christians work? And what, if anything, does our work have to do with our relationship with God? One might think that the Christian churches would have a long tradition of extensive theological reflection on the meaning of work. But such has not been the case. Like others, Christians have worked at paid employment, in their homes, and in various volunteer situations. But when they wanted to encounter God, they typically turned from work to read the Bible, participate in the Eucharist, pray on their knees, and so forth. In other words, they commonly inquired after God apart from their work.

Let me acknowledge a difficulty: no one, it seems, has devised a good definition for "work." Ordinary language gives us little help: for example,

---

* Second Vatican Ecumenical Council, Pastoral Constitution on the Church in the Modern World "Gaudium et Spes," 39: AAS 58 (1966), 1057.
† Ibid.

during Sunday worship the music director, who is a paid employee, "plays" an instrument at the "liturgy," a word that means the "work of the people." Or, in another context, an administrator "plays" a crucial role in her company. For relaxation she goes to the gym to "work out," or to the golf course where she will "work on" her putting. Meanwhile she pays someone to cut the grass which, if she did it herself, might be her leisure activity. The legendary Babe Ruth was stunned to learn that someone was going to pay him to play his favorite sport.

Almost any activity can become work. For example, we ordinarily do not think of sexual intercourse as work, but it might be work were one a prostitute or an experimental subject in a medical laboratory. On the other hand, many activities ordinarily thought of as work can become a hobby or leisure activity. For example, some people fix cars just for fun. Yet enjoyment does not turn work into play because many people genuinely enjoy their work; indeed for some, it is among their most satisfying activities. Conversely, the lack of pleasure does not make an activity work.

Usually, we do not say we are working if our actions are primarily directed to self-maintenance, to personal enjoyment, to self-development, or to sharing our personal life with another. Thus eating, reading a novel, or talking with a friend are ordinarily not work. Rather, work typically is an activity directed to producing some material object or desired state of affairs outside the self.[1] Because work usually involves overcoming some obstacle in achieving some goal, it demands attention and includes some expenditure of energy.[2] Because work is not an activity we do simply for its own sake, it also is partially motivated by a sense of obligation or by a desire for some absent good extrinsic to the action.

While the primary model for much of history has been the physical work of agriculture, today's workers engage in such a vast array of activities that it is difficult to offer a unified theology of work. In the first half of this essay, I examine how the Christian tradition has viewed work; in the second, I will propose a contemporary theology of work. My goal is to present a vision of how this large part of our daily lives coheres with our relationship with God.

Work in Christian Tradition

How have believers experienced or understood the connection between God and their work? First, I will briefly consider the Scriptures.[3] Then I will take up some helpful reflections from several major theologians of the subsequent Christian tradition.

First Testament

A foundation for a theology of work is laid in the first few chapters of Genesis. To begin, these texts describe God as a worker in two ways. On the one hand, the priestly writer depicts God as one who made things just by speaking, but this activity was sufficiently strenuous that after "God finished the work he had done," God rested for a seventh day (2:2). On the other hand, the Yahwistic writer portrays God as doing physical labor: God "makes" the earth (2:4), "forms" like a potter (2:7, 8, 19), "plants" (2:8), and "builds up" (2:22). Most intriguingly, God does not finish the work: no plants will grow since "there was no one to till the ground" (2:5); this task is given to the man (2:15) who himself needs a "helper as his partner" (2:18). Thus, just as God's activity of creation is completed by human procreation, so also God's project of a fruitful earth is completed by cooperative human work.

It is commonly known that the Ten Commandments contain the injunction to keep the Sabbath by resting. What is less commonly observed is that this command begins with the demand that "Six days you shall labor and do all your work" (Exod. 20:9). Thus we are commanded to work. On the other hand, the commandment to rest indicates that there are limits not only to the work that we do but also to the work done for us by other people, other living beings, and indeed the earth itself (Exod. 23:10–12).

As one might expect, the wisdom books of the Bible offer many common-sense recommendations: for example, hard work leads to abundant harvests, while laziness or mere talk leads to poverty (Prov. 10:5, 12:11, 14:23, 24:33–4); people are motivated by their hunger (Prov. 16:26), but without the right farm equipment they cannot produce a harvest (Prov. 14:4). More important for this theological inquiry is the recommendation that the believer should "Commit your work to the Lord, and your plans will be established" since "The human mind plans the way, but the Lord directs the steps" (Prov. 16:3, 9). That is, both God and human beings must each be involved in the same deed. This idea – which will be clarified – is basic to the thesis of the present essay. Isaiah admirably makes a similar point: "O Lord, all that we have done you have done for us" (Is. 26:12). Here we find a paradox that is essential to Christian life. We genuinely plan and work. But God too is actively present in our planning and working, and the good we do is truly done by God.

While work is a major source of the good things we need for life, it is also a locus of sin. To be sure, work itself is not a consequence of sin (Gen. 1:28). But because of sin human labor is marked by toil and sweat (Gen. 3:17, 19). Personal sin may also lead to poverty and misfortune (Deut. 28:15–68; Gen. 11:3–8). On the other hand, some people are poor not through their own fault, but because of the injustice of others (1 Sam. 8:10–18; Prov. 13:23; Mic. 2:2; Jer. 22:13). Israel knew this problem first-hand since it experienced long periods of forced slave labor in exile (Ex. 1:13–14; Deut. 26:6–7; Lev. 25:39–55).[4]

New Testament

The New Testament is at best only somewhat helpful for developing a positive theology of ordinary work. Christians who expected that everything would soon be destroyed in the fiery second coming of Christ had little incentive for thinking about the positive significance of "buying and selling, planning and building" (Luke 17:27–30; 2 Peter 3:10–13; 1 Cor. 7:29–31). More important, for Jesus the central concern was to preach faith and repentance, not to lay out the religious meaning of everyday work.

To be sure, Jesus himself probably was a carpenter (Mark 6:3),[5] a fact that served in subsequent centuries to validate manual work. Unfortunately, the New Testament authors seemed somewhat embarrassed about this part of Jesus' life. The hint that he was a carpenter comes as part of an accusation made by hecklers. Matthew changes the line to read not that Jesus was a carpenter but that he was a "son of a carpenter" (13:55), and the other two Gospels omit all mention of Jesus' manual work. In John, Jesus says: "My Father is still working, and I am also working" (5:17); and no doubt Jesus worked hard and asked the same of his disciples (Matt. 9:37–8, 10:10). But, in addition to performing miracles, their work was typically religious activity such as preaching and teaching the Gospel, not the ordinary work that occupies most people.

Jesus, of course, was aware of the workaday world. His parables and teachings refer to farms and field-laborers and vineyards and yokes. He employs these references to make some spiritual point. Unfortunately, however, his references also tend to subvert or qualify any importance we might want to find in work. Consider the portrait of Jesus in the Gospel of Luke. While it is true that Jesus calls ordinary workers such as fishermen or tax collectors to be his disciples, it is also true that he asks them to leave this sort of work in order to follow him (5:11, 28). When Martha complains that Mary is not doing her fair share of the work, Jesus sides with Mary and chastises Martha for worrying about many things (10:38–42). Jesus urges his followers to carry no purse, bag, or sandals but rather to live off provisions given by those they serve (10:4, 8). He recommends the lilies and birds of the field who don't do a lick of work yet who are wonderfully clothed and fed by God. Therefore, he warns, we should not worry about our food and drink, and if we already have any of the world's possessions, we should sell and give them away, since God will provide (12:22–33, 14:33, 18:22). Jesus warns those who are financially successful about the foolishness of their prudent decisions to conserve their good fortune (12:13–21); he speaks unfavorably of those who, instead of going to a party, choose rather to plow their fields (14:19). He tells us that the prodigal son who has squandered his inheritance is received with more exaltation than the son who for years has worked "like a slave" for his father (15:11–32). In one parable Jesus sets up the dishonest manager as a paradigm of shrewdness (16:1–9). He uses a story of reversal in which a rich man who had good things in life receives fiery torment after death, while a poor man who seemed to do nothing in life but beg now receives rich comfort (16:19–25). Indeed, according to Jesus, "it is easier for a camel to go through the eye of a needle than for someone who is rich to enter the kingdom of God" (18:25). Finally, in an incident that may serve as a metaphor for the problems that must be faced by those who want to relate work to God, Jesus drove out of the temple those who were selling things there (19:45).

The point of recalling these texts is *not* that these are Jesus' reflections on the meaning of work. In these texts Jesus is not criticizing work any more than in his parable of the ten talents he is cautioning against a conservative investment policy (19:11–27). Rather, all these texts point to the new kingdom that was appearing in Jesus. But they offer little about how our work fits within our relationship with God.

Curiously, an exhortation to slaves provides one of the few New Testament reflections on how we might connect our work with our Christian lives: "Whatever your task, put yourselves into it, as done for the Lord and not for your masters, since you know that from the Lord you will receive the inheritance as your reward; you serve the Lord Christ" (Col. 3:23–4). Still, when St. Paul explained why he continued to work as a tent-maker, he did not indicate that work is an important part of Christian life (Acts 18:3; 1 Cor. 9:6–15; 2 Thess. 3:6–9). Rather, by earning his own living he hoped to make clear that he did not preach for pay (1 Cor. 9:18). He exhorted others to work so that they would not have to depend on anyone (1 Thess. 4:9). The author of 2 Thessalonians added a famous rule that those who do not work will not eat (2 Thess. 3:8–10). The author of Ephesians gives two further reasons for work: it enables thieves to give up stealing, and it enables people to share with the needy (Eph. 4:28; also 1 Tim. 6:17–18). Paul reinforces the second reason in his speech to the Ephesians: "I worked with my own hands to support myself and my companions. In all this I have given you an example that by such work we must support the weak, remembering the words of the Lord Jesus, for he himself said, 'It is more blessed to give than to receive'" (Acts 20:34–5).

Various roles within the Church come from God, for example, apostles, prophets, or teachers; but these are for building up the body of Christ, not for building up the world (Eph. 4:11–12). Rather, the Colossians are told, "Set your minds on things that are above [where Christ is], not on things that are on earth" (Col. 3:1–2). In a deeply influential line Paul encouraged detachment from the affairs of this life: "let . . . those who buy [be] as though they had no possessions, and those who deal with the world as though they had no dealings with it. For the present form of this world is passing away" (1 Cor. 7:30–1).

Patristic tradition

After the New Testament period passed, Christians put forward various reasons for working, most of which had to do with helping workers avoid sin and attain virtue. Work involves suffering and sweat, and it thereby corrects the flesh which constantly seeks pleasures. Willingly endured, this suffering also serves as penance for sins. Work requires restraint and effort, and thus it promotes self-discipline. Work replaces idleness, which is the devil's workshop. Work requires submission to the demands of a task and often requires submission to someone in charge of the work, and thus it promotes obedience, a central Christian virtue. Work fosters humility and simplicity, counteracting the cardinal sin of pride. Reasons such as these lay behind the startling practice of some desert fathers who wove baskets by day and then at night either unwove or burned them. In short, the early Fathers of the Church tended to value work more for how it developed virtues and curbed vices than for how it supplied material goods or social services.[6]

Still, the monastic movement made significant contributions to a theology of work. The laboring monks showed that manual labor was not necessarily the work of slaves but could be freely chosen by persons of status in the Church. Furthermore, the monks developed healthy patterns of life that balanced prayer, study, and work. Many monasteries cultivated agriculture and the arts in ways that contributed significantly to western culture. By working the monks often were not a burden on others; instead they earned enough to be significant sources of help to others.

Medieval period

Since the harsh conditions of physical labor were grueling and demeaning, ordinary folk frequently connected their work with their Christianity through a theology of the cross.[7] They suffered with Christ crucified, and they hoped their toil would suffice as penance for sin. They practiced Christian resignation, and they hoped for a better life not here on earth but rather in heaven. The immensely popular book, *Imitation of Christ*, taught that any natural need such as for labor and rest "makes a devout soul feel wretched and harassed" since these things dragged the soul down and bound it to visible things.[8]

Thomas Aquinas added that work is not only inferior, but it also "hinders the contemplative, in so far as it is impossible for one to be busy with external action and at the same time give oneself to Divine contemplation."[9] On the other hand, Aquinas made major contributions to a theology of work. For him, God is actively present in our everyday work, and this presence in no way diminishes God's dignity.[10] God ordinarily acts not apart from creatures but through them, and in particular through our human effort.[11] It would be unreasonable and ungenerous, Aquinas thought, if God created us capable of acting, and then intervened to do what we can do by using our own intellect, freedom, and bodily powers. However, when we work, the action is wholly done by both God and ourselves, not by one or the other.[12] Thus, God does not replace human effort to better the world, but rather God and humans are integrally involved in human work.

Reformation theology

The Reformation brought forth a new, if still not well developed, theology of work. Why should Christians work? For Martin Luther, work is an activity commanded by God. Thus we please God by obedience in doing the work God gives us.[13] In this approach, however, work itself and what it accomplishes are not the relevant religious issue: "all works become equal. . . . all distinctions between works fall away, whether they be great, small, short."[14] Rather, what centrally matters to God and therefore should matter to us is obedience to God's call. Significantly, Luther also shifted the idea of "vocation" away from the monastery and into the workplace. God calls us to various "stations" in life, for example, marriage, government, or business.[15] Through our work within these stations God blesses humanity; and without God's blessing, we work in vain.[16]

John Calvin further stressed the idea of a vocation in the world: God "has assigned distinct duties to each in the different modes of life."[17] Calvin himself was hardly one to affirm a completely this-worldly spirituality. As he wrote, "When it comes to comparison with the life to come, the present life can not only be safely neglected but . . . must be utterly despised and loathed."[18] Still, Calvin's theology led to an intense concern for doing good in the world. The other-worldly asceticism of the medievals became a productive intra-worldly asceticism.[19] As Reginald White observed,

> All qualities which Calvin inculcated in the disciplined individual contributed toward the new industrial and commercial spirit – self-denial, frugality, honesty, sobriety, devotion to the general good, study, purposefulness, responsible stewardship in the handling of resources, the sense of vocation, the release of energy, the new valuation of work. Actual mental and physical toil was a Christian duty, not to be laid aside when physical needs were met.[20]

John Wesley's three rules easily followed: "Gain all you can"; "Save all you can"; "Give all you can."[21] The so-called Protestant work-ethic followed from the first rule. The second rule eventually served as a basis for capitalism. To many, the third rule became more or less dispensable. In a way unintended by the reformers, those who were successful in worldly terms often considered themselves specially close to God, since, as Paul Bernstein observed, "success in work was a sign of God's pleasure."[22] Calvin opened the door to such views when he wrote: "If the faith and devotion of the servants of God were perfect, the blessing of God . . . would be plainly visible."[23]

Recent papal teachings

In the past hundred years, Roman Catholic popes have frequently written to correct some of the excesses of both Marxism and capitalism that were so hard on the worker. Although prior papal teaching focused more on natural law arguments, Pope John Paul II grounded his understanding of work in a theological anthropology. Six points may be noted. First, people are created in the image of God; and, thus, workers must never be thought of as just another business expense.[24] Second, workers have a divine mandate to exercise dominion over the earth.[25] Human beings should "transform nature, adapting it to [their] own needs." Third, in working, a person "achieves fulfillment as a human being and indeed in a sense becomes 'more a human being'."[26] Fourth, God continues to create the world and develop it.[27] Thus, through work, people participate in God's creative activity. In this sense, they might be called co-creators[28] when they advance the course of culture and history through their discoveries and contributions.

Fifth, work participates in the redemptive activity of Christ in at least two ways. On the one hand, the toil and pain can be joined with the redemptive power of Christ's cross.[29] On the other, Christ's redemption is brought further to completion when Christians overcome the sins that commonly are associated with work – sloth, putting profits over people, allowing poverty amidst wealth, pitting one individual or group against another, wasting or misallocating resources, and so forth. Finally, John Paul II holds that work contributes to the eschatological coming of God's kingdom. What workers do will not be lost before God, and so they should see a connection between their work and eternity.[30]

Summary

When the early Christians thought that the end of the world would come soon, they had little impetus to improve either work conditions or the world.

Subsequent Christians held that the life of the spirit and eternal life after death were the truly important goods. The value of work for them lay, first, in providing the material conditions of life so that they could engage in explicitly religious devotions.[31] Second, work had value in the way it enabled them to help others and in the interior virtues it fostered, both of which were linked with aptness for heaven.

Something was missing in these approaches. In the post-medieval era, Christians began to view the world less as temporary scaffolding to heaven and more as a good in its own right. They valued embodiment, practical thinking, and engaged labor in this world not simply as necessary conditions for contemplation of eternal truths, but rather as graced enactments of their humanity.[32] They began to want to be fully involved in life on earth, not constantly pointed towards a life that takes place somewhere else and at some future time. They rejected any renunciation of the world as tantamount to scorning God's gift. Larry Rasmussen places this theme at the center of the Reformation: "Luther utterly rejects any flight from the creaturely and finite as the path to communion with God. [Luther] emphatically turns back Augustine's contention that Christ descended to help us ascend. He counters that Christ descended precisely to keep us from trying!"[33]

Rasmussen argues the extreme position that an earth-centered faith should replace a heaven-centered faith. A somewhat more cautious conclusion is that we must not just pass through this world, but we must also live fully here. We must do so because God's spirit dwells in this world. But we must also do so because, as we shall see, what we do here makes a difference to God's everlasting kingdom.

A Theology of Work

Cooperation with God

Why, then, should Christians work? My thesis is that the fundamental religious meaning of our daily work is that in it we collaborate or labor together with God.[34] Before developing that thesis, I should indicate my operative images for God, human beings, and the relationship between them. My basic theological image of God is that God is one who loves (1 John 4:16).[35] Out of an overflow of love, God creates this universe and pronounces it good. This God of love became incarnate in Jesus and is present in the Spirit among us. This God resists and challenges all that is evil in our lives and desires to liberate us from that evil. This God wants us to develop ourselves and our world. Finally, this God wants, above all, a mutual love relationship with us.

The basic theological anthropology I hold is that human beings are complex creatures whose good is realized through engaging in an array of activities that range from elemental bodily functioning to the highest of spiritual loves. Human beings are essentially relational and must learn to love themselves, one another, and this world. Above all, they must become ever more involved in a mutual love relationship with God.[36]

The relevant connection I make between God and humanity is that we should be collaborators with God.[37] Let me admit that, in describing divine–human interactions, biblical authors commonly play down the collaborative activity of creatures.[38] They may describe in detail what someone does, but then they proclaim that God alone has acted. For example, the Israelites take up the sword and do mighty battle; then they praise God that it was not by their sword but by God's might that they won (Josh. 6:21; Ps. 44:1–4). St. Paul says that he planted and Apollos watered, and then he says that only God was important in spreading the faith (1 Cor. 3:6–7).

Similarly, Luther and Calvin tend to write that God does all alone, but they insist that we too must act. For example, Luther wrote: "Having been justified by grace in this way, we then do good works, yes, Christ himself does all in us."[39] Calvin insisted that we must not give credit partially to God and partially to ourselves, but all to God. Nevertheless, he held that God "expects us to put to use whatever abilities we may have."[40] These classic theologians assert that God is the ultimate source of all our actions and that both God and human beings are involved in our good deeds. What has been missing is clarity about how both are involved.

There are, of course, many ways of understanding this collaboration. For example, the author of Colossians writes in terms of inspired energy: "I toil and struggle with all the energy that [Christ] powerfully inspires within me" (Col. 1:29). Aquinas held that God is primary cause and we exercise a secondary causality.[41] For Luther, our activities are "the work of our Lord God under a mask, as it were, beneath which he himself alone effects and accomplishes what we desire."[42] Calvin described our work as God's "instrument."[43] My own approach will build upon work I have done elsewhere.[44] Our collaboration with God flows from a mutual love relationship between God and ourselves. My broad thesis is this: we are loved by God; we return love to God; and, entering into a friendship with God, we share God's concerns and want to participate in God's activities. Since God is involved in this world, we want to be involved in the world. As a consequence, our work is best thought of not as a duty performed in obedience to God or as an act of fidelity to our own human nature. Rather, it is a way of enacting and fostering the friendship we have with God.[45]

We are, as Karl Barth wrote, God's "partners."[46] Obviously we never do good work without God; but in earthly matters God ordinarily does not (or, some would say, cannot) act independently of creaturely cooperation. Rather

God works through and with us. Since God is a creator, redeemer, and transformer of the world, and since "we have become partners of Christ" (Heb. 3:14), we can and should participate, in a human way, in these same activities. Put baldly, we should be co-creators, co-redeemers, and co-transformers, though always in a completely dependent way. This need not be arrogance, since Christ promised that we would be able to do not only the works that he did, but even greater than these (John 14:10–12).

Creator

Out of love, God creates not just human beings but the whole world. In Christ "all things in heaven and on earth were created, things visible and invisible" (Col. 1:16). Out of love for God, we should desire to develop, maintain, and enhance this world that God creates in Christ. We human beings, created in God's image, have a drive to be creative. When we Christians produce well-made objects or provide beneficial services, we are continuing God's on-going creative activity. We contribute positively or negatively to the shared history that God has with us and the world.[47] Even if our motives are selfish or sinful, what we produce may be excellent and may make a significant, perhaps even invaluable, contribution to the community's historical life. In this vein, the Second Vatican Council wrote that "by their labor [humans] are unfolding the creator's work ... and contributing by their personal industry to the realization in history of the divine plan."[48] As co-creators with God, we can create not only objects that enrich human life but also objects that are good in themselves (Gen. 1:24).

As collaborators with God, we not only create new products or services, but we also maintain what already exists. Much in our lives is a matter of natural rhythms: we plant and we reap. We eat and we eliminate. We expend our energies and we restore them. Our lives are greatly occupied with this sort of rhythmic, maintenance activity. In a theological perspective, what we are doing is cooperating with God's sustaining activity. Put simply, the work we do to prepare our food is one way that God maintains our life.

Redeemer

God not only creates and sustains all things, but also through Christ "God was pleased to reconcile to himself all things, whether on earth or in heaven" (Col. 1:20). God saves more than our free selves. God saves the world. As Calvin put it, Christ's "death was the real beginning of a right order and the full restoration of the world!"[49] Here it is helpful to contrast two approaches to redemption. In the west, the Latin Fathers tended to restrict the reach of redemption to the human spirit. Hence, asceticism often encouraged flight from the body and from the world. Work and the riches that come from work tended to be seen as an enemy or a distraction to a truly religious life. The

Greek Fathers of the east, however, tended to view redemption more broadly. They correctly saw that, in Christ's victory, all of creation, not just our inner selves, longs for the completion of redemption (Rom. 8:19–23).

Redemption is incomplete wherever alienation remains with respect to God, to ourselves, to one another, and to the earth.[50] Certainly, the basic alienation that has to be overcome is that between God and ourselves. Our redemption, I have elsewhere argued,[51] primarily consists in a mutual love relationship between God and ourselves. That cannot come about until God offers us friendship. But when God does offer, we can and must respond. God cannot save us without our free cooperation, since without our free response there is no friendship. Once we have accepted and begun to relish this friendship, we should then desire to cooperate, wherever possible, with God's healing projects for the rest of creation (1 Cor. 3:9; 2 Cor. 6:1; Phil. 1:22; Mark 16:20).

Much work involves violence and humiliation to both our spirit and our body.[52] We have a religious obligation to strive to overcome those inhumane qualities that are present in work. Not only followers of Karl Marx but also disciples of Jesus Christ recognize an obligation to reform alienating structures of labor. Work's difficulties are chiefly redeemed when we find meaning and purpose in our labor. We redeem the toil of our work through the awareness that we are cooperating with God in doing it. Just as within family life, hard tasks such as changing diapers or doing laundry have a certain sweetness when done out of love (see Prov. 15:15–17), so too work done as part of our love relationship with God can be infused with the deep-seated peace and even joy that arise from being faithful to this relationship.[53]

Work is also a locus where we can easily and seriously sin against our neighbor and thus refuse to cooperate with God's love for the neighbor. A redemptive practice of work must counteract such tendencies. Instead of using people, we affirm them in their abilities. Instead of harming people by shoddy or immoral products, we contribute to their lives by beneficial goods and enabling services. Indeed, our work will be the normal way that we feed the hungry, give drink to the thirsty, clothe the naked, and thereby serve Christ (Matt. 25:31–46).

There is also alienation between ourselves and earth. As Genesis 3:17–18 indicates, the earth itself is cursed or at odds with human needs. In turn, we are needlessly destructive of the earth and its environment. Redemption, therefore, requires a right relationship between ourselves and the earth. That relationship includes at times a receptive, hands-off admiration for the independent beauty and goodness of nature, but it also includes a respectful effort to mold nature to our will.[54] Thus, redemption ordinarily does not mean that we stop working, but rather that God's "chosen shall long enjoy the work of their hands" (Isa. 65:22–3; Jer. 31:5).

Finally and tentatively, some mention should be made of one traditional, redemptive meaning Christians have found in work, namely as a way of doing penance for sins. The New Testament insists not only that the cross of Christ atoned for our sins, but also that we must take up our daily cross (Luke 9:23). The Pauline author of Colossians rejoiced that in his suffering, he was "completing what is lacking in Christ's afflictions for the sake of the body, that is, the church" (Col. 1:24). While it has become obscure to many theologians how suffering can have redemptive value, this traditional view should not be hastily jettisoned. Those who have offended a beloved often are willing to endure hardship as a symbol of their desire to restore the relationship they have harmed. The hardships of work may serve this redemptive purpose.

Transforming reign

Christ's activity does not aim at simply restoring the world back to the way it was prior to sin. Rather, Christ's victory initiates a "new creation" (Gal. 6:15; Rev. 21:5). Images of the eschaton have, however, traditionally been a great obstacle to a positive theology of work.[55] Why build a bigger and better barn if tonight we shall die (Luke 12:13–21)? Why develop new goods if they will all eventually rust or fall apart (Matt. 6:19)? Why do work that increases personal and social wealth if riches make it nearly impossible to enter the kingdom of heaven (Matt. 19:23–4, 6:24)? If the present world will be consumed by fire, then should we not just wait patiently for God to establish a "new heaven and a new earth" (2 Peter 3:7, 13; Jam. 5:5–7; Rev. 21:1)? Much of what we build up will quickly be eroded by time's incessant ebb and flow. And very little of our work deserves to be called a significant contribution to history. Thus, the finitude, frustrations, and failures people inevitably experience in work have led Christians to look beyond this life and to long for heaven.[56]

Still, as we have seen, something is missing in such observations. In working with and for our neighbors and our world, many contemporary Christians have the sense that they are closely united to the transforming power of God. We must avoid two extremes. At one extreme, our earthly progress has nothing to do with the kingdom of God, and God alone brings about the kingdom; at the other, earthly progress by itself brings about the kingdom of God.[57] The middle-ground alternative is a transformationist view: we hope that our good works are, in a transformed state, eternally preserved in the kingdom of God.[58] That is, the contributions we make to the present world are taken up into God's realm. Just as our work makes a difference to us, so also our work makes a difference to God who is wholly engaged in it. Thus, not only will we abide with the eternal God, but so also will the work we have done (Rev. 14:13). Therefore, one reason we want to work is the hope that what we produce will become "fruit that will last" (John 15:16).

The goods of work

In the final section of this essay, I want to present several interlinking ways in which God's love for humanity and for the world is made concrete through our work.

Social

In loving God we are inclined to love those whom God loves, and that includes being concerned for all who are touched by our work. The metaphor of the body of Christ, used by Paul to describe the inner workings of the Church (1 Cor. 12), also applies to our more secular enterprises: different occupations promote the common good of all the people of God.

In at least four basic ways, work flows from our social nature and makes us more social.[59] First, we inherit from others the materials and machines we use, the science and ideas by which we reckon, the social organizations for production, and so forth. Thus, the judgment that any of us is a self-made success is illusory. Second, we usually work with others. One of the pleasures (and pains) of work is that it brings us into contact with other people. Third, when we work, we affect others. In fact, our most significant contribution to most people is through our work. Our good work contributes to the common life of our family, city, region, nation, and world. Fourth, and not so obvious, out of love for Christ, our work should benefit the downtrodden (Matt. 25:31–46; Acts 20:35). The writer to the Ephesians, not surprisingly, urges thieves to get a job, but, quite surprisingly, he encourages them to do so in order "to have something to share with the needy" (Eph. 4:28). This fourth point demands not only that all of us reach out to the poor when we have the means to do so, but also that we deliberately work so that we will have extra to give to those in need.[60]

Instrumental

Work is an instrumental activity. We need food, shelter, clothing. We desire improved culture, education, churches, and so forth. Through labor, we are able, usually through the medium of money, to obtain these things for ourselves and others. A paradox of human nature is that the more we satisfy our needs and wants, the more we tend to create new needs and wants. Obviously, an ever-increasing abundance of goods can also lead to distraction or, in its own way, to boredom. It can divert us from the deeper values in life, including our relationships with family and with God. But these goods can also be appreciated as gifts derived from our human creativity and God's overflowing and inexhaustible richness.

Our efforts to obtain various goods for ourselves should flow from our self-love. But self-love requires us to work for more than instrumental reasons. When we are not really interested in what we are doing but only interested, say, in the money we earn, we are alienated from the work itself.[61] Our work will then seem a "necessary evil" that we endure in order to get what we need and want.[62] We ought not be satisfied with the instrumental value of work, no matter how great the rewards. Our self-love demands more. Indeed, God demands more since self-love is the ordinary way that we cooperate with and enflesh God's love for us.[63]

Talent-developing

Karl Marx, and before him Adam Smith, noted that our abilities are in part determined by what we do. That is, not only do our individual abilities help determine the kind of work we can do, but also the work we do helps determine what kind of abilities we concretely have.[64] A "good work out" in the gym develops our muscles. Reading history books develops our minds. Caring for friends develops our hearts. Similarly, a division of labor that gives us nothing intelligent to do will dull our minds, while a job requiring world travel will stretch our imaginations. Thus, as intelligent beings, we should ideally be involved not only in the execution of our work but also in its planning and organizing. And, as persons with hearts, we should ideally be so engaged by our work that we take "ownership" of it.

When we cannot find suitable work, we are deprived of the development that comes from working. Thus, a lack of employment – even if we have sufficient money – tends to be dehumanizing. Our various abilities wither when they are not exercised. But work can be a pleasure (Eccles. 5:18) if it allows us to suitably exercise and expand our abilities.[65] To extend a New Testament image, we humans have multiple "talents." If we use these talents, they develop. If, however, we let those talents lie unused, the talents themselves disappear (Matt. 25:14–20).

Virtue-building

As we have seen, one aspect of work that in the past was uppermost in Christian spirituality was the way it instilled virtue and prevented vice. It should be obvious that God wants us to develop a life of virtue, that is, various capacities for easily being good and doing what is right. But in what ways does working help us to become virtuous?

Before addressing this question, we should recall that people work in an enormous variety of ways. "Work" includes not only the top executive whose tasks are mainly mental but also the company janitor who cleans the corporate bathrooms at night. Some forms of work involve the most energizing creativity but other forms require mind–numbing, assembly-line repetition. As a consequence, different kinds of work require and produce different kinds of virtue.

So-called "working class" jobs usually offer little scope for creativity or intelligence. Once a worker has figured out how to mop the floors, there is not much more to learn. Such work is usually supervised. Its time is regulated not by the internal needs of the worker, but by the cycles of a machine or by a clock. This kind of work promotes virtues such as obedience, endurance, patience, attention to external order, and self-abnegation. It discourages individual excellence or risk taking.[66] By contrast, the work of so-called white-collar workers is relatively free from close supervision, is non-routinized, is challengingly complex, and allows for individual self-development and personal expression. It fosters virtues of independence, responsibility, and creativity.

We must become keenly aware which virtues and vices our work may be promoting in us. Those of us who do menial work need other responsibilities that promote our independence and creativity while those of us whose daily work promotes such virtues need other tasks that promote our sense of dependence and limits. Thus, we must grow in a wide array of virtues that enhance our basic Christian vocation.

Identity-forming

Through work, we not only exercise our many and varied "talents," we also engage our freedom in deciding who we are becoming. While the focus of our consciousness is usually on the deed we are performing, in every free act we are also deciding about ourselves. When artists create a work, they not only develop their artistic abilities, they also solidify their identity as artists. This self-formation is usually far more important than any product produced. That is why, in the evaluation of work, one of the first questions should be "who are the workers becoming?" To the degree that work treats them as interchangeable cogs in a machine, it is dehumanizing and prima facie wrong.[67]

Through our work, we develop our identity. In theological terms, we accept and live out a call from God. This "call" is not a mysterious voice; rather, as Aquinas observed, it frequently arises simply "inasmuch as some people are more inclined to one kind of work than to another."[68] Informed by our friendship with God, our unique, multi-faceted self responds to current needs and available opportunities.

In responding to the world about us, we develop our distinctive identities. We develop the likes and dislikes as well as the preferences and perspectives that characterize a particular way of relating to the world. Of course, we can hold our worker-identity at a distance from ourselves, but we do so at the cost of self-alienation. Instead, we ordinarily should accept and foster this part of our identity.

Even though God may once have called us to a particular work, we do not have to keep doing it, especially when it is boring or deleterious (cf. 1 Cor. 7:21). Rather, God often calls us to make changes that further complexify our identity. Paradoxically, we must change in order to be faithful to our developing selves and to the God of history.

We must evaluate our work not only by what it does to and for and with human beings,[69] but also by what it does to and for and with other creatures. When we do so, as Pope John Paul II observed, we human beings freely participate in God's exercise of providence. That is, God guides the world of nature and the world of persons through our reasonable and responsible care.[70]

In sum, our work is not only central in our lives, but it is also a primary arena where we cooperate with God in building, maintaining, repairing, and enhancing creation. In our work, therefore, we contribute our small part in God's work to bring about the kingdom. And that is the most fundamental reason why we Christians should work.

Notes

1　Miroslav Volf, *Work in the Spirit: Toward a Theology of Work* (New York: Oxford, 1991), pp. 10–14; Peter Schoonenberg, SJ, *God's World in the Making* (Pittsburgh: Duquesne, 1964), pp. 143–4; Germain Grisez, *Way of the Lord Jesus: Living a Christian Life*, vol. 2 (Quincy, IL: Franciscan Press, 1993), pp. 754–5.

2　Martin Helldorfer, "Work: An Invitation to Growth and Self-confrontation," *Humanitas*, vol. 7 (Fall 1971), pp. 195–9.

3　Foster McCurley and John Reumann, "Work in the Providence of God," in George Forell and William Lazareth (eds), *Work as Praise* (Philadelphia: Fortress, 1979), pp. 26–42; Claus Westermann, "Work, Civilisation and Culture in the Bible," in Gregory Baum (ed.), *Work and Religion* (New York: Seabury, 1980), pp. 81–91.

4　Gunther Wittenberg, "Old Testament Perspectives on Labour," in James Cochrane and Gerald West (eds), *Three-Fold Cord: Theology, Work, and Labour* (Hilton, Republic of South Africa: Cluster, 1991), pp. 96–100.

5　Jonathan Draper, "Christ the Worker: Fact or Fiction?' in *Three-Fold Cord*, pp. 121–5.

6　Marie-Dominique Chenu, "Work," *Sacramentum Mundi*, vol. 6 (New York: Herder and Herder, 1970), p. 370.

7　Silvano Burgalassi, "Towards a Theology of Man as Worker," *Work and Religion*, pp. 105–7.

8　Thomas à Kempis, *Imitation of Christ*, trans. Joseph Tylenda, SJ (Wilmington, DE: Michael Glazier, 1984), pp. I:22.2, 4.

9　Thomas Aquinas, *Summa theologica*, 5 vols, trans. Fathers of the English Dominican Province (Westminster, MD: Christian Classics, 1981), pp. II–II.182.1.

10　Thomas Aquinas, *Summa contra gentiles*, trans. Vernon Bourke, vol. 3 (Notre Dame: University of Notre Dame Press, 1975), pp. 67, 75–6.

11 Ibid., pp. 77–8.
12 Ibid., pp. 69, 70, 73.
13 Paul Althaus, *Ethics of Martin Luther* (Philadelphia: Fortress, 1972), pp. 39, 41, 101.
14 Martin Luther, *The Christian in Society I*, in *Luther's Works*, ed. James Atkinson, vol. 44 (Philadelphia: Fortress, 1966), p. 26, also p. 23, but see p. 39.
15 Volf, *Work in the Spirit*, pp. 105–10; Althaus, *Ethics of Martin Luther*, pp. 36–42.
16 Martin Luther, *Christian in Society II*, in *Luther's Works*, ed. Walther Brandt, vol. 45 (Philadelphia: Muhlenberg, 1962), pp. 324–6.
17 John Calvin, *Institutes of the Christian Religion*, trans. Ford Lewis Battles, ed. John T. McNeill (Philadelphia: Westminster Press, 1960), p. 724, III:10.6.
18 Ibid., p. 716, III:9.4.
19 Waldo Beach and H. Richard Niebuhr, *Christian Ethics*, 2nd edn (New York: John Wiley, 1973), p. 273. John Calvin himself opposed such endless working; see *Calvin: Commentaries*, ed. and trans. Joseph Haroutunian (Philadelphia: Westminster, 1958), p. 342.
20 Reginald White, *Christian Ethics* (Atlanta: John Knox, 1981), p. 202.
21 John Wesley, "The Use of Money" [Sermon 50], *Works of John Wesley*, vol. 2 (Nashville, TN: Abingdon Press, 1985), pp. 266–80.
22 Paul Bernstein, "The Work Ethic that Never Was," in Vincent Barry (ed.), *Moral Issues in Business* (Belmont, CA: Wadsworth, 1986), p. 212.
23 *Calvin: Commentaries*, p. 343.
24 John Paul II, *On Human Work* (Washington, DC: United States Catholic Conference, 1982), nos. 4.2, 7.2.
25 Ibid., nos. 4.2, 5–6.
26 Ibid., no. 9.3.
27 Ibid., no. 25.3.
28 Ibid., no. 25; see my essay, "John Paul II and Cooperation with God," *Annual of the Society of Christian Ethics* (1990), pp. 81–108.
29 John Paul II, *On Human Work*, no. 27.3.
30 Ibid., no. 27.7.
31 Lee Cormie, "Work and Salvation," *Work and Religion*, p. 131; Aquinas, *Summa theologica*, pp. II–II.179.2, 182.3–4.
32 Gregory Baum, "Towards a Theology of Work," *Three-Fold Cord*, pp. 155–6.
33 Larry Rasmussen, *Earth Community, Earth Ethics* (Maryknoll, NY: Orbis, 1996), pp. 273–4.
34 Chenu, "Work," vol. 6, pp. 371–2; Grisez, *Way of the Lord Jesus*, vol. 2, pp. 755–6; Karl Barth, *Church Dogmatics*, trans. Henry A. Kennedy (Edinburgh: T. & T. Clark, 1961), p. III/4, 483.
35 Edward Vacek, SJ, *Love, Human and Divine* (Washington, DC: Georgetown University Press, 1994), pp. xiii–xv, 25, 61, 89–90, 117–26.
36 Vacek, "Love for God – Is it Obligatory?' *Annual of the Society of Christian Ethics* (1996), pp. 221–47.
37 Vacek, "John Paul II and Cooperation with God," pp. 81–108; Vacek, *Love, Human and Divine*, pp. 116–56.
38 John Mahoney, SJ, *Making of Moral Theology* (Oxford: Clarendon Press, 1987), p. 247.

39 Martin Luther, *Career of the Reformer IV*, in *Luther's Works*, ed. Lewis Spitz, vol. 34 (Philadelphia: Muhlenberg Press, 1960), pp. 111; also vol. 14, p. 115; vol. 45, pp. 324–6, 330–1.

40 *Calvin: Commentaries*, pp. 340–1.

41 Aquinas, *Summa contra gentiles*, vol. 3, pp. 67, also pp. 69, 70, 77.

42 *Luther's Works*, vol. 45, 331; also Luther, *Selected Psalms III*, in *Luther's Works*, ed. Jaroslav Pelikan, vol. 14 (St. Louis: Concordia, 1958), p. 115.

43 *Calvin: Commentaries*, p. 341.

44 Vacek, *Love, Human and Divine*, pp. 116–56, 280–318.

45 Vacek, "Divine-Command, Natural-Law, and Mutual-Love Ethics," *Theological Studies*, vol. 57 (December, 1996), pp. 633–53; also Volf, *Work in the Spirit*, p. 125.

46 Barth, *Church Dogmatics*, pp. III/4, 474, 482–3, 520–1.

47 Jean Lacroix, "Concept of Work," *Cross Currents*, vol. 4 (1954), p. 243.

48 Catholic Bishops, "Church in the Modern World," *Documents of Vatican II* (New York: Crossroad, 1989), no. 34.

49 *Calvin: Commentaries*, p. 339.

50 Volf, *Work in the Spirit*, pp. 157–200.

51 Vacek, *Love, Human and Divine*, pp. 98, 322–5.

52 Studs Terkel, *Working* (New York: Random House, 1972), p. xi.

53 Luther, *Luther's Works*, vol. 45, pp. 332–3.

54 Helldorfer, "Work," pp. 202–3.

55 Volf, *Work in the Spirit*, pp. 100–1.

56 Helldorfer, "Work," pp. 202–3.

57 Langdon Gilkey, *Message and Existence* (New York: Seabury, 1979), p. 220; Catholic Bishops, "Church in the Modern World," no. 39.

58 Vincent Genovesi, SJ, *In Pursuit of Love*, 2nd edn (Collegeville, MN: Liturgical Press, 1996), pp. 38–48.

59 Chenu, "Work," vol. 6, p. 372.

60 Volf, *Work in the Spirit*, pp. 189–90.

61 Ibid., pp. 53–61; Joe Holland, *Creative Communion: Toward a Spirituality of Work* (New York: Paulist, 1989), pp. 26–30.

62 Grisez, *Way of the Lord Jesus*, vol. 2, p. 756; Volf, *Work in the Spirit*, p. 50.

63 Vacek, *Love, Human and Divine*, pp. 198–275.

64 Volf, *Work in the Spirit*, pp. 26–7, 51.

65 Ibid., pp. 127–33.

66 Cormie, "Work and Salvation," pp. 130–1; Jean Rémy, "Work and Self-awareness," in *Work and Religion*, pp. 7–9.

67 Nondyebo Taki, "Elements of a Theology of Work," in *Three-Fold Cord*, pp. 170–72.

68 Aquinas, *Summa contra gentiles*, vol. 3, p. 134.

69 National Conference of Catholic Bishops, *Economic Justice for All* (Washington, DC: United States Catholic Conference, 1986), no. 13.

70 *Veritatis splendor* (Vatican City: Libreria Editrice Vaticana, 1993), no. 43; National Conference of Catholic Bishops, *Economic Justice for All*, no. 32.

5

Inquiring after God through Friendship

Christians have often summarized the essence of obedience to God as love of God and neighbor (Deut. 6:5; Lev. 19:18; Matt. 22:37–9). Reflection on these two commands is usually linked: loving God leads to loving one's neighbor, and love of neighbor is a form of loving God through caring for his creatures. Christianity, however, went beyond this traditional Jewish understanding to command love of enemies. From the many issues emanating from these themes three will be examined here: love of friends, love of strangers, and love of enemies.

The medieval text is the pivotal Christian classic on spiritual friendship written by St. Aelred, abbot of the Cistercian monastery at Rievaulx in northern England. In this treatise Aelred tells us that he entered the monastery in order to arrange his life that had been disordered by unruly "loves and affections" marked by untoward (sexual) behavior. He was educated at the court of the Scottish king where he became intimately involved with the king's sons. The relationships went sour, however, and he fell into depression and confusion. At the age of twenty-four he entered a monastery where he undertook a chaste and ordered life that helped him get his emotions and hormones under control.

He was so successful that he was made abbot of the monastery, where he had responsibility for the spiritual lives of hundreds of monks. He wrote the treatise on friendship to help others find intimacy in interpersonal relationships without falling prey to the manipulations and abuses of self and others that often accompany intimacy when it is ill-guided or gets out of control sexually.

Medieval monasticism is often characterized (perhaps caricatured) as having zero tolerance for the human needs for intimacy, fun, and sociality. Although it looks extreme to moderns there is thought behind the strict separation of women and men and the prohibition of "special friendships" among monks. Those who entered the monastery to live under a rule of life that would enable them to regain control of their behavior depended upon chastity to control sex and poverty to control greed. Living according to the opposite of where trouble lay established their lives on a new, healthy foundation. Addicts similarly have to separate themselves from the destructive behavior that enchains them. Recovering alcoholics may never consider themselves to be fully cured and so they abstain from alcohol completely for fear that even a bit of drink will reawaken destructive habits and patterns.

Aelred's abbatial responsibilities led him to offer his theological wisdom to those seeking a purer life. Instead of prohibiting intimacy as a way of nipping interpersonal problems in the bud, however, he counseled a risky path. He permitted close friendships within the monastery, but created a rule of friendship that located nonsexual intimacy under a theological canopy, since without guidance we do not instinctively know what is appropriate and helpful in friendship. For the monks such a risky option was supported by the vow of celibacy they took.

To find a rule for ordering friendship Aelred turned to the west's greatest authority on the subject, Marcus Tullius, the first-century B.C. Roman statesman, known as Tully or Cicero. Cicero's treatise on friendship helped Aelred up to a point. But he found, like Augustine before him when reading Platonic philosophy, that Cicero's understanding was only partial because he did not know Jesus Christ. That is, because he lived before Christianity he was unable to understand friendship theologically, for it begins in Christ, is preserved according to the Holy Spirit, and leads back to Christ.

In his treatise on spiritual friendship Aelred offers a distinctively Christian understanding of friendship in the service of God. To this end he distinguishes spiritual friendship from both carnal and worldly friendships. Carnal friendship focuses on sexual gratification, and worldly friendship focuses on economic gain that may be procured by means of the relationship. While carnal and worldly friendships are appropriate in their proper place, and have the potential to mature, spiritual friendship is the most refined, mature, and godly of the three. It disdains flighty emotions, jealousies, anger, slander, greed, and exploitation of any kind, and so develops the spiritual lives of both friends.

Now, since all complain that they cannot achieve this level of purity in personal relationships, Aelred offers a four-fold rule of friendship: choose friends slowly and carefully; test the friend for loyalty, proper intention, discretion, and patience before disclosing too much of oneself; only when the friend is tested should she or he be admitted fully as a spiritual friend with whom to grow in life with God; from then on one must always be a true spiritual friend to the persons admitted. Under this rule, one certainly has few spiritual friends.

Aelred knew from experience how much pain is caused by failed relationships, and so he concluded the treatise by suggesting that in order for spiritual friendships to endure one must cultivate one's own spiritual life. It is one thing to find a friend, another to be one. Perhaps his most challenging point is the need to protect one's friend by doing nothing unbecoming or demeaning that would by association reflect badly on one's friend. Thus, while the cultivation of spiritual friendship is for one's emotional and social enrichment, for Aelred friendship is a spiritual discipline that enables one to understand and obey God better by fostering the spiritual life of another.

Our contemporary interpreter pursues one of the paths Aelred does not follow. Professor Caroline Simon explores love of neighbor in the broad sense of Christian *agape*, or *caritas*, that extends to strangers and sinners. The Christian vision of living into our proper destiny is both constrained and made possible by God's grace. Neighbor-love is a command of God that calls one to recognize and foster the divine destiny and identity of another even if that destiny remains invisible to the person him or herself. In this way, Simon extends the high demands of personal friendship to estranged family members and street bums. Christian love embraces sinners, losers, and those who trespass against us.

Neighbor-love does not stop, perhaps does not even begin, with bringing food for the poor, or allowing the church building to be used by a worthy group. Rather it requires all one's compassion, tact, endurance, spiritual wisdom, and strength to help others grow into their God-given destiny. Neighbor-love – as Aelred also saw – is a great equalizer. Here issues of social station and biological differences are useless. For in helping another flourish one grows into God oneself – even when the experience is limited to a chance encounter among strangers. This is the power of divine grace. Simon presses beyond material charity to supernatural charity that gives the other the gift of a new vision of self grounded in the dignity and destiny of God. She distinguishes supernatural charity from sentimentality that may slide into condescension.

Like Aelred, Simon turns the camera around at the end of her essay and looks at what is required to receive supernatural charity, that is, forgiveness. Perhaps it takes as much largeness of spirit to receive Christian love as to give it. It takes what Simon calls supernatural gratitude, for it requires humbling oneself by seeing the truth about oneself.

Aelred of Rievaulx, *Spiritual Friendship*

Prologue

When I was still just a lad at school, and the charm of my companions pleased me very much, I gave my whole soul to affection and devoted myself to love amid the ways and vices with which that age is wont to be threatened, so that nothing seemed to me more sweet, nothing more agreeable, nothing more practical, than to love. And so, torn between conflicting loves and friendships, I was drawn now here, now there, and not knowing the law of true friendship, I was often deceived by its mere semblance. At length there came to my hands the treatise which Tullius [Cicero] wrote on friendship, and it immediately appealed to me as being serviceable because of the depth of his ideas, and fascination because of the charm of his eloquence. And though I saw myself unfitted for that type of friendship, still I was gratified that I had discovered a formula for friendship whereby I might check the vacillations of my loves and affections.

When, in truth, it pleased our good Lord to reprove the wanderer, to lift the fallen, and with his healing touch to cleanse the leper, abandoning all worldly hopes, I entered a monastery. Immediately I gave my attention to the reading of holy books, whereas prior to that, my eye, dimmed by the carnal darkness to which it had been accustomed, had not even a surface acquaintance with them. From that time on, Sacred Scripture became more attractive and the little learning which I had acquired in the world grew insipid in comparison. The ideas I had gathered from Cicero's treatise on friendship kept recurring to my mind, and I was astonished that they no longer had for me their wonted savor. For now nothing which had not been sweetened by the honey of the most sweet name of Jesus, nothing which had not been seasoned with the salt of Sacred Scripture, drew my affection so entirely to itself. Pondering over these thoughts again and again, I began to ask myself whether they could perhaps have some support from Scripture. . . . I decided to write my own book on spiritual friendship and to draw up for myself rules for a chaste and holy love. . . .

Book 1: The Origin of Friendship

Aelred. Here we are, you and I, and I hope a third, Christ, is in our midst. There is no one now to disturb us; there is no one to break in upon our friendly chat, no man's prattle or noise of any kind will creep into this pleasant solitude. Come now, beloved, open your heart, and pour into these friendly ears whatsoever you will, and let us accept gracefully the boon of this place, time, and leisure.

Just a little while ago as I was sitting with the brethren, while all around were talking noisily, one questioning, another arguing – one advancing some point on Sacred Scripture, another information on vices, and yet another on virtue – you alone were silent. At times you would raise your head and make ready to say something, but just as quickly, as though your voice had been trapped in your throat, you would drop your head again and continue your silence. Then you would leave us for a while, and later return looking rather disheartened. I concluded from all this that you wanted to talk to me, but that you dreaded the crowd, and hoped to be alone with me.

Ivo. That's it exactly, and I deeply appreciate your solicitude for your son. . . .

Aelred. . . . I am greatly pleased to see that you are not bent on empty and idle pursuits, but that you are always speaking of things useful and necessary for your progress. Speak freely, therefore, and entrust to your friend all your cares and thoughts, that you may both learn and teach, give and receive, pour out and drink in.

Ivo. . . . I wish that you would teach me something about spiritual friendship, namely, its nature and value, its source and end, whether it can be cultivated among all, and, if not among all, then by whom; how it can be preserved unbroken, and without any disturbance of misunderstanding be brought to a holy end. . . . I should like also to be instructed more fully as to how the friendship which ought to exist among us begins in Christ, is preserved according to the Spirit of Christ, and how its end and fruition are referred to Christ. For it is evident that Tullius was unacquainted with the virtue of true friendship, since he was completely unaware of its beginning and end, Christ. . . .

Aelred. . . . Friendship, therefore, is that virtue by which spirits are bound by ties of love and sweetness, and out of many are made one. Even the philosophers of this world have ranked friendship not with things casual or transitory but with the virtues which are eternal. Solomon in the *Book of Proverbs* appears to agree with them when he says: "He that is a friend loves at all times" [Prov. 17:17], manifestly declaring that friendship is eternal if it is true friendship; but, if it should ever cease to be, then it was not true friendship, even though it seemed to be so. . . .

Falsely do they claim the illustrious name of friends among whom there exists a harmony of vices; since he who does not love is not a friend, but he does not love his fellowman who loves iniquity. "For he that loves iniquity" does not love, but "hates his own soul" [Ps. 10:6]. Truly, he who does not love his own soul will not be able to love the soul of another. Thus it follows that they glory only in the name of friendship and are deceived by a distorted image and are not supported by truth. Yet, since such great joy is experienced in friendship which either lust defiles, avarice dishonors, or luxury pollutes, we may infer how much sweetness that friendship possesses which, in proportion as it is nobler, is the more secure; purer, it is the more pleasing; freer, it is the more happy. Let us allow that, because of some similarity in feelings, those friendships which are not true, be, nevertheless, called friendships, provided, however, they are judiciously distinguished from that friendship which is spiritual and therefore true. Hence let one kind of friendship be called carnal, another worldly, and another spiritual. The carnal springs from mutual harmony in vice; the worldly is enkindled by the hope of gain; and the spiritual is cemented by similarity of life, morals, and pursuits among the just.

The real beginning of carnal friendship proceeds from an affection which like a harlot directs its step after every passerby [see Ezek. 16:25], following its own lustful ears and eyes in every direction [Num. 15:39]. By means of the avenues of these senses it brings into the mind itself images of beautiful bodies or voluptuous objects. To enjoy these as he pleases the carnal man thinks is blessedness, but to enjoy them without an associate he considers less delightful. Then, by gesture, nod, words, compliance, spirit is captivated by spirit, and one is inflamed by the other, and they are kindled to form a sinful bond, so that, after they have entered upon such a deplorable pact, the one will do or suffer any crime or sacrilege whatsoever for the sake of the other. They consider nothing sweeter than this type of friendship, they judge nothing more equable, believing community of like and dislike to be imposed upon them by the laws of friendship. And so, this sort of friendship is undertaken without deliberation, is tested by no act of judgment, is in no wise governed by reason; but through the violence of affection is carried away through divers paths, observing no limit, caring naught for uprightness, foreseeing neither gains nor losses, but advancing toward everything heedlessly, indiscriminately, lightly and immoderately. For that reason, goaded on, as if by furies, it is consumed by its own self, or is dissolved with the same levity with which it was originally fashioned.

But worldly friendship, which is born of a desire for temporal advantage or possessions, is always full of deceit and intrigue; it contains nothing certain, nothing constant, nothing secure; for, to be sure, it ever changes with fortune and follows the purse. Hence it is written: "He is a fairweather friend, and he will not abide in the day of your trouble" [Sir. 6:8]. Take away his hope of profit, and immediately he will cease to be a friend. This type of friendship the following lines very aptly deride:

> A friend, not of the man, but of his purse is he,
> Held fast by fortune fair, by evil made to flee. [Anon.]

And yet, the beginning of this vicious friendship leads many individuals to a certain degree of true friendship: those, namely, who at first enter into a compact of friendship in the hope of common profit while they cherish in themselves faith in baneful riches, and who, in so far as human affairs are concerned, reach an acme of pleasing mutual agreement. But a friendship ought in no wise be called true which is begun and preserved for the sake of some temporal advantage.

For spiritual friendship, which we call true, should be desired, not for consideration of any worldly advantage or for any extrinsic cause, but from the dignity of its own nature and the feelings of the human heart, so that its fruition and reward is nothing other than itself. Whence the Lord in the Gospel says: "I have appointed you that you should go, and should bring forth fruit" [John 15:16–17], that is, that you should love one another. For true friendship advances by perfecting itself and the fruit is derived from feeling the sweetness of that perfection. And so spiritual friendship among the just is born of a similarity in life, morals, and pursuits, that is, it is a mutual conformity in matters human and divine united with benevolence and charity.

Ivo. Your explanation is certainly sufficient, and nothing else suggests itself to me for further inquiry. But before we go on to other things, I should like to know how friendship first originated among men. Was it by nature, by chance or by necessity of some kind? . . .

Aelred. . . . when God created man, in order to commend more highly the good of society, he said: "It is not good for man to be alone: let us make him a helper like unto himself" [Gen. 2:18]. It was from no similar, nor even from the same, material that divine Might formed this help mate, but as a clearer inspiration to charity and friendship he produced the woman from the very substance of the man [Gen. 2:21–2]. How beautiful it is that the second human being was taken from the side of the first, so that nature might teach that human beings are equal and, as it were, collateral, and that there is in human affairs neither a superior nor an inferior, a characteristic of true friendship. . . . Thus friendship, which nature has brought into being and practice has strengthened, has by the power of law been regulated. It is evident, then, that friendship is natural, like virtue, wisdom, and the like, which should be sought after and preserved for their own sake as natural goods. Everyone that possesses them makes good use of them, and no one entirely abuses them. . . .

Book 2: The Fruition and Excellence of Friendship

. . . *Walter.* Look, here I am, all ears to take in every word, the more avidly so since what I have read on friendship has so pleasant a taste. Since, therefore, I have read this excellent discussion on the nature of friendship, I should like to have you tell me what practical advantages it procures for those who cultivate it. For though it is a matter of such moment, as you seem to have thoroughly proved by means of unassailable arguments, yet it is only when its purpose and benefit are understood that it will be sought after with genuine ardor.

Aelred. . . . It manifests all the virtues by its own charms; it assails vices by its own virtue; it tempers adversity and moderates prosperity. As a result, scarcely any happiness whatever can exist among mankind without friendship, and a man is to be compared to a beast if he has no one to rejoice with [i.e. comfort] him in adversity, no one to whom to unburden his mind if any annoyance crosses his path or with whom to share some unusually sublime or illuminating inspiration. "Woe to him that is alone, for when he falls, he has none to lift him up" [Eccl. 4:10]. He is entirely alone who is without a friend.

But what happiness, what security, what joy to have someone to whom you dare to speak on terms of equality as to another self; one to whom you need have no fear to confess your failings; one to whom you can unblushingly make known what progress you have made in the spiritual life; one to whom you can entrust all the secrets of your heart and before whom you can place all your plans! What, therefore, is more pleasant than so to unite to oneself the spirit of another and of two to form one, that no boasting is thereafter to be feared, no suspicion to be dreaded, no correction of one by the other to cause pain, no praise on the part of one to bring a charge of adulation from the other. "A friend," says the Wise Man, "is the medicine of life" [Sir. 6:16]. Excellent, indeed, is that saying. For medicine is not more powerful or more efficacious for our wounds in all our temporal needs than the possession of a friend who meets every misfortune joyfully, so that, as the Apostle says, shoulder to shoulder, they bear one another's burdens [Gal. 6:2]. Even more each one carries his own injuries even more lightly than that of his friend. Friendship, therefore, heightens the joys of prosperity and mitigates the sorrows of adversity by dividing and sharing them. Hence, the best medicine in life is a friend. . . . And so it is that the rich prize friendship as their glory, the exiles as their native land, the poor as their wealth, the sick as their medicine, the dead as their life, the healthy as their charm, the weak as their strength and the strong as their prize. So great are the distinction, memory, praise and affection that accompany friends that their lives are adjudged worthy of praise and their death rated as precious. And, a thing even more excellent than all these considerations, friendship is a stage bordering upon that perfection which consists in the love and knowledge of God, so that man from being a friend of his fellowman becomes the friend of God, according to the words of the Savior in the Gospel: "I will not now call you servants, but my friends" [John 15:15]. . . .

Nevertheless, turn your attention briefly to the manner in which friendship is, so to say, a stage toward the love and knowledge of God. Indeed, in friendship there is nothing dishonorable, nothing deceptive, nothing feigned; whatever there is, is holy, voluntary, and true. And this itself is also a characteristic of charity [see 1 Cor. 13]. In this, truly, friendship shines forth with a special light of its own, that among those who are bound by the tie of friendship all joys, all security, all sweetness, all charms are experienced. Therefore, in the perfection of charity we love very many who are a source of burden and grief to us, for whose interest we concern ourselves honorably, not with hypocrisy or dissimulation, but sincerely and voluntarily, but yet we do not admit these to the intimacy of our friendship. And so in friendship are joined honor and charm, truth and joy, sweetness and goodwill, affection and action. And all these take their beginning from Christ, advance through Christ, and are perfected in Christ. Therefore, not too steep or unnatural does the ascent appear from Christ, as the inspiration of the love by which we love our friend, to Christ giving himself to us as our Friend for us to love, so that charm may follow upon charm, sweetness upon sweetness and affection upon affection. And thus, friend cleaving to friend in the spirit of Christ, is made with Christ but one heart and one soul [Acts 4:32], and so mounting aloft through degrees of love to friendship with Christ, he is made one spirit with him in one kiss [1 Cor. 6:17]. . . .

Walter. Since, therefore, it is agreed that many are deceived by the mere semblance of friendship, tell us, pray, what sort of friendship we ought to avoid and what sort we ought to seek, cherish and preserve.

Aelred. Since we have said that friendship cannot endure except among the good, it is easy for you to see that no friendship which would be unbecoming to the good is acceptable.

Gratian. But perhaps we are not clear on the distinction between what is becoming and what is unbecoming.

Aelred. I shall comply with your wishes and state in a few words what friendships ought to be avoided should they present themselves to us. There is the puerile friendship begotten of an aimless and playful affection, directing its step after every passerby without reason, without weight, without measure, without consideration of advantage or disadvantage. This type of friendship for a time affects one strongly, it draws one rather closely, and entices one rather flatteringly. But affection without reason is an animal movement, inclined to everything illicit, nay, unable to discern licit from illicit. Moreover, although affection, for the most part, commonly precedes friendship yet it ought never be followed unless reason lead it, honor temper it, and justice rule it. Hence, this friendship which we have styled puerile, because it is chiefly in children that feelings hold sway, ought, as a thing unfaithful, unstable, and always mixed with impure loves, to be guarded against in every way by those who take delight in the sweetness of spiritual friendship. . . . For that reason the beginnings of spiritual friendship ought to possess, first of all, purity of intention, the direction of reason and the restraint of moderation; and thus the very desire for such friendship, so sweet as it comes upon us, will presently make friendship itself a delight to experience, so that it will never cease to be properly ordered.

. . . It is clear, then, from this whole discussion, what the fixed and true limit of spiritual friendship is: namely, that nothing ought to be denied to a friend, nothing ought to be refused for a friend, which is less than the very precious life of the body, which divine authority has taught should be laid down for a friend [John 15:13]. Hence, since the life of the soul is of far greater excellence than that of the body, any action, we believe, should be altogether denied a friend which brings about the death of the soul, that is, sin, which separated God from the soul and the soul from life. . . .

Book 3: The Conditions and Characters Requisite for Unbroken Friendship

...*Aelred*.... We have said that love is the source of friendship, not love of any sort whatever, but that which proceeds from reason and affection simultaneously, which, indeed, is pure because of reason and sweet because of affection. Then we said that a foundation of friendship should be laid in the love of God, to which all things which are proposed should be referred, and these ought to be examined as to whether they conform to the foundation or are at variance with it. Then we thought that one should pay attention to the four steps which lead up to the heights of perfect friendship; for a friend ought first to be selected, next tested, then finally admitted, and from then on treated as a friend deserves. And speaking of selection, we excluded the quarrelsome, the irascible, the fickle, the suspicious, and the loquacious; and yet not all, but only those who are unable or unwilling to regulate or restrain these passions. For many are affected by these disturbances in such a manner that their perfection is not only in no way injured, but their virtue is even more laudably increased by the restraint of these passions. For men, who, as though unbridled, are carried away headlong under the impulse of these passions, inevitably slip and fall into those vices by which friendship, as Scripture testifies, is wounded and dissolved; namely, insults, reproaches, betrayal of secrets, pride, and the stroke of treachery [see Sir. 27:27]. If, nevertheless, you suffer all these evils from him whom you once received into friendship, we said that your friendship should not be broken off immediately, but dissolved little by little, and that such reverence should be maintained for the former friendship, that, although you withdraw your confidence from him, yet you never withdraw your love, refuse your aid, or deny him your advice. But if his frenzy breaks out even to blasphemies and calumny, do you, nevertheless, yield to the bonds of friendship, yield to charity, so that the blame will reside with him who inflicts, not with him who bears, the injury. Furthermore, if he is found to be a peril to his father, to his country, to his fellow-citizens, to his dependents or to his friends, the bond of familiarity ought to be broken immediately; love for one man should not take precedence over the ruin of many. To prevent such misfortunes one should be cautious in choosing a friend, that one be chosen whom fury does not goad on to such evils, nor levity induce, nor loquacity drive headlong, nor suspicion carry off; especially should one be chosen who does not differ too much from your character, and is not of harmony with your temperament. But since we are speaking of true friendship, which cannot exist except among the good, we make no mention of those concerning whom there can be no doubt that they ought not to be chosen, namely, those who are base, avaricious, ambitious, slanderous. Now, then, if we have discussed selection sufficiently for you, let us then pass on to probation....

There are four qualities which must be tested in a friend: loyalty, right intention, discretion, and patience, that you may entrust yourself to him securely. The right intention, that he may expect nothing from your friendship except God and its natural good. Discretion, that he may understand what is to be done in behalf of a friend, what is to be sought from a friend, what sufferings are to be endured for his sake, upon what good deeds he is to be congratulated; and, since we think that a friend should sometimes be corrected, he must know for what faults this should be done, as well as the manner, the time, and the place. Finally, patience, that he may not grieve when rebuked, or despise or hate the one inflicting the rebuke, and that he may not be unwilling to bear every adversity for the sake of his friend. . . .

There are many other ways in which the fidelity of a friend is proved, though ill-fortune is the best. For, as we have said before, there is nothing which wounds friendship more than the betrayal of one's secret counsels. Indeed, the Gospel sentence reads: "He that is faithful in that which is little, will be faithful in that which is great" [Luke 10:16]. Therefore, to those friends, for whom thus far we have thought probation necessary, we ought not confide to them all our profound secrets, but at first, external or little things about which one does not care a great deal whether they be concealed or exposed; yet this should be done with very great caution as if these smaller matters should do harm if betrayed, but would be of service if concealed. If your friend has been found faithful in these smaller matters, do not hesitate to test him in greater. . . .

Our Lord and Savior himself has written for us the formula of true friendship when he said: "You shall love your neighbor as yourself" [Matt. 22:39; Lev. 19:18]. Behold the mirror. You love yourself. Yes, especially if you love God, if you are such a person as we have described as worthy of being chosen for friendship. But tell me, do you think you should expect any reward from yourself for this love of yours? No, indeed, not the least, for from the very nature of things each one is dear to himself. Unless, therefore, you transfer [t]his same affection to the other, loving him gratuitously, in that from the very nature of things in himself your friend seems dear, you cannot savor what true friendship is. For then truly he whom you love will be another self, if you have transformed your love of self to him. "For friendship is not tribute," as St. Ambrose says, "but a thing full of beauty, full of grace. It is a virtue, not a trade, because it is bought with love, not money, because it is acquired by competition in generosity, not by a haggling over its prices" [*Duties*, 3:133]. Therefore the intention of the one whom you have chosen must subtly be tested, that he may not wish to be joined in friendship to you according to the hope of some advantage, thinking friendship mercenary and not gratuitous. . . . And so towards the wealthy one acts flatteringly, but towards the poor no one pretends to be other than he is. Whatever is given to a poor man is a true gift, for the friendship of the poor is devoid of envy. . . .

This is that extraordinary and great happiness which we await, with God himself acting and diffusing, between himself and his creatures whom he has uplifted, among the very degrees and orders which he has distinguished, among the individual souls whom he has chosen, so much friendship and charity, that thus each loves another as he does himself; and that, by this means, just as each one rejoices in his own, so does he rejoice in the good fortune of another, and thus the happiness of each one individually is the happiness of all, and the universality of all happiness is the possession of each individual. There one finds no hiding of thoughts, no dissembling of affection. This is true and eternal friendship, which begins in this life and is perfected in the next, which here belongs to the few where few are good, but there belongs to all where all are good. . . .

Walter. This friendship is so sublime and perfect that I dare not aspire to it. For me and our friend Gratian that type of friendship suffices which your Augustine describes: namely, to converse and jest together, with good-will to humor one another, to read together, to discuss matters together, together to trifle, and together to be in earnest; to differ at times without ill-humor, as a man would do with himself, and even by a very infrequent disagreement to give zest to our very numerous agreements; to teach one another something, or to learn from one another; with impatience to long for one another when absent, and with joy to receive one another when returning. By these and similar indications emanating from the hearts of those who love and are loved in turn, through the countenance, the tongue, the eyes, and a thousand pleasing movements, to fuse our spirits by tinder, as it were, and out of many to make but one. This is what we think we should love in our friends, so that our conscience will be its own accuser, if we have not loved him who in turn loves us, or if we have not returned love to him who first loved us.

Aelred. This type of friendship belongs to the carnal, and especially to the young people, such as they once were, Augustine and the friend of whom he was then speaking. And yet this friendship except for trifles and deceptions, if nothing dishonorable enters into it, is to be tolerated in the hope of more abundant grace, as the beginnings, so to say, of a holier friendship. By these beginnings, with a growth in piety and in constant zeal for things of the spirit, with the growing seriousness of maturer years and the illumination of the spiritual senses, they may, with purer affections, mount to loftier heights from, as it were, a region close by, just as yesterday we said that the friendship of man could be easily translated into a friendship for God himself because of the similarity existing between both. . . .

Men would lead a very happy life, says the Wise Man, if these two words were taken from their midst: namely, "mine" and "yours." For holy poverty certainly bestows great strength upon spiritual friendship, poverty which is holy for the reason that it is voluntary. For since cupidity makes heavy demands on friendship, friendship once attained is the more easily preserved in proportion as the soul is found more fully purified of this pest. There are, moreover, other resources in spiritual love, by means of which friends can be of aid and advantage to one another. The first is to be solicitous for one another, to pray for one another, to blush for one another, to rejoice for one another, to grieve for one another's fall as one's own, to regard another's progress as one's own.

By whatever means are in one's power, one ought to raise the weak, support the infirm, console the afflicted, restrain the wrathful. Furthermore one ought so to respect the eye of a friend as to dare to do nothing which is dishonorable, or dare to say nothing which is unbecoming. For when one fails one's self in anything, the act ought so to well over to one's friend, that the sinner not only blushes and grieves within himself, but that even the friend who sees or hears reproaches himself as if he himself has sinned...

"Therefore," as Saint Ambrose says, "if you perceive any vice in your friend, correct him secretly; if he will not listen to you, correct him openly. For corrections are good and often better than a friendship which holds its peace. And even though your friend think himself wronged, nevertheless correct him. Even though the bitterness of correction wound his soul, nevertheless cease not to correct him. For the wounds inflicted by a friend are more tolerable than the kisses of flatterers [Prov. 27:6]. Therefore, correct the erring friend" [*Duties*, 3:127].

And yet, above all things, one ought to avoid anger and bitterness of spirit in correction, that he may be seen to have the betterment of his friend at heart rather than the satisfaction of his own ill humor.

... Added to this there is prayer for one another, which, coming from a friend, is the more efficacious in proportion as it is more lovingly sent to God, with tears which either fear excites or affection awakens or sorrow evokes. And thus a friend praying to Christ on behalf of his friend, and for his friend's sake desiring to be heard by Christ, directs his attention with love and longing to Christ; then it sometimes happens that quickly and imperceptibly the one love passes over into the other, and coming, as it were, into close contact with the sweetness of Christ himself, the friend begins to taste his sweetness and to experience his charm [Ps. 34:8]. Thus ascending from that holy love with which he embraces a friend to that with which he embraces Christ, he will joyfully partake in abundance of the spiritual fruit of friendship, awaiting the fullness of all things in the life to come. Then, with the dispelling of all anxiety by reason of which we now fear and are solicitous for one another, with the removal of all adversity which it now behooves us to bear for one another, and, above all, with the destruction of the sting of death together with death itself [1 Cor. 15:54f.], whose pangs now often trouble us and force us to grieve for one another, with salvation secured, we shall rejoice in the eternal possession of Supreme Goodness; and this friendship, to which here we admit but few, will be outpoured upon all and by all outpoured upon God, and God shall be all in all [1 Cor. 15:28].

CONTEMPORARY REFLECTION

Inquiring after God through our Neighbor

Caroline J. Simon

Love and Destiny

At the heart of the Christian tradition is the deep, inextricable linkage between loving one another and loving God. What we have done to or for our sisters and brothers, our neighbors, the infirm, widows, orphans, prisoners, and strangers within our gates, we have done to or for Christ (Matt. 25). John's first epistle puts this in no uncertain terms:

> We love because he first loved us. Those who say, "I love God," and hate their brothers or sisters, are liars; for those who do not love a brother or sister whom they have seen, cannot love God whom they have not seen. The commandment we have from him is this: those who love God must love their brothers and sisters also.   (1 John 4:19–21, NRSV)

Much of the history of Christian theology is the story of our trying to get our minds around this mystery. Much of the history of the Church is the story of our stumbling attempts to grow into this mystery and live it out.

Aelred of Rievaulx, a twelfth-century Cistercian monk and abbot, and his book *Spiritual Friendship* are chapters in this story. Aelred's life spanned two worlds: his early life included the world of the Scottish court; from his mid-twenties on, his life revolved around the monastery at Rievaulx. His education at court included an exposure to Cicero's *De amicitia*, echoes of which are heard throughout his own reflections.

Spiritual Friendship is in many ways a courageous work. Living in a time when monastics were suspicious of particular human affections, Aelred insisted on seeing true friendship as having both its source and fruition in the love of God. Living in a time when some were suspicious of classical pagan thinkers, Aelred baptized the wisdom that Cicero had borrowed from Aristotle and wove it into a deeply Christian theology of human affection. Although indebted to Cicero, Aelred transforms Cicero's wisdom by

◆ 121

giving it a distinctively Christian stamp. Cicero knew nothing of charity, the peculiar love that Christians are enjoined to have even toward their enemies. Nor is Cicero in a position to see that true friendship has its *telos* in something more than human excellence. For Aelred, both charity and spiritual friendship "take their beginning from Christ, advance through Christ, and are perfected in Christ." These loves for our fellow human beings are stages toward the love and knowledge of God (2:18–21). Growing in Christian love for our fellow human beings is inquiring after God. Knowing and loving our neighbors and friends is caught up in a sacred tangle with knowing and loving God.

There are puzzles about love that need to be sorted out here. There is, in any kind of love, a kind of tension. To love is to esteem and to prize. But if our love takes a specific, concrete human being as its focus, there will be many reasons not to esteem or to prize the person. Every particular person has faults and failings. Yet love seems committed to overlooking these imperfections. This is puzzling, because if love must be "blind," in what sense is love directed to this particular person? If love refuses to see what is there in all its sometimes distressing reality, then does love by its nature involve fantasy and falsification?

Despite adages like "love is blind," I share with Aelred the belief that genuine love, in all its forms, provides insight into the loved one's true self. Infatuation, manipulation, and sentimentality are prone to whimsical reaction and wishful, self-interested projection. In contrast, love involves knowledge: of God, ourselves, and others.

One important aspect of the biblical story takes our stories to be more than they appear to be: "Beloved, we are God's children now; it does not yet appear what we shall be, but we know that when he appears we shall be like him, for we shall see him as he is" (1 John 3:2). Love gives insight into the true end toward which we aspire, which (humanly) does not yet appear. Love, in all its forms, involves and makes possible the work of attention necessary to have such insight; as such it is both hard-won and a gift of grace. In contrast, fiction-making is the construction and projection of a narrative for oneself or another which is unconnected with that person's true self.

Political philosopher Glenn Tinder calls each person's true self a "destiny." Tinder says, "My destiny is my own selfhood, given by God, but given not as an established reality, like a rock or a hill, but as a task lying under a divine imperative."[1] Destiny is unlike fate in that a destiny can be failed or refused; it is what God intends, but does not compel, me to be. When Tinder talks of failing one's destiny, he refers to having made choices which make it impossible for one to actualize some of the potentials which constitute one's destiny.

Christians believe that no one's destiny is completely fulfilled in time;

rather everyone's destiny has an eternal aspect. Because of this, "they insist that a human being in essence is not something here and now in front of us, which we can examine and understand, as we might an automobile or a building, but is something that has yet to be discovered and realized; this they believe, can finally be accomplished only beyond the limitations of space and time."[2] Tinder asserts that each person's destiny is unique and personal, but our destinies intertwine in complex and mysterious ways.[3] Destinies can be failed and refused, but God confers on humans the dignity of being creators of their own destinies within the limits set by God's intentions.

Apart from grace, we are incapable of fulfilling, or in some cases even glimpsing, our destinies. Left to our own devices, our natural bent is toward fiction-making. To the extent that our view of ourselves is a product of fiction-making, we cannot love ourselves, and that in turn affects our relationships with others. Our pride fails to see that the brokenness of others is not unlike our own brokenness. In order to know and love ourselves and others, we need to cultivate the correctives to pride: the faith that allows us to face the truth about ourselves because the depth of our brokenness finds its answer in grace; the hope that, though we often wander from the path, grace will make straight what we have bent; and the love, compassion, and gratitude that follow seeing our own and others' stories as part of God's story. The correctives to pride that make love of others possible thus are tied up with inquiring after God. As Stanley Hauerwas observes, "We can act within the world rightly only as we are trained to see. We do not come to see merely by looking, but must develop disciplined skills through initiation into that community that attempts to live faithful to the story of God."[4] The faithful community does not give us a theory to follow, but a practice: pray without ceasing.

As Aelred notes, there is a difference between neighbor-love and friendship. He tells us, "in the perfection of charity we love very many who are a source of burden and grief to us, for whose interest we concern ourselves honorably, not with hypocrisy or dissimulation, but sincerely and voluntarily, but yet we do not admit these to the intimacy of our friendship. And so in friendship are joined honor and charm, truth and joy, sweetness and good-will, affection and action" (2:19–20).

Neighbor-love involves seeing a person as having a destiny even when there is little overt evidence that this is so. Neighbor-love can be had toward people about whom we know little, or toward those we think are living in misguided and tragic ways. In neighbor-love, one is given, through grace, the creative imagination to see another as having a destiny even when all outward signs are against it. We can see the person as having a destiny without having any clear idea of what his destiny is beyond the general Christian belief that it will somehow involve Christlikeness.

Friendship and Supernatural Charity

Friendship involves imagination as well, but here it plays a quite different role. Because of its nature, friendship is a special relationship that involves endorsing a friend's own conception of who she is or at least aspires to be. This role of imagination in friendship follows from the fact that friendship is a relationship between equals in which paternalism is inappropriate. Imagination's function in friendship is to affirm that my friend's view of her destiny is substantially correct. Friendship commits itself to helping a person attain her vision of herself. If the judgment that the friend's self-concept approximates her destiny is true, it must be based on insight. Friendship involves not just endorsing someone's self-concept, but caring deeply enough about her achieving her destiny to go out of one's way to help.

Søren Kierkegaard emphasizes connections between hope and love, observing, "The true lover says: 'Hope all things; give up no man, for to give him up is to abandon your love for him – and if you do not give it up, then you hope. But if you abandon your love for him, then you yourself cease to be a lover.'"[5] This is nowhere more vividly displayed than in Christian love for one's neighbor.

William Kennedy's Pulitzer Prize winning novel *Ironweed*[6] can be seen as an exploration of the validity of a love which hopes all things. Kennedy's main character, Francis Phelan, calls himself "just a bum." He sees himself as a blood brother to all those "for whom life has been a promise unkept . . . a promise now and forever unkeepable" (50). Part of the glory of the Christian tradition is that by enjoining us to love our neighbor, it refuses to let us see anyone's life as an unkeepable promise. Is this foolishness or imagination's genuine insight into human destiny?

Phelan is, to put it mildly, a man down on his luck. Having at one point in his life worked his way up baseball's minor leagues to a brief span of glory as a popular infielder for the Washington Senators, Phelan has spent the last twenty-two years as part of a brotherhood of survival within desolation. He belongs to the company of the afflicted. Simone Weil points out that affliction combines three elements: physical pain, distress of soul, and social degradation. Together these result in blows that "leave a being struggling on the ground like a half-crushed worm."[7] Our natural tendency when placed in contact with those in affliction is recoil – "passing by on the other side" – because of our fear or disgust or indifference (see Luke 10:31–2). The face of the afflicted is not one on which we have any natural desire to gaze. The power of *Ironweed* is that it makes us look closely enough to see the humanity of those in affliction. That this is a major goal of the novel is evidenced by the movie version of the book, for which Kennedy was the screenwriter. The opening sequence of the movie pans from the heavens down, and down, to focus on a wall. As the camera pans in, the viewer notices the trash lying in front of the wall, being ruffled by the wind. As the camera zooms slowly in, one begins to realize that some of the "trash" is in fact a man, staggering up from his makeshift bed of cardboard and newspapers. I take this to be a visual depiction of the thesis of both the novel and the movie.

To see the afflicted as human is to care about their story. What is Phelan's story? How has he come to this sorry state?

Phelan's story is, in part, the story of a runner. In one of the many acts of violence which punctuate his life, he cracks the skull of a bum who has tried to cut off his feet in order to steal his shoes. In this context, Kennedy tells us that the compulsion to flight was among the most familiar notions Phelan had ever entertained. His life was a "quest for pure flight" (75): flight from blame and from family and from destitution of spirit. In 1901 he flees Albany temporarily to avoid prosecution, after having thrown a stone with lethal accuracy at a scab during a trolley strike. Many seasons after that, he has a sense of relief in temporarily fleeing each spring and summer from the confines of his family to play his beloved game. And in 1916 he completely abandons his family after, in boozy clumsiness, picking up his infant son Gerald by a sagging diaper and having the baby wriggle into a fatal plunge to the floor.

The novel opens as Phelan, having returned to Albany and gained employment as a day-laboring gravedigger, enters the graveyard in which his father, mother, and infant son are buried. The action of the novel takes place on Hallowe'en and All Saints' Day, and Kennedy plays with the relationship between living and dead, saints and sinners, future and past. In what Kennedy indicates may be the beginning of a process of regeneration, Phelan finds himself drawn to his son's grave. Phelan has learned from his older son, Billy, that Annie, Phelan's wife, has kept the circumstances of their son's death secret for twenty-two years. Knowing of her loyalty enables Phelan to face what he has done. Reminiscing over Gerald's grave, he asks, "Do you suppose now that I can remember this stuff out in the open, I can finally start to forget it?" (19). This sets the major question of the novel. For twenty-two years Phelan has been living out the story of a man with a secret so terrible that he does not deserve to live. His confession may be the beginning of his liberation from the trap of the story he's told for himself. As long as sin remains hidden, fiction-making becomes a fate. Can his owning up to his past redeem his present and future?

In a startling depiction of the communion of the saints, the dead are attentive to Phelan's redemption throughout *Ironweed*. In one vivid scene, the dead set up bleachers in the backyard of Annie's house in order to watch the drama of Phelan's homecoming unfold (176ff). Will Phelan's guilt be expiated? Will he receive grace? Will he finally be able to stop wanting to die because of what he's done to Gerald?

These are not questions to which Kennedy is willing to give easy answers. The drama of Phelan's life is displayed as a tug-of-war between gravity and grace. In this Phelan is, of course, Everyman. But he is also the lowest of the low. To allow imagination's insight into our common humanity with him is to see our need of grace. And in an even more dramatic reversal, imagination grants us the vision of Phelan not just as our needy neighbor but as a person who, given his humanity, is capable of graciously extending neighbor love to others.

Ronald S. Wallace's study of Calvin's doctrine of the Christian life displays the nature of neighbor-love as an abiding theme of Calvin's commentaries and sermons. Wallace says, "the very fact that we are human creatures means that 'we cannot but behold, as in a mirror, our own face in those who are poor and despised, who have come to an end of their own power to help themselves, and who groan under their burden, even though they are utter strangers to us.'"[8] Calvin saw neighbor-love as a response to the image of God that is part of humanity's created nature.

In her discussion of the parable of the Good Samaritan, Simone Weil eloquently sets out the role of imagination's creative attention in neighbor-love. She claims that neighbor-love's creative attention is analogous to genius. For those who pass, the stranger on the road is a nameless, inert piece of flesh. The Samaritan gives this lump of flesh the kind of attention which is creative, compassionate, and generous. He sees not just inert flesh but a human life that calls on his empathy and help. Weil observes,

> It is not surprising that a man who has bread should give a piece to someone who is starving. What is surprising is that he should be capable of doing so with so different a gesture from that with which we buy an object. Almsgiving when it is not supernatural is like a sort of purchase. It buys the sufferer.[9]

Weil's insight regarding neighbor-love is similar to Dietrich Bonhoeffer's. In *Life Together* he describes a merely human love of neighbor that seeks control and gratitude in exchange for help. He says that this is the type of love that Paul says gains us nothing in 1 Corinthians 13:3.[10] Kennedy's Phelan can teach us a good deal about what it is to be a neighbor.

Paradoxically, an unselfconscious compassion is as characteristic of Phelan as is violence. One incident in which this is displayed, which has significant parallels with Weil's rendition of the story of the Samaritan, is Phelan's encounter with Sandra. Phelan and his friend Rudy come upon Sandra lying face down in the dust, arms forward, legs spread:

"She dead?"

. . .

"She's just drunk," Rudy said, standing up. "She can't hold it no more. She falls over."

"She'll freeze there and the dogs'll come along and eat her ass off."

"If she's drunk she can't go inside the mission," Francis said.

"That's right," said Rudy. "She comes in drunk, he kicks her right out. He hates drunk women more'n he hates us."

"Why the hell's he preachin' if he don't preach to people that need it?"

"Drunks don't need it," Rudy said. "How'd you like to preach to a room full of bums like her?"

"She a bum or just a heavy drunk?"

"She's a bum."

"She looks like a bum."

"She's been a bum all her life."

"No," said Francis. "Nobody's a bum all their life. She hada been somethin' once."

"She was a whore before she was a bum."

"And what about before she was a whore?"

"I don't know," Rudy said. "She just talks about whorin' in Alaska. Before that I guess she was just a little kid."

"Then that's somethin'. A little kid's somethin' that ain't a bum or a whore." (29–30)

Whether or not Kennedy has read Weil or Bonhoeffer, these three are clearly operating with the same conception of neighbor-love. Phelan sees Sandra as more than an inert body, more than a bum and more than a former whore. He pays her creative attention, finding her lost shoe, sneaking soup and a blanket to her from the Mission whose rules will not let her in. Phelan, who describes himself as "just a bum," refuses to see Sandra as just a bum, and thus can reach out to her with true neighbor-love that does not try to buy the sufferer. Although he has not yet learned for himself how not to see his story as a fate rather than a destiny, he will not let Sandra be fated by her past.

Because those in charge of the Mission lack the creative attention that is supernatural charity, they will not give to those who are unwilling or unable to barter for their bread. By contrast, Phelan insists on seeing her as someone who was once "a kid," someone who once was, and perhaps still is, full of unrealized potential. A child is someone who is not a bum and not a whore, someone such that to her belongs the kingdom of heaven (Mark 10:14).

What Kennedy and Weil describe is much more than just having the general belief that everyone, by virtue of being human, has a destiny, a life narrative which is well worth living. Conscientious people may act on this general belief, but this may not involve any genuine sight, and thus no imagination. Such action may be merely dutiful. This, however, would be very different, both intellectually and emotionally, from a love which *sees someone as having a destiny*. Cognitively, the difference is between a belief formed on the basis of taking someone to be an instance of the general truth "Every human being has a destiny" and a belief based on attending to him as the *Gestalt*: perceiving this-person-with-a-destiny. The former need not involve any emotions at all. The latter both depends on and engenders what Lawrence Blum calls the altruistic emotions.[11] Even this case where Phelan knows too little and sees too dimly to have any notion of what Sandra's destiny is – even when she appears to be no more than inert flesh – imagination in the form of neighbor-love allows him to see her as more than she appears to be.

Neighbor-love thus involves seeing someone as having a destiny even when there is little overt evidence that this is so. Because Christians refuse to see people from a merely human point of view (2 Cor. 5:16–17), we take this exercise in imagination to be more than fiction-making. But there is, of course, something superficially similar to neighbor-love which does involve fiction-making – sentimentality. Sentimentality assumes that thinking nice thoughts will solve all problems, that pretending that things are less grim than they are will somehow magically make them better.

It is part of the power of Kennedy's novel that it deals with its subject without succumbing to sentimentality or condescension. While neighbor-love is redemptive, sentimentality is not. In life, of course, it is no less difficult to tell neighbor-love from sentimentality than to distinguish true romantic love from fantasy. There are no algorithms; here as elsewhere we can attempt to exercise practical wisdom but will sometimes also need to walk by faith, not by sight.

Often, from a human point of view, seeing people as having a destiny will look like foolishness. Many of Phelan's gestures of love seem ineffectual. Yet one can ask: how should effectiveness be judged? And what makes acting out of love significant? When Phelan gives away his last bits of food to parents living with their infant son in a hobo jungle, "the man accepted the gifts with an upturned face that revealed the incredulity of a man struck by lightning in the rainless desert; and his benefactor was gone before he could acknowledge the gift" (213). It is likely that this family was killed shortly afterwards by raiders who, intent on removing a public eyesore, knock down and burn the shacks and lean-tos, clubbing anyone within reach. How shall this act be evaluated? Or what are we to make of Phelan's attempt to save Aldo, the horse thief who is fleeing the police? Phelan attempts to pull Aldo onto a moving freight train. Phelan saw this as "a spectacle," a display of the truth that "a proffered hand in a moment of need is a beautiful thing," and "Francis still remembered Aldo's face as it came toward him. It looked like his own, which is perhaps why Francis put himself in jeopardy: to save his own face with his own hand" (28). Aldo is shot before Phelan can save him. What good does it do to pay close attention to a drunk or to find her shoe? What good does it do to feed the poor if they will shortly die anyway? What good to risk one's life in a futile attempt to save another? Perhaps none; humanly, all seem a waste. But perhaps in the mysterious fullness of things, extravagant compassion will work toward our neighbors' redemption, or ours.

Receiving Grace

In her discussion of the parable of the Good Samaritan quoted above, Weil points out that "Christ taught us that supernatural love of our neighbor is the exchange of compassion and gratitude which happens in a flash between two beings."[12] Compassion seems almost as natural to Phelan as running; he can clearly give in love for his neighbor. The crucial question regarding Phelan's redemption becomes whether he is willing to receive it. Will he allow himself to receive grace?

Perceptive writers have noted that gracious receptivity is more difficult than one might first expect. That giving is difficult seems natural, but what could be easier than receiving? Gilbert C. Meilaender correctly observes, however, that "a glad receptivity, free of any desire to receive solely on our own terms" is something of which we are not often capable.[13] In this he concurs with C. S. Lewis, who, like Weil, distinguishes two movements within charity, supernatural Gift-love and supernatural Need-love. Of the latter, Lewis says, "I mean a love which does not dream of disinterestedness, a bottomless indigence. Like a river making its own channel, like a magic wine which in being poured out should simultaneously create the glass that was to hold it, God turns our need of Him into Need-love of Him."[14] Such a gift is a severe mercy, because to take it requires humility; "how difficult it is to receive, and to go on receiving, from others a love that does not depend on our own attraction."[15] Genuine self-love requires humility. Receptivity to supernatural Need-love, and the supernatural gratitude that responds to grace, also require humbling ourselves – it requires allowing our story to be rewritten to take into account the truth about ourselves, God, and others.

There are many senses in which one might be tempted to think that Francis Phelan has no pride. He is, after all, willing to dig graves, cart debris for a junk dealer, even beg when necessary. He is perhaps more cognizant than many of the multitude of his sins. He is willing to own his violence and degradation. And though it has taken him twenty-two years, he is willing to re-establish contact with the family he has so deeply wounded.

After he learns from his son Billy that his wife Annie has kept the secret of his role in Gerald's death all this time, Francis arrives on her doorstep on All Saints' Day with a turkey which has cost him almost his whole day's wages. Annie, the embodiment of loyal love, welcomes him. She has never blamed him for Gerald's death; she long ago stopped being angry at him for leaving. She has not only kept his things in the attic awaiting his return, but has arranged for a grave for him in the family plot. Annie's love is more than natural; she is a woman who hopes all things. She has never doubted that he is a part of her family; he must take this to heart and accept himself back into the fold.

Will her hope and love be enough to heal Phelan's brokenness? Only if he is willing to have his story taken out of his hands. She sets no conditions on his return, but Phelan's self-conception does:

> . . . he was, yes, a warrior, protecting a belief that no man could ever articulate, especially himself; but somehow it involved protecting saints from sinners, protecting the living from the dead. And a warrior, he was certain, was not a victim. Never a victim.
>
> In the deepest part of himself that could draw an unutterable conclusion, he told himself: My guilt is all that I have left. If I lose it, I have stood for nothing, done nothing, been nothing.   (216)

To give up his guilt will be to admit that much of his life has been a flight from self. He would prefer to see himself as the family killer than as a man who has lacked the courage to face himself. "Francis is no coward," he stoutly asserts (10). At the end of the novel he still harbors the seemingly impotent intention to return home permanently – someday, after things "got to be absolutely right, and straight" (227).

If this is taken as Kennedy's last word of Phelan, then it would appear that a love that hopes all things is, in Phelan's case, ineffectual. He is still running. But two important passages complicate this picture. The framing metaphor of Phelan's life is baseball, and the grand old game is never over till it's over. In looking through the collection of his mementos and clippings that Annie has stored in the attic, Phelan contemplates an old photograph. It shows him tossing a baseball from one hand to another and has caught the ball clutched in one hand but also in flight.

> What the camera had caught was two instants in one: Time separated and unified, the ball in two places at once, an eventuation as inexplicable as the Trinity itself. Francis now took the picture to be a Trinitarian talisman (a hand, a glove, a ball) for achieving the impossible: for he had always believed it impossible for him, ravaged man, failed human, to reenter history under this roof. . . . But the ball was not really caught, except by the camera. . . . And

> Francis is not yet ruined. . . . The ball still flies.
> Francis still lives to play another day.
> Doesn't he? (169)

In space and time, Francis is still running; from a human point of view this appears to be a pattern too entrenched to be overcome. He looks to be forever a person whose pride will, perversely, make him try to manufacture the straightness from which grace will flow. But, as Kennedy reminds us on the book's last page, space and time are but two of reality's dimensions.

> The empyrean, which is not spatial at all, does not move and has no poles. It girds, with light and love, the *primum mobile*, the utmost and swiftest of the material heavens. Angels are manifested in the *primum mobile* (227).

The references here are to ancient cosmology. The empyrean was the highest reaches of heaven, a realm of pure light in which God dwells. The *primum mobile* was thought to be the tenth and outermost ring of the physical heavens. Phelan still lives, entertaining angels unawares. Where there is life, there is hope.

How is loving our neighbor inquiring after God? When we can see our own face in the face of others, even the lowest of the low, when we can understand that our need for forgiveness and help is no more shallow and no deeper than Phelan's, we can grasp what Pascal called our wretchedness. When we can see the image of God in others, even the lowest of the low, we can grasp that this wretchedness, as Pascal tells us, is the wretchedness of displaced royalty. When we can see that, contrary to Phelan's tragic belief, we do not save our own face or another's with our own hand, but that the hand that will save us is the very hand of God, our hard-heartedness and anxiety can be transformed into a doxology. When that doxology is not just sung, but lived, we will love as God loves us. Here we can close with the words of Aelred: ". . . to be solicitous for one another, to pray for one another, to blush for one another, to rejoice for one another, to grieve for one another's fall as one's own, to regard another's progress as one's own. By whatever means are in one's power, one ought to raise the weak, support the infirm, console the afflicted, restrain the wrathful" (3:101–2). By grace, love's imagination can allow us to see ourselves and others as having a destiny, a destiny which, even despite all contrary appearances, may yet be fulfilled. For love hopes all things.

Notes

1 Glenn Tinder, *The Political Meaning of Christianity* (Baton Rouge: Louisiana State University Press, 1989), p. 28.
2 Ibid., p. 29.
3 Ibid., p. 30.
4 Stanley Hauerwas, *The Peaceable Kingdom* (Notre Dame: Notre Dame University Press, 1983), pp. 29–30.
5 Søren Kierkegaard, *Works of Love*, trans. Howard and Edna Hong (New York: Harper Torchbooks, 1962), p. 239.
6 William Kennedy, *Ironweed* (New York: Penguin Books, 1984). Subsequent page references will be noted in parentheses within the text.
7 Simone Weil, "The Love of God and Affliction," *Waiting for God*, trans. Emma Craufurd (New York: Harper and Row, 1951), p. 120.
8 Ronald S. Wallace, *Calvin's Doctrine of the Christian Life* (Grand Rapids: Eerdmans, 1959), p. 150.
9 Weil, "Forms of the Implicit Love of God," in *Waiting for God*, p. 1467.
10 Dietrich Bonhoeffer, *Life Together*, trans. John W. Dobersein (New York: Harper and Row, 1954), pp. 33–4.
11 Lawrence Blum, *Friendship, Altruism and Morality* (London: Routledge and Kegan Paul, 1980).
12 Weil, "Forms of the Implicit Love of God," p. 146.
13 Gilbert C. Meilaender, *Friendship: A Study in Theological Ethics* (Notre Dame: Notre Dame University Press, 1981), p. 50.
14 C. S. Lewis, *The Four Loves* (New York: Harcourt, Brace Jovanovich, 1960), p. 178.
15 Ibid., p. 182.

6

Inquiring after God in Marriage

Early Christianity, like some other ancient religions, distrusted sex, and not without reason. Although sex is the exercise of a natural pleasurable urge and assures the survival of the species, that urge is unstable, a raw instinct capable of great damage and harm to society, to other individuals, and to oneself. Civilization requires people to transcend brute copulation by regulating sexual desire. Yet sexual and emotional maturity have always been difficult to cultivate. Christian marriage, which rejected polygamy, frowned on divorce, restricted sexual activity to marriage, and encouraged the rearing of children in marriage, has provided the foundation of western civilization ever since.

Although they are not in direct conversation with one another, the two works we consider in this chapter on Christian marriage communicate through two key New Testament passages on sex and marriage: 1 Corinthians 7 and Ephesians 5 – the former written by St. Paul, the latter dependent upon his theology. Paul's own writing reflects the preference for sexual abstinence promoted by early Christians to help them separate from the sexual unholiness of their day. Nevertheless it develops a theology of sexuality to counsel those who are married as well as those who are not. He begins by adumbrating a theology of Christian marriage. Husbands and wives are to protect one another's holiness by caring for each other sexually, as well as in other ways. He then discusses the responsibilities of persons married to pagans who do not necessarily share in the commitment to sexual holiness that Christians take upon themselves in baptism. Finally, he discusses the situation of unmarried Christians, virgins who decide not to marry, and widows, all to the end of supporting high standards of sexual holiness within the Church.

The second scriptural teaching considered by the authors of this chapter is a segment of the letter to the Ephesians that occurs in the context of contrasting the Christian to the pagan way of life. The difference, not surprisingly, turns on the figure of Christ. The foundation of the Christian life is that Christians take Christ as their savior and lord, and seek to be guided and judged by him in all things. This section applies Christ's authority to the running of households, focusing especially on the relationships between husband and wife, parents and children, servants and masters, all of whom made up the basic family unit in ancient Roman society. The issue is how to live out one's obedience to Christ in these everyday relationships.

While all are under the lordship of Christ, the writer still maintains traditional Roman lines of authority in which male heads of household are the human authority and others follow lines of mutual duty and responsibility to one another. Thus, while there is universal submission to Christ, the social status of individuals remains ranked. While it is true that for any society to survive there must be role differentiation and a workable division of authority and responsibility, the social and legal ranking that was taken for granted in that day appears to many contemporary readers to conflict with another Christian principle of complete equality among persons such as that given in Galatians 3:28: "There is neither Jew nor Greek, there is neither slave nor free, there is neither male nor female; for all of you are one in Christ Jesus." That all are equal before God but not equal in social and legal terms is today problematic. The fact that the earliest Christians did not see this tension has had serious negative consequences throughout history. While the legal and social structures that bear the imprint of this teaching have largely been undone in the modern west, this should not obscure the fact that the fundamental issue for the writer of Ephesians was holy living under the guidance of God, which calls for theological reflection whatever social and legal arrangements may prevail.

The birth of Christianity was surrounded by apocalyptic expectation, and the decay of Greco-Roman civilization did nothing to quell the pessimism and sense of tragedy that was at the root of Roman fatalism and Roman religion. It seemed that the end of the world was near. Into this atmosphere Christianity brought hope of resurrection after death. Christians believed that Jesus would soon return to rescue them from the evil world in which they felt trapped. In such a circumstance, celibacy was preferable to marriage because it provided a dramatic way to protest against an indulgent and bloated culture, and offered the safety of not bringing children into a world soon to be abandoned by God.

As it turned out, the Last Judgment and the general resurrection did not happen. Christians learned to make their long-term, if penultimate, home in this world. The great and prolific bishop, Augustine of Hippo, saw that the Church would sustain western civilization as Roman civilization decayed and died. Christianity could nurture and shape a morally and socially stronger civilization than could paganism. Augustine worked to bring this about through his writings. One of the many significant and enduring ideas that he introduced into Christianity was his reinterpretation of eschatology. Rather than predict the imminent end of the world, Augustine prepared Christians to rule themselves for the long haul.

Marriage was central to the idea that Christianity prepared the world to survive irruptions of evil, social chaos, and confusion, including war, disease, famine, and social breakdown. Without openly arguing with Christian writers before him, like Paul, who preferred that Christians remain celibate, Augustine built on Paul's incipient theology of marriage, and argued that sex within marriage is a holy state of life, not simply a way to control brute instinct. Although he is infamous for teaching that original sin is conveyed from generation to generation in the act of copulation, this did not suggest to him that sex is "dirty," only that it is volatile. Therefore he counseled Christians to marry and have children. His famous treatise on this theme is included here in edited form.

Augustine offered three reasons why marriage is good. First, it provides for the proper rearing and nurture of children who are dependent on adult care and guidance for many years. Second, it controls sexuality by encouraging fidelity, necessary for stable family and social life. Third – and this was the Augustinian innovation that shaped the Church's teaching more than any other – marriage was good because it binds the partners together in a sacramental relationship in the presence of God. The Church sanctified married life in the context of Christian community. In Augustine's hands, marriage became not simply a way to control sexuality but a holy way of life.

The Christian calling to love one another and bear one another's burdens is most intimately and regularly lived out in marriage and the rearing of children. Loyalty and faithfulness to others – especially if their quirks and weaknesses become irksome – is a true test of Christian strength and nobility. Marriage itself is a spiritual discipline because it trains one to care for others.

Although Protestants did not retain marriage as a sacrament, Richard Foster, himself a Protestant, picks up Augustine's mantel in his discussion of fidelity in marriage. Today, when casual sex without commitment or responsibility is increasingly common, commitment to Christian marriage appears strenuous, anachronistic, even oppressive, even though the psychological damage from bad sexual and romantic relationships causes immense damage to people, especially girls and women. Marriage as an institution is contended although it remains an ideal for many.

Foster acknowledges that we are all sexual beings, and many people desire the intimacy of close interpersonal relationships; but he denies that genital sex is the only or the necessary means by which one's sexuality or desire for intimacy may be expressed. Celibacy is an honorable way of life, the proper way of life for Christians who are not married. Celibacy honors closeness and friendship without genital expression. Similarly, genital sex belongs only in marriage, but nonerotic touching may be a part of many close and meaningful relationships in appropriate contexts.

Christian marriage calls for a lifelong pledge of monogamous love and loyalty, sexual fidelity and fulfilment, and mutual submission in Christ, a standard hinted at although not fully achieved in the letter to the Ephesians. While not dwelling on it, Foster would surely censure exploitation, abuse or physical violence in marriage as clearly counter to the norm of mutual Christic submission. Although he does not see marriage as a sacrament, Foster suggests that the Church should nurture young marriages.

Neither Augustine nor Foster specifically links marriage to theological inquiry *per se*, but they do see Christian marriage as a holy way of life that honors God and the goodness and fragility of creation by maintaining a healthy awe for the psychological, physical, and social dangers posed by sexuality and the tenuousness of the social fabric. Indeed, current studies indicate that marriage supports the well-being of society since married people are happier, healthier, wealthier, and live longer than the unmarried. Perhaps Christian marriage, then, as strenuous as it is, itself provides a point of entry into the holiness of God.

CLASSIC TEXT

St. Augustine of Hippo, *The Good of Marriage*

Every human being is part of the human race, and human nature is a social reality and possesses a great and natural good, the power of friendship. For this reason God wished to create all human beings from one, so that they would be held together in human society, not only by the similarity of [the human] race, but also by the bond of blood relationship. Therefore, the first natural union of human society is the husband and wife. God did not create even these as separate individuals and join them together as if they were alien to each other, but he created the one from the other. The power of the union was also signified in the side from which she was taken and formed, for they are joined to each other's side, when they walk together and together look where they are walking. The result is the bonding of society in children, who are the one honorable fruit, not of the union of male and female, but of sexual intercourse. . . .

This is what we now say: according to that state of birth and death, which we experience and in which we were created, the union of male and female is something good. The divine Scripture commends this alliance to such an extent that a woman who is divorced by her husband is not allowed to marry another, while her husband is still alive; and a man who is divorced by his wife may not take another, unless the wife who has left him has died. It is right, therefore, to inquire why the good of marriage is a good, which even the Lord confirmed in the gospel, not only because he prohibited divorce, except in cases of fornication [see Matt. 19:9], but also because when he was invited to the wedding, he attended [see John 2:1–11].

I do not believe that marriage is a good solely because of the procreation of children; there is also the natural association (*societas*) between the sexes. Otherwise, we would no longer speak of a marriage between elderly people, especially if they had lost or had never produced children. But now in a good marriage, even if it has lasted for many years and even if the youthful ardor between the male and female has faded, the order of charity between husband and wife still thrives. The earlier they begin to refrain from sexual intercourse, by mutual consent, the better they will be. This is not because they will eventually be unable to do what they wish, but because it is praiseworthy not to wish to do what they are able to do.

If, therefore, they keep faithful to the honor and the conjugal duties that each sex owes the other, even if both of their bodies grow weak and almost corpselike, yet the chastity of spirits joined in a proper marriage will endure; the more it is tested, the more genuine it will be; the more it is calmed, the more secure it will be. There is an additional good in marriage, namely the fact that carnal or youthful incontinence, even the most wicked, is directed toward the honorable task of procreating children. As a result, conjugal intercourse makes something good out of the evil of lust (libido), since the concupiscence of the flesh, which parental affection moderates, is then suppressed and in a certain way burns more modestly. For a sort of dignity prevails over the fire of pleasure, when in the act of uniting as husband and wife the couple regard themselves as father and mother.

To this we would add that in the very act of paying the conjugal debt, even if they demand it somewhat intemperately and incontinently, the spouses still owe to each other mutual fidelity (*fides*). The apostle attributed to this fidelity so much authority that he called it a "power," saying: "A wife does not have power over her body, but her husband does; likewise, a husband has no power over his body, but his wife does" [1 Cor. 7:4]. The violation of this fidelity is called adultery, when one has intercourse with another man or woman contrary to the marriage agreement, either at the instigation of one's own lust or out of consent to another's lust. In this way fidelity, which is a great good of the spirit even in the insignificant affairs of the body, is broken. Therefore, it is certain that fidelity ought to be preferred even to the health of the body, by which life itself is sustained. A little straw may be almost nothing compared to a great amount of gold; yet, when fidelity is genuinely preserved in a matter of straw as if in one of gold, it is no less valuable because it is preserved in a thing that is less valuable.

When fidelity is used to commit sin, of course, we wonder whether it should still be called fidelity. But whatever it is, if one acts contrary to it, one becomes worse, unless one is abandoning it in order to return to a true and legitimate fidelity, that is, in order to make amends for a sin by correcting the wickedness of the will. Take, for example, someone who is unable to rob a man by himself and so finds an accomplice and agrees with him that they will commit the crime together and then share the loot; but after the crime is committed, he takes it all himself. The accomplice, of course, will be sad and will complain that fidelity to him was not kept. But in his very complaint he ought to realize that he should have kept his fidelity to human society by leading a good life and by not unjustly plundering another human being, if he recognizes how unjust it was that fidelity to him in the society of sin was not preserved.

Of course, the first robber, who is guilty of infidelity on two counts, should be judged the more guilty of the two. But if the first regretted the evil they had done and for this reason refused to share the loot with his accomplice, in order to return it to the man from whom it was stolen, not even the unfaithful accomplice would call him unfaithful. Thus, if a wife who has violated the fidelity of marriage keeps her fidelity to the adulterer, she is still evil; but if she is not faithful even to the adulterer, she is worse. Yet if she repents of her wickedness and returns to her marital chastity, thereby repudiating her adulterous agreements and purposes, I do not think that even the adulterer will regard her as violating fidelity.

It is often asked whether this situation should be called a marriage: when a man and a woman, neither of whom is married to another, have intercourse with each other, not in order to have children, but out of incontinence solely to have sex, and yet faithfully pledge not to do this with anyone else. Perhaps it would not be absurd to call this a marriage, if they made this agreement to last until the death of one of them, and if, although they have not come together for the sake of procreation, they at least do not avoid it, either by not wishing to have children or by acting in an evil way to prevent children from being born. But if one or both of these conditions are absent, I do not see how we could call this a marriage.

For if a man is living with a woman only until he finds someone else who is worthy either of his position or of his wealth, whom he can marry as an equal, in his heart he is an adulterer, not with the woman whom he would like to find, but with the woman with whom he is living but not in a marital union. The same applies to the woman, if she is aware of this and is still willing to have unchaste intercourse with a man, with whom she does not have a commitment as a wife. But if she preserves her fidelity to him as to a spouse after he has taken a wife, and if she refuses to marry and decides to remain completely continent, I would not find it easy to call her an adulteress. Yet who would not call it a sin, knowing that she had intercourse with a man who was not her husband?

But if all the woman wanted from the sexual relations was to have children, and if she unwillingly bore whatever else was involved beyond the desire for procreation, surely this woman ranks higher than many matrons. Some of them, even if they are not guilty of adultery, force their husbands, who often desire to be continent, to pay the debt of the flesh. They make intemperate use of their right, not out of a desire for offspring, but solely out of the passion of concupiscence. Nonetheless, in the marriages of such women there is this good, namely that they are married. For this is why they were married, so that concupiscence itself might be directed toward a legitimate bond and thereby cease to flow in a disordered and disgraceful way. Concupiscence has in itself a weakness of the flesh that cannot be restrained, but in marriage it has an association of fidelity that cannot be dissolved. On its own, concupiscence leads to immoderate intercourse, but in marriage it finds a means of chaste procreation. Even if it is shameful to use a husband in a lustful way, nevertheless it is honorable to choose to have sex only with a husband and to bear children only with a husband.

Likewise, there are men who are so incontinent that they do not spare their wives even during pregnancy. But whatever immodest, shameful, and sordid acts are committed by married persons with each other, these are the result of human vice, not the fault of marriage itself.

Furthermore, even when people make an excessive demand for the payment of the carnal debt – which the apostle did not give them as a command but granted as a concession [cf. 1 Cor. 7:6] – so that they engage in intercourse even without the purpose of procreation; even if immoral conduct leads them to this sort of intercourse, nevertheless marriage protects them from adultery and fornication. It is not that this sort of behavior is permitted because of marriage; rather, it is forgiven because of marriage. Therefore, not only do married people owe each other the fidelity of sexual intercourse for the sake of procreation, which is the first association of the human race in this mortal life, but they also owe each other a sort of mutual service for the sustaining of each other's weakness, so that they may avoid illicit intercourse. As a result, even if one of them would prefer to adopt perpetual continence, it is not permitted without the consent of the partner. For in this matter "a wife does not have power over her body, but her husband does; likewise, a husband has no power over his body, but his wife does" [1 Cor. 7:4].

Therefore, they should not deny one another that which the husband seeks from matrimony and that which the wife seeks from her husband, even if this proceeds not from a desire to have children but only from weakness and incontinence. This is to prevent them from falling into damnable seductions at the temptation of Satan because of the incontinence of one or both of them. Conjugal intercourse for the sake of procreation carries no fault; intercourse for the sake of satisfying lust, provided that it takes place with a spouse, carries a forgivable fault (*venialis culpa*) because of marital fidelity; but adultery or fornication carries a mortal fault. . . .

"Let marriage be held in honor by all and the marriage bed be undefiled" [Heb. 13:4]. We do not say that marriage is a good merely in comparison with fornication; in that case there would be two evils, one of which is worse. In that sense even fornication would be a good because adultery is worse – since to violate another person's marriage is worse than to have sex with a prostitute; and adultery would be a good because incest is worse – since it is worse to have intercourse with your mother than with another man's wife; and on it would go until you reach things which, as the apostle said, "it is disgraceful even to mention" [Eph. 5:12]. On this rendering all things would be good in comparison with something worse. But who has any doubts that this is false?

Marriage and fornication, therefore, are not two evils, one of which is worse, but marriage and continence are two goods, one of which is better. Similarly, bodily health and sickness are not two evils, one of which is worse, but health and immortality are two goods, one of which is better. Likewise, knowledge and vanity are not two evils, of which vanity is the worse, but knowledge and love are two goods, of which love is the better. For "knowledge will be destroyed," the apostle says, and yet it is a necessity in the present life; but "love will never fail" [1 Cor. 13:8]. In the same way, the procreation of mortal bodies, which is the purpose of marriage, will be destroyed; but freedom from all sexual relations is a participation in the angelic life (*angelica meditatio*) here and now, and it will remain so forever. . . .

. . . just as Martha did something good when she ministered to the saints, but her sister Mary did something better when she sat at the Lord's feet and listened to his words [cf. Luke 10:38–42], so likewise we praise the good of Susanna in her conjugal chastity, and yet we rank more highly the good of the widow Anna, and much more highly the good of the virgin Mary. It was a good thing that they did, when they supplied Christ and his disciples with the necessities out of their own resources; but those who abandoned all their resources in order to follow the same Lord more readily did an even better thing. Yet, in both of these goods, whether that of Martha and Mary or that of the disciples, the better thing could not be done without bypassing or abandoning the lesser good.

It must be understood, therefore, that marriage is not to be regarded as an evil simply because abstention from it is necessary in order to achieve the chastity of a widow or the integrity of a virgin. It is not the case that what Martha did was an evil simply because her sister had to abstain from it in order to do the better thing. Nor is it an evil to invite a just man or a prophet into one's house simply because the person who wishes to follow Christ perfectly is required to abandon his house in order to do the better thing.

Surely, it must be acknowledged that God gave us some goods to be sought for their own sake, such as wisdom, good health, and friendship, and other goods that are necessary for the sake of something else, such as learning, food, drink, sleep, marriage, and sexual intercourse. Some of these goods are necessary for wisdom, such as learning; some are necessary for good health, such as food and drink and sleep; and some are necessary for friendship, such as marriage and sexual intercourse, for these lead to the propagation of the human race, in which a friendly association is a great good.

Thus the person who does not use these goods, which are necessary because of something else, for the purpose for which they were intended, sometimes sins in a forgivable way, sometimes in a damnable way. But the person who uses them for the purpose for which they were given does well. Therefore, the person who abstains from using things that are unnecessary does better. In the same way, when we have need of these things, we do well to want them; but we do better not to want them than to want them, since we possess them in a better way when we do not possess them as necessities.

For this reason, it is good to marry, since it is good to produce children, to be the mother of a family. But it is better not to marry, since it is better, even in regard to human society itself, not to have any need of marriage. For the state of the human race is such that not only do some make use of marriage because they are unable to be continent, but also many others indulge in illicit intercourse. Since the good Creator sees to it that good comes of their evils, numerous offspring are born and an abundant succession is produced, out of which holy friendships may be sought.

This leads me to conclude that in the earliest times of the human race the saints were required to make use of the good of marriage, not as something to be sought for its own sake, but as a good necessary for something else, namely the propagation of the people of God, through which the Prince and Savior of all peoples was both prophesied and born. But in the present, since there is abundant opportunity for spiritual kinsmen to enter into holy and genuine associations everywhere and among all nations, even those people who wish to marry solely for the sake of procreation are urged to practice the better good of continence.

But I know what they will murmur: "What if all people wish to abstain completely from sexual intercourse? How would the human race survive?" If only all people had this desire, as long as it proceeds from "a pure heart and a good conscience and a sincere faith" [1 Tim. 1:5]! The City of God would be filled up much more quickly, and the end of time would be hastened. What else does the apostle seem to encourage when he says: "I would like everyone to be as I am" [1 Cor. 7:7]? Or, in another place: "What I mean, my friends, is that the time is short. From now on even those who have wives should live as if they had none; those who mourn, as if they were not mourning; those who rejoice, as if they were not rejoicing; those who buy, as if they were not buying; and those who use this world, as if they were not using it. For the form of this world is passing away. I want you to be without care". Then he adds: "The man without a wife is concerned about the Lord's affairs, how to please the Lord. But the married man is concerned about the affairs of the world, how to please his wife, and he is divided. And the unmarried woman and virgin, she is concerned about the Lord's affairs, that she may be holy in body and spirit. But the married woman is concerned about the affairs of the world, how to please her husband" [1 Cor. 7:29–34]. For this reason, it seems to me that in the present time only those who do not restrain themselves should marry, in accord with that saying of the same apostle: "But if they cannot control themselves, they should marry, for it is better to marry than to burn" [1 Cor. 7:9].

Not even in this case, however, is marriage a sin. For if marriage were preferable only by comparison with fornication, it would be a lesser sin than fornication, but still it would be a sin. But, as it is now, what shall we say in response to the very clear message that the apostle declares: "He may do whatever he wishes; he does not sin; let him marry [1 Cor. 7:36]?" And: "If you have taken a wife, you have not sinned; and if a virgin marries, she does not sin [1 Cor. 7:28]?" This is now clear evidence that it is wrong to have any doubts about the sinlessness of marriage.

Therefore, it was not marriage that the apostle granted *as a concession* – for would it not be quite absurd to say that a concession is granted to those who did not sin? Rather, he granted *as a concession* that sexual union which takes place because of incontinence, not solely for the sake of procreation and sometimes not even for the sake of procreation at all. Marriage does not force this sort of intercourse to occur, but it does obtain for it a pardon, as long as it is not so excessive that it impedes the times that ought to be set aside for prayer, and as long as it does not lead to that use which is contrary to nature.

The apostle was unable to remain silent about this when he spoke about the extreme depravities that impure and wicked people practice. The intercourse that is necessary for the sake of procreation is without fault, and only this belongs properly to marriage. Intercourse that goes beyond the need of procreation follows the dictates of lust (libido), not of reason. Nevertheless, to render this to a spouse (though not to demand it), so that the spouse may avoid the damnable sin of fornication, is a duty of the married person. But if both partners are subject to such a desire (*concupiscentia*), they are doing something that clearly does not belong to marriage.

Nevertheless, if in their union they love what is honorable more than what is dishonorable (that is, if they love what belongs to marriage more than they love what does not belong to marriage), this is granted to them *as a concession* by the authority of the apostle. Their marriage does not encourage this fault; rather, it intercedes for it, if they do not turn away from the mercy of God, either by failing to abstain on certain days in order to be free for prayer (since abstinence, like fasting, lends support to one's prayers) or by exchanging a natural use for one that is contrary to nature, for this is more damnable in a spouse. . . .

It is clear that a couple who have [*sic*] entered into an illicit union [i.e. concubinage] can still contract a valid marriage, if they subsequently make an honorable agreement. But once they have entered into a marriage in the City of our God, where even from the very first intercourse of two human beings marriage derives a kind of sacramental quality (*quoddam sacramentum*), the marriage cannot be dissolved in any way, except by the death of one of the spouses. For the bond of marriage remains, even if children, for the sake of which the marriage was entered into, do not result because of a clear case of sterility. Therefore, it is not permissible for married persons who know that they will not have children to separate from each other and have intercourse with others, even for the sake of having children. If they do so, they commit adultery with those with whom they have intercourse because they remain married persons. . . .

Therefore, the married women of our own day, of whom it is said: "If they cannot control themselves, they should marry" [1 Cor. 7:9],* ought not to be compared even to the holy women who married in ancient times. Marriage itself, of course, in all nations exists for the same purpose, the procreation of children. No matter how these children turn out in the end, marriage was instituted in order that they might be born in an ordered and honorable way. Now people who are unable to control themselves have taken a step up in honor, as it were, by marrying; but those who without a doubt would have controlled themselves, had the conditions allowed this, have taken a step down in piety, so to speak, by marrying. Because of this, even though the marriages of both types of people are equally good, in respect to the marriage itself, since they both exist for the sake of procreation, nevertheless the married people of our day are not to be compared to the married people of ancient times.

Married people today have something that is granted to them *as a*

---

* Paul's text is actually directed to "the unmarried and the widows" (1 Cor. 7:8, NRSV), not married women.

concession because of the honorable state of marriage, although this concession does not pertain to the essence of marriage itself; I am referring to the use of intercourse beyond the need of procreation, something that was not conceded to the ancients. Even if some married people today desire and seek in marriage only that for which marriage was instituted, even these spouses cannot be compared to the people of ancient times. For in people today the very desire for children is carnal, whereas in the ancients it was spiritual because it was in harmony with the sacred mystery (*sacramentum*) of the times. In fact, in our day no one who is perfect in piety seeks to have children except in a spiritual way, whereas in the past to have children in a carnal way was itself an act of piety, since the propagation of that people was a proclamation of future events and participated in the dispensation of prophecy [see Gen. 12:2; 15:5, et al.]. . . .

The good of marriage, therefore, among all nations and peoples lies in the purpose of procreation and in the faithful preservation (*fides*) of chastity. But for the people of God the good of marriage lies also in the holiness of the sacramental bond (*sacramentum*). Because of this holiness, it is wrong for a woman to marry another man, even if she leaves with a bill of divorce, as long as her husband is alive, even if she does this for the sake of having children. Even if the first marriage took place solely for the sake of procreation and even if that for the sake of which the marriage was made did not happen, the marriage bond is not dissolved until the spouse dies.

In a similar way, if a cleric is ordained in order to form a congregation and if the congregation does not come into being, nonetheless the sacramental sign of ordination remains in those who have been ordained. If a cleric is removed from office because of some fault, he will not lose the sacramental sign of the Lord that was imposed once and for all, although it remains as a mark of judgment.

The apostle, therefore, testifies that marriage was made for the purpose of procreation. "I want the younger widows to marry," he said [1 Tim. 5:14]. Then, as if someone had asked him, "But why?" he immediately added: "to bear children, to become the mothers of the households." This passage also pertains to the faithful preservation of chastity: "A wife does not have power over her body, but her husband does, likewise, a husband has no power over his body, but his wife does" [1 Cor. 7:4]. This passage also speaks of the holiness of the sacrament: "A wife should not separate from her husband; but if she does separate, she must remain unmarried or else be reconciled to her husband, and a man may not divorce his wife" [1 Cor. 7:10–11]. All these are the goods on account of which marriage is a good: offspring, fidelity, sacrament. . . .

CONTEMPORARY REFLECTION

from *Money, Sex & Power*

Richard J. Foster

The Vow of Fidelity

Fidelity is the ethical element which enhances natural love.   (Emil Brunner)

The sex issue demands a new and vigorous response. It cannot be a negative or reactionary response; rather, it must be active, creative, positive. We need a response that bears witness to the rich, positive attitude of Scripture toward human sexuality. We need a response that is for all Christians and can be experienced in ordinary life. And we need a response that deals compassionately and forthrightly with our distortions of sexuality's God-given functions. That response is best crystallized in the vow of fidelity. All believers – whether male or female, whether single, married, divorced, widowed, or remarried – are called to fidelity in their sexual relationships.

Fidelity means to affirm our sexuality in all its manifold complexity. We celebrate the fact that we are sexual beings with needs for tenderness and compassion, love and friendship. We stoutly refuse to think of ourselves in nonsexual terms. We know that to make a person sexless is to dehumanize that person, and we will not do that to ourselves or anyone else. We will be faithful to our God-created nature as sexual beings.

Fidelity means loyalty to our calling. Some are called to the single life. When that call is given by God and is confirmed in the community of faith, then the disciple of Christ can rest contented in this provision of God's grace. There is no need to fret and stew or cast about for other options. The believing community welcomes this calling and gift without casting disparaging innuendos about the failure to find a mate.

Others are called to marriage. They welcome their calling and do not begrudge the time and energy needed to fulfill it. The Church understands and seeks to enhance their efforts to cultivate a strong marriage and family. The Church refuses to frustrate these goals by proliferating meetings and commitments that separate the family unit.

Fidelity means directing genital sex into its God-given channel in the covenant of marriage. We say no to promiscuity before marriage and adultery after marriage. We scorn the modern myth that sexual prowess is validated by sexual conquest. We confess the wholeness, the fullness, of sexual expression found in a permanent "one flesh" relationship in marriage.

Fidelity means an enduring commitment to the well-being and growth of each other. We commit ourselves to our partner's wholeness and happiness. We desire that every gift, every talent, every ability be given every opportunity to blossom and flower. Husband and wife are each called to sacrifice for the advancement of the other.

Fidelity means mutuality. Our faithfulness means a refusal to lord it over one another. No power plays, no phony superiority, no artificial hierarchy.

Fidelity means honesty and transparency with each other. Our commitment is to take off our masks, to come out from behind our facades. Our sharing is no "trivial pursuit," but a willingness to speak the deep inner language of the heart.

Fidelity means to explore the interior world of the spiritual life together. We pledge ourselves to pray together, to worship together, to celebrate together. We invite our mates into the inner sanctuary of our own soul. We invite them to be witnesses to our struggles, our doubts, our breakthroughs, our growth.

The Meaning of Fidelity for Singles

Human sexuality has many aspects, only one of which is genital intercourse. If single persons will nurture and cultivate the many other aspects of their sexuality, the genital needs will come into perspective.

In fact, what we call sexual needs are not really needs at all but wants. The body needs food, air, and water – without these human life cannot long survive. But no one has yet died from a lack of sexual intercourse. Many have lived quite full and satisfying lives without genital sex – including Jesus!

So sexual intercourse is a human want, not a human need, and the difference is significant. To understand this difference can be tremendously liberating for singles. They are not half people, unfulfilled and incomplete. They do not need sexual intercourse to experience wholeness in their sexuality.

The apostle Paul dealt specifically with this matter of "sexual needs" in his epistle to the Christians at Corinth. They lived in a sexually charged environment, and some, sensing the liberty that is in the Gospel, assumed that this meant total sexual freedom, including sexual relations with prostitutes. Evidently their slogan was "All things are lawful in Christ." Paul responded, "'All things are lawful for me,' but not all things are helpful. 'All things are lawful for me,' but I will not be enslaved by anything" (1 Cor. 6:12).

The Corinthians then raised the issue of sex as a normal physical need, just like food. In other words, if sex is a natural physical appetite like the appetite for food, what is wrong with satisfying our sexual need whenever the urge arises? Paul's answer was that "food is meant for the stomach," but "the body is meant for the Lord" (1 Cor. 6:13). He went on to argue that the digestive system is temporal and biological and has meaning only in earthly existence. But the body is the temple of the Holy Spirit and is destined for resurrection and filled with eternal significance. Therefore, we should "shun immorality." Promiscuous sex is such a travesty of the "one flesh" principle that it violates the spiritual aspect of our bodies. "Do you not know that he who joins himself to a prostitute becomes one body with her? For as it is written, 'The two shall become one.' But he who is united to the Lord becomes one spirit with him" (1 Cor. 6:16–17). Paul's word to us, then, is that sexual intercourse is so filled with eternal significance that it should always be reserved for the permanency of marriage. Therefore, believers who are single will want to abstain from genital sex; at the same time, they will want to develop fully the many other aspects of their sexuality.

Intimacy is one facet of our human sexuality that singles should nurture. The giving and receiving of love is essential; in fact, people have literally died from its absence. We need to find friendships that are caring and life-giving. Loneliness is epidemic today, and many singles suffer from it because they have tended to equate intimacy with coitus. But the truth is that many intimate and affectionate relationships can be cultivated without sexual intercourse.

Singles can find intimacy with people by entering into their lives on many different levels. Sharing books, ideas, goals, conversation, and much more helps us to become intimate with one another. Friendships can be with both men and women, both single and married. People are rich tapestries, and learning the varied and intricate weave of each life can be great fun.

Closely associated with intimacy is that aspect of our sexuality that is revealed by touch. Touching, holding, stroking – these are valid aspects of our sexuality that should not necessarily be tied to genital sex. In fact, Ashley Montagu, in his book *Touching*, has noted that, "In the Western world it is highly probable that sexual activity, indeed the frenetic preoccupation with sex that characterizes Western culture, is in many cases not the expression of a sexual interest at all, but rather a search for the satisfaction of the need for contact."[1]

Singles should welcome the touch, the hug, the warm embrace. These are essential ingredients in our human sexuality, and it is not wise to cut ourselves off from them. Nonerotic touching is of growing interest to those in the healing professions. Nurses are learning how to stroke and cuddle babies; psychiatric workers are learning the power of simply holding a hand; and people like Mother Teresa of Calcutta have helped us all discover the healing power of the compassionate touch.

Older singles especially need the life-giving experience of touch. Many go for months without ever being touched by another human being. If people in the churches, for example, were to go to the older members of the fellowship and simply give them a friendly hug or a backrub, they would be astonished at the emotional boost they would be providing.

Another aspect of our sexuality is the appreciation of beauty and physical attractiveness. Many single people draw back from the natural appreciation we have for a handsome man or a beautiful woman for fear that it will lead to the lust of the heart that Jesus condemned. But that is not necessary. It is quite possible to admire beauty of face and figure without lust. We can learn to enjoy the eyes, the hair, the smile, the strength of shoulders and arms, the curve of hips and legs, without leering and lusting. They are lovely gifts from the Creator's hand. How dare we despise them!

The enjoyment of beauty does not need to be wicked; it simply needs to be controlled. And it can be. We can appreciate the lovely curve of bicep or breast without falling headlong into uncontrolled passion. Just because the media tries [*sic*] to tie every attractive figure and every sensuous move to erotic sexuality does not mean that we have to buy into such a fantasy world. As children of the light, let us have beauty without lust and sensuousness without sensuality.

Still another aspect of our sexuality is the experience of communication. Initially this takes the form of simply talking about big and little things. Often it includes laughing. There are times too when it goes beyond human speech, so that quietly sitting together becomes a profound experience of communication.

In my first pastorate there was one individual whose home I would frequent just for conversation. We would often sit in his study and talk over great ideas and dream about what could be. Sometimes we would pause and pray together; often we would laugh together. But what I remember most are the times we would simply stop talking and sit together in profound silence. Enduring bonds are built through such experiences of communication, and they broaden and enhance our ability to be intimate.

Very often we in the Church place single people in a real bind regarding their sexuality. We hang them on the horns of a genuine dilemma: either marry, or bury your sexuality. But that dilemma is false, and they do not need to break it by opting for genital sex outside of marriage. There is another option. It is possible to affirm and celebrate one's sexuality and still reserve genital sex for the covenant of marriage.

Singles have the freedom in Christ to bring to the fore and develop to the full sexuality's many other aspects of intimacy and fellowship. This is the meaning of the vow of fidelity for single people.

The Meaning of Fidelity for the Married

Marriage that is Christian is covenantal.[2] A covenant is a promise – a pledge of love, loyalty, and faithfulness. A covenant involves continuity – the sense of a common future to look forward to and a history to look back on together. A covenant means belonging – a commitment to a rich and growing relationship of love and care. Let us seek, then, to flesh out the meaning of fidelity within the covenant of marriage.

First, fidelity in marriage means monogamy. We argue for monogamy and against polygamy, but not on the basis of biblical laws on the subject. In fact, some people would be surprised to realize that for every verse of Scripture we could marshal in the defense of monogamy we could find two for polygamy. No, the Christian witness to monogamy is based upon the revelation of agape that we have in Jesus Christ. The love that Christ bequeathed to us is an "existence-for-the-other-person" reality.[3] To be blunt, polygamy dehumanizes the woman.[4] The woman is made to be part of the herd for the pleasure of the man. Polygamy is an affront to the law of love. Even in the Old Testament, we can see some of the harmful results of such an arrangement.

This does not mean that we insist that people in polygamous situations immediately change to monogamy upon conversion. I know a bright student from Nigeria who has a wife and four lovely children. His father, however, had seven wives. Recently his father died, and by custom the seven wives reverted to the son. Now, for my friend to throw these women out would be terribly destructive, and so he has decided to keep all of them as his wives. He will be a husband to them in the sense of providing for their physical needs; however, he has told all seven that he will not be a husband to them sexually and therefore has given them freedom for sexual expression outside of marriage. If later they have a chance to marry someone else, he will give them a divorce – an "honorable discharge," if you will. These are certainly difficult decisions for a Christian caught in a polygamous culture, but I, for one, applaud his efforts.

Second, fidelity in marriage means a lifelong pledge to love and loyalty. Disciples must refuse to look for a way out of the covenant just because difficulties arise or romantic love cools. Difficulties are not a sign of a bad marriage; indeed, they often indicate health in the marriage. People who care for each other will have arguments and disagreements because they prize the relationship. If there never are any, it may be an indication that they just do not care any more.

The disagreements and the arguments are not the problem but how we handle them. In *Letters to Karen*, Charlie Shedd has given his "Seven Official Rules for a Good Clean Fight" that have guided him and Martha throughout their marital disagreements, and I recommend them to you.[5] To this wise counsel I would add only one comment: never, but never, allow the conflict to become physically violent. Physical abuse damages the relationship far more deeply than we know. (And if one is looking for biblical grounds for divorce, certainly physical abuse should rank at the top.)

There are times when the conflict that a couple experiences seems unbearable. "Why try any longer?" they ask. We keep trying longer because the stakes are so high, the reward of success is so great! And if we value a long life together, we will believe that our marriage is worth a great deal of effort and struggle. Our love is too good a thing to lose.

Having said this, I also know that in certain situations there may come a time when the conflict not only seems unbearable, it is unbearable. In such circumstances, fidelity suggests that wherever it is feasible the question of divorce be brought before the Christian fellowship for loving counsel and discernment. The Church is supposed to be in the business of healing ruptured marriages, or failing that, of healing the wounds of divorce.

No one is more keenly aware than I that many churches simply could not handle such a delicate and awesome responsibility. Often elders or other officially designated leaders are so divided on the issues of divorce and remarriage that they cannot help at all. Prejudice often reigns and blots out spiritual insight. Many leaders honestly feel that the business of the Church is to monitor budgets and maintain buildings, not to be amateur marriage counselors.

Yet amazing healing can come from a loving fellowship that is allowed to put its arms around a broken and bleeding marriage. It must be done with tenderness and humility. There can be no arrogance, no gossip, and no moralistic advice. The couple must feel assured that the fellowship accepts them and stands with them in their pain whatever the outcome. The main means of support are sympathetic listening and empathetic prayer. Sometimes what emerges from such experiences seems almost as real a resurrection as when Lazarus walked out of the tomb. Not always, but sometimes!

Third, fidelity in marriage means mutual subordination out of reverence for Christ. The apostle Paul places the principle of mutual subordination over all family relationships: "Be subject to one another out of reverence for Christ" (Eph. 5:21). He then proceeds to explain the details of how mutual subordination is to operate within the Christian household. It is truly amazing the responsibility for submission that Paul places upon the male, who, after all, stood at the top of the Hebrew patriarchal society. Paul calls for Christly submission through sacrificial love. First-century marriage customs did not view a woman as a full person, much less as someone to whom sacrificial love was due.

To be sure, Paul places a special responsibility for submission upon the wife: "Wives, be subject to your husbands, as to the Lord" (Eph. 5:22). He also places a special function upon the man: "The husband is the head of the wife as Christ is the head of the church" (Eph. 5:23).[6] There are those who wish Paul had not put it quite that way, since so often this teaching has been twisted into a way of keeping women under the male thumb. However, we must remember that here Paul is using the teaching approach of connection that is so common in Scripture. He is connecting with where people are and moving them to where he would like them to be.[7]

What Paul is doing in this passage is really quite astonishing. Informed by the gospel liberty that came from the example of Christ, he makes a radical break with the authoritarian, hierarchical system of the past – "be subject to one another out of reverence for Christ." But in the next breath he connects with tradition of the past – "wives be subject . . . for the husband is the head." Regarding this passage, Elizabeth Achtemeier has noted:

> The passage is ingenious. It has preserved the traditional view of the male as the head of the family, but that headship is a function only, not a matter of status or superiority. The understanding of the headship and of the wife's relation to it has been radically transformed. There is no lording it over the other here, no exercise of sinful power, no room for unconcern or hostility toward the other. Instead there is only the full devotion of love, poured out for the other, in imitation of Christ's faithfulness and yearning and sacrifice for his church, and of the church's like response to him.[8]

In all honesty, I think it must be said that the apostle Paul does not rush into the arms of egalitarian marriage. But neither does he fit in the embrace of authoritarian, hierarchical marriage. Certainly his strong words of mutual subordination and mutual marital responsibility are moving his readers, and us, along a continuum from a patriarchal or authoritarian approach toward a partnership or companionship approach. And all of us must find our marriage place somewhere along this continuum.

The direction Paul is heading in all of this is most clearly seen in his famous statement of Galatians 3:28, "There is neither Jew nor Greek, there is neither slave nor free, there is neither male nor female; for you are all one in Christ Jesus." In the Jerusalem Council of Acts 15, the Church dealt with the issue of cultural religion – "neither Jew nor Greek." Over many painful centuries the Church finally dealt with the issue of chattel slavery – "neither slave nor free." We can hope and pray that in the providence of God the Church will soon be able to deal successfully with the issue of sexism – "neither male nor female."

What does all this mean to you and me in a practical sense? Well, to borrow from Paul's language, each of us must work out our own marriage style in fear and trembling (see Phil. 2:12). Disciples of Christ are free and equal in the Gospel to work through the meaning of mutuality and submission. But there must be no lording it over one another and no headstrong rebellion. Tenderness, love, and mutual respect must govern all decisions. Always remember that the "one flesh" experience of "bone of my bones and flesh of my flesh" gives us a predisposition to walk through life's decisions in concert. Mutuality is one of fidelity's many facets.

Fourth, fidelity in marriage means sexual restraint outside of the marital covenant. When I speak of sexual restraint I mean two things: no extramarital genital sex; and expression of non-genital sexuality that is controlled by the good of the marriage and the well-being of the spouse.

The first statement needs little clarification. Adultery is not acceptable in any form for those who are followers of Jesus Christ. It does violence to the "one flesh" reality of the marriage covenant and damages the marriage relationship.

The second statement may need to be explained a bit more. Although "all things are lawful . . . not all things are helpful," as Paul put it (1 Cor. 6:12). In one sense, after marriage we are no longer our own, no longer free to choose and act as we please. Every choice, every act, affects our spouse and our marriage. Now, we may not like that, but it is a fact of life and we might just as well make peace with it. Our spouse and marriage are more profoundly affected for good or for ill by the way we express our sexuality than by nearly anything else in our lives.

This does *not* mean that we repress our sexuality outside marriage. Oh, no, hardly anything will damage the marriage more. We must be human; we need intimacy, touch, meaningful conversation, and much more outside the marriage bonds. Otherwise we will be asking the marriage to carry more than is reasonable for even the healthiest relationship. . . .

. . . fifth, fidelity in marriage means sexual liberty within the marital covenant. Here we must truly let the liberty bells ring! When sex is in its own free, full channel of marriage, it is a rich and fulfilling adventure. At times the channel is fast and exciting, like the Colorado River. At other times it is quiet and placid, like the Mississippi. Often it is deep and strong, like the Columbia.

Paul sounded the high note of sexual liberty within marriage when he declared, "The husband should give to his wife her conjugal rights, and likewise the wife to her husband" (1 Cor. 7:3). Now, you might be thinking that that sounds a lot more like obligation than liberty, but I can tell you the women in Paul's day saw liberty in every word of that command, and so did the men, I am sure, once they understood all that it meant. The call is to give ourselves sexually to each other freely and without reserve. Note the equality of rights. It is not the husband's rights and the wife's duties. There is mutual giving and receiving. Men, your wife deserves to be satisfied sexually. You are free within the covenant of marriage to do whatever would delight, whatever would please, whatever would satisfy. And women have the same liberty.

Coitus has larger purposes than procreation. Children are great, to be sure, but we must never confine sex to "baby making." Intimacy, self-disclosure, vulnerability, recreation – these and more all inform the sexual experience.

One of the great things about sex is the warmth, the love, the indefinable sense of knowing someone in the most intimate way possible. It is no accident that the Hebrew term for coitus is *yada'*, "to know." The sexual experience somehow ushers us into the subterranean chambers of each others' being.

No doubt the experience of self-disclosure and vulnerability that goes hand in hand with sexual intercourse contributes to this mysterious sense of knowing. There is something to the unashamed nakedness, the total giving of oneself that allows a couple to crash through the sound barrier of external niceties and into the inner circle of nearness. There is a sense in which the physical coupling is indicative of a deeper coupling – a uniting of heart, mind, soul, and spirit. It's wonderful, it's good, and even more, it's fun.

It is this aspect of fun, of recreation, that is, in many ways, the richest experience of all. Sex at its best, at its highest, at its holiest, is play. It is festivity; it is delight. As C. S. Lewis said, "Banish play and laughter from the bed of love and you may let in a false goddess."[9]

We get to know each other in recreation in a way that is not possible when we are serious. Sex is an adventure; it is also a game. We delight in each other's bodies in a light, airy, happy way. We play together; we romp and frolic together. This is an essential element in our celebration of sex.

The Meaning of Fidelity for the Church

We have tried to consider what the vow of fidelity might mean to single people and to married couples, but what about the corporate fellowship of believers? What does fidelity mean to the Church?

The first thing that we need to say to that question is that our understanding of what fidelity means must be drawn from the model we are given in God's covenant relationship with his people, and specifically Christ's fidelity to the Church. God's dogged faithfulness to his children in the Old Testament and Christ's tenacious love of his Church in the New Testament give us the content for the vow of fidelity. Our understanding of marriage must always be brought back to and judged by this paradigm. Paul puts it most graphically when he is dealing with the marriage union: "This is a great mystery, and I take it to mean Christ and the church" (Eph. 5:32).

When we understand marriage in light of God's covenant love for us, we are catapulted onto a new, positive level. Lewis Smedes writes:

> The Christian concept of fidelity is based on the model offered to us by the marriage between God and his people. . . . If we use this model, we will avoid the sterile, passive caricature of fidelity that is mere absence of adultery. We will have a picture of someone who makes a solemn vow to enduring partnership and whose fidelity is measured in terms of creative love for his partner.[10]

This model, however, can never remain theoretical. It must work its way into our practice. Let us turn, then, to the practical implications in the life of the Church.

The Church is first called to a ministry of prayer and spiritual direction. This is the business of the Church. Would to God that the Christian fellowship could provide an environment in which, for example, young couples could bring their questions about marriage and their leanings toward marriage to the fellowship for discernment, counsel, and blessing. . . .

For the Church to "witness" and "bless" a marriage involves ongoing accountability for its success. We have dozens of useless committees; how about a useful one charged with encouraging the healthy growth and maturing of young marriages? Visiting homes, suggesting reading material, friendship counseling, and much more could make up the committee's agenda. And why not have another committee concerned with the health of established marriages?

We have a special service to begin marriages, why not a special service for the healing and blessing of existing marriages? Couples could come to the altar together; ministers could lay hands on them and offer prayers for the marriage to go from strength to strength. . . .

Fidelity in Perspective

We have sought to travel a long way. We have looked at the vow of fidelity for the single, for the married, and for the Church. . . . Always remember, fidelity is not a static set of regulations; it is a vibrant, living adventure. It is not so much a way to suppress lust as a way to orient our lives toward a unifying goal. Fidelity is the *sine qua non* of unity and focus.

Notes

1   Ashley Montagu, *Touching: The Human Significance of Skin*, 2nd edn (New York: Harper & Row, 1978), p. 166.

2   Letha Dawson Scanzoni, *Sexuality* (Philadelphia: Westminster Press, 1984), pp. 60–2.

3   Helmut Thielicke, *The Ethics of Sex*, trans. John V. Doberstein (New York: Harper & Row, 1964), p. 90.

4   I am aware that technically *polygamy* refers to multiple mates of either sex. (*Polyandry* means many husbands and *polygyny* means many wives.) Most people, however, think of polygamy in terms of multiple wives, and the practice of polygamy in most cultures has been in that direction.

5   Charlie Shedd, *Letters to Karen* (New York: Avon Books, 1978), pp. 61–9.

6   There have been more recent attempts to translate *kephale* not as "head" but as "source" and therefore distance the passage from a hierarchical model for the husband–wife relationship. Also, the verb "to submit" does not appear in verse 22; it says simply "wives to your husband." Obviously the verb must be supplied from verse 21 and therefore is precisely the same kind of submission that is required of all believers. For a thoughtful study of this issue, see Berkeley and Alvera Mickelsen, "The 'Head' of the Epistles," *Christianity Today* (20 February 1981), pp. 20–3.

7   Jesus, for example, used this principle of connection when he said, "Think not that I have come to abolish the law and the prophets" (Matt. 5:17). But given what he had just been teaching them they could not think anything other than that he had come to abolish the law and the prophets! So without backing down on his radical disjuncture with the past, Jesus proceeds to show how his teaching connects with the past and fulfills it. Paul is doing the same thing in the Ephesians passage.

8   Elizabeth Achtemeier, *The Committed Marriage* (Philadelphia: Westminster Press, 1976), p. 86.

9   C. S. Lewis, *The Four Loves* (New York: Harcourt Brace Jovanovich, 1960), p. 140.

10   Lewis Smedes, *Sex for Christians* (Grand Rapids: Wm. B. Eerdmans, 1976), p. 169.

Inquiring after God when Afflicted

Modernity has seen attention turned to the alleviation of suffering, by vanquishing disease, developing technology, and addressing social ills. On this last point, over the past 150 years social, economic, and political suffering have been prominent concerns. Both communist and liberal democratic welfare states have actively addressed social problems. As noted in the Introduction, in the last quarter of the twentieth century, against the background of Walter Rauschenbusch's earlier Social Gospel Movement, liberal theology took a Marxist turn and reinterpreted Christian beliefs in political and economic terms that urge the powerless to cease expecting their tormentors to become benevolent and to rise up on their own behalf.

Liberation theology has reinterpreted salvation as political and economic freedom and power. Wealth and power should be redistributed to address grievances. Failure to do so further exploits the weak because without direct intervention wealth and power tend to accumulate in the hands of a few. Structures of injustice rigidify and perpetuate themselves as the powerful seek to protect their privileged status. Suffering, injustice, and alienation deepen.

Latin American, black, and feminist liberation theologies have reinterpreted not only salvation but also sin and election. Sin is primarily social rather than personal and the elect are the victims of social injustice. God is on the side of the oppressed, who cry out – like the Israelites of old – for justice. The crucified Jesus knows their affliction and dwells in their midst, carrying them aloft and strengthening them until the day of their vindication. The oppressors are called to repent and obey God by alleviating the suffering they have caused.

While considerable attention has been paid to the economic, political, and social dimensions of affliction, less attention has been given to the spiritual circumstances of the afflicted. This chapter takes up this concern. Both selections predate contemporary liberation theology, although the latter anticipates it in important ways. One is from the fourth century and one from the twentieth. Neither takes what is sometimes assumed to be the traditional view that people suffer because of their sins, or that suffering itself is redemptive. Rather, both essays point to the possibility of spiritual freedom and dignity even in dire circumstances. Although they are quite different from one another in striking ways, the essays presented here agree that it is possible, albeit difficult, to experience spiritual dignity even in affliction.

St. John Chrysostom ("the golden-mouthed"), a prolific and gifted preacher who flourished in Antioch (Syria) in the fourth century, was a highly influential figure in his day, and remains so in Eastern Orthodoxy. In his day, as in ours, it was assumed that the suffering of the innocent was the fault of others. To raised eyebrows (then and now) John questioned this seemingly self-evident position by writing "A treatise to prove that no one can harm the man who does not injure himself."

John acknowledges that the wealthy treat the poor badly, that the courts are bought by the powerful, so that the weak have no recourse against them, and that the wealthy flaunt their goods rudely and viciously. He has no sympathy for the cruelty that so often corrupts the holders of wealth and power, and exposes their moral vacuity mercilessly. His exhortation, however, is not to them alone. In a striking twist of subtle rhetoric he addresses sinners through the sinned against.

Chrysostom's intentionally provocative title conveys his concern. No matter what happens to us, life with God provides the key to our dignity and freedom. No matter how much deprivation one may suffer, no matter how much external control another may have over one, each person has an arena of freedom and power under one's own control. This space, which escapes any torturer, John says, is one's moral integrity. For surely, in a situation in which one party acts indecently and the other remains virtuous, the one who is damaged is the perpetrator, while the one who remains godly under pressure takes the moral high ground. The oppressed are injured materially, but that is not the whole story. Honor consists in perseverance in righteousness. Spiritual welfare is the true measure of one's stature.

By highlighting spiritual well-being, Chrysostom is not implying that material well-being is not important. He is pointing out that preoccupation with material well-being is corrupting, for one comes to focus on the wrong goods and to oppress others in pursuit of one's own ends; that is the greatest danger of all. There is, of course, the danger that such a view may easily be abused and distorted to justify oppression of the weak. John certainly did not intend this. And its possibility should not be permitted to obscure his point: self-esteem lies in spiritual strength, not in worldly wealth and power. Perhaps he understood that a direct attack on wealthy people would probably fall on deaf ears. Additionally, perhaps he realized how easily the afflicted are tempted by anger and bitterness that would destroy them spiritually. He seems to be preaching to both.

While Chrysostom's perspective may be intriguing, converting the haughty indirectly and encouraging the afflicted to define their freedom and dignity spiritually must be considered with great care. The whole project might backfire. The wealthy might misunderstand and the afflicted may be tempted by yet another spiritual trap: self-righteousness. And Chrysostom missed the spiritual damage done to souls that are twisted and corrupted by affliction.

Fifteen hundred years separate John Chrysostom and Simone Weil (1909–1943). The latter was a French woman born of a moderately comfortable family who had heightened sensitivities to the plight of the poor, especially factory workers in the days before protective legislation. Although of the educated middle class, she spent her brief life trying to share the suffering of workers, soldiers, and the poor by either placing herself voluntarily in their situation, or imitating their deprivation as best she could. Unlike Chrysostom, Weil strenuously objected to the physical pain, distress, and social degradation that combine in what she calls affliction (*malheur*). Yet she saw the spiritual danger that Chrysostom missed. Affliction destroys the soul unless one can dwell in God's love.

In addition to her acute social conscience and need to share the suffering of others physically, Weil was also a deeply religious person, who came under the influence of the Roman Catholic Church as an adult. Her reflections on affliction blend her keen analysis of the psychological impact of affliction with her conviction that the cross of Christ is the only hope for the afflicted. The only way to preserve one's soul is for those flung at the foot of the cross in affliction to retain the power to love God hanging there where the agony of affliction and love is made known. The ability to love God in affliction is the defeat of the dehumanization of affliction, and hence, the dignity of the afflicted.

We have then three theological approaches to affliction: God sides with the afflicted against their oppressors; the afflicted are comforted and retain their dignity in their godliness; and the afflicted retain the freedom to love God. Each has its strengths and weaknesses. None countenances affliction; all seek the repentance of the sinner.

St. John Chrysostom, *A Treatise to Prove that no one can Harm the Man who does not Injure Himself**

1.   I know well that to coarse-minded persons, who are greedy in the pursuit of present things, and are nailed to earth, and enslaved to physical pleasure, and have no strong hold upon spiritual ideas, this treatise will be of a strange and paradoxical kind: and they will laugh immoderately, and condemn me for uttering incredible things from the very outset of my theme. Nevertheless, I shall not on this account desist from my promise, but for this very reason shall proceed with great earnestness to the proof of what I have undertaken. For if those who take that view of my subject will please not to make a clamour and disturbance, but wait to the end of my discourse, I am sure that they will take my side, and condemn themselves, finding that they have been deceived hitherto, and will make a recantation, and apology, and crave pardon for the mistaken opinion which they held concerning these matters, and will express great gratitude to me, as patients do to physicians, when they have been relieved from the disorders which lay siege to their body.

For do not tell me of the judgment which is prevailing in your mind at the present time, but wait to hear the contention of my arguments and then you will be able to record an impartial verdict without being hindered by ignorance from forming a true judgment. For even judges in secular causes, if they see the first orator pouring forth a mighty torrent of words and overwhelming everything with his speech, do not venture to record their decision without having patiently listened to the other speaker who is opposed to him; and even if the remarks of the first speaker seem to be just to an unlimited extent, they reserve an unprejudiced hearing for the second. In fact, the special merit of judges consists in ascertaining with all possible accuracy what each side has to allege and then bringing forward their own judgment.

Now in the place of an orator we have the common assumption of mankind

---

* We have altered the punctuation and paragraphing of this essay for easier reading.

which, in the course of ages, has taken deep root in the minds of the multitude, and declaims to the following effect throughout the world. "All things," it says, "have been turned upside down." The human race is full of much confusion and many are they who every day are being wronged, insulted, subjected to violence and injury, the weak by the strong, the poor by the rich. And as it is impossible to number the waves of the sea, so is it impossible to reckon the multitude of those who are the victims of intrigue, insult, and suffering; and neither the correction of law, nor the fear of being brought to trial, nor anything else can arrest this pestilence and disorder. But the evil is increasing every day, and the groans, and lamentations, and weeping of the sufferers are universal.

And the judges who are appointed to reform such evils, themselves intensify the tempest, and inflame the disorder. . . . Hence many of the more senseless and despicable kind, seized with a new kind of frenzy, accuse the providence of God, when they see the forbearing man often violently seized, racked, and oppressed, and the audacious, impetuous, low and low-born man waxing rich, and invested with authority, and becoming formidable to many, and inflicting countless troubles upon the more moderate: and this perpetrated both in town and country, and desert, on sea and land.

This discourse of ours of necessity comes in by way of direct opposition to what has been alleged, maintaining a contention which is new, as I said at the beginning, and contrary to opinion, yet useful and true, and profitable to those who will give heed to it and be persuaded by it. For what I undertake is to prove (only make no commotion) that no one of those who are [*sic*] wronged is wronged by another, but experiences this injury at his own hands.

But in order to make my argument plainer, let us first of all enquire what injustice is, and of what kind of things the material of it is wont to be composed; also what human virtue is, and what it is which ruins it; and further what it is which seems to ruin it but really does not. For instance (for I must complete my argument by means of examples), each thing is subject to one evil which ruins it: iron to rust, wool to moth, flocks of sheep to wolves. . . . And not to lengthen the list by going through all possible examples, our own flesh is subject to fevers, and palsies, and a crowd of other maladies.

As then each one of these things is liable to that which ruins its virtue, let us now consider what it is which injures the human race, and what it is which ruins the virtue of a human being. . . . The multitude then, having erroneous opinions, imagine that there are many different things which ruin our virtue. Some say it is poverty, others bodily disease, others loss of property, others calumny, others death, and they are perpetually bewailing and lamenting these things. And whilst they are commiserating [with] the sufferers and shedding tears, they excitedly exclaim to one another, "What a calamity has befallen such and such a man! He has been deprived of all his fortune at a blow." Of another again one will say: "Such and such a man has been attacked by severe sickness and is despaired of by the physicians in attendance." Some bewail and lament the inmates of the prison, some those who have been expelled from their country and transported to the land of exile, others those who have been deprived of their freedom, others those who have been seized and made captives by enemies, others those who have been drowned, or burnt, or buried by the fall of a house, but no one mourns those who are living in wickedness. On the contrary, which is worse than all, they often congratulate them, a practice which is the cause of all manner of evils. Come then (only, as I exhorted you at the outset, do not make a commotion), let me prove that none of the things which have been mentioned injure the man who lives soberly, nor can ruin his virtue. For tell me if a man has lost his all either at the hands of calumniators or of robbers, or has been stripped of his goods by knavish servants, what harm has the loss done to the virtue of the man?

But, if it seems well, let me rather indicate in the first place what is the virtue of a man, beginning by dealing with the subject in the case of existences of another kind, so as to make it more intelligible and plain to the majority of readers.

3.   What then is the virtue of a horse? Is it to have a bridle studded with gold and girths to match, and a band of silken threads to fasten the housing, and clothes wrought in divers colors and gold tissue, and head gear studded with jewels, and locks of hair plaited with gold cord? Or is it to be swift and strong in its legs, and even in its paces, and to have hoofs suitable to a well bred horse, and courage fitted for long journeys and warfare, and to be able to behave with calmness in the battle field, and if a rout takes place to save its rider? Is it not manifest that these are the things which constitute the virtue of the horse, not the others? Again, what should you say was the virtue of asses and mules? Is it not the power of carrying burdens with contentment, and accomplishing journeys with ease, and having hoofs like rock? Shall we say that their outside trappings contribute anything to their own proper virtue? By no means. And what kind of vine shall we admire? One which abounds in leaves and branches, or one which is laden with fruit? Or what kind of virtue do we predicate of an olive? Is it to have large boughs, and great luxuriance of leaves, or to exhibit an abundance of its proper fruit dispersed over all parts of the tree? Well, let us act in the same way in the case of human beings also.

Let us determine what is the virtue of man, and let us regard that alone as an injury, which is destructive to it. What then is the virtue of man? Not riches that thou shouldest fear poverty, nor health of body that thou shouldest dread sickness, nor the opinion of the public, that thou shouldest view an evil reputation with alarm, nor life simply for its own sake, that death should be terrible to thee, nor liberty that thou shouldest avoid servitude: but carefulness in holding true doctrine, and rectitude in life. Of these things not even the devil himself will be able to rob a man, if he who possesses them guards them with the needful carefulness. And that most malicious and ferocious demon is aware of this. For this cause also he robbed Job of his substance, not to make him poor, but that he might force him into uttering some blasphemous speech. . . . He tortured his body, not to subject him to infirmity, but to upset the virtue of his soul. But nevertheless, when he had set all his devices in motion, and turned him from a rich man into a poor one (that calamity which seems to us the most terrible of all), and had made him childless who was once surrounded by many children, and had scarified his whole body more cruelly than the executioners do in the public tribunals (for their nails do not lacerate the sides of those who fall into their hands so severely as the gnawing of the worms lacerated his body). . . . When he had fastened a bad reputation upon him (for Job's friends who were present with him said, "thou hast not received the chastisement which thy sins deserve," and directed many words of accusation against him): . . . after he had not merely expelled him from city and home and transferred him to another city, but had actually made the dunghill serve as his home and city. After all this, he not only did him no damage but rendered him more glorious by the designs which he formed against him. And he not only failed to rob him of any of his possessions, although he had robbed him of so many things, but he even increased the wealth of his virtue. For after these things he enjoyed greater confidence, inasmuch as he had contended in a more severe contest.

Now, if he who underwent such sufferings – and this not at the hand of man, but at the hand of the devil who is more wicked than all men – sustained no injury, which of those persons who say such and such a man injured and damaged me will have any defense to make in future? For if the devil, who is full of such great malice, after having set all his instruments in motion, and discharged all his weapons, and poured out all the evils incident to man, in a superlative degree upon the family and the person of that righteous man, nevertheless did him no injury – but as I was saying rather profited him – how shall certain [people] be able to accuse such and such a man, alleging that they have suffered injury at their hands, not at their own?

4   . . . Or what harm was done to Joseph [Gen. 37–50] by his getting evil reported of, both in his own land, and in the land of strangers? For he was supposed to be both an adulterer and fornicator. Or what harm did servitude do him or expatriation? Is it not specially on account of these things that we

regard him with admiration and astonishment? And why do I speak of removal to a foreign land, and poverty, and evil report, and bondage? For what harm did death itself inflict on Abel [Gen. 4:1–8], although it was a violent and untimely death, and perpetrated by a brother's hand? Is not this the reason why his praise is sounded throughout the whole world? Seest thou how the discourse has demonstrated even more than it promised? For not only has it disclosed the fact that no one is injured by anybody, but also that they who take heed to themselves derive the greater gain (from such assaults). What is the purpose then, it will be said, of penalties and punishments? What is the purpose of hell? What is the purpose of such great threatenings, if no one is either injured or injures? What is it thou sayest? Why dost thou confuse the argument? For I did not say that no one injures, but that no one is injured. And how is it possible, you will say, for no one to be injured when many are committing injury? In the way which I indicated just now. For Joseph's brethren did indeed injure him, yet he himself was not injured; and Cain laid snares for Abel, yet he himself was not ensnared. This is the reason why there are penalties and punishments. For God does not abolish penalties on account of the virtue of those who suffer; but he ordains punishments on account of the malice of those who do wickedly. For, although they who are evil entreated [*sic*: evilly treated?] become more illustrious in consequence of the designs formed against them, this is not due to the intention of those who plan the designs, but to the courage of those who are the victims of them. Wherefore, for the latter, the rewards of philosophy are made ready and prepared, for the former the penalties of wickedness. . . .

5. When then, neither loss of money, nor slander, nor railing, nor banishment, nor diseases, nor tortures, nor that which seems more formidable than all, namely death, harms those who suffer them, but rather adds to their profit, whence can you prove to me that any one is injured when he is not injured at all from any of these things? For I will endeavor to prove the reverse, showing that they who are most injured and insulted, and suffer the most incurable evils are the persons who do these things. For what could be more miserable than the condition of Cain, who dealt with his brother in this fashion? What more pitiable than that of Phillip's wife, who beheaded John [Matt. 14:1–12]? Or the brethren of Joseph who sold him away, and transported him into the land of exile? Or the devil who tortured Job with such great calamities? For not only on account of his other iniquities, but at the same time also for this assault he will pay no trifling penalty.

Dost thou see how here the argument has proved even more than was proposed, shewing that those who are insulted not only sustain no harm from these assaults, but that the whole mischief recoils on the head of those who contrive them? For since neither wealth nor freedom, nor life in our native land, nor the other things which I have mentioned, but only right actions of the soul, constitute the virtue of man, naturally, when the harm is directed against these things, human virtue itself is in no wise harmed.

What then? Supposing some one does harm the moral condition of the soul? Even then if a man suffers damage, the damage does not come from another but proceeds from within, and from the man himself. "How so," do you say? When any one having been beaten by another, or deprived of his goods, or having endured some other grievous insult, utters a blasphemous speech, he certainly sustains a damage thereby, and a very great one. Nevertheless it does not proceed from him who has inflicted the insult, but from his own littleness of soul. For what I said before I will now repeat, no man, if he be infinitely wicked, could attack any one more wickedly or more bitterly than that revengeful demon who is implacably hostile to us, the devil. But yet, this cruel demon had not power to upset or overthrow him who lived before the law, and before the time of grace, although he discharged so many and such bitter weapons against him from all quarters. Such is the force of nobility of soul. . . .

6.   But I am injured in other ways, one will say, and even if I do not blaspheme, yet when I am robbed of my money I am disabled from giving alms. This is a mere pretext and pretense. For if you grieve on this account know certainly that poverty is no bar to almsgiving. For even if you are infinitely poor you are not poorer than the woman who possessed only a handful of meal [1 Kgs. 17:12], and the one who had only two mites [Luke 21:2], each of whom, having spent all her substance upon those who were in need, was an object of surpassing admiration. And such great poverty was no hindrance to such great lovingkindness, but the alms bestowed from the two mites was so abundant and generous as to eclipse all who had riches, and in wealth of intention and superabundance of zeal to surpass those who cast in much coin. Wherefore, even in this matter thou art not injured but rather benefited, receiving by means of a small contribution, rewards more glorious than they who put down large sums. . . .

Now, tell me why is wealth an object of ambition? For it is necessary to start from this point, because to the majority of those who are afflicted with this grievous malady it seems to be more precious than health and life, and public reputation, and good opinion, and country, and household, and friends, and kindred and everything else. Moreover, the flame has ascended to the very clouds; and this fierce heat has taken possession of land and sea. Nor is there any one to quench this fire. But all people are engaged in stirring it up, . . . those who have been already caught by it, and those who have not yet been caught, in order that they may be captured. And you may see every one, husband and wife, household slave, and freeman, rich and poor, each according to his ability, carrying loads which supply much fuel to this fire by day and night: loads not of wood or faggots (for the fire is not of that kind), but loads of souls and bodies, of unrighteousness and iniquity. For such is the material of which a fire of this kind is wont to be kindled. . . .

7. And how might we cure those who are thus disposed? It would be possible if they would open their ears to us, and unfold their heart, and receive our words. For it is impossible to turn and divert the irrational animals from their unclean habit; for they are destitute of reason. But this, the gentlest of all tribes, is honored by reason and speech. I mean, human nature, might, if it chose, readily and easily be released from the mire and the stench, and the dung hill and its abomination. For wherefore, O man, do riches seem to thee worthy [of] such diligent pursuit? Is it on account of the pleasure which no doubt is derived from the table? Or on account of the honor and the escort of those who pay court to thee, because of thy wealth? Is it because thou art able to defend thyself against those who annoy thee, and to be an object of fear to all? For you cannot name any other reasons, save pleasure, and flattery, and fear, and the power of taking revenge. For wealth is not generally wont to make any one wiser, or more self-controlled, or more gentle, or more intelligent, or kind, or benevolent, or superior to anger, or gluttony or pleasure. It does not train any one to be moderate, or teach him how to be humble, nor introduce and implant any other piece of virtue in the soul. Neither could you say for which of these things it deserves to be so diligently sought and desired. For not only is it ignorant [of] how to plant and cultivate any good thing, but even if it finds a store of them it mars and stunts and blights them; and some of them it even uproots, and introduces their opposites – unmeasured licentiousness, unseasonable wrath, unrighteous anger, pride, arrogance, foolishness.

But let me not speak of these; for they who have been seized by this malady will not endure to hear about virtue and vice, being entirely abandoned to pleasure and therefore enslaved to it. Come then, let us forgo for the time being the consideration of these points, and let us bring forward the others which remain, and see whether wealth has any pleasure, or any honor. For in my eyes the case is quite the reverse. And first of all, if you please, let us investigate the meals of the rich and poor, and ask the guests which they are who enjoy the purest and most genuine pleasure. Is it they who recline for a full day on couches, and join breakfast and dinner together, and distend their stomach, and blunt their senses, and sink the vessel by an overladen cargo of food, and waterlog the ship, and drench it as in some shipwreck of the body, and devise fetters, and manacles, and gags, and bind their whole body with the band of drunkenness and surfeit more grievous than an iron chain, and enjoy no sound pure sleep undisturbed by frightful dreams, and are more miserable than madmen and introduce a kind of self-imposed demon into the soul and display themselves as a laughing stock to the gaze of their servants, or rather to the kinder sort amongst them as a tragic spectacle eliciting tears, and cannot recognize any of those who are present, and are incapable of speaking or hearing, but have to be carried away from their couches to their bed? Or, is it they who are sober and vigilant, and limit their eating by their need, and sail with a favorable breeze, and find hunger and thirst the best relish in their food and drink? For nothing is so conducive to enjoyment and health as to be hungry and thirsty when one attacks the viands, and to identify satiety with the simple necessity of food, never overstepping the limits of this, nor imposing a load upon the body too great for its strength.

But, if you disbelieve my statement, study the physical condition and the soul of each class. Are not the bodies vigorous of those who live thus moderately? (For do not tell me of that which rarely happens, although some may be weak from some other circumstance. But form your judgment from those instances which are of constant occurrence.) I say, are they not vigorous, and their senses clear, fulfilling their proper function with much ease? Whereas the bodies of the others are flaccid and softer than wax, and beset with a crowd of maladies? For gout soon fastens upon them, and untimely palsy, and premature old age, and headache, and flatulence, and feebleness of digestion, and loss of appetite. . . . They require constant attendance of physicians, and perpetual dosing, and daily care. Are these things pleasurable? Tell me. Who of those that know what pleasure really is would say so? For pleasure is produced when desire leads the way, and fruition follows. Now, if there is fruition, but desire is nowhere to be found, the conditions of pleasure fail and vanish. On this account also invalids, although the most charming food is set before them, partake of it with a feeling of disgust and sense of oppression, because there is no desire which gives a keen relish to the enjoyment of it.

For it is not the nature of the food or of the drink, but the appetite of the eaters which is wont to produce the desire, and is capable of causing pleasure. Therefore, also a certain wise man who had an accurate knowledge of all that concerned pleasure, and understood how to moralize about these things said "the full soul mocketh at honeycombs" [Prov. 28:7], showing that the conditions of pleasure consist not in the nature of the meal, but in the disposition of the eaters. Therefore, also the prophet, recounting the wonders in Egypt and in the desert, mentioned this in connexion with the others: "He satisfied them with honey out of the rock" [Ps. 81:16]. And yet, nowhere does it appear that honey actually sprang forth for them out of the rock; what then is the meaning of the expression? Because the people, being exhausted by much toil and long traveling, and distressed by great thirst, rushed to the cool spring, their craving for drink serving as a relish, the writer, wishing to describe the pleasures which they received from those fountains, called the water honey, not meaning that the element was converted into honey, but that the pleasure received from the water rivalled the sweetness of honey, inasmuch as those who partook of it rushed to it in their eagerness to drink.

Since then, these things are so and no one can deny it, however stupid he may be, is it not perfectly plain that pure, undiluted, and lively pleasure is to be found at the tables of the poor? Whereas at the tables of the rich there is discomfort, and disgust and defilement? As that wise man has said "even sweet things seem to be a vexation" [see Prov. 22:7].

9.   But riches, some one will say, procure honor for those who possess them, and enable them to take vengeance on their enemies with ease. And is this a reason, pray, why riches seem to you desirable and worth contending for – that they nourish the most dangerous passion in our nature, leading on anger into action, swelling the empty bubbles of ambition, and stimulating and urging men to arrogance? Why these are just the very reasons why we ought resolutely to turn our backs upon riches, because they introduce certain fierce and dangerous wild beasts into our heart. [They] depriv[e] us of the real honor which we might receive from all, and introduc[e] to deluded men another which is the opposite of this, only painted over with its colors, and persuad[e] them to fancy that it is the same, when by nature it is not so, but only seems to be so to the eye. For, as the beauty of courtesans, made up as it is of dyes and pigments, is destitute of real beauty, yet makes a foul and ugly face appear fair and beautiful to those who are deluded by it, when it is not so in reality, even so also riches force flattery to look like honor. For I beg you not to consider the praises which are openly bestowed through fear and fawning, for these are only tints and pigments. But unfold the conscience of each of those who flatters you in this fashion, and inside it you will see countless accusers declaring against you, and loathing and detesting you more than your bitterest adversaries and foes. And if ever a change of circumstances should occur which would remove and expose this mask which fear has manufactured – just as the sun when it emits a hotter ray than usual discloses the real countenances of those women whom I mentioned – then you will see clearly that all through the former time you were held in the greatest contempt by those who paid court to you, and you fancied you were enjoying honor from those who thoroughly hated you, and in their heart poured infinite abuse upon you, and longed to see you involved in extreme calamities. For there is nothing like virtue to produce honor – honor neither forced nor feigned, nor hidden under a mask of deceit, but real and genuine, and able to stand the test of hard times.

But do you wish to take vengeance on those who have annoyed you? This, as I was saying just now, is the very reason why wealth ought specially to be avoided. For it prepares thee to thrust the sword against thyself, and renders thee liable to a heavier account in the future day of reckoning, and makes thy punishment intolerable. For revenge is so great an evil that it actually revokes the mercy of God, and cancels the forgiveness of countless sins which has been already bestowed. For he who received the remission of the debt of ten thousand talents, and, after having obtained so great a boon by merely asking for it, then made a demand of one hundred pence from his fellow servant – a demand, that is, for satisfaction for his transgression against himself – in his severity towards his fellow servant recorded his own condemnation. For this reason and no other he was delivered to the tormentors, and racked, and required to pay back the ten thousand talents; and he was not allowed the benefit of any excuse or defense, but suffered the most extreme penalty, having been commanded to deposit the whole debt which the lovingkindness of God had formerly remitted [Matt. 18:23–35].

Is this then the reason, pray, why wealth is so earnestly pursued by thee, because it so easily conducts thee into sin of this kind? Nay verily, this is why you ought to abhor it as a foe and an adversary teeming with countless murders. But poverty, some one will say, disposes men to be discontented and often also to utter profane words, and condescend to mean actions. It is not poverty which does this, but littleness of soul. For Lazarus also was poor, aye! Very poor; and besides poverty he suffered from infirmity, a bitterer trial than any form of poverty, and one which makes poverty more severely felt. . . . In addition to infirmity there was a total absence of protectors, and difficulty in finding any to supply his wants, which increased the bitterness of poverty and infirmity [Luke 16:19–31].

For each of these things is painful in itself, but when there are none to minister to the sufferer's wants, the suffering becomes greater, the flame more painful, the distress more bitter, the tempest fiercer, the billows stronger, the furnace hotter. And if one examines the case thoroughly, there was yet a fourth trial besides these – the unconcern and luxury of the rich man who dwelt hard by. . . . But the poor man, and he so very poor, and encompassed with so many miseries, was not even vouchsafed the crumbs which fell from that table, although he greatly desired them. . . . Yet, none of these things injured him, he did not give vent to a bitter word, he did not utter a profane speech. But, like a piece of gold which shines all the more brilliantly when it is purified by excessive heat, even so he, although oppressed by these sufferings, was superior to all of them, and to the agitation which in many cases is produced by them. For, if generally speaking poor men, when they see rich men, are consumed with envy and racked by malicious ill-will, and deem life not worth living – and this even when they

are well supplied with necessary food, and have persons to minister to their
wants – what would the condition of this poor man have been had he not
been very wise and noble-hearted? . . .

12.   Thus, in no case will any one be able to injure a man who does not
choose to injure himself. But, if a man is not willing to be temperate, and
to aid himself from his own [spiritual] resources, no one will ever be able
to profit him. Therefore, also that wonderful history of the Holy Scriptures,
as in some lofty, large, and broad picture, has portrayed the lives of the men
of old time, extending the narrative from Adam to the coming of Christ. . . .
It exhibits to you both those who are upset, and those who are crowned with
victory in the contest, in order that it may instruct you by means of all
examples that no one will be able to injure one who is not injured by himself,
even if all the world were to kindle a fierce war against him. For it is not
stress of circumstances, nor variation of seasons, nor insults of men in power,
nor intrigues besetting thee like snow storms, nor a crowd of calamities, nor
a promiscuous collection of all the ills to which mankind is subject, which
can disturb even slightly the man who is brave, and temperate, and watchful.
Just as, on the contrary, the indolent and supine man who is his own betrayer,
cannot be made better, even with the aid of innumerable ministrations.
   This, at least, was made manifest to us by the parable of the two men, of
whom the one built his house upon the rock, the other upon the sand [Matt.
7:24–7]. Not that we are to think of sand and rock, or of a building of stone,
and a roof, or of rivers, and rain, and wild winds, beating against the
buildings, but we are to extract virtue and vice as the meaning of these things,
and to perceive from them that no one injures a man who does not injure
himself. Therefore, neither the rain, although driven furiously along, nor the
streams dashing against it with much vehemence, nor the wild winds beating
against it with a mighty rush, shook the one house in any degree. But it
remained undisturbed, unmoved – that thou mightest understand that no
trial can agitate the man who does not betray himself. But the house of the
other man was easily swept away, not on account of the force of the trials
(for in that case the other would have experienced the same fate), but on
account of his own folly. For it did not fall because the wind blew upon it,
but because it was built upon the sand, that is to say, upon indolence and
iniquity. For before that tempest beat upon it, it was weak and ready to fall.
For buildings of that kind, even if no one puts any pressure upon them, fall
to pieces of themselves, the foundation sinking and giving way in every
direction. . . . Even so, also they who do not injure themselves become
stronger, even if they receive innumerable blows. But they who betray
themselves, even if there is no one to harass them, fall of themselves, and
collapse and perish. For even thus did Judas perish, not only having been

unassailed by any trial of this kind, but having actually enjoyed the benefit of much assistance [Matt. 27:3–5].

17. ... I will now conclude my discourse by repeating what I said at the beginning, that if any one be harmed and injured he certainly suffers this at his own hands, not at the hands of others, even if there be countless multitudes injuring and insulting him. So that, if he does not suffer this at his own hands, not all the creatures who inhabit the whole earth and sea, if they combined to attack him would be able to hurt one who is vigilant and sober in the Lord. Let us then, I beseech you, be sober and vigilant at all times, and let us endure all painful things bravely that we may obtain those everlasting and pure blessings in Christ Jesus our Lord, to whom be glory and power, now and ever throughout all ages. Amen.

CONTEMPORARY REFLECTION

The Love of God and Affliction

Simone Weil

In the realm of suffering, affliction is something apart, specific, and irreducible. It is quite a different thing from simple suffering. It takes possession of the soul and marks it through and through with its own particular mark, the mark of slavery. Slavery as practiced by ancient Rome is only an extreme form of affliction. The men of antiquity, who knew all about this question, used to say: "A man loses half his soul the day he becomes a slave."

Affliction is inseparable from physical suffering and yet quite distinct. With suffering, all that is not bound up with physical pain or something analogous is artificial, imaginary, and can be eliminated by a suitable adjustment of the mind. Even in the case of the absence or death of someone we love, the irreducible part of the sorrow is akin to physical pain, a difficulty in breathing, a constriction of the heart, an unsatisfied need, hunger, or the almost biological disorder caused by the brutal liberation of some energy, hitherto directed by an attachment and now left without a guide. A sorrow that is not centered around an irreducible core of such a nature is mere romanticism or literature. Humiliation is also a violent condition of the whole corporal being, which longs to surge up under the outrage but is forced, by impotence or fear, to hold itself in check.

On the other hand pain that is only physical is a very unimportant matter and leaves no trace in the soul. Toothache is an example. An hour or two of violent pain caused by a decayed tooth is nothing once it is over.

It is another matter if the physical suffering is very prolonged or frequent, but in such a case we are dealing with something quite different from an attack of pain; it is often an affliction.

Affliction is an uprooting of life, a more or less attenuated equivalent of death, made irresistibly present to the soul by the attack or immediate apprehension of physical pain. If there is complete absence of physical pain there is no affliction for the soul, because our thoughts can turn to any object. Thought flies from affliction as promptly and irresistibly as an animal flies from death. Here below, physical pain, and that alone, has the power to chain down our thoughts; on condition that we count as physical pain certain phenomena that, though difficult to describe, are bodily and exactly equivalent to it. Fear of physical pain is a notable example.

When thought is obliged by an attack of physical pain, however slight, to recognize the presence of affliction, a state of mind is brought about, as acute as that of a condemned man who is forced to look for hours at the guillotine that is going to cut off his head. Human beings can live for twenty or fifty years in this acute state. We pass quite close to them without realizing it. What man is capable of discerning such souls unless Christ himself looks through his eyes? We only notice that they have rather a strange way of behaving and we censure this behavior.

There is no real affliction unless the event that has seized and uprooted a life attacks it, directly or indirectly, in all its parts, social, psychological, and physical. The social factor is essential. There is not really affliction unless there is social degradation or the fear of it in some form or another.

There is both continuity and the separation of a definite point of entry, as with the temperature at which water boils, between affliction itself and all the sorrows that, even though they may be very violent, very deep and very lasting, are not affliction in the strict sense. There is a limit; on the far side of it we have affliction but not on the near side. This limit is not purely objective; all sorts of personal factors have to be taken into account. The same event may plunge one human being into affliction and not another.

The great enigma of human life is not suffering but affliction. It is not surprising that the innocent are killed, tortured, driven from their country, made destitute, or reduced to slavery, imprisoned in camps or cells, since there are criminals to perform such actions. It is not surprising either that disease is the cause of long sufferings, which paralyze life and make it into an image of death, since nature is at the mercy of the blind play of mechanical necessities. But it *is* surprising that God should have given affliction the power to seize the very souls of the innocent and to take possession of them as their sovereign lord. At the very best, he who is branded by affliction will keep only half his soul.

As for those who have been struck by one of those blows that leave a being struggling on the ground like a half-crushed worm, they have no words to express what is happening to them. Among the people they meet, those who have never had contact with affliction in its true sense can have no idea of what it is, even though they may have suffered a great deal. Affliction is something specific and impossible to describe in any other terms, as sounds are to anyone who is deaf and dumb. And as for those who have themselves been mutilated by affliction, they are in no state to help anyone at all, and they are almost incapable of even wishing to do so. Thus compassion for the afflicted is an impossibility. When it is really found we have a more astounding miracle than walking on water, healing the sick, or even raising the dead.

Affliction constrained Christ to implore that he might be spared, to seek consolation from man, to believe he was forsaken by the Father. It forced a just man to cry out against God, a just man as perfect as human nature can be, more so, perhaps, if Job is less a historical character than a figure of Christ. "He laughs at the affliction of the innocent!" This is not blasphemy but a genuine cry of anguish. The Book of Job is a pure marvel of truth and authenticity from beginning to end. As regards affliction, all that departs from this model is more or less stained with falsehood.

Affliction makes God appear to be absent for a time, more absent than a dead man, more absent than light in the utter darkness of a cell. A kind of horror submerges the whole soul. During this absence there is nothing to love. What is terrible is that if, in this darkness where there is nothing to love, the soul ceases to love, God's absence becomes final. The soul has to go on loving in the emptiness, or at least to go on wanting to love, though it may only be with an infinitesimal part of itself. Then, one day, God will come to show himself to this soul and to reveal the beauty of the world to it, as in the case of Job. But if the soul stops loving it falls, even in this life, into something almost equivalent to hell.

That is why those who plunge men into affliction before they are prepared to receive it kill their souls. On the other hand, in a time such as ours, where affliction is hanging over us all, help given to souls is effective only if it goes far enough really to prepare them for affliction. That is no small thing.

Affliction hardens and discourages us because, like a red hot iron, it stamps the soul to its very depths with the scorn, the disgust, and even the self-hatred and sense of guilt and defilement that crime logically should produce but actually does not. Evil dwells in the heart of the criminal without being felt there. It is felt in the heart of the man who is afflicted and innocent. Everything happens as though the state of soul suitable for criminals had been separated from crime and attached to affliction; and it even seems to be in proportion to the innocence of those who are afflicted.

If Job cries out that he is innocent in such despairing accents, it is because he himself is beginning not to believe in it; it is because his soul within him is taking the side of his friends. He implores God himself to bear witness, because he no longer hears the testimony of his own conscience; it is no longer anything but an abstract, lifeless memory for him.

Men have the same carnal nature as animals. If a hen is hurt, the others rush upon it, attacking it with their beaks. This phenomenon is as automatic as gravitation. Our senses attach all the scorn, all the revulsion, all the hatred that our reason attaches to crime, to affliction. Except for those whose whole soul is inhabited by Christ, everybody despises the afflicted to some extent, although practically no one is conscious of it.

This law of sensibility also holds good with regard to ourselves. In the case of someone in affliction, all the scorn, revulsion, and hatred are turned inward. They penetrate to the center of the soul and from there color the whole universe with their poisoned light. Supernatural love, if it has survived, can prevent this second result from coming about, but not the first. The first is of the very essence of affliction; there is no affliction without it.

Christ . . . being made a curse for us. It was not only the body of Christ, hanging on the wood, that was accursed; it was his whole soul also. In the same way every innocent being in his affliction feels himself accursed. This even goes on being true for those who have been in affliction and have come out of it, through a change in their fortunes, that is to say, if the affliction ate deeply enough into them.

Another effect of affliction is, little by little, to make the soul its accomplice, by injecting a poison of inertia into it. In anyone who has suffered affliction for a long enough time there is a complicity with regard to his own affliction. This complicity impedes all the efforts he might make to improve his lot; it goes so far as to prevent him from seeking a way of deliverance, sometimes even to the point of preventing him from wishing for deliverance. Then he is established in affliction, and people might think he was satisfied. Further, this complicity may even induce him to shun the means of deliverance. In such cases it veils itself with excuses which are often ridiculous. Even a person who has come through his affliction will still have something left in him compelling him to plunge into it again, if it has bitten deeply and forever into the substance of his soul. It is as though affliction had established itself in him like a parasite and were directing him to suit its own purposes. Sometimes this impulse triumphs over all the movements of the soul toward happiness. If the affliction has been ended as a result of some kindness, it may take the form of hatred for the benefactor; such is the cause of certain apparently inexplicable acts of savage ingratitude. It is sometimes easy to deliver an unhappy man from his present distress, but it is difficult to set him free from his past affliction. Only God can do it. And even the grace of God itself cannot cure irremediably wounded nature here below. The glorified body of Christ bore the marks of the nails and spear.

One can only accept the existence of affliction by considering it at a distance.

God created through love and for love. God did not create anything except love itself, and the means to love. He created love in all its forms. He created beings capable of love from all possible distances. Because no other could do it, he himself went to the greatest possible distance, the infinite distance. This infinite distance between God and God, this supreme tearing apart, this agony beyond all others, this marvel of love, is the crucifixion. Nothing can be further from God than that which has been made accursed.

This tearing apart, over which supreme love places the bond of supreme union, echoes perpetually across the universe in the midst of the silence, like two notes, separate yet melting into one, like pure and heart-rending harmony. This is the Word of God. The whole creation is nothing but its vibration. When human music in its greatest purity pierces our soul, this is what we hear through it. When we have learned to hear the silence, this is what we grasp more distinctly through it.

Those who persevere in love hear this note from the very lowest depths into which affliction has thrust them. From that moment they can no longer have any doubt.

Men struck down by affliction are at the foot of the Cross, almost at the greatest possible distance from God. It must not be thought that sin is a greater distance. Sin is not a distance, it is a turning of our gaze in the wrong direction.

It is true that there is a mysterious connection between this distance and an original disobedience. From the beginning, we are told, humanity turned its gaze away from God and walked in the wrong direction for as far as it could go. That was because it could walk then. As for us, we are nailed down to the spot, only free to choose which way we look, ruled by necessity. A blind mechanism, heedless of degrees of spiritual perfection, continually tosses men about and throws some of them at the very foot of the Cross. It rests with them to keep or not to keep their eyes turned toward God through all the jolting. It does not mean that God's Providence is lacking. It is in his Providence that God has willed that necessity should be like a blind mechanism.

If the mechanism were not blind there would not be any affliction. Affliction is anonymous before all things; it deprives its victims of their personality and makes them into things. It is indifferent; and it is the coldness of this indifference – a metallic coldness – that freezes all those it touches right to the depths of their souls. They will never find warmth again. They will never believe any more that they are anyone.

Affliction would not have this power without the element of chance contained by it. Those who are persecuted for their faith and are aware of the fact are not afflicted, although they have to suffer. They only fall into a state of affliction if suffering or fear fills the soul to the point of making it forget the cause of the persecution. The martyrs who entered the arena, singing as they went to face the wild beasts, were not afflicted. Christ was afflicted. He did not die like a martyr. He died like a common criminal, confused with thieves, only a little more ridiculous. For affliction is ridiculous.

Only blind necessity can throw men to the extreme point of distance, right next to the Cross. Human crime, which is the cause of most affliction, is part of blind necessity, because criminals do not know what they are doing.

There are two forms of friendship: meeting and separation. They are indissoluble. Both of them contain some good, and this good of friendship is unique, for when two beings who are not friends are near each other there is no meeting, and when friends are far apart there is no separation. As both forms contain the same good thing, they are both equally good.

God produces himself and knows himself perfectly, just as we in our miserable fashion make and know objects outside ourselves. But, before all things, God is love. Before all things God loves himself. This love, this friendship of God, is the Trinity. Between the terms united by this relation of divine love there is more than nearness; there is infinite nearness or identity. But, resulting from the Creation, the Incarnation, and the Passion, there is also infinite distance. The totality of space and the totality of time, interposing their immensity, put an infinite distance between God and God.

Lovers or friends desire two things. The one is to love each other so much that they enter into each other and only make one being. The other is to love each other so much that, with half the globe between them, their union will not be diminished in the slightest degree. All that man vainly desires here below is perfectly realized in God. We have all those impossible desires within us as a mark of our destination, and they are good for us when we no longer hope to accomplish them.

The love between God and God, which in itself *is* God, is this bond of double virtue: the bond that unites two beings so closely that they are no longer distinguishable and really form a single unity and the bond that stretches across distance and triumphs over infinite separation. The unity of God, wherein all plurality disappears, and the abandonment, wherein Christ believes he is left while never ceasing to love his Father perfectly, these are two forms expressing the divine virtue of the same Love, the Love that is God himself.

God is so essentially love that the unity, which in a sense is his actual definition, is the pure effect of love. Moreover, corresponding to the infinite virtue of unification belonging to this love, there is the infinite separation over which it triumphs, which is the whole creation spread throughout the totality of space and time, made of mechanically harsh matter and interposed between Christ and his Father.

As for us men, our misery gives us the infinitely precious privilege of sharing in this distance placed between the Son and his Father. This distance is only separation, however, for those who love. For those who love, separation, although painful, is a good, because it is love. Even the distress of the abandoned Christ is a good. There cannot be a greater good for us on earth than to share in it. God can never be perfectly present to us here below on account of our flesh. But he can be almost perfectly absent from us in extreme affliction. This is the only possibility of perfection for us on earth. That is why the Cross is our only hope. "No forest bears such a tree, with such blossoms, such foliage, and such fruit." . . .

Joy and suffering are two equally precious gifts both of which must be savored to the full, each one in its purity, without trying to mix them. Through joy, the beauty of the world penetrates our soul. Through suffering it penetrates our body. We could no more become friends of God through joy alone than one becomes a ship's captain by studying books on navigation. The body plays a part in all apprenticeships. On the plane of physical sensibility, suffering alone gives us contact with that necessity which constitutes the order of the world, for pleasure does not involve an impression of necessity. It is a higher kind of sensibility, capable of recognizing a necessity in joy, and that only indirectly through a sense of beauty. In order that our being should one day become wholly sensitive in every part to this obedience that is the substance of matter, in order that a new sense should be formed in us to enable us to hear the universe as the vibration of the word of God, the transforming power of suffering and of joy are equally indispensable. When either of them comes to us we have to open the very center of our soul to it, just as a woman opens her door to messengers from her loved one. What does it matter to a lover if the messenger be polite or rough, so long as he delivers the message?

But affliction is not suffering. Affliction is something quite distinct from a method of God's teaching.

The infinity of space and time separates us from God. How are we to seek for him? How are we to go toward him? Even if we were to walk for hundreds of years, we should do no more than go round and round the world. Even in an airplane we could not do anything else. We are incapable of progressing vertically. We cannot take a step toward the heavens. God crosses the universe and comes to us.

Over the infinity of space and time, the infinitely more infinite love of God comes to possess us. He comes at his own time. We have the power to consent to receive him or to refuse. If we remain deaf, he comes back again and again like a beggar, but also, like a beggar, one day he stops coming. If we consent, God puts a little seed in us and he goes away again. From that moment God has no more to do; neither have we, except to wait. We only have not to regret the consent we gave him, the nuptial yes. It is not as easy as it seems, for the growth of the seed within us is painful. Moreover, from the very fact that we accept this growth, we cannot avoid destroying whatever gets in its way, pulling up the weeds, cutting the good grass, and unfortunately the good grass is part of our very flesh, so that this gardening amounts to a violent operation. On the whole, however, the seed grows of itself. A day comes when the soul belongs to God, when it not only consents to love but when truly and effectively it loves. Then in its turn it must cross the universe to go to God. The soul does not love like a creature with created love. The love within it is divine, uncreated; for it is the love of God for God that is passing through it. God alone is capable of loving God. We can only consent to give up our own feelings so as to allow free passage in our soul for this love. That is the meaning of denying oneself. We are created for this consent, and for this alone.

Divine Love crossed the infinity of space and time to come from God to us. But how can it repeat the journey in the opposite direction, starting from a finite creature? When the seed of divine love placed in us has grown and become a tree, how can we, we who bear it, take it back to its origin? How can we repeat the journey made by God when he came to us, in the opposite direction? How can we cross infinite distance?

It seems impossible, but there is a way – a way with which we are familiar. We know quite well in what likeness this tree is made, this tree that has grown within us, this most beautiful tree where the birds of the air come and perch. We know what is the most beautiful of all trees. "No forest bears its equal." Something still a little more frightful than a gibbet – that is the most beautiful of all trees. It was the seed of this tree that God placed within us, without our knowing what seed it was. If we had known, we should not have said yes at the first moment. It is this tree that has grown within us and has become ineradicable. Only a betrayal could uproot it.

When we hit a nail with a hammer, the whole of the shock received by the large head of the nail passes into the point without any of it being lost, although it is only a point. If the hammer and the head of the nail were infinitely big it would be just the same. The point of the nail would transmit this infinite shock at the point to which it was applied.

Extreme affliction, which means physical pain, distress of soul, and social degradation, all at the same time, is a nail whose point is applied at the very center of the soul, whose head is all necessity spreading throughout space and time.

Affliction is a marvel of divine technique. It is a simple and ingenious device which introduces into the soul of a finite creature the immensity of force, blind, brutal, and cold. The infinite distance separating God from the creature is entirely concentrated into one point to pierce the soul in its center.

The man to whom such a thing happens has no part in the operation. He struggles like a butterfly pinned alive into an album. But through all the horror he can continue to want to love. There is nothing impossible in that, no obstacle, one might almost say no difficulty. For the greatest suffering, so long as it does not cause the soul to faint, does not touch the acquiescent part of the soul, consenting to a right direction.

It is only necessary to know that love is a direction and not a state of the soul. If one is unaware of this, one falls into despair at the first onslaught of affliction.

He whose soul remains ever turned toward God though the nail pierces it finds himself nailed to the very center of the universe. It is the true center; it is not in the middle; it is beyond space and time; it is God. In a dimension that does not belong to space, that is not time, that is indeed quite a different dimension, this nail has pierced cleanly through all creation, through the thickness of the screen separating the soul from God.

In this marvelous dimension, the soul, without leaving the place and the instant where the body to which it is united is situated, can cross the totality of space and time and come into the very presence of God.

It is at the intersection of creation and its Creator. This point of intersection is the point of intersection of the arms of the Cross.

Saint Paul was perhaps thinking about things of this kind when he said: "That ye, being rooted and grounded in love, may be able to comprehend with all saints what is the breadth, and length, and depth, and height; and to know the love of Christ, which passeth knowledge" [Eph. 3:17–19].

8

Inquiring after God by Repentance and Forgiveness

The duplex theme of repentance and forgiveness runs throughout this book. Here it is the central focus. The classic text for this chapter, from the *Dialogue* of Caterina di Giacomo di Benincasa, St. Catherine of Siena (1347–80), sees repentance and forgiveness as essential to Christian faithfulness and life. Catherine was an extraordinary woman. She was a spiritual director, a theologian, a social activist, a political activist, and a Church reformer, whose voluminous correspondence testifies to her conviction that Christian faithfulness, while it requires solitude and prayer, inevitably carries one into the world of politics. Her extraordinary piety and care for the poor as well as the powerful attracted a band of followers during her life, and her theological work is designed to lead both individuals and the Church to holiness. She lived at a time of political division and crisis in the Church and worked hard to reunite it, based on her spiritual and theological vision. She was canonized in 1461 and declared a Doctor of the Church in 1970.

Catherine's major theological work is written neither as a treatise nor as a systematically ordered set of questions and answers as was customary in her day. Rather it took the form of a dialogue between herself, presented as a "soul," and God, through what she believed God would say to her in response to her concerns. There is also a narrator (indicated in the text by italics) who provides the readers with a window into Catherine's own thinking. It is a rather sophisticated format, for she is both baring her soul and inviting others into a deeper spiritual life following her lead. This was her way of correcting the corruption and abuse of the Church and its members by its ministers. In an age when women had no voice in the Church, Catherine dared to lift her own against the vices of her age, not because she believed she was right but because she was being obedient to the lifelong dialogue with God that she entertained through prayer. Like many before her, Catherine pleaded for the reform of the Church almost two hundred years before Martin Luther sparked the Protestant Reformation. Her vision of clerical reform was taken up by the Catholic Reformation in the latter half of the sixteenth century.

Catherine gives us a general picture of late medieval theology in the west. She finds her identity in being created in God's image, an image that was lost through sin but restored through the Incarnation, God's becoming one of us. People are redeemed by the Incarnation and death of Christ once and for all. Although they are in the image of God, people are born wounded by original sin. This wound is healed by baptism into Christ when one receives the power of the Holy Spirit, leaving only a scar. Redemption reclaims the freedom of the will to resist evil. Seeing the redemption in Christ and God's grace and love arouses a yearning and love for God and the desire and freedom to serve him only.

Although all Christians have regained the freedom to love and serve God, many turn back to evil ways, even though God's mercy and goodness toward them is evident for all to see. Thus, Catherine divides Christians into two groups: true servants of God and those who ought to serve God but do not yet, especially the clergy. God is very angry at the latter, and Catherine, herself a true servant of God, is deeply grieved and embarrassed by those ministers who were so selfish that they failed to lead the Church properly.

In this circumstance, however, she does not succumb to righteous indignation or despair. Rather, she sets to work. Perhaps this is the reason she was such a valiant fighter, traveling long distances under dangerous conditions to plead with the break-away segment of the Church in France to reunite with Rome, and for warring city-states to make peace. While she used outward forms of political intervention, the theological power behind her political activity is disclosed in the *Dialogue*. Here she presents the idea that Jesus Christ is the bridge between God and ourselves. We climb up his body, beginning at his feet. In Catherine's able hands the Christian teaching that God became human in the Incarnation becomes something that one can taste, touch, and smell. For in the Eucharist believers eat, drink, and are strengthened by this very bridge.

This moving theology was written in the midst of a time of widespread misunder-standing and misuse of the faith for personal gain. Catherine's work both urges clerics to repent of their selfishness and offers a plan of action for the simple faithful, embodied by her own disciples. The prayers, tears, and sweat of faithful servants constitute a powerful rebuke to corrupt ministers, and this in two ways. First, seeing the tears and hearing the prayers of the faithful God controls his anger at the corrupt ministers of the Church, giving the pious a chance to bring the sinners to account. The faithful laity sustain the reconciling work of Christ by their holiness. Holiness is not withdrawal from political activity but an instance of it. Nor is it a means to one's own salvation, for that has already been assured by Christ's Incarnation and death. Catherine believes that God prefers not the death but the return of the wicked. And it is the faithful who are the instruments of that return. Therefore, by going to work to purify the Church they still God's wrath. Prayer and piety both serve one's neighbor and purify the Church.

Catherine has turned the hierarchical structure of the Church on its head with her startling insight that corruption in the Church is eradicated by obeying Jesus' command to love one's enemies (or, in this case God's enemies) and praying for God's persecutors who lead the Church! The real power here is in the hands of the laity. And so she urges her disciples to continue to receive the sacraments at the hands of corrupt ministers. In an ironic twist, the pious laity are strengthened in their resolve to entreat God to bring the guilty to their knees by being fed the body and blood of the Lord by those very same corrupt ministers.

The second way that a holy life serves others is by example. Surely Catherine's disciples shame the priest-nobles by showing them the life they ought to be living. In Catherine's day, for women and the laity to show themselves more faithful than the ministers of the Church was indeed chastisement. In short, to tend the garden of one's own spiritual life is to tend to the spiritual purity of the whole body of Christ. A powerful way to reform the Church, she teaches, is by being faithful to God. The weak redeem the strong. Or rather, the "weak" are the "strong" and the "strong" are the "weak". Of course, Catherine's political activism demonstrates that the reform of the Church also required organizing and strategizing. But here again, as we have seen before, the spiritual and the political are never separated from each other.

Dean Gregory Jones's essay in this chapter locates Catherine's theology and piety within the great tradition of Christian spirituality that traces back to St. Augustine. Jones relies on the spiritual writings of Bernard of Clairvaux (1090–1153), who portrays the spiritual life as a journey into friendship and intimacy with God that cleanses the self of its impure orientation and desires and transforms it. St. Bernard was a great spiritual master who taught his students how to love God. He taught that the Christian walk is a lifelong discipline of moving from obeying God simply out of duty or fear of punishment to joyfully loving God for his own sake, not because of an ulterior gain for ourselves. To teach this he preached from the Bible's book of love, the Song of Songs. The spiritual or mystical life is growth in maturity and inner strength by coming to love God primarily.

Practicing disciplined Christian righteousness is a long and slow process of unlearning and learning. It depends upon repentance and forgiveness and the cultivation of gentleness, patience, humility, and vigilance in letting go of the ways of distorted desire and practicing the ways of desire ordered toward God. This journey is not taken outside of God, but by "locating ourselves in the fountain of God's love" as well as by cultivating these skills by practicing them with our neighbors. So, God is at once the means and the end of disciplined Christian spirituality.

In addition to diligently reorienting one's inner life it is essential to have companions who also acknowledge the need for friendship with God. The Church's rites are also markers that carry the seeker forward. Here the power of the ancient Church's rites of initiation are highlighted. In North Africa it took up to two years to be trained and prepared for membership in the body of Christ, the completion of which was greeted with great celebration. The process was slow yet dramatic because the transition from being a pagan to being a Christian was nothing less than the transformation of one's whole identity.

On a Catholic view, inquiring after God by practicing repentance and forgiveness enables one to understand God better. And when we do we love him more, and when we love God more we become more like him.

St. Catherine of Siena, *Dialogue*

Then the soul was restless and aflame with tremendous desire because of the unspeakable love she had conceived in God's great goodness when she had come to see and know the expanse of his charity. How tenderly he had deigned to answer her petition and give her hope in her bitterness – bitterness over God's being offended and holy Church's being ravaged, and bitterness over her own wretchedness, which she saw through knowledge of herself! Her bitterness was softened and at the same time grew, for the supreme eternal Father, now that he had shown her the way of perfection, was showing her in a new light how he was being offended and souls were being harmed.

As the soul comes to know herself she also knows God better, for she sees how good he has been to her. In the gentle mirror of God she sees her own dignity: that through no merit of hers but by his creation she is the image of God. And in the mirror of God's goodness she sees as well her own unworthiness, the work of her own sin. For just as you can better see the blemish on your face when you look at yourself in a mirror, so the soul who in true self-knowledge rises up with desire to look at herself in the gentle mirror of God with the eye of understanding sees all the more clearly her own defects because of the purity she sees in him [cf. 1 John 3:2 and Jas. 1:24].

Now as light and knowledge grew more intense in this soul, a sweet bitterness was both heightened and mellowed. The hope that first Truth had given her mellowed it. But as a flame burns higher the more fuel is fed it, the fire in this soul grew so great that her body could not have contained it. She could not, in fact, have survived had she not been encircled by the strength of him who is strength itself.

Thus cleansed by the fire of divine charity, which she had found in coming to know herself and God, and more hungry than ever in her hope for the salvation of the whole world and the reform of holy Church, she stood up with confidence in the presence of the supreme Father. She showed him the leprosy of holy Church and the wretchedness of the world, speaking to him as with the words of Moses [see Exod. 32:11]:

... For what would it mean to me to have eternal life if death were the lot of your people, or if my faults especially and those of your other creatures should bring darkness upon your bride, who is light itself? It is my will, then, and I beg it as a favor, that you have mercy on your people with the same eternal love that led you to create us in your image and likeness. You said, "Let us make humankind in our image and likeness" [Gen. 1:26]. And this you did, eternal Trinity, willing that we should share all that you are, high eternal Trinity! You, eternal Father, gave us memory to hold your gifts and share your power. You gave us understanding so that, seeing your goodness, we might share the wisdom of your only-begotten Son. And you gave us free will to love what our understanding sees and knows of your truth, and so share the mercy of your Holy Spirit.

Why did you so dignify us? With unimaginable love you looked upon your creatures within your very self, and you fell in love with us. So it was love that made you create us and give us being just so that we might taste your supreme eternal good.

Then I see how by our sin we lost the dignity you had given us. Rebels that we were, we declared war on your mercy and became your enemies. But stirred by the same fire that made you create us, you decided to give this warring human race a way to reconciliation, bringing great peace out of our war. So you gave us your only-begotten Son, your Word, to be mediator between us and you. He became our justice [see 1 Cor. 1:30] taking on himself the punishment for our injustices. He offered you the obedience you required of him in clothing him with our humanity, eternal Father, taking on our likeness and our human nature!

O depth of love! What heart could keep from breaking at the sight of your greatness descending to the lowliness of our humanity? We are your image, and now by making yourself one with us you have become our image, veiling your eternal divinity in the wretched cloud and dung heap of Adam. And why? For love! You, God, became human and we have been made divine! In the name of this unspeakable love, then, I beg you – I would force you even! – to have mercy on your creatures.

God let himself be forced by her tears and chained by her holy desire. And turning to her with a glance at once full of mercy and of sadness he said:

Dearest daughter, because your tears are joined to my charity and are shed for love of me, your weeping has power over me and the pain in your desire binds me like a chain. But look how my bride has disfigured her face! She is leprous with impurity and selfishness. Her breasts are swollen because of the pride and avarice of those who feed there: the universal body of Christianity and the mystic body of holy Church. I am speaking of my ministers who feed at her breasts. They ought not only to feed themselves, but hold to those breasts the whole body of Christianity as well as whoever would rise from the darkness of unbelief and be bound into the body of my Church.

Do you see how ignorantly and blindly they serve out the marvelous milk and blood of this bride – how thanklessly and with what filthy hands? And do you see with what presumption and lack of reverence it is received? And so the precious life-giving blood of my only-begotten Son, which dispelled death and darkness, confounded falsehood, and brought the gift of light and truth, all too often, because of their sinfulness, brings them death instead.

For those who are receptive this blood bestowed and accomplished all that they need to be saved and made perfect. But since its gift of life and grace is in proportion to the soul's readiness and desire, it deals death to the wicked. So it gives death rather than life to those who receive it unworthily, in the darkness of deadly sin. The fault for this is not in the blood. Nor does it lie in the ministers. The latter may be just as evil or worse, but their sin cannot spoil or contaminate the blood or lessen its grace and power, nor can it harm those they serve. They are, however, bringing on themselves the evil of sin, which will certainly be punished unless they set themselves right through true contrition and contempt for sin. . . .

This is why I gave the Word, my only-begotten Son. The clay of humankind was spoiled by the sin of the first man, Adam, and so all of you, as vessels made from that clay, were spoiled and unfit to hold eternal life. So to undo the corruption and death of humankind and to bring you back to the grace you had lost through sin, I, exaltedness, united myself with the baseness of your humanity [see Gal. 4:4–5; 1 John 4:9]. For my divine justice demanded suffering in atonement for sin. But I cannot suffer. And you, being only human, cannot make adequate atonement. Even if you did atone for some particular thing, you still could make atonement only for yourself and not for others. But for this sin you could not make full atonement either for yourself or for others since it was committed against me, and I am infinite Goodness.

Yet I really wanted to restore you, incapable as you were of making atonement for yourself. And because you were so utterly handicapped, I sent the Word, my Son; I clothed him with the same nature as yours – the spoiled clay of Adam – so that he could suffer in that same nature which had sinned, and by suffering in his body even to the extent of the shameful death of the cross he would placate my anger.

And so I satisfied both my justice and my divine mercy. For my mercy wanted to atone for your sin and make you fit to receive the good for which I had created you. Humanity, when united with divinity, was able to make atonement for the whole human race – not simply through suffering in its finite nature, that is, in the clay of Adam, but by virtue of the eternal divinity, the infinite divine nature. In the union of those two natures I received and accepted the sacrifice of my only-begotten Son's blood, steeped and kneaded with his divinity into the one bread, which the heat of my divine love held nailed to the cross. Thus was human nature enabled to atone for its sin only by virtue of the divine nature. . . .

Only the scar remains of that original sin as you contract it from your father and mother when you are conceived by them. And even this scar is lifted from the soul – though not completely – in holy baptism, for baptism has power to communicate the life of grace in virtue of this glorious and precious blood. As soon as the soul has received holy baptism, original sin is taken from her and grace is poured in. The inclination to sin, which is the trace that remains from original sin, is a weakness as I have said, but the soul can keep it in check if she will. . . .

But such is the freedom of your humanity, and so strong have you been made by the power of this glorious blood, that neither the devil nor any other creature can force you to the least sin unless you want it. You were freed from slavery so that you might be in control of your own powers and reach the end you were created for. How wretched you would be, then, to wallow in the mud like an animal, ignoring the great gift I had given you! A miserable creature full of such foolishness could not receive more.

I want you to understand this, my daughter: I created humankind anew in the blood of my only-begotten Son and reestablished them in grace, but they have so scorned the graces I gave them and still give them! They go from bad to worse, from sin to sin, constantly repaying me with insults. And they not only fail to recognize my graces for what they are, but sometimes even think I am abusing them – I who want nothing but their sanctification! I tell you it will go harder for them in view of the grace they have received, and they will be deserving of greater punishment. They will be more severely punished now that they have been redeemed by my Son's blood than they would have been before that redemption, before the scar of Adam's sin was removed [see John 15:22]. . . .

So sin is punished far more severely after people have been redeemed by the blood than before. For they have received more, but they seem to ignore it and to take no notice of their evil deeds. Though I once reconciled them to myself through the blood of my Son, they have become my enemies.

But I have one remedy to calm my wrath: my servants who care enough to press me with their tears and bind me with the chain of their desire. You see, you have bound me with that chain – and I myself gave you that chain because I wanted to be merciful to the world. I put into my servants a hunger and longing for my honor and the salvation of souls so that I might be forced by their tears to soften the fury of my divine justice.

Bring, then, your tears and your sweat, you and my other servants. Draw them from the fountain of my divine love and use them to wash the face of my bride. I promise you that thus her beauty will be restored. Not by the sword or by war or by violence will she regain her beauty, but through peace and through the constant and humble prayers and sweat and tears poured out by my servants with eager desire.

And so I will fulfill your desire by giving you much to suffer, and your patience will spread light into the darkness in all the world's evil. Do not be afraid: Though the world may persecute you, I am at your side and never will my providence fail you [see Isa. 43:1–5; John 16:33].

Then that soul stood before the divine majesty deeply joyful and strengthened in her new knowledge. What hope she had found in the divine mercy! What unspeakable love she had experienced! For she had seen how God, in his love and his desire to be merciful to humankind in spite of their enmity toward him, had given his servants a way to force his goodness and calm his wrath. So she was glad and fearless in the face of the world's persecution, knowing that God was on her side. And the fire of her holy longing grew so strong that she would not rest there, but with holy confidence made her plea for the whole world.

In her second petition she had concerned herself with the good that both Christians and unbelievers would reap from the reform of holy Church. But as if that were not enough, she now stretched out her prayer, like one starved, to the whole world, and as if he himself were making her ask it, she cried out:

Have mercy, eternal God, on your little sheep, good shepherd that you are! Do not delay with your mercy for the world, for already it almost seems they can no longer survive! Everyone seems bereft of any oneness in charity with you, eternal Truth, or even with each other: I mean, whatever love they have for each other has no grounding in you. . . .

So in obedience to the most high Father, she raised her eyes, and she saw within his closed fist the entire world. And God said:

My daughter, see now and know that no one can be taken away from me [see John 10:28]. Everyone is here as I said, either in justice or mercy. They are mine; I created them, and I love them ineffably. And so, in spite of their wickedness, I will be merciful to them because of my servants, and I will grant what you have asked of me with such love and sorrow.

The fire within that soul blazed higher and she was beside herself as if drunk, at once gloriously happy and grief-stricken. She was happy in her union with God, wholly submerged in his mercy and savoring his vast goodness; but to see such goodness offended brought her grief. She knew, though, that God had shown her his creatures' sinfulness to rouse her to intensify her concern and longing. And so she offered thanks to the divine majesty.

As she felt her emotions so renewed in the eternal Godhead, the force of her spirit made her body break into a sweat. (For her union with God was more intimate than was the union between her soul and her body.) The holy fire of love grew so fierce within her that its heat made her sweat water, but it was not enough. She longed to see her body sweat blood, so she said to herself:

Alas, my soul! You have frittered your whole life away, and for this have all these great and small evils come upon the world and holy Church! So I want you to heal them now with a sweat of blood.

Indeed, this soul remembered well what Truth had taught her: that she should always know herself and God's goodness at work in her, and that the medicine by which he willed to heal the whole world and to soothe his wrath and divine justice was humble, constant, holy prayer. So, spurred on by holy desire, she roused herself even more to open the eye of her understanding. She gazed into divine charity and there she saw and tasted how bound we are to love and seek the glory and praise of God's name through the salvation of souls. She saw that God's servants are called to this – and in particular eternal Truth had called and chosen her spiritual father,* whom she brought before the divine goodness, asking God to light within him a lamp of grace by which he might in truth pursue this Truth.

Then, in answer to her third petition, which came from her hunger for her [spiritual] father's good, God said:

Daughter, this is what I want: that he seek to please me, Truth, by his deep hunger and concern for the salvation of souls. But neither he nor anyone else can achieve this without accepting whatever sufferings I grant.

As much as you long to see me honored in holy Church, just so much must you conceive the love it takes to suffer willingly and with true patience. By this will I know that he and you and my other servants are seeking my honor in truth. Then will he be my very dear son, and he will rest, along with the others, on the breast of my only-begotten Son. And I will make of my Son a bridge by which you can all reach your goal and there receive the fruit of all the labors you have borne for my love. So carry on courageously!

I told you that I have made a bridge of the Word, my only-begotten Son, and such is the truth. I want you to realize, my children, that by Adam's sinful disobedience the road was so broken up that no one could reach everlasting life. Since they had no share in the good for which I had created them, they did not give me the return of glory they owed me, and so my truth was not fulfilled. What is this truth? That I had created them in my image and likeness so that they might have eternal life, sharing in my being and enjoying my supreme eternal tenderness and goodness. But because of

---

* The reference is to Raymond of Capua, Catherine's spiritual director and biographer.

their sin they never reached this goal and never fulfilled my truth, for sin closed heaven and the door of my mercy. . . .

But I wanted to undo these great troubles of yours. So I gave you a bridge, my Son, so that you could cross over the river, the stormy sea of this darksome life, without being drowned. . . .

But first I want you to look at the bridge of my only-begotten Son, and notice its greatness. Look! It stretches from heaven to earth, joining the earth of your humanity with the greatness of the Godhead. This is what I mean when I say it stretches from heaven to earth – through my union with humanity.

This was necessary if I wanted to remake the road that had been broken up, so that you might pass over the bitterness of the world and reach life. From earth alone I could not have made it great enough to cross the river and bring you to eternal life. The earth of human nature by itself, as I have told you, was incapable of atoning for sin and draining off the pus from Adam's sin, for that stinking pus had infected the whole human race. Your nature had to be joined with the height of mine, the eternal Godhead, before it could make atonement for all of humanity. Then human nature could endure the suffering, and the divine nature, joined with that humanity, would accept my Son's sacrifice on your behalf to release you from death and give you life.

So the height stooped to the earth of your humanity, bridging the chasm between us and rebuilding the road. And why should he have made of himself a roadway? So that you might in truth come to the same joy as the angels. But my Son's having made of himself a bridge for you could not bring you to life unless you make your way along that bridge.

Here the eternal Truth was showing that, although he had created us without our help, he will not save us without our help. He wants us to set our wills with full freedom to spending our time in true virtue. So he continued:

You must all keep to this bridge, seeking the glory and praise of my name through the salvation of souls, bearing up under pain and weariness, following in the footsteps of this gentle loving Word. There is no other way you can come to me [see John 14:6].

You are the workers I have hired for the vineyard of holy Church [see Matt. 20:1–6]. When I gave you the light of holy baptism I sent you by my grace to work in the universal body of Christianity. You received your baptism within the mystic body of holy Church by the hands of my ministers, and these ministers I have sent to work with you. You are to work in the universal body. They, however, have been placed within the mystic body to shepherd your souls by administering the blood to you through the sacraments you receive from them, and by rooting out from you the thorns of deadly sin and planting grace within you. They are my workers in the vineyard of your souls, ambassadors for the vineyard of holy Church.

Each of you has your own vineyard, your soul, in which your free will is the appointed worker during this life. Once the time of your life has passed, your will can work neither for good nor for evil; but while you live it can till the vineyard of your soul where I have placed it. This tiller of your soul has been given such power that neither the devil nor any other creature can steal it without the will's consent, for in holy baptism the will was armed with a knife that is love of virtue and hatred of sin. This love and hatred are to be found in the blood. For my only-begotten Son gave his blood for you in death out of love for you and hatred for sin, and through that blood you receive life in holy baptism. . . .

So if you would receive the fruit of this blood, you must first rouse yourself to heartfelt contrition, contempt for sin, and love for virtue. . . .

Therefore, if you do not produce the fruit of good and holy deeds you will be cut off from this vine and you will dry up. For those who are cut off from this vine lose the life of grace and are thrown into the eternal fire, just as a branch that fails to bear fruit is cut off the vine and thrown into the fire, since it is good for nothing else [see John 15:6]. So those who are cut off because of their offenses, if they die still guilty of deadly sin, will be thrown into the fire that lasts forever, for they are good for nothing else. . . .

But that is not how my servants act, and you should be like them, joined and engrafted to this vine. Then you will produce much fruit, because you will share the vital sap of the vine. And being in the Word, my Son, you will be in me, for I am one with him and he with me [see John 10:30]. If you are in him you will follow his teaching, and if you follow his teaching you will share in the very being of this Word – that is, you will share in the eternal Godhead made one with humanity, whence you will draw that divine love which inebriates the soul. All this I mean when I say that you will share in the very substance of the vine.

Do you know what course I follow, once my servants have completely given themselves to the teaching of the gentle loving Word? I prune them, so that they will bear much fruit – cultivated fruit, not wild [see Isa. 5:1–4]. Just as the gardener prunes the branch that is joined to the vine so that it will yield more and better wine, but cuts off and throws into the fire the branch that is barren, so do I the true gardener act. When my servants remain united to me I prune them with great suffering so that they will bear more and better fruit, and virtue will be proved in them. But those who bear no fruit are cut off and thrown into the fire.

These are the true workers. They till their souls well, uprooting every selfish love, cultivating the soil of their love in me. They feed and tend the growth of the seed of grace that they received in holy baptism. And as they till their own vineyards, so they till their neighbors' as well, for they cannot do the one without the other. You already know that every evil as well as every good is done by means of your neighbors. . . .

Keep in mind that each of you has your own vineyard. But every one is joined to your neighbors' vineyards without any dividing lines. They are so joined together, in fact, that you cannot do good or evil for yourself without doing the same for your neighbors.

All of you together make up one common vineyard, the whole Christian assembly, and you are all united in the vineyard of the mystic body of holy Church from which you draw your life. In this vineyard is planted the vine, which is my only-begotten Son, into whom you must be engrafted [see Rom. 11:17–24]. Unless you are engrafted into him you are rebels against holy Church, like members that are cut off from the body and rot.

It is true that while you have time you can get yourselves out of the stench of sin through true repentance and recourse to my ministers. They are the workers who have the keys to the wine cellar, that is, the blood poured forth from this vine. (And this blood is so perfect in itself that you cannot be deprived of its benefits through any fault in the minister.)

It is charity that binds you to true humility – the humility that is found in knowing yourself and me. See, then, that it is as workers that I have sent you all. And now I am calling you again, because the world is failing fast. The thorns have so multiplied and have choked the seed so badly that it will produce no fruit of grace at all.

I want you, therefore, to be true workers. With deep concern help to till the souls in the mystic body of holy Church. I am calling you to this because I want to be merciful to the world as you have so earnestly begged me.

And the soul, restless in her great love, answered:

O immeasurably tender love! Who would not be set afire with such love? What heart could keep from breaking? You, deep well of charity, it seems you are so madly in love with your creatures that you could not live without us! Yet you are our God, and have no need of us. Your greatness is no greater for our well-being, nor are you harmed by any harm that comes to us, for you are supreme eternal Goodness. What could move you to such mercy? Neither duty nor any need you have of us (we are sinful and wicked debtors!) – but only love! . . .

CONTEMPORARY REFLECTION

A Fire of Holy Longing

L. Gregory Jones

Many modern people are interested in matters of spirituality; comparatively few, however, are as interested in inquiring after the God of Jesus Christ. We are interested in spiritual searches because they help us get in touch with a realm beyond ourselves. However, too often we want to do so on our own terms, even if such searches are ultimately unsatisfying and leave us continually waiting for, and vulnerable to, another spiritual fad or technique.

We find it difficult genuinely to inquire after the God of Jesus Christ, even if such inquiry proves to enable our restless hearts to find their rest in the truth of God's gracious love. We find it difficult because it is costly, requiring us to engage in activities of repentance and forgiveness. Why? Because otherwise we are tempted, even in matters of "spirituality," to become devoted to false gods and distorted desires. We are tempted to endorse "feel-good" spiritualities that do not challenge us in our propensities for self-indulgent fantasies and distorted, individualistic desires.

Through repentance and forgiveness, conjoined to other practices such as prayer, we cultivate disciplines that cleanse our lives and enable us to understand and love God more truthfully. God confronts us with the recognition that, in the midst of our sinful desires, we would rather *not* know the truth – about ourselves, about God, about the world around us. But the assurance of God's grace, learned through practices of repentance and forgiveness, enables us both to learn the truth and, eventually, to learn to love the truth.

We can discover a great deal about what it means to inquire after God through repenting and forgiving by reflecting on the works of our forebears, particularly saints such as Catherine of Siena and Bernard of Clairvaux, and activities such as the ancient church's baptismal catechumenate. They help us understand how our self-knowledge is linked to truthful knowledge of God, and how God's forgiving grace shapes us into people who learn to desire holiness. We will do so in three steps: first, by reflecting on *why* repentance and forgiveness are necessary to inquiring after God; second, by exploring *how* repentance and forgiveness make a difference; and third, by displaying how practices of the baptismal catechumenate initiate people into life with God and with others in Christian community shaped by repentance and forgiveness.

Authentic Self-Knowledge

St. Catherine of Siena's *Dialogue* begins with a powerful vision of a prayerful person's relationship with God. She writes:

> A soul rises up, restless with tremendous desire for God's honor and the salvation of souls. She has for some time exercised herself in virtue and has become accustomed to dwelling in the cell of self-knowledge in order to know better God's goodness toward her, since upon knowledge follows love. And loving, she seeks to pursue truth and clothe herself in it.
>
> But there is no way she can so savor and be enlightened by this truth as in continual humble prayer, grounded in the knowledge of herself and of God. For by such prayer the soul is united with God, following in the footsteps of Christ crucified, and through desire and affection and the union of love he makes of her another himself. So Christ seems to have meant when he said, "If you will love me and keep my word, I will show myself to you, and you will be one thing with me and I with you." And we find similar words in other places from which we can see it is the truth that by love's affection the soul becomes another himself.[1]

Catherine sees the transformative relationship that occurs when one is inclined both to be enlightened by the truth and to savor it in friendship. But she also recognizes that such enlightenment does not occur apart from repentance and forgiveness, the kind of humble prayer by which people come to knowledge of themselves and of God.

Yet, we might wonder, why should this be so? Why should we both desire such a union between love and knowledge of God *and* find ourselves incapable of fulfilling such desire apart from activities of repentance and forgiveness? We see the dynamics of this desire quite clearly in Bernard of Clairvaux's series of sermons on the Song of Songs.

Bernard aims in his sermons to show people how to seek the One by whom they are themselves sought. As he describes it in another work, the *De diligendo Deo*: "No one has the strength to seek you unless he has first already found you. For it is a fact that you will to be found in order that you may be sought and you will to be sought in order that you may be found. It is possible, therefore, to seek you and to find you, but it is not possible to anticipate you."[2] This seeking and being sought is shaped by Bernard's understanding of the natural human desire for God. We have such natural desire because human beings are created in the divine image. Our inquiring after God, then, is already shaped by God's gift in creation. Human desire describes that longing, that thirst, for God which God's grace has already instilled in human hearts – and which remains unfulfilled except through friendship with God. There can be no knowledge of ourselves apart from knowledge of God.

Unfortunately, however, the effects of sin and evil have led human beings to wrong desires and to failures in knowledge – particularly failures in self-knowledge. Fundamentally, we human beings are tempted to mistake our present condition in the world with the purpose for which we were created. So it is that, for Bernard, authentic self-knowledge begins with a sober acknowledgment of how "unlike" God we have become as a result of human sin and evil. Bernard writes:

> There must be no dissimulation, no attempt at self-deception, but a facing up to one's real self without flinching and turning aside. When a [person] thus takes stock of himself in the clear light of truth, he will discover that he lives in a region where likeness to God has been forfeited, and groaning from the depths of a misery to which he can no longer remain blind, will he not cry out to the Lord as the Prophet did: "In your truth you have humbled me"?[3]

It is in this light that our desire for God is awakened and renewed in the acknowledgment of the ways in which our desires have been distorted, our quests for knowledge corrupted by self-deception, and our lives damaged by the sin and evil we have done and had done to us. If our acknowledgment of our life in this "region of unlikeness" leads to prayers for forgiveness and renewal, then the love of God will be deepened and growth toward friendship with God – ultimately, for Bernard, toward "spiritual marriage" – will become possible.[4] All of this is initiated and sustained through the gift of God through Jesus Christ, the Word by whom all human beings are created and with whom human beings are destined for spiritual union.

Bernard suggests that the waters of our desire for God are drawn from the well of charity – that charity which is none other than God's self-gift in Jesus Christ and the Spirit. For Bernard, Jesus is the source of all virtues and knowledge (Sermon 13), of wisdom, justice, holiness, and redemption (Sermon 22), of life and fruitfulness (Sermon 48).[5] At the heart of Bernard's account is God's charity, which transforms our desire from selfish acquisitiveness into that self-giving love reflected in the indwelling love of Father, Son, and Spirit. Hence, Christian living involves a journey of learning to know oneself precisely as one who is known by God. This journey of self-knowledge requires awareness both of our absence from God, our "unlikeness," and also of our presence with God, our renewal of the divine image by God's Spirit learned through such practices as prayer and almsgiving. For it is through our self-knowledge of our "unlikeness" from God that self-knowledge becomes a step towards the knowledge of God; as Bernard continues, God "will become visible to you according as his image is being renewed within you. And you, gazing confidently on the glory of the Lord with unveiled face, will be transformed into that same image with ever increasing brightness, by the work of the Spirit of the Lord" (36.6).

Christian spiritual living thus moves on a journey shaped by both the absence and presence of God. Self-knowledge – understood both as awareness of our estrangement from God and, by God's forgiving grace, our delightful knowledge of God – is the context in which we engage in those practices that move us forward in the journey toward spiritual marriage with God. Our awareness of estrangement from God, and of our sense of God's absence, move us to repentance through compunction over sin, recognizing in response to God's gracious love the ways in which it inhibits our friendship with Christ. He describes our self-knowledge of being unlike God as a "sowing in tears." Indeed, Bernard elsewhere characterizes those tears which accompany our compunction over sin and estrangement from God as a "kind of baptism."[6]

Our tears, our good desires, and our good works are the seeds which enable us to "sow righteousness" through engaging in particular practices of Christian living:

> You therefore have sown righteousness for yourself if by means of true self-knowledge you have learned to fear God, to humble yourself, to shed tears, to distribute alms and participate in other works of charity; if you have disciplined your body with fastings and prayers, if you have wearied your heart with acts of penance and heaven with your petitions. This is what it means to sow righteousness. (37.2)

These practices contribute to our knowledge of God, enabling what we sow in tears in relation to our self-knowledge to be reaped in joy in our knowledge of God. That is, we reap the joy associated with awareness of the gift of God's grace, God's charity, the ways in which we are being renewed in the divine image through the workings of the Holy Spirit. In this sense, we are drawn ever closer to God through the delight of loving friendship, a closeness that is nourished through careful attention to, and embodiment of, practices of repentance and forgiveness.

At the same time, however, there is another sense of tears which is not so much attributable to human sin as to the predicament of living in this time between the times. That is, we should mourn as we long for God's kingdom, for the consummation of the lover's desire to be with the beloved, for the time when there will be no more suffering, no more tears, no more injustice. As Bernard puts it, "Why should the absence of Christ not move me to frequent tears and daily groaning? 'O Lord, all that I long for is known to you, my sighing is no secret from you'" (59.4; the internal citation is to Ps. 37:10).

Thus, Christian living set in the context of the desire to know God sees the ongoing need for disciplined practices of righteousness, sees the relations between God's forgiveness and our holiness, sees our tears – both of compunction and of mourning – as means to witness to God more faithfully. As Michael Casey describes Bernard's view, the one who seeks God and possesses a "sober mind" will:

> be circumspect with regard to himself, regretfully recognising his failures; he will strive always to be pleasing to God; and finally, with regard to his neighbours, he will aim to serve and to prove himself useful [see Sermon 57.11]. In other words, vigilance for the coming of the bridegroom is not a passive matter of looking down the road with longing, but it is expressed through attention to the details of evangelical living.[7]

In the same ways that Christian spiritual living involves seeking the One who has already sought us, so also our attentive movements along the journey of encountering both the absence and the presence of God require an active receptivity. We must become aware both of that sense of absence, that lack, by which our desire is awakened and we yearn for a better life on the one hand, and of the presence of God through which we find a response to our yearning on the other. To have only the former would tempt us to despair; but, at least in this world, to have only the latter would tempt us to a false sense of self-sufficiency.

As such, Christian spiritual practices of repentance and forgiveness teach us both to become detached from those features of our world which separate us from God and to cling to the One who alone can satisfy our desire for communion. By this means we will then learn how to love the world in the light of God's love. Unlearning the patterns of disordered desire and then learning rightly to order our affections involves ongoing attention throughout the journey of Christian living; though there is growth in this life, our unlearning and learning await fulfillment in God's kingdom. This is also true of our desire, which in this life knows both surplus and lack. In God's kingdom, according to Bernard, we will discover the desire to know and love God – a desire which will know no lack, which will have no sense of unrest but will find fulfillment in the endless delight of God. The practices of Christian spiritual disciplines constitute the school for this divine pedagogy, teaching us how to find the fulfillment which human beings naturally – but all too often desperately and misguidedly – desire.

At the same time, however, Bernard is acutely aware of the slowness by which human beings typically learn this divine pedagogy. As Bernard sketches it, there is a threefold movement as human beings grow through participation in Christian spiritual disciplines. In the first, human beings respond to grace by acting through will-power and self-restraint, compelling themselves to do what is right. After a period of practice, however, they develop good habits and so learn that external constraints and coercion are less necessary; hence they are learning to act virtuously for virtue's own sake. Finally, in a third movement, they find that good behavior is increasingly easy to practice and delightful in itself.[8] These movements require ongoing practice, and Bernard notes that to act perfectly from delight is a possibility only in the next life.[9]

In this sense, then, Bernard believes that virtuous living is the natural result of cultivating a desire to know God. As he puts it, "God is sought by good works" (75.4). This should not be confused with the infamous idea of "works-righteousness," for Bernard clearly holds that even our natural desire for God is a gift of grace. Virtuous living is found in our active receptivity, the active contemplative living of repentance and forgiveness through which our desires are transformed by the love and knowledge of God as we journey towards friendship with God.

It should be clear that, for Bernard, this journey is neither simple nor easy. It requires disciplined practices to engage God through both the darkness of God's absence and the light of God's presence. Complacency must be avoided, and growth in the knowledge of both God and of the self will require repentance, forgiveness, and the practice of virtue – including, especially, such virtues as patience, gentleness, a "zeal for justice," gratitude, and charity. Further, we should not trust our own judgments; there is a need for friends on the journey, particularly as we turn to others who provide guidance, correction, and support as we seek to unlearn sin and learn to become friends of God. At the same time, Bernard is aware that disciplined practices are necessary also to combat the dangers, temptations, and enemies that will be faced on the journey. Hence, the practice of Christian spiritual living requires us to be both humble and vigilant, drawn forward in the Christian path by the love of God and the forces of memory and hope.[10]

We learn to inquire after God through the repentance which puts our distorted self-knowledge into question, the forgiveness which cleanses us of such distortions, and the holiness by which we learn to offer God what Catherine calls "the fragrance of virtue rooted in truth."[11] But, the question might be asked, how do we go about doing so? If Bernard offers us a rich theological context for understanding *why* we inquire after God through repentance and forgiveness, *how* do we do so?

Locating Oneself in the Fountain of God's Love

We do so, Catherine suggests, by locating our lives in the fountain of God's love. Friendship, the Father tells her,

> is just like a vessel that you fill at the fountain. If you take it out of the fountain to drink, the vessel is soon empty. But if you hold your vessel in the fountain while you drink, it will not get empty. Indeed, it will always be full. So the love of your neighbor, whether spiritual or temporal, is meant to be drunk in me, without any self-interest.[12]

As Catherine elsewhere describes it, the fountain is "the heart of Christ, and the love that we drink in perfect friendship is his blood, the fire of charity, the Holy Spirit of God."[13]

Apart from that fountain, apart from the love which is the fire of charity, the Holy Spirit of God, our lives become empty. By so locating our lives in that fountain – our habits, our practices, and our friendships – we will be continually refreshed and nourished by the joy of Christ, the peace of God. We do this both liturgically, and through our daily activities of repentance and forgiveness of others.

In order to live in the fountain of God's love, we cultivate practices of repentance and forgiveness that shape virtuous holiness. At the most basic level, this emphasis on practices reflects common sense. We know that the habits we develop, or that we instill in children, make a difference – we know they are crucial for learning to play the piano, or learning to become a basketball player. We know that "practice makes perfect." We also know, as did our saintly forebears, that habits and practices of sin are often the most difficult to break.

The underlying point is that, as our lives are fundamentally social, so also must be our salvation. Practices suggest the importance of our being placed in particular social contexts and activities where we can have our lives shaped by the grace of Christ. As Pope John Paul II puts it in his encyclical, *Veritatis Splendor*: "To imitate and live out the love of Christ is not possible for man by his own strength alone. He becomes *capable of this love only by virtue of a gift received.*"[14]

This emphasis on practices in which we receive that which comes as a gift is indispensable for our spiritual lives, for shaping our life in God as holy people. These practices are how we live in the fountain of God's love, for they are oriented toward the passion of Christ. They school us as people of repentance and forgiveness.

That is to say that life in the fountain of God's love, the Christian practices by which we receive God's grace, require our openness to transformation

– in evangelical terms, our openness to ongoing conversion. The fountain in which we are continually nourished is the heart of Christ, the one who calls us away from sin and destruction to follow him. We cannot do so if we think that the purpose of spirituality, or of the Church, is to have my or our needs met. Our focus, so Bernard and Catherine teach us, is to inquire after God through repentance and forgiveness so that we will have "the mind of Christ" (Phil. 2:5).

At some level, we all know that success in any craft requires openness to transformation. Nobody has ever become an excellent pianist or sculptor or golfer who thought they already knew what they needed to know. Learning any craft, especially the craft of discipleship, takes time and involves a willingness to be changed by those who teach us. The fire of divine charity, the working of God's Holy Spirit, is like the refiner's fire: our sin needs to be burned away as we are formed in the beauty of God's love. We need, like David in Psalm 51, to confess our sin and be given a clean heart. Our self-knowledge does not come through navel-gazing spirituality; it comes through being known by God, having our lives penetrated by the divine refiner's fire, and having our desire shaped by Christ's infinite desire for our salvation.

How might we learn to inquire after God through practices of repentance and forgiveness? We can take a clue from ancient practices of baptismal catechesis, practices which are now being recovered through such programs as the Roman Catholic "Rite of Christian Initiation of Adults." These practices emphasize that our learning to inquire after God occurs as we begin a lifelong journey into the power of baptism through repentance and forgiveness.

Preparation for Baptism

At the heart of ancient practices of baptismal catechesis is the conviction that Christian living involves a dramatic journey of conversion, a process of turning – typically over time, and with testing – from one way of life to another. This journey typically moved through four stages, which Thomas Finn summarizes as follows: "(1) a period of preparation that emphasized instruction and testing and involved personal struggle; (2) penultimate preparations for baptism also characterized by instruction, testing, and ritual struggle; (3) baptismal immersion; and (4) post-baptismal "homecoming" celebrations, which included the eucharist."[15]

In this context I can only offer brief descriptions of each of these stages, attempting throughout to highlight some of the salient features of these practices and texts. The first period was when those who had become seriously interested in Christianity would seek basic instruction in the Christian faith. Those whose interest increased were then entered into the catechumenate, signaled by inscription. This included formal questioning concerning the person's intention, making the sign of the cross on the forehead, exorcism, imposition of hands, and consumption of a tiny bit of salt. Being designated as "catechumens" meant that they could be present at worship for scriptural readings and homilies, though they would be dismissed prior to the eucharist in order to preserve the mysteries (hence the designation of the "discipline of secrecy").

During this first period as catechumens, the focus was on instruction and a gradual inclusion into the Christian community. The process typically took two years, as people began to learn the faith and pattern of Christian life through repentance and forgiveness. The "instruction" the catechumens would receive included learning Scripture through study and hearing homilies, *and* reshaping their affections – "educating desire," as some have felicitously termed it – *and* being mentored in actual Christian living.

In addition to "formal" instruction, catechumens were assigned sponsors whose task it was to model Christian living and to apprentice the catechumens during this period of formation. As Augustine proclaimed in one of his sermons, "Christ is announced through Christian friends."[16] As this apprenticeship occurred, it was presumed that the catechumens' patterns of life would exhibit – albeit often slowly and painfully – transformations in their thinking, feeling, and living. The ancient Christian preacher Quodvultdeus chided both catechumens and Christians who wanted to keep in view both the saving scriptural "spectacles" of mystery and miracle and the withering, far-from-scriptural spectacles of theatre, racetrack, and the fights. Becoming a Christian involved repentance, a turning away from some activities in order to turn toward God.[17]

Catechumens who appeared ready for baptism were encouraged to submit their names at the beginning of Lent. Those who did so began the second pivotal stage in their journey.[18] Those who became formally enrolled did so as part of a liturgy in which Psalm 42 would be sung, including the famous words: "As a deer longs for flowing streams, so my soul longs for you, O God. My soul thirsts for God, for the living God. When shall I come and behold the face of God?" (Ps. 42:1–2). This liturgical practice linked the process of enrollment to the catechumens' transformation of desire – to live in communion with the Triune God.

Those who enrolled were identified as *competentes*. The focus of this second period was on prayer, further instruction in Scripture, exorcism, and a strict observance of Lent: no wine, no meat, no baths, no public entertainment, and celibacy within marriage.[19] During this time the homilies in worship focused particularly on moral formation. This theme, which focused on the *competentes*, also had an effect on the congregations more generally. After all, baptismal catechesis served not only to initiate new persons into God's reign, it also could renew the practices of the larger congregation.[20]

More generally, the Lenten period combined for the *competentes* an intensive period of repentance and renunciation with a continuous deepening of their formation in relation to the Triune God. The renunciations entailed both an inward cleansing and an outward mission toward engaging injustice. Often this renunciation of the Devil was linked to the Exodus narrative, identifying the work of the Devil with the Pharaoh, and the people's sins with the Egyptian armies drowned in the Red Sea.[21]

The preacher drew his listeners into the dramatic narrative of God's dealings with God's people. The hearers were invited to see themselves as participants in a grand drama of repentance and forgiveness.

Most significantly for the *competentes*, the renunciation of sin and evil involved both exorcisms and the event known as the "scrutiny," a physical and psychological examination which culminated in the renunciation of the devil and all of his works. Quodvultdeus described the rite as follows:

> From a secret place you were each presented before the entire church, and then with your head bowed, which was proudly upright before, and standing barefoot on goat skin, the scrutiny was performed on you, and while the humble and most noble Christ was invoked, the proud devil was rooted out of you. All of you were humble of demeanor and humbly you pleaded by praying, chanting and saying, "Probe me, Lord, and know my heart" (Ps. 139:3). Then the *competens* says: "I renounce the devil, his pomps, and his angels."[22]

The result of the rite of scrutiny was that, in Augustine's words, the *competentes* were "free from their former master (*immunis*) and healthy (*sanitas*) in body and heart."[23]

As Lent moved toward Holy Week, the *competentes* received instruction in both the Creed and the Lord's Prayer. In North Africa, instruction in the Creed would involve both memorization of the actual words (typically, guided by their sponsors) and instruction concerning their meaning. Part of the reason for memorization was that it helped to preserve the secrecy of the mystery; but, more deeply, Augustine thought that memorizing the Creed would help the *competentes* internalize the truth and the ways of God.[24]

For Augustine, doctrinal clarity is crucial and must be set in the context of Christian living, learned and discerned in the context of other practices. That is, for Augustine there was a reciprocal relation between Christian living and understanding the Creed: "May this belief imbue your hearts and guide you in professing it. On hearing this, believe so that you may understand, so that by putting into practice what you believe you may be able to understand it."[25]

The *competentes* had already been learning to pray, but during the week preceding baptism, instruction in the Lord's Prayer was a particular focus. Augustine's instructions tended to focus most on the petition concerning forgiveness. In part, this is because of its prominence in Matthew's text (6:14–15); but in part it was because he knew that lack of forgiveness was a local vice, and so this petition seemed "especially applicable" to the people. Indeed, Augustine noted in one of his sermons that his people tended to bring their fierce resentments and their desires for revenge to prayer: "Each day, people come, bend their knees, touch the earth with their foreheads, sometimes moistening their faces with tears, and in all this great humility and distress say: 'Lord, avenge me. Kill my enemy.'" Augustine insisted that his listeners recognize that their enemies were also children of God, and told them that, when praying for those enemies, "Let your prayer be against the malice of your enemy; may his malice die, but may he live. . . . If his malice should die, then you would have lost an enemy and gained a friend."[26]

Augustine emphasized that God would forgive them only if they also forgave others. Further, he stressed that the Lord's Prayer offered a "daily baptism" for forgiveness, noting that he too was a sinner who needed the cleansing of forgiveness: "You might ask, 'And you, too?' I [must] answer back: 'Yes, me too!' 'You, reverend bishop – you, a debtor?' 'Yes, I am debtor as you are.' "[27] And Augustine also linked prayer to practice, most typically by linking the importance of forgiveness to justice – specifically, loving the neighbor through sharing material resources. As he put it in a sermon:

> [As for justice,] do as much as you can do, give from what you can muster, do it with joy, and send up your prayer fearlessly. It will have two wings, a double alms. What do I mean, a "double alms"? "Forgive and it will be forgiven you; give and it will be given you." One "almsgiving" is what you do from the heart when you forgive your neighbor his sin. The other "almsgiving" is what you do with your resources – when you hand out bread to the poor. Do both: that your prayer not be grounded because it lacks one wing.[28]

Hence, Augustine closely linked prayer and Christian living.

On Easter morning, the third stage of the journey occurred: the baptismal immersion itself. Finn describes the drama of this event:

> (1) baptismal water was consecrated; (2) the *competentes* processed to the font while chanting the now familiar Ps. 41 (42); (3) they removed their garments (the coarse leather penitential tunic); (4) they responded to a final inquiry into

their faith and firm will as they stood waist-deep in the font; and (5) they were immersed three times in the name of the Father, of the Son, and of the Holy Spirit. When they emerged the bishop imposed his hand on them, anointed their heads with chrism, and traced the sign of the cross on their foreheads, probably also with chrism. The newly-baptized then dressed in white, including a linen head cover. They then received a baptismal candle and the embrace of the congregation.[29]

After the baptisms were completed, the newly baptized received their first eucharist, and a cup of milk and honey. After that service, the newly baptized returned later on Easter morning for a second eucharist (and perhaps in the afternoon for a third). In Augustine's homilies for the whole congregation on Easter morning, he pointed to the newly baptized, noting that they themselves had become the first day of a new creation; they who "were once darkness" were now "light in the Lord" (Eph. 5:8).[30] He called them to live in that light.

With the celebration of these eucharists on Easter Sunday, the newly baptized had moved into the fourth stage of their journeys of conversion. As a part of their "homecoming," the newly baptized received a new name to signify their new life in Christ. Further, their homecoming typically included liturgies and continuing instruction over a period of eight days. For those eight days, they continued to wear white robes and came each day for a celebration of the eucharist, including a homily. The newly baptized were given pride of place in these liturgies, as their white garments testified to the completion of their journey into God's reign. They served as living icons of God's new Creation.

The primary concern of Christian leaders at this point was whether the people would continue to walk in the ways of light after this catechetical journey into baptism had been completed.[31] As Augustine saw it, the only cloud on the horizon was the question of how to keep unstained the inner renovation symbolized by their robes, which they would wear for the last time on the octave day of their baptism: would they also put away what had been accomplished in baptism?[32] Augustine reminded the congregation that the neophytes would continue to need mentoring as they ventured forth into the world without their robes.

Further, Augustine was more worried about the influence unfaithful Christians would have on these neophytes than he was about the effects of pagan society. In the same sermon, he noted: "We know that many who are called 'faithful' live badly and that their mores do not square with the grace they have received; that they praise God with the tongue and blaspheme him with their lives."[33] Augustine also warned the neophytes about specific vices and "thorns" they needed to guard against, including business fraud and usury, drunkenness and luxurious living, lying and gossip, consulting fortune tellers and wearing amulets, fornication and adultery. They needed to learn that practices of repentance and forgiveness are a daily task for all Christians; indeed, the Lord's Prayer is a daily renewal of that baptismal life.

Even amidst the dangers, many of the newly baptized continued along the journey of holiness toward full communion with God. Indeed, by the time the catechumens had passed through the various stages of baptismal catechesis, they not only desired new life in Christ, they had already begun to see transformations occurring in their lives – transformations accomplished by the Holy Spirit, yet not apart from the disciplines and practices the new believers had been initiated into through their catechumenate.

Even so, Augustine did not offer the newly baptized any illusions about life on the far side of baptism. Drawing on the Exodus imagery so common in baptism, he reminded them that while they had crossed the Red Sea, they were not yet in the Promised Land. Desert wanderings still lay ahead of them. Yet Augustine reminded the neophytes that they had been initiated into eschatological living; he pointed to the Octave, the eighth day, as a symbol for the new life in the Kingdom: "Today is a great sacrament, [a sign] for us of unending joy. Today itself will pass away, but the life it symbolizes will not pass away. . . . For this day, the Octave, symbolizes the new life at the world's end."[34] This eighth day, the day of Christ's resurrection, thus focused the neophytes' attention on the destiny – the *telos* – of human life: the unending joy of fellowship in communion with the Triune God. As he called them to keep their "concentration fixed on the eighth day," so he also reminded them of the power and the importance of eschatological living – particularly on behalf of the poor.

Overall, this dramatic journey of baptismal catechesis highlights the centrality of initiation into the spectacular drama of God's creating, redeeming, and consummating work. Finn draws on Quodvultdeus's description of the "new spectacles" of Christian life to describe the process as follows: "Here in Roman Africa at the end of the fourth century and in the early fifth the ritual drama of baptism and its Lenten preparations were the *spectacula christiana* – the new theatre, the new racetrack, and the new boxing ring. It is difficult to overestimate the impact of this long-extended ritual drama on convert and community alike."[35] Through a combination of scriptural preaching and teaching, formal instruction, dramatic ritual, spiritual direction, and apprenticeship in the deeds of holy living, the practices of baptismal catechesis fostered a spectacular vision – and, more importantly, embodiment – of what it means to inquire after God through repentance and forgiveness.

In a time when we are particularly tempted by the appeal of spirituality without discipline, of illusions that our desires and thoughts are already where they should be, we need to reclaim a more truthful vision of the ways in which God calls us to be people of repentance and forgiveness. As ancient forebears have taught us, our lives will be truthful only to the extent that we allow ourselves, our desires, and our thoughts to be questioned by God. Our spiritual lives cannot be divorced either from theological convictions or from social and political realities. The cultivation of desire for God entails holy living and, more specifically, a recurring suspicion of the temptation to grasp for self-interested power. Christian living requires a willingness to inquire after the God of Jesus Christ, an inquiry which shapes us as people of repentance and forgiveness. As such, we learn to live in the fountain of God's love, to have that fire of holy longing for God and God's people which fosters a zeal for justice, awareness of the forces that seek to divide and destroy both oneself and others, and a commitment to having one's own desires and relationships shaped by the self-gift of God in Jesus Christ and the Spirit.

Notes

1 Catherine of Siena, *The Dialogue*, trans. Suzanne Noffke (New York: Paulist Press, 1980), p. 25.
2 Bernard of Clairvaux, *De diligendo Deo* 22, cited in Michael Casey, *A Thirst for God* (Kalamazoo, MI: Cistercian Publications, 1988), p. 85.
3 Bernard of Clairvaux, Sermon 36.5, in *On the Song of Songs II*, trans. Killian Walsh (Kalamazoo, MI: Cistercian Publications, 1976). Further citations to sermons will be to this edition and translation, and will be cited parenthetically in the text.
4 For Bernard, "spiritual marriage" occurs when the soul gives itself wholeheartedly and unreservedly to responding to its experience of the love of God. See Casey, *A Thirst for God*, esp. pp. 191–200.
5 See also Casey, *A Thirst for God*, pp. 54ff., 94.
6 Bernard of Clairvaux, *Sermo in octava Paschae* 1.7, cited in Casey, *A Thirst for God*, p. 126.
7 Casey, *A Thirst for God*, p. 268.
8 See Bernard's comment at the close of Sermon 57 (57.11): "We find a contemplative Mary in those who, co-operating with God's grace over a long period of time, have attained to a better and happier state. By now confident of forgiveness they no longer brood anxiously on the sad memory of their sins, but day and night they meditate on the ways of God with insatiable delight, even at times gazing with unveiled face, in unspeakable joy, on the splendor of the Bridegroom, being transformed into his likeness from splendor to splendor by the Spirit of the Lord."
9 See Bernard, Sermon 23, and the treatise *On Grace and Free Choice*. See Casey, *A Thirst for God*, pp. 245–51.
10 See Casey, *A Thirst for God*, pp. 54–9, with specific citations to various sermons in

which Bernard deals with these themes.

11 Catherine of Siena, *The Dialogue*, p. 47.

12 Ibid., p. 121.

13 Suzanne Noffke, *Catherine of Siena: Vision through a Distant Eye* (Collegeville, MN: Liturgical Press, 1996), p. 36.

14 John Paul II, *Veritatis Splendor* (Vatican City: Liberia Editrice Vaticana, 1993), #22.

15 Thomas M. Finn, *Early Christian Baptism and the Catechumenate* (Collegeville, MN: The Liturgical Press, 1992), p. 3.

16 Augustine, *Tractatus in evangelium Ioannis* 15.33, cited in William Harmless, *Augustine and the Catechumenate* (Collegeville, MN: Liturgical Press, 1995), p. 152.

17 See Thomas M. Finn, "It Happened One Saturday Night: Ritual and Conversion in Augustine's North Africa," *Journal of the American Academy of Religion*, vol. 58, no. 4 (Winter, 1990), p. 591.

18 As the number of people affiliated with Christianity increased, many catechumens would delay baptism for extensive periods. This problem was a status of "nominal" Christianity, neither pagan nor subject to the full expectations of being Christian. In the east, John Chrysostom and Gregory of Nazianzus used both scathing criticism and enticing rhetoric to discourage delays in baptism and to encourage becoming formally enrolled.

19 See Finn, "It Happened One Saturday Night," p. 591.

20 Note Augustine's description that in his sermons he presented a "cross-weave" of doctrine and of moral admonition and that "both were given to catechumens, both to the faithful"; in this way, the "catechumens were instructed," while the "faithful were roused from forgetfulness" (*De fide et operibus*, 7.11, cited in Harmless, *Augustine and the Catechumenate*, p. 156).

21 Augustine, Sermon 213.8, cited in Harmless, *Augustine and the Catechumenate*, p. 282.

22 Quodvultdeus, *Sermo de symbolo* 1.1.4–7, cited in an unpublished typescript of Robert L. Wilken, "Moral Formation in the Early Church," p. 16.

23 Cited in Finn, "It Happened One Saturday Night," p. 597.

24 See Augustine's account of his own recitation of the Creed at his baptism in Book VII of the *Confessions*.

25 Augustine, Sermon 214.10, cited in Harmless, *Augustine and the Catechumenate*, p. 277. Augustine's formulation here has broader implications in his work concerning the importance of authority in relation to reason, an issue particularly pertinent to his arguments with the Manichaeans. It also suggests the importance of "submitting" to participation in disciplined practices as a necessary part of learning to understand what it means to be a Christian.

26 Augustine, Sermons 56.13, 211.6, and 56.14; cited in Harmless, *Augustine and the Catechumenate*, p. 290–1.

27 Augustine, Sermon 56.11, cited in Harmless, *Augustine and the Catechumenate*, p. 293.

28 Augustine, Sermon 58.10, cited in Harmless, *Augustine and the Catechumenate*, p. 292.

29 Finn, "It Happened One Saturday Night," p. 594.

30 See Augustine, Sermons 225 and 226; see Harmless, *Augustine and the Catechumenate*, pp. 313–14.

31 It is important to remember, however, that their journey of conversion would never be fully complete; it would continue as an ongoing process throughout Christian living, as Augustine's reference to the Lord's Prayer as a "daily baptism" signifies.

32 This is the focus of Augustine's sermons 259 and 260. I am indebted to Finn, "It Happened One Saturday Night," p. 594, for this way of phrasing Augustine's concern.

33 Augustine, Sermon 376A.2, cited in Harmless, *Augustine and the Catechumenate*, p. 332. Note also the following passage from John Chrysostom: "I see many after their baptism living more carelessly than the uninitiated, having nothing particular to distinguish them in their way of life. It is, you see for this cause, that neither in the market nor in the Church is it possible to know quickly who is a believer and who an unbeliever; unless one be present at the time of the mystery, and see the one sort dismissed, the others remaining within – whereas they ought to be distinguished *not by their place, but by their way of life*." In *S. Matthaei evangelium*, 4.14, cited in Harmless, *Augustine and the Catechumenate*, p. 74.

34 Augustine, Sermon 259.1–2, cited in Harmless, *Augustine and the Catechumenate*, p. 334.

35 Finn, "It Happened One Saturday Night," p. 595. For a first-hand description of the effect of the baptismal liturgy on a pilgrim visiting Jerusalem, see *Egeria: Diary of a Pilgrimage*, trans. George E. Gingras (New York: Newman Press, 1970).

9

Inquiring after God when Meditating on Scripture

Scripture has always been central to Christian theological inquiry. Perhaps as much as 40 percent of the New Testament is scripture interpretation, that is, reinterpretation of what Christians came to regard as the Old Testament. But the Christians were not the first to do this. The Hebrew Bible or Old Testament itself does this. Because the Hebrew Bible was written and edited over the course of many centuries, different books and authors "talk" to one another across the ages, incorporating earlier texts into later ones or rereading some in light of changed circumstances.

Authors of New Testament writings quoted the Greek translation of the Bible that they had and, like their predecessors, reinterpreted it, only now in light of the teaching and death of Jesus that changed their understanding of God, the people of God, the nature of obedience to God, and proper worship of God. The New Testament is the accumulation of that reflection. Subsequently, Christians took both sets of scripture as their own, but interpreted the Hebrew and Aramaic writings of the Jews by means of the Christian principles followed by the Christian interpreters of scripture in the New Testament.

Most of what would eventually be accepted as Christian scripture was written by the end of the first century. And that meant that Christians of the second, third, and fourth centuries who accepted these writings as authoritative read them through the convictions of their faith within the context in which they lived. This process constitutes the development of Christian scriptural interpretation.

Until the seventeenth century it was assumed that the scriptures were from God and given to human beings to disclose "his" truth and goodness and to guide their lives according to God's instruction. But modernity began to challenge these assumptions. Scripture came to be read as historical documents that reveal little more than the time and place in which they were written and the contended issues of that day. For the past three centuries or more, the Bible has been read like any other literature as well as the revelation of God. Thus, in one sense, biblical scholars have become historians who inquire after the culture or social issues that gave rise to the text rather than theologians who inquire after God.

The interpretive essay in this chapter argues for again taking up theological inquiry as a proper task of biblical interpretation. It contends that the social, historical, and cultural aspects of and issues behind the texts do not exhaust their meaning, for the texts assume that God is real. The biblical documents were written to disclose to readers the God they discuss. To disregard this textual intention is to fail to understand the texts themselves. It carries the concomitant danger of using them for the interpreter's purpose and ignoring the purpose for which they were composed. To fail to take the texts seriously as religious documents is to fail to understand the purpose of reading: to be enlarged, not simply informed.

The chapter undertakes theological meditation both by looking at St. Augustine's interpretation of the First Letter of John, and by listening to the suggestion of one contemporary student of the Bible who seeks to reclaim theological reflection for biblical study. As we have already seen throughout this book, classically, theological reflection occurred in a large variety of genres. Here we have Augustine preaching to his parishioners. There was not then the strict division between first- and second-order reflection that came to be the case in modern theology. But this does not mean that Augustine is not self-conscious about his task as an interpreter of scripture.

While he is eager to draw his listeners' attention to the message that he takes from the well of Johannine literature – that the central Christian teaching is love – he is mindful of the fact that he questions the text, just as modern interpreters do. In the eighth homily he is bothered by a seeming contradiction between the Christian moral norm of love of enemies proclaimed in the Synoptic Gospels, and the seemingly parochial norm of 1 John to love other Christians in the fellowship of the Church. If the central message of the faith is love, and God is love, then God must stretch us beyond our friends into realms that make us uncomfortable.

It could be that Augustine did not grasp that the author of the Epistle was admonishing love of fellow Christians in the context of a deep division in the Church that turned believers against one another, so that the admonition to love one's brother was an admonition to love one's enemy. But it may also be the case that Augustine was quite aware of this fact about the text itself. The problem may not be that Augustine was not bright enough or as informed as a modern biblical historian but that he was calling attention to the issue for another reason.

At the time he wrote these homilies Augustine himself was deeply embroiled in a long and divisive controversy called the Donatist controversy, named after Donatus, the bishop of another North African province of the Church. Donatists upheld a rigorous standard of Christian purity, in which the efficacy of Christian rites depends upon the holiness of the administrator. Augustine opposed the Donatists, arguing that the sacraments are effective even if administered by unworthy ministers because God, not the local minister, is the one who is at work in the sacraments. As we have seen, Catherine of Siena, along with the whole western church, followed Augustine on this.

On the political side of the matter, Augustine went so far as to admit that civil authority might be used to bring the schismatics back into the Christian fold. This decision led to the practice of religious coercion for many centuries to come. Thus, his admonition to love one's enemies as the Christian moral standard reflects not only his awareness that Church struggles may turn brothers and sisters into opponents, but his own spiritual struggle to love those whom he believed were undermining the integrity of the Catholic faith.

As an artful Christian listener to scripture Augustine was drawing out a feature of the text that spoke both to himself and his audience about what God requires of them. It also enabled genuine reflection on the variety of teachings offered by the various authors. Augustine did not have to choose between critical study of scripture and pastoral nurture. He deftly did both at once.

Professor C. Clifton Black apprentices himself to Augustine to be taught of his deftness, to learn how to do theological exegesis that inquires after God through scripture, since modern scholarship often focuses exclusively on historical questions. Black identifies how Augustine goes about his task and discerns that the master is able to "see" three different concerns simultaneously: the text at hand, its place within the larger scope of scripture, and his audience. Augustine's exegetical task is to bring each point of this triangle into conversation with each other point. With that method in hand, Black points to the message the master delivers about his central concern: the Christian teaching on love. The ability to live lovingly divides faithful from unfaithful Christians. Yet, as we saw with Anselm's treatise on God and Aelred's teaching on spiritual friendship, the ability to live lovingly is so difficult that it must be a gift of the Holy Spirit. The Christian task is to be obedient to God's law of love instead of following one's natural inclinations. This gift is honed in worship in the company of other Christians, even though practicing it extends well beyond the church's walls.

Black concludes that Augustine's contribution to biblical scholarship is to aid the listener in conforming his or her own will with God's by arousing one's love for God. But scripture meditation also leads the seeker to know God who is love. Finally, then, properly done, scripture teaches how to love: as God loves.

1 John

[2:18–25] Children, it is the last hour! As you have heard that antichrist is coming, so now many antichrists have come. From this we know that it is the last hour. They went out from us, but they did not belong to us; for if they had belonged to us, they would have remained with us. But by going out they made it plain that none of them belongs to us. But you have been anointed by the Holy One, and all of you have knowledge. I write to you, not because you do not know the truth, but because you know it, and you know that no lie comes from the truth. Who is the liar but the one who denies that Jesus is the Christ? This is the antichrist, the one who denies the Father and the Son. No one who denies the Son has the Father; everyone who confesses the Son has the Father also. Let what you heard from the beginning abide in you. If what you heard from the beginning abides in you, then you will abide in the Son and in the Father. And this is what he has promised us, eternal life.

[4:1–21] Beloved, do not believe every spirit, but test the spirits to see whether they are from God; for many false prophets have gone out into the world. By this you know the Spirit of God: every spirit that confesses that Jesus Christ has come in the flesh is from God, and every spirit that does not confess Jesus is not from God. And this is the spirit of the antichrist, of which you have heard that it is coming; and now it is already in the world. Little children, you are from God, and have conquered them; for the one who is in you is greater than the one who is in the world. They are from the world; therefore what they say is from the world, and the world listens to them. We are from God. Whoever knows God listens to us, and whoever is not from God does not listen to us. From this we know the spirit of truth and the spirit of error.

Beloved, let us love one another, because love is from God; everyone who loves is born of God and knows God. Whoever does not love does not know God, for God is love. God's love was revealed among us in this way: God sent his only Son into the world so that we might live through him. In this is love, not that we loved God but that he loved us and sent his Son to be the atoning sacrifice for our sins. Beloved, since God loved us so much, we also ought to love one another. No one has ever seen God; if we love one another, God lives in us, and his love is perfected in us.

By this we know that we abide in him and he in us, because he has given us of his Spirit. And we have seen and do testify that the Father has sent his Son as the Savior of the world. God abides in those who confess that Jesus is the Son of God, and they abide in God. So we have known and believe the love that God has for us.

God is love, and those who abide in love abide in God, and God abides in them. Love has been perfected among us in this: that we may have boldness on the day of judgment, because as he is, so are we in this world. There is no fear in love, but perfect love casts out fear; for fear has to do with punishment, and whoever fears has not reached perfection in love. We love, because he first loved us. Those who say, "I love God," and hate their brothers or sisters, are liars; for those who do not love a brother or sister whom they have seen, cannot love God whom they have not seen. The commandment we have from him is this: those who love God must love their brothers and sisters also.

St. Augustine of Hippo, *Homilies on the First Epistle of John*

Prologue

... [M]y people, ... [the First Epistle of John] is a book very sweet to every healthy Christian heart that savours the bread of God; and it should be constantly in the mind of God's Holy Church. But I choose [to preach on] it more particularly because what it specially commends to us is charity. The man who has in himself that of which he hears must rejoice at the hearing. To him this reading will be like oil on the flame: if there is matter in him for nourishment, it will be nourished, it will grow and abide. For some, the Epistle should be like flame to firewood; if it was not already burning, the touch of the word may kindle it. In some, then, what is present is to be nourished: in some, what may be lacking is to be kindled; so that we may all rejoice together in one single charity. Where there is charity, there is peace: where there is humility, there is charity. ...

Seventh Homily (on 1 John 4:4–12)

2. "Now ye are children of God, and ye have overcome him." Overcome, that is, the Antichrist; for he had said above: "Every one that dissolveth Jesus Christ, and denies that he is come in the flesh, is not of God." We have explained, as you remember, that all who violate charity deny Jesus Christ's coming in the flesh, because there was no cause but charity for the coming of Jesus. It is that same charity here enjoined upon us, which he himself enjoins in the Gospel: "Greater love can no man have than this, that a man lay down his life for his friends" (John 15:13). By no means could the Son of God lay down his life for us, but by clothing himself with the flesh in which he might die. Therefore whoever violates charity, let his tongue say what it will, by his life denies Christ's coming in the flesh; and that man is Antichrist, wherever he is and into whatever place he has made his way. And to them who are citizens of the home-land after which we sigh, John says: "ye have overcome him." How? "Because greater is he that is in you than he that is in this world." He would not have them ascribe the victory to their own strength, and so be overcome by the presumption of pride; for the devil overcomes every man that he makes proud. So, with intent that they may keep humble, John says, first, "ye have overcome him." That word "overcome" might make any man raise his head, hold himself upright, and look for praise. But be not uplifted, see whose is the victory in you: you have overcome, "because greater is he that is in you than he that is in this world." Be humble, carry your Master, go quietly under your rider. It is good for you that he have the reins, and use them. If you have not him on your back, you may throw up your head and heels, but riderless, it will go ill with you: that freedom will dispatch you to the wild beasts as their prey.

3. "They are of the world: therefore speak they of the world, and the world heareth them." They who speak of the world, you must observe, are they who speak against charity. You have heard the Lord's saying: "If ye forgive men their sins, your heavenly Father also will forgive you your sins; but if ye forgive not, neither will your Father forgive you your sins" (Matt. 6:14–15). There is the sentence of truth: deny it, if it be not the Truth who speaks. If you are a Christian and believe the Christ, he said: "I am the truth" (John 14:6): that sentence is true and fast. Now hear the men that speak of the world: "Are you not to have your revenge? Is he to tell the tale of what he has done to you? No, let him feel that he is dealing with a man!" We hear that sort of thing every day, from those who "speak of the world"; and the world hears them. Such things are said only by those who love the world; and only by those who love the world are they listened to.

You have been told that he who loves the world and is regardless of charity, denies the coming of Jesus in the flesh. What if the Lord himself had so acted in the flesh: if when struck by men's hands, he had been moved to avenge himself; if, hanging on the cross, he had not said: "Father, forgive them, for they know not what they do"? If he, who had the power, would use no threatenings, why should you, that are subject to another's power, go puffing and blowing? He died because he willed to die, and threatened not: are you to threaten, who know not when your death shall be?

4. "We are of God." Let us see why this is so: whether there is any reason but charity. "We are of God: he that knoweth God, heareth us; he that is not of God, heareth us not. Hereby know we the spirit of truth and of error." Because he that hears us, has the spirit of truth, and he that hears us not, has the spirit of error. Now let us see how he counsels us, and let us hear his counsel as given in the spirit of truth: counsel given not to Antichrists, not to lovers of the world, not to the world. . . . Our attention is roused: he that knows God, hearkens, he that knows not, hearkens not; and here lies the discerning of the spirit of truth and of error. Let us see what is to be the counsel, wherein we should hear him. "Beloved, let us love one another." Why? Because this is a man's counsel? "Because love is of God." It is a strong commendation of love, to say that it is of God; but there is more to come, and let us listen with all our ears. "Love," he has said, "is of God; and everyone that loveth is born of God, and knoweth God. He that loveth not, knoweth not God." Why? "For God is love." My brothers, what more could be said? If nothing else were said in praise of love, in all the pages of this Epistle, nothing else whatever in any other page of Scripture, and this were the one and only thing we heard from the voice of God's Spirit – "For God is love" – we should ask for nothing more.

5. See now, that to act contrary to love is to act contrary to God. Let no man say: "When I do not love my brother, I sin against a man;" – note this well – "sin against a man is a small thing, it is only against God I may not sin." How can you not be sinning against God, when you sin against love? "God is love." The words are not mine. If it were I that said, "God is love," any of you might take offence, and say, "What was that? What did he mean, 'God is love'? God has given love, God has granted love." – "Love is of God: God is love." There, my brethren, is God's Scripture before you: this is a canonical Epistle, read in every nation, maintained by universal authority, on which the world itself has been built up. Here you are told by the Spirit of God, "God is love." Now, if you dare, act against God, and refuse to love your brother. . . .

8. . . . When we look at differing actions, we find that charity may cause a man to be fierce, and wickedness to speak smoothly. A boy may be struck by his father, and have fair words from a slave-dealer. Were you to offer a choice between blows and smooth words, who would not choose the fair

213

words and shun the blows? But if you look to the persons from whom they come, it is charity that strikes and wickedness that ingratiates. You see the point we are making, that the actions of men are discerned only according to their root in charity. Many things can be done that look well, yet do not issue from the root of charity. Thorns too have their flowers. Some actions seem harsh or savage, but are performed for our discipline at the dictate of charity. Thus a short and simple precept is given you once for all: Love, and do what you will. Whether you keep silence, keep silence in love; whether you exclaim, exclaim in love; whether you correct, correct in love; whether you forbear, forbear in love. Let love's root be within you, and from that root nothing but good can spring. . . .

10. "No man hath seen God at any time." God is an invisible reality: he is to be sought, not with the eye, but with the heart. If we would see the light of the sun, we must keep clear the bodily eye which is our means of beholding it. So if we would see God, let us cleanse the eye with which God can be seen. And the place of that eye we may learn from the Gospel: "Blessed are the pure in heart, for they shall see God" (Matt. 5:8). Only let not the "desire of the eyes" fashion our thought of God. One may easily imagine for oneself some vast form, or some measureless immensity extended through space, as it might be this light which our eyes can see, increased to the limit and flooding the landscape; or one may picture some old man of venerable aspect. But our thoughts are not to go that way. There is true matter for your thought, if you would see God. "God is love." What outward appearance, what form, what stature, hands or feet, has love? None can say; and yet love has feet, which take us to the Church, love has hands which give to the poor, love has eyes which give intelligence of him who is in need – as the Psalm says: "Blessed is he who bethinks himself of the needy and the poor" (Ps. 41:1). Love has ears, of which the Lord says: "He that hath ears for hearing, let him hear" (Luke 8:8). All these are not members set each in their own place: he that has charity sees the whole at once with the understanding's grasp. Dwell there, and you shall be dwelt in: abide, and there shall be abiding in you. My brothers, one does not love what one cannot see. Why then, when you hear the praise of charity, are you stirred to acclamation and applause? What have I displayed to your eyes? No vivid colors, no gold or silver, no gems of the treasure-house. My own face has not changed in speaking: this body of mine looks as it did when I entered the church, and so do all of you. You hear the praise of charity, and your voices ring out. Certainly there is nothing for you to see. But let that same delight in charity which makes you acclaim it, lead you to hold it fast in your heart. Listen to me, my brothers: here is a great treasure, which I would urge you with all the power that God gives me to win for yourselves. Suppose you were shown some cup, finely wrought and gilded, which charmed your

eye and compelled your admiration, delighting you by the artist's skill, the weight of the silver and the gleam of the metal. Any of you might exclaim: "If only that cup were mine!" The words would be wasted, for you could not make them come true. Or if one were bent upon possessing it, he might meditate the stealing of it out of the owner's house. Now you have heard the praise of charity: if it delights you, take it for your own – no need to commit any robbery, no need to think of the purchase price. It is yours for nothing. Take hold of it, clasp it to yourself: no possession can be sweeter. If it be such to the hearing of it, what must it be in the owning! ...

Eighth Homily (on 1 John 4:12–16)

4. It may have occurred to some of you, since we have been expounding this Epistle of John, to ask why the charity which he so strongly commends is only brotherly love. He speaks of "him that loveth his brother," and of the "commandment given to us that we love one another." Brotherly charity is continually spoken of; but of the charity of God, the charity (that is) whereby we love God, there is not such constant mention – though it is not altogether passed over in silence. On the other hand, there is scarcely a word in the whole Epistle about the love of enemies. In all his urgent preaching and commendation of charity, he does not tell us to love our enemies, only to love our brethren. Yet, just now, in our reading of the Gospel, we heard the text: "If ye love them that love you, what reward have you? Do not the publicans the same?" (Matt. 5:46). How is it then that John the Apostle enjoins brotherly love upon us as the great means toward our perfecting, while our Lord says that it is not enough for us to love our brothers, but that love itself must stretch so far as to reach our enemies? The reaching to enemies does not mean the passing over of brothers. . . . Love for those who are linked to you is much the same as love for yourself. Extend it to such as you do not know, who yet have done no harm to you; and now go further than them, and reach to the love of enemies. That, certainly, is our Lord's command. Why then has John said nothing of loving an enemy?

5. All love, even the love we call carnal . . ., my dear brothers, implies necessarily an element of goodwill towards those who are loved. . . . we should not, indeed we cannot love men in the sense in which a glutton will say, "I love partridges": the object of his love being the killing and eating of them. He says he loves, but the effect for the partridges is to put an end to their existence: he loves their destruction. The love of food can only purport its consumption and our own refreshment. Men are not to be loved as things to be consumed, but in the manner of friendship and goodwill, leading us to do things for the benefit of those we love. And if there is nothing

we can do, goodwill alone is enough for the lover. We should not want there to be unfortunates, so that we may exercise works of mercy. You give bread to the hungry; but it would be better that no one should hunger, and that you should not have to give. You clothe the naked; would that all were so clothed so that there were no need for it! You bury the dead: but we long for that life in which there is no dying. You reconcile men at law with one another: but we long for the everlasting peace of Jerusalem where all quarrels are at an end. All these are the services called out by man's needs. Remove distress, and there will be no place for works of mercy. Works of mercy will cease, but there will be no quenching of the fire of charity. You may have the truest love for a happy man, on whom you have nothing to bestow: such love will have a greater sincerity and a far more unspoilt purity. Once you have bestowed gifts on the unfortunate, you may easily yield to the temptation to exalt yourself over him, to assume superiority over the object of your benefaction. He fell into need, and you supplied him: you feel yourself as the giver to be a bigger man than the receiver of the gift. You should want him to be your equal, that both may be subject to the one on whom no favor can be bestowed.

8. The true Christian will never set himself up over other men. God gave you a place above the beasts, in which you are of more value than they. That is your natural privilege, always to be better than a beast. If you would be better than another man, you will grudge to see him as your equal. You ought to wish all men equal to yourself; and if you have gone beyond another man in wisdom, you should want him too to show himself wise. While he is still backward, he may learn of you: while he is ignorant, he has need of you; and you appear as teacher, he as learner. As teacher, you are the superior; as learner, he is the inferior. Unless you want him to be your equal, you will be for having him always as the learner, and that will make you a grudging teacher. But what sort of teaching will a grudging teacher give? I can only beg of you not to teach your grudgingness. Listen to the apostle's words, which come from the true heart of charity: "I would that all men were such as I myself" (1 Cor. 7:7). See how he wanted all to be his equals; and just because charity made him so desire, he was raised above all. Man has transgressed his proper limit: created higher than the beasts, he has let covetousness carry him away, so that he might be higher than other men. And that is pride.

9. Consider now the works that pride may do: notice how they may resemble or even equal those of charity. Charity feeds the hungry, so does pride: charity, to the praise of God, pride, to the praise of itself. Charity clothes the naked, so does pride; charity fasts, so does pride; charity buries the dead, so does pride. All the good works that are willed and done by charity, may be set in motion by its contrary[,] pride, like horses harnessed to a car. But when charity is the inward driver, pride must give place – pride which is not so much

misgoverning as misgoverned. It goes ill with the man who has pride for his charioteer, for he is sure to be overturned. How can we know or see that it be not pride which governs the good deed? Where is the proof? . . . In the works themselves we can see no difference. I would go further – though it is not I, but Paul, who says it: charity goes to death, a man (that is) who has charity confesses the name of Christ and becomes a martyr, and pride also may do both. . . . "If I give all my goods to the poor, and if I give my body to burn, and have not charity, it profiteth me nothing" (1 Cor. 13:3). So Holy Scripture recalls us from all this outward showing, recalls us from the surface appearance displayed before men, to the inward truth. Come back to your own conscience, and question it: pay heed, not to the visible flowering but to the root beneath the ground. Is covetousness at the root? Then you may have a show of good deeds, but of works truly good there can be none. Is charity at the root? Be easy, for no evil can be the issue. . . . The stroke of charity is more to be welcomed than the alms of pride. Come back, then, my brothers, into the place within, and in whatsoever you do, look for the witness of God. See, as he sees, the intention of your acts. If your heart does not accuse you of acting for the sake of display, it is well, you may be easy. And when you do well, have no fear of another's seeing. Fear only to act so that you may have praise for yourself; let the other see, so that God may have the praise. . . . There are two parties for whose benefit you give alms, two are hungry, the one for bread, the other for righteousness; for it is written, "Blessed are they that hunger and thirst after righteousness, for they shall be filled" (Matt. 5:6). Between these two hungering ones, you are set for the working of good: if charity is the worker, it has compassion for both, it seeks to give help to both. For while the one looks for food, the other looks for an example to follow. As you feed the first, offer yourself to the second, and you have given alms to both. You have enabled the one to give thanks for the ending of his hunger, the other to imitate the example shown him.

10. Let your works of mercy, then, proceed from a merciful heart; for then even in your love of enemies you will be showing love of brothers. Do not think that John has given no charge concerning love of one's enemy; for he has said much of brotherly charity, and it is always the brother that you love. How so? you ask. I ask in turn, Why do you love your enemy? Because you wish him to have good health in this life? but suppose that is not in his interest? Because you wish him to be rich? but if riches themselves should rob him of his sight? To marry a wife? but if that should bring him a life of bitterness? To have children? but suppose they turn out badly? Thus there is uncertainty in all things you seem to desire for your enemy, because you love him: uncertainty everywhere. Let your desire for him be that together with you he may have eternal life: let your desire for him be that he may be your brother. And if that is what you desire in loving your enemy – that

he may be your brother – when you love him, you love a brother. You love in him, not what he is, but what you would have him be. Once before, if I remember right, my dear people, I put to you this parable: Imagine the trunk of a tree lying before you: a good carpenter may see such a piece of timber, unhewn, as it was cut in the forest. He loves it at sight, but because he means to make something of it. The reason for his love is not that it may always remain as it is: as a craftsman, he has looked at what it shall be, not as lover at what it is; and his love is set upon what he will make of it, not upon its present state. Even so has God loved us sinners. God, we say, has loved sinners; for we have his word, "They that are whole need not a physician, but they that are sick" (Matt. 9:12). But surely his love for us sinners is not to the end that we remain in our sin. Like trees from the wood, we have been looked on by the Carpenter, and his thought turns to the building he will make of us, not the timber that we were. So may you look upon your enemy, standing against you with his angry passion, his biting words, his provoking insults, his unrelenting hate. But in all this you need think only that he is a *man*. You see all the hostility to yourself as of the man's making; and you see in himself God's making. That he was made to be a man, is the act of God; his hatred of you, his malice against you, is his own. And what do you say in your heart? "Lord have mercy upon him: forgive him his sins: put fear in him, and change him." You love in him, not what he is but what you would have him be; and thus when you love your enemy, you love a brother. Therefore, the perfection of love is the love of an enemy, and this perfect love consists in brotherly love. . . . John, indeed, instructs us to love our brothers, Christ to love even our enemies. But you must consider why Christ has bidden you love your enemies. It cannot be with the intent that they should always remain such: that would be an instruction to hate, not to love. Consider the manner of his own love for them, which was a will that they should not continue his persecutors: "Father," he says, "forgive them, for they know not what they do" (Luke 23:34). The will for their pardoning was a will for their transformation: in willing that they should be transformed, he deigned to make brothers out of enemies; and so in very truth he did. He was killed, and buried. He rose again and ascended into heaven, he sent the Holy Spirit upon his disciples. They began with confidence to preach his name, they worked miracles in the name of the crucified and slain; and those who had done the Lord to death saw what was done: that blood which they had shed in fury, they drank in faith.

11. . . . If there is in you nothing of charity, all I have said comes to nothing. But if it exists at all in you, my words should be as oil upon the flames, and perhaps they may have kindled it even where it was not. . . . I have spoken in order to stir up your backwardness in the love of enemies. If a man is passionate against you, meet his passion with prayer: if he hates

you, meet his hatred with pity. It is the fever in his soul that hates you: when he is cured, he will show his gratitude. Think of the physician's love for the sick: he does not love them *as* sick men. If he did, he would want them always to be sick. He loves the sick, not so that they may remain sick men but so that they may become healthy instead of sick. And how much he may have to suffer from them in their delirium – abuse, not seldom blows! The physician attacks the fever and excuses the man: is this loving his enemy? Truer to say that he is hating his real enemy, disease: that is what he hates, while he loves the man that strikes at him. His hatred, then, is for the fever; for the blows are struck at him by the disease, the sickness, the fever. The physician takes away the thing that shows hostility to him, in order that the man may live to give him thanks. So with you. If your enemy hates you, and hates you unjustly, you know that it is because the lusts of this world have mastery in him. If you meet his hate with hate, you are returning evil for evil; and what comes of that? I had to lament for one sick man, who hated you: now if you are hating also, I must mourn for two. But, you say, he has attacked your property, he is robbing you of some earthly possession or other: you hate him, because he is making this life strait for you. You need not suffer such straitening: for you can take your journey into the heaven above, lifting up your heart to the wide realm of freedom where in the hope of life eternal there is no straitness to be borne. Think what it really is of which he would rob you, and remember that he could not even do that, were he not permitted by the Father who "chasteneth every son that he receiveth" (Heb. 12:6). Your enemy himself is as it were God's operating instrument to work your own healing: if God knows it to be for your good that he should despoil you, he allows it; if God knows it to be for your good to be beaten, he allows your enemy to strike you. God is using him to make you whole; pray that he too may be given healing.

12. . . . "If we love one another, God shall abide in us, and his love shall be perfected in us." Make a beginning of love, and you shall be made perfect. For if you have begun to love, God has begun to dwell in you: love him who has begun to dwell in you, so that by a more perfect indwelling he may make you perfect. "Hereby we know that we abide in him, and he in us, because he has given us of his Spirit." It is well: thanks be to God! We know that he dwells in us; and how do we know that we know it? Because John himself tells us, that, "he has given us of his Spirit." How do we know that? How do we know that he has given you of his Spirit? Ask your heart: if it is full of charity, you have the Spirit of God. How do we know that this is evidence for you of God's Spirit dwelling in you? Ask Paul the apostle, "Because the charity of God is shed abroad in our hearts through the Holy Spirit that is given us" (Rom. 5:5).

13. . . . Sick men, be at your ease: if such a physician has come to you,

there can be no despairing. Grave were your diseases, incurable your wounds, desperate your sickness. But if you think of the gravity of your trouble, think also of the omnipotence of the Physician. . . .

14. "Whosoever confesses that Jesus is the Son of God, God abideth in him, and he in God." We need not now insist at length, that this confessing must be not in word but in deed not of the tongue but of the life; for there are many that confess in words what their deeds deny. "And we have known, and have believed, what love God hath in us." Again, how have you known this? "God is love." He has said it before, and now says it again. You could not have a fuller commendation of love than the naming of it with God's name. You might possibly have thought little of God's gift, but can you think little of God? "God is love, and he that abideth in love, abideth in God and God abideth in him." There is a mutual indwelling of the holder and the held: your dwelling in God means that you are held by him, God's dwelling in you means that he holds you, lest you fall. Think of yourself as being made a house of God, but not like the house of bricks and mortar that carries you in the body. If that house should go from under you, you fall; but God does not fall, if you go from under him. He is whole and entire, when you desert him, whole and entire when you return to him. Your healing brings no gift to him: it is you that are cleansed, you that are amended and re-created. He is medicine to the unhealthy, rule to the crooked, light to the darkened, dwelling to the homeless. The imparting is all to you, and you may not suppose that when you come to God there is aught imparted to him – even the possession of a slave. God will not lack servants, though you refuse, though all refuse his service. God has no need of servants, but servants have need of God. Hence the words of the Psalm: "I have said unto the Lord, thou art my God" – yes, God is the true Lord – "because thou needest not my goods" (Ps. 16:2). . . . The true Lord is he who seeks nothing from us; and it goes ill with us, if we seek not him. He seeks nothing from us, yet he sought us when we were not seeking him. One sheep had gone astray: he found it and brought it home upon his shoulders rejoicing (Luke 15:4–5). Was the sheep a necessity for the shepherd, or not rather the shepherd a necessity for the sheep?

I am loath, you see, to reach the end of this Epistle, just because there is no theme on which I would fainer speak than charity; and no other Scripture extols charity with greater warmth. For you there can be no sweeter matter of discourse, no food more healthful for your souls – but only if by good living you confirm in yourselves the gift of God. Be not unthankful for this wondrous grace of God – God, who, possessing one only-begotten Son, willed not that Son to be alone, but adopted us to be his brothers and share with him eternal life.

Augustinian Exegesis and the Nature of Christian Inquirers

C. Clifton Black

As pursued in most mainline departments of religion and schools of theology, modern biblical interpretation tends to be more religiously descriptive than theologically engaged. This is to say, biblical study has become an inquiry into the history and the historically recoverable convictions of Jews and Christians in antiquity, through those literary deposits they left behind and eventually canonized within their respective religious communities. This, in a nutshell, is the historical-critical enter- prise, inherited by modern scholars from their Enlightenment predecessors. As a multifaceted lens in the hands of skillful and sensitive interpreters, historical criticism has taught us much about the Bible and ought not to be despised by academia or the Church. Judiciously executed, historical criticism has enhanced our understanding of that dimension to which the Church's earliest mothers and fathers referred as Scripture's *literalis*, its historical sense.

Yet patristic interpreters were interested in more than merely the literal sense. As later popularized by the Franciscan theologian Nicholas of Lyra (*c.* 1270–1349),

> Littera gesta docet,
> Quid credas allegoria,
> Moralis quid agas,
> Quo tendas anagogia.
> The letter carries the teaching;
> Allegory, what [the church] believes;
> Tropology, its conduct;
> Anagogy, [that future] to which it strives.

For pre-modern interpreters, the Bible was not simply ancient literature whose history invited scientific analysis. It was scripture, pervaded by many levels of meaning, which continued to address the Church to which those

221

biblical books were indigenous.[1] Indeed, throughout most of the Church's existence, there was no divorce of biblical study from scriptural meditation. The reader who sought to understand the biblical word was prepared to obey God's living Word, assumed to be revealed on scripture's pages. This we can observe within the Bible itself: thus, the First Letter of John (*c.* 110) exemplifies an inquiry after God through meditation on the first-century Johannine tradition, known to us through the Gospel of John. That kind of inquiry continued beyond the New Testament into the Patristic era, as represented by Saint Augustine's homiletical interpretations of 1 John (*c.* 415). This essay suggests that Augustine's approach to Johannine interpretation strives for that in which modern historical criticism as such was neither interested nor equipped: namely, the formation of the interpreter into a more knowledgeable, faithful, loving, and mature creature of God.

Historical Background

Because theological inquiry never occurs in a vacuum, Augustine's homilies on 1 John invite historical location. These sermons were originally delivered during Eastertide, 415, in the African harbor-town of Hippo Regius. Assembled to hear them was the same great congregation before whom, twenty-four years earlier, some agents of Valerius, his episcopal predecessor, had literally dragged Augustine to the priest's bench (in rough accordance with the ecclesiastical practice of the day). Hippo's Christians were for the most part poor, hot-tempered, illiterate, and superstitious, "still bogged up to the neck" in the mores of paganism. Their lives, if not Hobbesian in solitude, were indeed poor, nasty, brutish, and short. By the time Augustine ascended the *cathedra* of the Hippo diocese in 396, its Christians could hear him preach almost daily. Still, on even the coldest and rawest Sundays, they turned out in droves to stand listening, from thirty minutes to two hours at a stretch, to their bishop's subtle ruminations on John and 1 John.[2]

Critical Issues in Augustine's Seventh and Eighth Homilies on 1 John

Augustine's interpretive *modus operandi* sustains a sophisticated conversation among (a) every verse of the text before him, (b) that text's conceptual relationship with a broad range of Old and New Testament citations, and (c) the theological implications of this biblical synthesis for Augustine's listeners. If such a procedure seems to veer at times wildly from that employed in modern commentaries, then that deviation betokens to some degree our truncated preoccupation with self-contained textual analysis, often with minimal comparison to other biblical texts and even less with contemporary reflection on the topics raised by those texts. By contrast, Augustine's exposition of scripture is inclined towards the cultivation of a deeper theological imagination, based on epistemological premises whose dimensions I shall consider momentarily.

The most intricately developed theme in Augustine's seventh and eighth homilies is *caritas*: charity, or love. Here is no eisegesis: even by the standards of modern exegetical scholarship, there is no more extensive, arguably no more profound biblical treatment of the topic of love than that found in 1 John 4. Following 1 John's lead, what claims does Augustine make about *caritas*?

1.   Augustine's seventh sermon opens on a negative note: to live in a way that violates the command of love is to set oneself against Christ, or (in 1 John's terminology) to play the "antichrist." The reason for this is that "there was no cause but charity for the coming of Jesus . . . in the flesh" (7.2).[3] Still following 1 John's train of thought, Augustine asserts, "They who speak of the world . . . are they who speak against charity" (7.3). To illustrate this point, Augustine contrasts Jesus' warning from the Sermon on the Mount with the conventional wisdom of fifth-century Hippo:

> You have heard the Lord's saying: "If ye forgive men their sins, your heavenly Father also will forgive you your sins; but if ye forgive not, neither will your Father forgive you your sins" [Matt. 6:14–15]. . . . Now hear the men that speak of the world: "Are you not to have your revenge? Is he to tell the tale of what he has done to you? No, let him feel that he is dealing with a man!" We hear that sort of thing every day . . .   (7.3)

Augustine is equally quick to expose any spuriously spiritual division between our love for God and our Christian siblings: "Let no man say: 'sin against a man is a small thing, it is only against God I may not sin.' How can you not be sinning against God, when you sin against love? 'God is love.' . . . Now, if you dare, act against God, and refuse to love your brother" (7.5).

2.   The preceding remarks anticipate another emphasis of Augustine in his treatment of *caritas*: Aided by Paul's wording in Romans Augustine infers, "we may understand that in love is the Holy Spirit" (7.6). Those who violate the command of love (the antichrists) may enter our churches, may have been baptized, may possess the gift of prophecy, can receive the eucharist, can even bear the name of Christ. In these respects they are no different from the loving. But those who are unloving cannot receive the Holy Spirit. "This

... is the peculiar gift of the Spirit: he is the one and only fountain. To drink of it, God's Spirit calls you: God's Spirit calls you to drink of himself" (7.6).

From this claim follow three corollaries, all of which Augustine develops in his eighth sermon on 1 John. The first corollary is anthropological:

> Men are not to be loved as things to be consumed, but in the manner of friendship and goodwill, leading us to do things for the benefit of those we love. ... Once you have bestowed gifts on the unfortunate, you may easily yield to the temptation to exalt yourself over him, to assume superiority over the object of your benefaction. ... [Rather] you should want him to be your equal, that both may be subject to the one on whom no favour can be bestowed. The true Christian will never set himself up over other men. (8.5, 8)

Augustine's second corollary is theological in the narrower sense:

> For if you have begun to love, God has begun to dwell in you. ... "God is love, and he that abideth in love, abideth in God and God abideth in him" [John 4:16b]. There is a mutual indwelling of the holder and the held: your dwelling in God means that you are held by him, God's dwelling in you means that he holds you, lest you fall. (8.12, 14)

The third corollary pertains to the ongoing struggle in this life between human sin, chiefly expressed as *superbia* – pride – and the ultimate triumph of God among those who submit their wills to the operation of grace. While the God of *caritas* is the proper, beneficent pilot of every human life, in Augustine's analysis it is clear that human beings may submit their wills to base motives instead of love. Both dove and snake may be angered and fight. "The dove," however, "has no bitterness; yet it struggles to defend its nest with its beak and its wings; it strikes without harshness" (7.11).[4] Accordingly, the quality of human conduct cannot be discerned from its outward appearance. "The difference in intention makes a difference in the acts" (7.7).

> Come back to your own conscience, and question it: pay heed, not to the visible flowering but to the root beneath the ground. ... Many things can be done that look well, yet do not issue from the root of charity. Thorns too have their flowers. Some actions seem harsh or savage, but are performed for our discipline at the dictate of charity. (8.9; 7.8)

3. Wherein is *caritas* cultivated, since "No one has ever beheld God" (1 John 4:12a)? Love is inculcated within and expressed by the Church, under the wings of the baptismal Spirit. Yet love cannot, must not, be confined within the Church's walls, dispensed solely among one's siblings in Christ.

On this point Augustine moves beyond 1 John's explicit, seemingly restrictive, injunctions of love for one another and considers also love for one's enemies: "Let your desire for [your enemy] be that together with you he may have eternal life: let your desire for him be that he may be your brother" (8.10).

Such charity is by no means one-directional, but potentially painful in its reciprocity:

> Your enemy himself is as it were God's operating instrument to work your own healing: if God knows it to be for your good that he should despoil you, he allows it; if God knows it to be for your good to be beaten, he allows your enemy to strike you. God is using him to make you whole; pray that he too may be given healing. (8.11)

To summarize Augustine's description of *caritas* in these sermons on 1 John: love is not an inherent capability within human beings; it is, to the contrary a spiritual gift from the merciful God. This understanding coheres with Augustine's well-known definition of love as "the impulse of one's mind to enjoy God on his own account and to enjoy oneself and one's neighbor on account of God,"[5] an ascent that is prompted by the prior descent of a loving, redeeming God. Charity fosters neither manipulation nor patronization among human beings but, rather, equalizes them before God. Right intention proceeds solely from the root of charity, and charity is the sole canon by which human conduct is to be blessed or execrated; praised or damned. To accept this world's values, anchored in pride, is to repudiate charity; to violate charity is to oppose the reason for Christ's having come in flesh; to deny charity to one in need is nothing other than sin against God, who is love. By contrast, to love God's creatures is to cooperate in their restoration as God's children and our siblings, just as God uses our fellow creatures – even our enemies – as instruments of our own healing.

Scriptural Interpretation as Christian Nurture

Scholars of our day are likely to find various aspects of Augustine's biblical interpretation unsatisfactory and occasionally dismaying. Judged by modern standards, his treatment does not offer a systematic, verse-by-verse analysis of the historical, traditional, or literary dimensions of the 1 John. For something approximating technical exegesis, as we understand the term, I think that we must await Calvin's commentaries, whose adherence to Renaissance norms yields an exposition more in line with modern expectations.[6] Moreover, Augustine's equipment in biblical languages was weak, and it is clear that he used some pre-Vulgate, Latin translation of 1 John in preparing his sermons.[7] Augustine's handling of particular passages also seems forced, as exemplified by his ingenious reconciliation of the characteristically Johannine principle of love for one another within the Christian community (John 15:12–17) with the more generous form of Jesus' love-command, in the Synoptics, to encompass the enemy as well (Matt. 5:43–8; Luke 6:27–36). Augustine's theology emphasizes the incomparable honor bestowed on human beings who have been created and are being perfected in the image of God. When plucked from that indispensable context, Augustine's suggestion that God may allow us to be hurt for our own healing runs outrageously roughshod across not only modern sensibilities but Augustine's own. Finally, a modern exegete, trained to approach the text with scientific objectivity and sharp focus on minute detail, may be more than a little unnerved by the highly personal, expansive, emotional style of Augustine's treatment – even after allowances are made for the fact that these are not polished tractates but sermons probably delivered *ad libitum*, without Bible or manuscript, transcribed by secretaries present as the bishop preached.[8] In these respects and others, on first encounter, Augustine's exegesis of scripture seems to exhibit, materially and methodologically, many traps that modern interpreters discipline themselves to avoid.

From Augustine, nevertheless, we have much to learn about an important matter that transcends the qualms of historical criticism. I refer to biblical interpretation in the service of nurturing Christians. I do not think that Augustine is merely setting forth a program of catechesis, for which biblical exegesis provides theological prolegomena or raw material. Rather, he is catechizing through exegesis, demonstrating for us how scriptural interpretation actually functions as Christian nurture. That demonstration, I submit, is every bit as needful in our century as in Augustine's. In his sermons on 1 John, Augustine boldly proposes that, when we approach the Bible as scripture – when we inquire after God through assiduous reading of the biblical text – it is there that we encounter the God who is relentlessly inquiring after us.

Were we to take seriously his interpretive endeavors, what might Augustine teach us about biblical interpretation and the business of theology in our day?

1. To begin with, Augustine never allows us to imagine that scriptural interpretation, properly understood, is an end in itself. Surely he would have been monumentally bored – if not appalled – by philological, philosophical, historical, traditional, or literary studies of the Bible undertaken for their own sake, divorced from humanity's restless quest for that God to whom the biblical witness points, the God who uses many media – the sacraments

and their observance, prayer and its practice, scripture and its exegesis – to graciously conform our wills to God's own.

Biblical study as merely an end in itself – or as nothing more than a means to such secondary objectives as fulfilling requirements for a degree or eliciting facile answers to the burning questions of the day – would be, to Augustine's thinking, a practical expression of that idolatry summed up by Paul in Romans 1:25: humanity's radically confused worship and service of the creature rather than of the Creator (2.11).

Augustine believes that education is anchored in love. The ultimate aim of education is the discovery and arousal of our love for God. Although we may think we have begun to search for God through the interpretation of scripture, in Augustinian perspective the truth is actually the reverse. *It is we who are interpreted by scripture, which reveals the God who is searching after us*. Nor is that inquiry ours to begin: if we turn to the Bible as a means of grace, it is only because God has bestirred us in that divinely appointed direction. The only fountain that can slake humanity's deepest thirst is the Holy Spirit, and "God's Spirit calls you to drink of himself" (7.6).

2.   What does that tell us about the nature of God? For Augustine, the words of 1 John 4:8b crystallize what human beings can know of God: "If nothing else were said in praise of love, in all the pages of this Epistle, nothing else whatever in any other page of Scripture, and this were the one and only thing we heard from the voice of God's Spirit – 'For God is love' – we should ask for nothing more" (7.4). "Eternal Truth, true Love, beloved Eternity – all this, my God, you are": so confesses Augustine.[9] Likewise, "the plentitude and end of the law and of all the sacred scriptures is the love of a Being who is to be enjoyed and of a Being who can share that enjoyment with us".[10] With God, as with scripture, the touchstone is *caritas*. And in his homilies on 1 John, Augustine's fundamental characterization of love is of a love that *heals*. Thus, his Prologue to these sermons: "[1 John] is a book very sweet to every healthy Christian heart that savors the bread of God, and it should be constantly in the mind of God's Holy Church." Such an understanding unlocks Augustine's portrayal of Christ: Jesus is preeminently the omnipotent physician who heals the desperately ill who are incapable of healing themselves.

> Think of the physician's love for the sick: he does not love them *as* sick men. If he did, he would want them always to be sick. He loves the sick, not so that they may remain sick men but so that they may become healthy instead of sick. And how much he may have to suffer from them in their delirium – abuse, not seldom blows! . . . The physician takes away the thing that shows hostility to him, in order that the man may live to give thanks. So with you.   (8.11)

Augustine believes that, through scripture as through the Incarnation, *God's sole intention is to restore all human beings to their proper dignity, to that perfection of love indigenous to their creation in God's own image.* In an age such as ours, seemingly enthralled by a Nietzschean "hermeneutics of suspicion," Augustine may offer us the most cogent, powerful justification for our adoption of a "hermeneutics of trust."[11] Indeed, if his appraisal be accepted, we have a reason *par excellence* to entrust ourselves to the God who meets us on scripture's pages, a reason articulated elsewhere by Augustine in the poignant language of maternal nurture:

> . . . it is to you [my God] that I sigh night and day. . . . I realized that I was far away from you. It was as though I were in a land where all is different from your own and I heard your voice calling from on high, saying, "I am the food of full-grown adults. Grow and you shall feed on me. But you shall not change me into your own substance, as you do with the food of your body. Instead you shall be changed into me."[12]

3.   With Augustine as a partner in our conversations about theological inquiry, we can acknowledge *God's power to transform us, through scripture, as interpreters of love "in deed and in truth"* (1 John 3:18). We can begin to understand that the discovery of "authorial intention" in the biblical text is practically impossible unless our own "lectorial intention" is in alignment with the grace and love of God that scripture reveals. In this connection it is critical to recall Augustine's emphasis on the intentionality of our actions, and on *caritas* as the only root of excellent performance. "Open your heart's ear!" cries Augustine to his people (6.12).

For this reason "purity in heart" – a soul continuously aspiring to love for God, that *caritas* which is the only basis for proper love of one's self – is for Augustine a *sine qua non* for the biblical theologian. What if we took seriously, as did Augustine, the transformative power of scripture? What would this mean for the ways in which we view ourselves, our neighbors, and our benevolent projects? We would recognize that the love of God and the love of neighbor are inseparably entwined. In a given moment, one of these two may receive greater emphasis, but each necessarily implies the other:

> Does it then follow that he who loves his brother loves God also? Of necessity he must love God: of necessity he must love love itself. He cannot love his brother and not love love; he cannot help loving love. And if he loves love, he needs must love God: [for] in loving love, he is loving God. . . . If God is love, whoever loves love, loves God. Therefore, love your brother, and have no other care.   (9.10)

From this it follows that, according to Augustine, no material distinction exists between what we sometimes contrast as "theology" and "praxis," or, as Augustine puts it, the contemplative life and the active life. Love for the neighbor is actually a form of contemplation in the midst of action. In no case of which I am aware does Augustine suggest that love for the neighbor is exclusively coterminous with the active life, or that the province of love for God is exclusively defined as the contemplative life. Any detachment of spirituality from social witness can only corrupt them both. Jesus is honored by both Mary at his feet and Martha in her kitchen.[13]

Further, if guided by Augustine in our inquiry after God, we would recognize that humility is the proper sense of self for those who bear the name of Christ, who humbled himself for our healing. "God has humbled himself – and still man is proud!"[14] Let us be clear that Augustine never confused humility with self-contempt, as have too many Christians after him. Created in the image of God, with the capacity to be elevated to a God who desires us, human beings possess extraordinary dignity in Augustinian thought. This Augustine dared to believe amidst a civilization collapsing around him, a blood-drenched society in which "a real man" or a "real woman" would demand vendetta when injured (7.3). Yet Augustine insistently reminded his people of the gospel's utterly counter-cultural strategy, predicated not on "nature red in tooth and claw,"[15] but on God's subversive love, which enkindles within us that God-given nobility within ourselves from which we have gotten so far out of touch. To understand scripture is to *stand under* its paradoxical yet invincible convictions: that humanity's future lies not in revenge but in reconciliation; that only under Christ's discipline can his disciples know healthy freedom; that the needy whom we benefit are every bit our benefactors, through whom God is re-forming us in Christ.

4.   Finally, if we pay attention to Augustine the exegete, we will learn afresh that *scripture's native habitat is the church catholic*, which is neither interchangeable with nor reducible to any party, sect, or denomination. A child of monastic spirituality, Augustine could appreciate more easily than we that scripture is as much a source of *understanding* as of information. By confessing the Bible to be scripture ("inspired") and canon ("regulative") for that family of God into which they have been baptized, Christians have found *in* scripture their hermeneutic (their framework for understanding) and in the Holy Spirit their epistemic instrument (the means by which they are able to understand). Across history, however, scripture has not been the Church's solitary canon. Scripture has been, and in most congregations continues to be, read within the authoritative context of the Church's prayers, liturgies, creeds, disciplines, and practices. Such was certainly the

case for Augustine, who loved Christ's Church as "the mother of us all"[16] and who came to accept that it is, indeed, the walls of the Church that make the Christian (8.2).

In an important study of the role of scripture in early Christian monasticism, Douglas Burton-Christie suggests that the desert mothers and fathers "saw the sacred texts as projecting worlds of possible meaning that they were called upon to enter."[17] Others have argued that patristic allegorists did not so much assimilate scripture to their ambient culture as they profoundly Christianized that culture's dominant worldview.[18] I can think of no mandate more pressing upon Christian theology in our day than this: to entrust the children of God, within the embrace of the Church's prayers and praise, to those radically new possibilities of divine imagination and holy conduct that God offered us through scripture.

Some Conclusions

In an illuminating essay first published almost twenty years ago, David Steinmetz argued that medieval hermeneutical theory was superior to historical criticism in at least this respect: "The medieval theory of levels of meaning in the biblical text, with all its undoubted defects, flourished because it is true, while the modern theory of a single meaning" – namely, that which was originally intended by the author of the biblical text – "with all its demonstrable virtues, is false."[19] Relatively few biblical interpreters would now cling to the exegetical quest for a single, original meaning. On the contrary: owing to the complexities of texts and their reception, the Bible is currently subject to an interpretive range so broad, at times seemingly limitless, that it would have left a medieval allegorist's head spinning.

It now appears that, for all its inadequacies, an Augustinian hermeneutical theory is superior to that of our own in another, even more crucial respect. Augustine defended the proposition, increasingly alien to modernity, that scripture discloses to its inquirers the God who is utterly desirous and uniquely able, by means of such instruments as scripture itself, to heal a diseased creation. Properly interpreted, scripture is for us both a mirror of our own flawed nobility and a window through which God's love radiates the healing of our conduct, our imagination, our most truthful understanding of ourselves and others. Although scripture, like any good gift, is susceptible to abuse, the nourishment for which we are most famished lies, not in ourselves, but in the scripture that nurtures.

Notes

1   See Harry Caplan, "The Four Senses of Scriptural Interpretation and the Mediaeval Theory of Preaching," *Speculum*, vol. 4 (1929), pp. 282–90.
2   F. van der Meer, *Augustine the Bishop: The Life and Work of a Father of the Church* (London and New York: Sheed & Ward, 1961), p. 46.
3   Parenthetical references are to Augustine's homilies on 1 John in *Augustine: Later Works*, ed. John Burnaby (Philadelphia: Westminster, 1955).
4   As translated by Mary T. Clark, *Augustine of Hippo: Selected Writings* (New York, Ramsey and Toronto: Paulist Press, 1984), p. 307.
5   Augustine, *De Doctrina Christiana*, trans. R. P. H. Green (Oxford: Clarendon Press, 1995), pp. 149, 3.10.16.
6   See John Calvin, *The Gospel According to St. John 11–12 and the First Epistle of John*, in David W. Torrance and Thomas F. Torrance (eds), *Calvin's Commentaries* (Grand Rapids: Eerdmans, 1959), pp. 227–315.
7   Gerald Bonner, "Augustine as Biblical Scholar," in P. R. Ackroyd and C. F. Evans (eds), *The Cambridge History of the Bible*, vol. 1 (Cambridge: Cambridge University Press, 1970), pp. 550–1.
8   See R. J. Deferrai, "Augustine's Method of Composing and Delivering Sermons," *American Journal of Philology*, vol. 40 (1922), pp. 193–219.
9   Augustine, *Confessions*, trans. R. S. Pine-Coffin (London: Penguin, 1961), pp. 147, 7.10.
10 Augustine, *On Christian Doctrine*, trans. D. W. Robertson, Jr. (Indianapolis: Bobbs-Merrill, 1958), pp. 30, 1.35.39.
11 Thus, Richard B. Hays, "Salvation by Trust? Reading the Bible Faithfully," *Christian Century*, vol. 114 (February 26, 1997), pp. 218–23.
12 Augustine, *Confessions*, pp. 147, 7.10.
13 See Augustine, Sermons 53 and 54 in *The Nicene and Post-Nicene Fathers*, 1st series, vol. 6, ed. Philip Schaff, trans. R. G. MacMullen (Peabody, MA: Hendrickson, 1994), pp. 427–30.
14 Augustine, Sermon 162.6.
15 Tennyson, *In Memoriam* 55.4.
16 Augustine, *Confessions*, pp. 31, 1.11.
17 Douglas Burton-Christie, *The Word in the Desert: Scripture and the Quest for Holiness in Early Christian Monasticism* (New York and Oxford: Oxford University Press, 1993), p. 299.
18 David Dawson, *Allegorical Readers and Cultural Revision in Ancient Alexandria* (Berkeley: University of California Press, 1992); Francis M. Young, *Biblical Exegesis and the Formation of Christian Culture* (Cambridge: Cambridge University Press, 1997).
19 David Steinmetz, "The Superiority of Pre-critical Exegesis," *Theology Today*, vol. 37 (1980), p. 38.

Inquiring after God when Preaching

The western reading of the gospel may be summed up by saying that God has reconciled sinners to himself in Jesus Christ. Disregarding our sins because of the sacrifice of Christ's life on our behalf is good news. We can let go of our shame before God if, indeed, that is what we suffer from, trusting that God accepts us, warts and all.

While this good news brings a rush of relief, the Christian life that follows thereupon is not based on a devil-may-care attitude but a life of responsibility. The emotional liberation of the gospel brings responsibility in its wake. For by turning our attention to his power and goodness, God requires one to follow him rather than make one's way in the world unguided. Christ is the proper comforter and guide.

Most people encounter the gospel by hearing, by reading, or by example. Understanding God does not come naturally but is conveyed from one to another. Being told about him is not enough, however. Something in the soul must crave God's wisdom in order to respond. And craving something outside oneself means to some extent being dissatisfied with oneself. It means that one recognizes a lack in oneself that needs to be filled. Otherwise, words about God's truth cannot ring true, even if they are true. So, as John Calvin says, each Christian must engage in self-scrutiny in order to arrive at a degree of self-despair and then yearn to change. And that being the case, it is necessary for life with God to offer a refreshing way out of ourselves. This is the yearning that Augustine sought and found, and the argument made by the Christian tradition.

Augustine is the first Church Father to allow us to overhear his lifelong conversation with God. His *Confessions* is the first spiritual autobiography in history, and its effect on western civilization has been immense. Like the psalmists before him, he shares his inner life with us, written as a prayer-conversation with God. As he imagines this conversation over the years his theology takes shape as a quest to understand God and to grow in wisdom from the increase of understanding. By allowing us into his mind and heart Augustine gave us the very notion of the inner life, life as a prayer of gratitude. We have seen that Catherine of Siena adapted this genre in her own dialogue with God. By taking us into their confidence these Doctors of the Church preach the gospel in a deeply personal style.

Calvin concurs with Augustine's teaching that self-understanding and understanding God are mutually interdependent. We cannot get very far on our own. Or, perhaps it is better to say that we may think we get far only to find out later that we were going in the wrong direction. While Augustine was acutely sensitive to God's nearness to himself as a guide, Calvin pulled the camera back and was awed by the majesty of God that he saw displayed in the world and explained through scripture. For both teachers, facing God is a process of self-critical discernment in which one seeks to be admonished and challenged by the encounter.

When we see ourselves contrasted with the awesome strength and greatness of God we are humbled. But, as we noted at the outset of this journey, even being able to look toward God must be accounted for. Calvin argued, in agreement with St. Augustine, that people have an instinctual feel for God and are eventually drawn to spiritual self-confrontation by following this instinct guided by scripture and the teaching of the Church. Some think of this intuitive sense as conscience. It may be as weak as a vague gnawing that something is not quite right with us, or as intense as a drive to seek God above all else.

With the loss of a religious ethos one may wonder whether there really is such a universal instinct for God in people. Perhaps the desire for God is truly a gift of divine grace. Regardless of its origin, the desire for God needs to be cultivated by the Christian community. The preaching of the story of salvation by the Church's ministers has been a chief instrument for forming, goading, or instigating a deeper understanding of God and of ourselves. It presses beyond simply acknowledging the existence of God to a more robust spiritual life that takes effect in the world.

Our interpretive essay presses tepid believers, for it contends that trusting God is only the first step in Christian faithfulness. For those who successfully defend themselves against the call of God for a while, submitting to him may be a great relief. They may be surprised to learn that the hard work is only just beginning, for the temptation to fall back into life without God recurs and recurs. Being a Christian requires continuous conversion.

Professor Cornelius Plantinga suggests that the task of preaching to Christians is to bring the reality of God home repeatedly, in order to aim them in the right direction. An especially needy group within the Christian family is those he identifies as practical atheists, Church members who become distracted by pursuits into which they would rather not have God intrude. This "disease of the religious," as he calls it, is a form of self-deception where a believer may be active in the church but not seriously engaged in the life of faith to the point at which it scrutinizes one's life. It renders churchly life a way of avoiding and evading God.

A variant of this self-deception is to bend God to support or represent one's favorite cause, especially when the cause advances one's own political interests. This is to recreate God in one's own image, so that one no longer has to examine one's motives. For on close examination, one's ego, desire for honor, status, and power, may take over even virtuous projects, such as helping the downtrodden. Good preaching can help such persons learn of God better and overcome their self-righteousness.

Another temptation of the faithful is to sentimentalize God so that he no longer challenges them to think hard about their lives. It is tempting to think that God favors one for one's piety, and is completely supportive, following the sign outside a church that reads "God loves you and so do we." This neglects the fact that God is not always pleased with us or all that we do, but also calls us to account. The task of the preacher, then, is to break through the enormous capacity people have for self-justification and self-deception so that they come into contact with who they really are before God, and can begin again the process of repentance and renewal. For the beginning of wisdom is "the fear of the Lord" (Prov. 1:7).

The challenge of bringing God home to people is the entry point for inquiring after God, the kind of serious reflection that is free enough to move from self-concern to questions about God himself. And this more reflective and sober knowledge enables one to preach sermons that invite others to inquire after God.

SACRED TEXTS

Psalm 14:1–2

Fools say in their hearts, "There is
no God."
They are corrupt, they do
abominable deeds;
there is no one who does good.

The Lord looks down from heaven
on humankind
to see if there are any who are
wise,
who seek after God.

2 Corinthians 4:1–7

Therefore, since it is by God's mercy that we are engaged in this ministry, we do not lose heart. We have renounced the shameful things that one hides; we refuse to practice cunning or to falsify God's word; but by the open statement of the truth we commend ourselves to the conscience of everyone in the sight of God. And even if our gospel is veiled, it is veiled to those who are perishing. In their case the god of this world has blinded the minds of the unbelievers, to keep them from seeing the light of the gospel of the glory of Christ, who is the image of God. For we do not proclaim ourselves; we proclaim Jesus Christ as Lord and ourselves as your slaves for Jesus' sake. For it is the God who said, "Let light shine out of darkness," who has shone in our hearts to give the light of the knowledge of the glory of God in the face of Jesus Christ. But we have this treasure in clay jars, so that it may be made clear that this extraordinary power belongs to God and does not come from us.

St. Augustine of Hippo, *Confessions*

Book I

"You are great, Lord, and highly to be praised (Ps. 47[48]: 2): great is your power and your wisdom is immeasurable" (Ps. 146[147]:5). Man, a little piece of your creation, desires to praise you, a human being "bearing his mortality with him" (2 Cor. 4:10), carrying with him the witness of his sin and the witness that you "resist the proud" (1 Pet. 5:5). Nevertheless, to praise you is the desire of man, a little piece of your creation. You stir man to take pleasure in praising you, because you have made us for yourself, and our heart is restless until it rests in you.

"Grant me Lord to know and understand" (Ps. 118[119]: 34, 73, 144) which comes first – to call upon you or to praise you, and whether knowing you precedes calling upon you. But who calls upon you when he does not know you? For an ignorant person might call upon someone else instead of the right one. But surely you may be called upon in prayer that you may be known. Yet "how shall they call upon him in whom they have not believed? and how shall they believe without a preacher?" (Rom. 10: 14). "They will praise the Lord who seek for him" (Ps. 21[22]: 27).

In seeking him they find him, and in finding they will praise him. Lord, I would seek you, calling upon you – and calling upon you is an act of believing in you. You have been preached to us. My faith, Lord, calls upon you. It is your gift to me. You breathed it into me by the humanity of your Son, by the ministry of your preacher. . . .

Who then are you, my God? What, I ask, but God who is Lord? For "who is the Lord but the Lord," or "who is God but our God? (Ps. 17: 32 [18:31]). Most high, utterly good, utterly powerful, most omnipotent, most merciful and most just, deeply hidden yet most intimately present, perfection of both beauty and strength, stable and incomprehensible, immutable and yet changing all things, never new, never old, making everything new and "leading" the proud "to be old without their knowledge" (Job 9:5, Old Latin version); always active, always in repose, gathering to yourself but not in need, supporting and filling and protecting, creating and nurturing and bringing to maturity, searching even though to you nothing is lacking: you love without burning, you are jealous in a way that is free of anxiety, you "repent" (Gen. 6:6) without the pain of regret, you are wrathful and remain tranquil. You will a change without any change in your design. You recover what you find, yet have never lost. Never in any need, you rejoice in your gains (Luke 15:7); you are never avaricious, yet you require interest (Matt. 25:27). We pay you more than you require so as to make you our debtor, yet who has anything which does not belong to you? (1 Cor. 4:7). You pay off debts, though owing nothing to anyone; you cancel debts and incur no loss. But in these words what have I said, my God, my life, my holy sweetness? What has anyone achieved in words when he speaks about you? Yet woe to those who are silent about you because, though loquacious with verbosity, they have nothing to say.

Who will enable me to find rest in you? Who will grant me that you come to my heart and intoxicate it, so that I forget my evils and embrace my one and only good, yourself? What are you to me? Have mercy so that I may find words. What am I to you that you command me to love you, and that, if I fail to love you, you are angry with me and threaten me with vast miseries? If I do not love you, is that but a little misery? What a wretch I am! In your mercies, Lord God, tell me what you are to me. "Say to my soul, I am your salvation" (Ps. 34 [35]:3). Speak to me so that I may hear. See my ears of my heart are before you, Lord. Open them and "say to my soul, I am your salvation." After that utterance I will run and lay hold on you. Do not hide your face from me (see Ps. 26[27]:9). Lest I die, let me die so that I may see it.

The house of my soul is too small for you to come to it. May it be enlarged by you. It is in ruins: restore it. In your eyes it has offensive features. I admit it, I know it; but who will clean it up? Or to whom shall I cry other than you? . . .

Book X

My love for you, Lord, is not an uncertain feeling but a matter of conscious certainty. With your word you pierced my heart, and I loved you. But heaven and earth and everything in them on all sides tell me to love you. Nor do they cease to tell everyone that "they are without excuse" (Rom. 1:20). But at a profounder level you will have mercy on whom you will have mercy and will show pity on whom you will have pity (Rom. 9:15). Otherwise heaven and earth would be uttering your praises to the deaf. But when I love you, what do I love? It is not physical beauty nor temporal glory nor the brightness of light dear to earthly eyes, nor the sweet melodies of all kinds of songs, nor the gentle odour of flowers and ointments and perfumes, nor manna or honey, nor limbs welcoming the embraces of the flesh; it is not these I love when I love my God. Yet there is a light I love, and a food, and a kind of embrace when I love my God – a light, voice, odour, food, embrace of my inner man, where my soul is floodlit by light which space cannot contain, where there is sound that time cannot seize, where there is a perfume which no breeze disperses, where there is a taste for food no amount of eating can lessen, and where there is a bond of union that no satiety can part. That is what I love when I love my God. . . .

Late have I loved you, beauty so old and so new: late have I loved you. And see, you were within and I was in the external world and sought you there, and in my unlovely state I plunged into those lovely created things which you made. You were with me, and I was not with you. The lovely things kept me far from you, though if they did not have their existence in you, they had no existence at all. You called and cried out loud and shattered my deafness. You were radiant and resplendent, you put to flight my blindness. You were fragrant, and I drew in my breath and now pant after you. I tasted you, and I feel but hunger and thirst for you. You touched me, and I am set on fire to attain the peace which is yours. . . .

John Calvin, *Institutes of the Christian Religion*

Book One: The Knowledge of God the Creator

Chapter I: The Knowledge of God and that of Ourselves are Connected. How they are Interrelated

1. Without knowledge of self there is no knowledge of God
Nearly all the wisdom we possess, that is to say, true and sound wisdom, consists of two parts: the knowledge of God and of ourselves. But, while joined by many bonds, which one precedes and brings forth the other is not easy to discern. In the first place, no one can look upon himself without immediately turning his thoughts to the contemplation of God, in whom he "lives and moves" [Acts 17:28]. For, quite clearly, the mighty gifts with which we are endowed are hardly from ourselves; indeed, our very being is nothing but subsistence in the one God. Then, by these benefits shed like dew from heaven upon us, we are led as by rivulets to the spring itself. Indeed, our very poverty better discloses the infinitude of benefits reposing in God. The miserable ruin, into which the rebellion of the first man cast us, especially compels us to look upward. Thus, not only will we, in fasting and hungering, seek thence what we lack; but, in being aroused by fear, we shall learn humility. For, as a veritable world of miseries is to be found in mankind, and we are thereby despoiled of divine raiment, our shameful nakedness exposes a teeming horde of infamies. Each of us must, then, be so stung by the consciousness of his own unhappiness as to attain at least some knowledge of God. Thus, from the feeling of our own ignorance, vanity, poverty, infirmity, and – what is more – depravity and corruption, we recognize that the true light of wisdom, sound virtue, full abundance of every good, and purity of righteousness rest in the Lord alone. To this extent we are prompted by our own ills to contemplate the good things of God; and we cannot seriously aspire to him before we begin to become displeased with ourselves. For what man in all the world would not gladly remain as he is – what man does not remain as he is – so long as he does not know himself, that is, while content with his own gifts, and either ignorant or unmindful of his own misery? Accordingly, the knowledge of ourselves not only arouses us to seek God, but also, as it were, leads us by the hand to find him.

2. Without knowledge of God there is no knowledge of self
Again, it is certain that man never achieves a clear knowledge of himself unless he has first looked upon God's face, and then descends from

contemplating him to scrutinize himself. For we always seem to ourselves righteous and upright and wise and holy – this pride is innate in all of us – unless by clear proofs we stand convinced of our own unrighteousness, foulness, folly, and impurity. Moreover, we are not thus convinced if we look merely to ourselves and not also to the Lord, who is the sole standard by which this judgment must be measured. For, because all of us are inclined by nature to hypocrisy, a kind of empty image of righteousness in place of righteousness itself abundantly satisfies us. And because nothing appears within or around us that has not been contaminated by great immorality, what is a little less vile pleases us as a thing most pure – so long as we confine our minds within the limits of human corruption. Just so, an eye to which nothing is shown but black objects judges something dirty white or even rather darkly mottled to be whiteness itself. Indeed, we can discern still more clearly from the bodily senses how much we are deluded in estimating the powers of the soul. For if in broad daylight we either look down upon the ground or survey whatever meets our view round about, we seem to ourselves endowed with the strongest and keenest sight; yet when we look up to the sun and gaze straight at it, that power of sight which was particularly strong on earth is at once blunted and confused by a great brilliance, and thus we are compelled to admit that our keenness in looking upon things earthly is sheer dullness when it comes to the sun. So it happens in estimating our spiritual goods. As long as we do not look beyond the earth, being quite content with our own righteousness, wisdom, and virtue, we flatter ourselves most sweetly, and fancy ourselves all but demigods. Suppose we but once begin to raise our thoughts to God, and to ponder his nature, and how completely perfect are his righteousness, wisdom, and power – the straightedge to which we must be shaped. Then, what masquerading earlier as righteousness was pleasing in us will soon grow filthy in its consummate wickedness. What wonderfully impressed us under the name of wisdom will stink in its very foolishness. What wore the face of power will prove itself the most miserable weakness. That is, what in us seems perfection itself corresponds ill to the purity of God.

3. Man before God's majesty
Hence that dread and wonder with which Scripture commonly represents the saints as stricken and overcome whenever they felt the presence of God. Thus it comes about that we see men who in his absence normally remained firm and constant, but who, when he manifests his glory, are so shaken and struck dumb as to be laid low by the dread of death – are in fact overwhelmed by it and almost annihilated. As a consequence, we must infer that man is never sufficiently touched and affected by the awareness of his lowly state until he has compared himself with God's majesty. . . .

Chapter II: What it is to Know God, and to What Purpose the Knowledge of him Tends

1. Piety is requisite for the knowledge of God

Now, the knowledge of God, as I understand it, is that by which we not only conceive that there is a God but also grasp what befits us and is proper to his glory, in fine, what is to our advantage to know of him. Indeed, we shall not say that, properly speaking, God is known where there is no religion or piety. Here I do not yet touch upon the sort of knowledge with which men, in themselves lost and accursed, apprehend God the Redeemer in Christ the Mediator; but I speak only of the primal and simple knowledge to which the very order of nature would have led us if Adam had remained upright. In this ruin of mankind no one now experiences God either as Father or as Author of salvation, or favorable in any way, until Christ the Mediator comes forward to reconcile him to us. Nevertheless, it is one thing to feel that God as our Maker supports us by his power, governs us by his providence, nourishes us by his goodness, and attends us with all sorts of blessings – and another thing to embrace the grace of reconciliation offered to us in Christ. First, as much in the fashioning of the universe as in the general teaching of Scripture the Lord shows himself to be simply the Creator. Then in the face of Christ [cf. 2 Cor. 4:6] he shows himself the Redeemer. Of the resulting twofold knowledge of God we shall now discuss the first aspect; the second will be dealt with in its proper place.

Moreover, although our mind cannot apprehend God without rendering some honor to him, it will not suffice simply to hold that there is One whom all ought to honor and adore, unless we are also persuaded that he is the fountain of every good, and that we must seek nothing elsewhere than in him. This I take to mean that not only does he sustain this universe (as he once founded it) by his boundless might, regulate it by his wisdom, preserve it by his goodness, and especially rule mankind by his righteousness and judgment, bear with it in his mercy, watch over it by his protection; but also that no drop will be found either of wisdom and light, or of righteousness or power or rectitude, or of genuine truth, which does not flow from him, and of which he is not the cause. Thus we may learn to await and seek all these things from him, and thankfully to ascribe them, once received, to him. For this sense of the powers of God is for us a fit teacher of piety, from which religion is born. I call "piety" that reverence joined with love of God which the knowledge of his benefits induces. For until men recognize that they owe everything to God, that they are nourished by his fatherly care, that he is the Author of their every good, that they should seek nothing beyond him – they will never yield him willing service. Nay, unless they establish their complete happiness in him, they will never give themselves truly and sincerely to him. . . .

Chapter III: The Knowledge of God has been Naturally Implanted in the Minds of Men

1. The character of this natural endowment

There is within the human mind, and indeed by natural instinct, an awareness of divinity. This we take to be beyond controversy. To prevent anyone from taking refuge in the pretense of ignorance, God himself has implanted in all men a certain understanding of his divine majesty. Ever renewing its memory, he repeatedly sheds fresh drops. Since, therefore, men one and all perceive that there is a God and that he is their Maker, they are condemned by their own testimony because they have failed to honor him and to consecrate their lives to his will. If ignorance of God is to be looked for anywhere, surely one is most likely to find an example of it among the more backward folk and those more remote from civilization. Yet there is, as the eminent pagan says, no nation so barbarous, no people so savage, that they have not a deep-seated conviction that there is a God. And they who in other aspects of life seem least to differ from brutes still continue to retain some seed of religion. So deeply does the common conception occupy the minds of all, so tenaciously does it inhere in the hearts of all! Therefore, since from the beginning of the world there has been no region, no city, in short, no household, that could do without religion, there lies in this a tacit confession of a sense of deity inscribed in the hearts of all.

Indeed, even idolatry is ample proof of this conception. We know how man does not willingly humble himself so as to place other creatures over himself. Since, then, he prefers to worship wood and stone rather than to be thought of as having no God, clearly this is a most vivid impression of a divine being. So impossible is it to blot this from man's mind that natural disposition would be more easily altered, as altered indeed it is when man voluntarily sinks from his natural haughtiness to the very depths in order to honor God! . . .

3. Actual godlessness is impossible

Men of sound judgment will always be sure that a sense of divinity which can never be effaced is engraved upon men's minds. Indeed, the perversity of the impious, who though they struggle furiously are unable to extricate themselves from the fear of God, is abundant testimony that this conviction, namely, that there is some God, is naturally inborn in all, and is fixed deep within, as it were in the very marrow. Although Diagoras* and his like may jest at whatever has been believed in every age concerning religion, and Dionysius† may mock the heavenly judgment, this is sardonic laughter, for

---

* Diagoras of Melos, called "the atheist" (a contemporary of Socrates).
† Dionysius, tyrant of Syracuse, 407–367 B.C.

the worm of conscience, sharper than any cauterizing iron, gnaws away within. I do not say, as Cicero did, that errors disappear with the lapse of time, and that religion grows and becomes better each day. For the world (something will have to be said of this a little later) tries as far as it is able to cast away all knowledge of God, and by every means to corrupt the worship of him. I only say that though the stupid hardness in their minds, which the impious eagerly conjure up to reject God, wastes away, yet the sense of divinity, which they greatly wished to have extinguished, thrives and presently burgeons. From this we conclude that it is not a doctrine that must first be learned in school, but one of which each of us is master from his mother's womb and which nature itself permits no one to forget, although many strive with every nerve to this end. . . .

Chapter IV: This Knowledge is either Smothered or Corrupted, Partly by Ignorance, Partly by Malice

1. Superstition

As experience shows, God has sown a seed of religion in all men. But scarcely one man in a hundred is met who fosters it, once received, in his heart, and none in whom it ripens – much less shows fruit in season [cf. Ps. 1:3]. Besides while some may evaporate in their own superstitions and others deliberately and wickedly desert God, yet all degenerate from the true knowledge of him. And so it happens that no real piety remains in the world. But as to my statement that some erroneously slip into superstition, I do not mean by this that their ingenuousness should free them from blame. For the blindness under which they labor is almost always mixed with proud vanity and obstinacy. Indeed, vanity joined with pride can be detected in the fact that, in seeking God, miserable men do not rise above themselves as they should, but measure him by the yardstick of their own carnal stupidity, and neglect sound investigation; thus out of curiosity they fly off into empty speculations. They do not therefore apprehend God as he offers himself, but imagine him as they have fashioned him in their own presumption. When this gulf opens, in whatever direction they move their feet, they cannot but plunge headlong into ruin. Indeed, whatever they afterward attempt by way of worship or service of God, they cannot bring as tribute to him, for they are worshiping not God but a figment and a dream of their own heart. Paul eloquently notes this wickedness: "Striving to be wise, they make fools of themselves" [Rom. 1:22] He had said before that "they became futile in their thinking" [Rom. 1:21]. In order, however, that no one might excuse their guilt, he adds that they are justly blinded. For not content with sobriety but claiming for themselves more than is right, they wantonly bring darkness upon themselves – in fact, they become fools in their empty and perverse haughtiness. From this it follows that their stupidity is not excusable, since it is caused not only by vain curiosity but by an inordinate desire to know more than is fitting, joined with a false confidence. . . .

Book Two: The Knowledge of God the Redeemer

Chapter VI: Fallen Man Ought to Seek Redemption in Christ

1. Only the Mediator helps fallen man
The whole human race perished in the person of Adam. Consequently that original excellence and nobility which we have recounted would be of no profit to us but would rather redound to our greater shame, until God, who does not recognize as his handiwork men defiled and corrupted by sin, appeared as Redeemer in the person of his only-begotten Son. Therefore, since we have fallen from life into death, the whole knowledge of God the Creator that we have discussed would be useless unless faith also followed, setting forth for us God our Father in Christ. The natural order was that the frame of the universe should be the school in which we were to learn piety, and from it pass over to eternal life and perfect felicity. But after man's rebellion, our eyes – wherever they turn – encounter God's curse. This curse, while it seizes and envelops innocent creatures through our fault, must overwhelm our souls with despair. For even if God wills to manifest his fatherly favor to us in many ways, yet we cannot by contemplating the universe infer that he is Father. Rather, conscience presses us within and shows in our sin just cause for his disowning us and not regarding or recognizing us as his sons. Dullness and ingratitude follow, for our minds, as they have been blinded, do not perceive what is true. And as all our senses have become perverted, we wickedly defraud God of his glory.

We must, for this reason, come to Paul's statement: "Since in the wisdom of God the world did not know God through wisdom, it pleased God through the folly of preaching to save those who believe" [1 Cor. 1:21]. This magnificent theater of heaven and earth, crammed with innumerable miracles, Paul calls the "wisdom of God." Contemplating it, we ought in wisdom to have known God. But because we have profited so little by it, he calls us to the faith of Christ, which, because it appears foolish, the unbelievers despise.

Therefore, although the preaching of the cross does not agree with our human inclination, if we desire to return to God our Author and Maker, from whom we have been estranged, in order that he may again begin to be our Father, we ought nevertheless to embrace it humbly. Surely, after the fall of the first man no knowledge of God apart from the Mediator has had power unto salvation [cf. Rom. 1:16; 1 Cor. 1:24]. For Christ not only speaks of his own age, but comprehends all ages when he says: "This is eternal life, to know the Father to be the one true God, and Jesus Christ whom he has sent" [John 17:3]. . . .

CONTEMPORARY REFLECTION

Bringing God Home through Preaching

Cornelius Plantinga, Jr.

In "The God with Whom We Can be Confident" (1984), the final sermon of his ministry at the Fourth Presbyterian Church of Chicago, the great Welsh preacher Elam Davies told of an incident that had stuck in his mind.[1] During their years in Chicago, Davies and his wife Grace used to return to Wales on holiday, and every so often they would visit a favorite spot, a giant rock on the coast called the Great Orme. The Great Orme is at land's end, right at the seaside, and people gather on it to watch sunsets. On clear evenings, people watch the yellow sun drop steadily into the pewter sea, backlighting strands of clouds in such a way that the whole horizon turns into a kaleidoscope. Because the sunsets are so spectacular and because the people who watch them are so Welsh, the spectators on the Great Orme sometimes weep.

On one particular night, the Davies were parked there, taking in the beauty, when a beat-up car drew alongside. In this car were a couple of elderly people and also a man who seemed to be their son, likely the son of their middle-age. Some accident or illness had come to this son along the way, with the result that he was clearly disabled. There he lay in the back seat behind his parents, limp, and maybe exasperated with the condition that held him captive.

Then, as the great ball of fire began its final descent toward the sea, the two old folks got out of their junker and came around to the back seat. They reached in, hoisted their son up to a sitting position, and maneuvered him forward to the edge of the seat. And, according to Davies's account, just as the sun in its full flame, in a final burst of glory, dropped below the rim of the world – just then the old parents reached under their boy's chin, raised his head, and "pointed him out there toward the horizon."

"And I knew at that moment," said Elam Davies in his sermon, "that God can dazzle us with all the magnificence of the universe, but that the *secret* of the universe lies in a love that comes to us in our weakness and in our need."

God's glory was in the sunset that night. Of course. That's what everybody on the Great Orme came to see. But the greater glory of God was in the hearts of two old parents and in the fingers that lifted the chin of their son. And the simple name of this glory is love.

What Does Preaching Do?

Let's say that Christian preaching is the presentation of God's word at a particular time to particular people by someone authorized to do it. Like telling others of one's spiritual experiences (some Christians call it "sharing" or, in intellectually chaste moods, "just sharing"), good preaching is personal and concrete. A sermon is not a lecture. But even a highly personal and concrete preacher, such as Elam Davies, does not create his message from scratch. He works out of the Bible, which is his community's book. And how he personally feels about his message matters, but it matters less than how faithfully he brings it. After all, he himself is addressed by his message, just as his listeners are. In fact, the sermon's message ultimately comes only through, and not from, the preacher, and it centers on the same God who sends it. "For we do not proclaim ourselves," as St. Paul puts it, "we proclaim Jesus Christ as Lord" (2 Cor. 4:5).

Then Paul adds these words (vv. 6–7): "For it is the God who said, 'Let light shine out of darkness,' who has shone in our hearts to give the light of the knowledge of the glory of God in the face of Christ. But we have this treasure in clay jars, so that it may be made clear that this extraordinary power belongs to God and does not come from us."

Imagine a preacher at work on this text. In a classic way of proceeding, he or she studies the text for a time, listening to it, questioning it, probing it, looking at it from several angles of vision. The preacher compares it with kindred texts in scripture and reads what biblical scholars have said about the text and its family. The preacher also attempts to fit this text into his or her biblical and theological network of understanding, so that the text can speak from its context there. All along, the preacher imagines strategies or "moves" for getting the text's message across to listeners – apt illustrations, dramatic contrasts, perhaps the use of a refrain that stitches the sermon together. Then one day the preacher stands before a congregation and preaches this text.

How so? Classically speaking, to preach a text is to do in other words what the text does. Thus, depending on the text, the preacher might warn people one Sunday and comfort them the next. She might prophesy, counsel, teach, or rebuke. She might provoke people if her text is provocative enough. She might begin by challenging a popular opinion and end by reinforcing it, but only after moving this opinion inside a biblical view of the world. She might reproduce an interrogative text by turning a big part of her sermon into a repeated question.

If she is preaching 2 Corinthians 4:6, perhaps she will tell her listeners a story like the one of the people on the Great Orme, not just because the story inspires, but especially because the story inspires listeners right along the same line as the text does. This is a line that runs from creation to redemption, showing us, at both ends of the line, a God who says "Let there be light."

We should notice that redemption is the harder piece of work. The reason is that in redemption God cannot start fresh. Instead, God must salvage human beings who have already been damaged by years of sin and misery. The difficulty of this salvage project may be measured by the kind of pain it takes, namely the self-giving passion and death of Jesus Christ, the Son of God, who had to cut the loop of retaliation by absorbing evil without passing it on.

The death and resurrection of Jesus Christ occupy the center of human history, according to Christians, and the center of Christian preaching. In the death of Christ, God adopts a "like-cures-like" strategy of defeating death by way of another death. Then God follows up with a similar strategy for passing along the death benefits of Christ to his followers. Remarkably, God elects to salvage human beings by deputizing other human beings to preach Christ to them – other human beings who are just as damaged and foolish as their audience. In 2 Corinthians 4:7 Paul compares the preacher (he has himself especially in mind) to a baked clay jar. To find the flame of love in such homely ware, to find the flame of God's glory in human hearts, Elam and Grace Davies found it one night on the Great Orme, is to find a kind of miracle.

What the Davieses found that night also provides a first-rate sermon illustration, which reminds us that the preacher's job is not just to repeat a text, but also to outfit it for the hearing of a congregation. The preacher not only does in other words what the text does. She also says in other words what the text says – dressing it up or down, shaping and coloring and amplifying it in such a way that when people hear the preached text they hear God's word to them. For example, they might hear a warning that sin is not only an offense against God and neighbor, but also a form of self-abuse. They might hear that we do not belong to ourselves, that we are not our own authors or centers, and that, surprisingly, this is a comfort. They might hear that idolaters want to carry their gods around with them, but that the God of Scripture carries us, and that a central question of religion is therefore "Who is carrying whom?"

When preaching works well, the result is eventful. People feel pierced, or assured, or blessed. They sense that they are somehow joined to God by this religious event, just as they are by partaking of baptism or the Lord's Supper. Indeed, Christians think of a preached and heard sermon as "an audible sacrament," to use a phrase attributed to Augustine.[2] Sacraments are ligaments of the covenant between God and believers – covenant "binders," we might say. So preaching naturally binds believers to God by making God audible to them. But a sermon may also take hold of others. A well-designed sermon may make God audible to unbelievers, or to seekers, or to people who are so consciously ambivalent about God that they would hardly know what to call themselves.

Bringing God Home

In fact, we may generalize: one of the main functions of preaching is to make God real to listeners, including to the preacher who is always a sermon's "pioneer listener."[3] Of course God is real whether people in church think so or not. Presuming to "activate" God by preaching a sermon would be a prime piece of arrogance.

In another way, though, sermons do render God actual to listeners. I mean that in healthy preaching God's grace and power come home to people: these qualities are brought to mind, raised up in consciousness, affirmed by the heart. A godly life is at least a God-conscious life, and the preacher stimulates such a life by re-presenting God to listeners. When this is effectively done – that is, when the preacher's good efforts are energized and focused by the power of the Holy Spirit (the unpredictable variable or "x-factor" in preaching) – then once more God seems large and luminous to people who are listening.

However, because a sermon bears God's word, it also calls for a response on the part of those who hear it. A dynamic sermon goes to human hearts and stirs them. When people hear such a sermon they feel faith rising in them. They feel passion rising in them. They may feel very much like *doing* something. When Martin Luther King, Jr. preached one of the great prophetic texts of scripture such as Micah 6:8 ("What does the Lord require of you but to do justice, and to love kindness, and to walk humbly with your God?"), or when he made a political speech that arose from this text, the effect was the same. People were moved to believe that God was on the side of racial justice. They were moved with a passion for seeking this justice. But, especially, people listening to King were moved in their hearts to shout "*Yes!*" and then to start marching. Sometimes King would urge them on: "Let us march on ballot boxes!" he would proclaim. "Let us march on ballot boxes till we send to . . . the United States Congress men who will not fear to do justice!"[4]

"True religion," said Jonathan Edwards, "consists in great measure in . . . the fervent exercises of the heart."[5] Edwards meant that, at its core, true religion has to do not just with kindling our passions, but also with aiming them in the right direction. The world is full of good. The godly person must say "Yes" to it with all his heart and then act accordingly. The world is also full of evil. The godly person must say "No" to it with all his heart and then act accordingly. The world is full of the mixture of good and evil so that the godly person sometimes needs the gift of discernment before he knows *what* to say or *how* to act.

In any event, true religion always begins from the central place in us where we "hate what is evil" and "hold fast to what is good" (Rom. 12:9). A sequence of hearty yes's and no's lies at the center of true religion, said Edwards, and this is why we sing our praise instead of merely saying it. This is why we preach the word instead of simply reading it. This is why in the Lord's Supper we "eat and drink our God." The reason in each case is that we want to get our hearts going again, and we want the passions of our hearts to find their true target.[6] For example, we want love and joy to start up, and we especially want these "affections," as Edwards called them, to be aimed at God. We want the reality of God to be big enough to see with the eyes of faith and good enough to taste with the mouth of faith. To "taste and see that the Lord is good" (Ps. 34:8) means for Edwards, and for many writers on spirituality before him, that we need preaching and other spiritual exercises to give us a sense of God's "sweetness" and "glorious brightness."[7]

Here a caution is in order. To say that preaching helps to make God real to us does not mean that it helps to make God obvious. Nor, certainly, does the preached God somehow become our possession to be shaped and used as we see fit. Any attempt to possess God or the word of God in this way would be raw idolatry. "Bringing God home" to believers gives nobody a license to domesticate God.

The truth is that God may be known, but God is also hard to know. God does approach us in sermons and sacraments, but only by grace. The mystery of God's grace and the majesty of God's nature combine to generate one of the most basic of biblical paradoxes: God is both present to us and absent from us, both immanent and transcendent, both available and also perfectly free in power and grace. Karl Barth, a theologian who never met a paradox he didn't like, wrote that God was both veiled and unveiled, and veiled in his unveiling.[8] Although Barth sharpened the point of the paradox more than most, he was working from a solid biblical base. On the one hand, "the Lord used to speak to Moses face to face, as one speaks to a friend"; on the other hand, "The Lord said to Moses . . . 'you shall see my back; but my face shall not be seen.'" So basic is this paradox to biblical thinking that in Exodus these two testimonies appear next door to each other (Ex. 33:11, 23).

Human suffering seems to heighten the paradox instead of collapsing it. On the one hand, believers who suffer great pain sometimes lament what feels like the withdrawal of God: "My God, my God, why have you forsaken me?" (Ps. 22:1, Matt. 27:46). On the other hand, many believers testify that it is just when they are imperilled that they most fully experience the presence of God: "Even though I walk through the darkest valley, I fear no evil; for you are with me" (Ps. 23:4). In one of the eloquent passages of his *Confessions*, Augustine states the paradox with simple depth: "Who then are you, my God? . . . deeply hidden, yet most intimately present."[9]

A biblical word that is faithfully preached and believed will usually bring the reality of God home to people at both of these depths – both at the depths of God's hiddenness and also at the depths of God's intimate nearness.

While taking part in the drama of bringing these things home, a preacher inevitably clothes a text not only with stories and images, but also with many features of his own mind and personality. God is personal, and it is therefore fitting that the gospel of God should be preached by persons. Thus, when a preacher stands before a congregation, his posture, energy level, choice of language, tone of voice, degree of eye contact with his audience – even his manners – may all serve to make God real to us. Some of his "fruit of the Spirit," such as generosity and patience, will help as well. If he has a history of self-giving strength, the God of whom he speaks may seem especially plausible to hearers.

Such plausibility is crucial, because it is the matrix of faith. To play his part in creating this matrix, the preacher must bend heart, mind, and voice to his calling. He must preach the word of God quite deeply into our lives. He must give up the hope of thrilling people all the time, and of amusing them, and of confirming their favorite ideas. Because he must rebuke as well as comfort, he must give up the hope of regularly endearing himself to listeners. Moving to the pulse of God's word and not to the breezes of fashion, he must give up the hope of mere popularity. In short, he must give up anything that threatens his integrity as a preacher.

By guarding his integrity, the preacher becomes available to God as a lamp.

When he preaches – when he says in other words what the text says, and does in other words what the text does – a part of the glory of God may shine from him. And then his audience may spot "the light of the knowledge of the glory of God in the face of Jesus Christ." God's light shines from acts of love and justice, as Elam Davies discovered on the Great Orme and as the followers of Martin Luther King discovered when he shamed a whole nation into passing civil rights legislation. But God's light shines especially from God's Word made flesh and from God's Word made audible. To praise God, says Augustine, we must call upon God; to call upon God we must know God; to know God we must believe in God. And to believe in God we need a preacher.[10]

Preaching to Practical Atheists

The preacher's job of bringing God home to human beings is necessary not because most of the people in earshot of the preacher are atheists, but rather because many of them are "practical" atheists. I do not deny that even devout believers sometimes doubt the sheer existence of God. So luminous a believer as C. S. Lewis testified that just as he had once doubted his atheism, so too, after he had become a Christian, he endured certain moods in which the whole Christian religion seemed "very improbable" to him.[11] So sturdy a Puritan as Increase Mather wrote in his diary for 29 July 1664 that he was "grieved, grieved, grieved with temptations to Atheisme."[12]

Nevertheless, such temptations are rare enough among believers as to be remarkable. What is more common among them is to forget about God. It happens all the time, and it happens right in the middle of a religious life. Religious people get distracted by the traffic of daily living – getting educated, making a living, juggling the responsibilities of various relationships. They get distracted by their joys, forgetting to thank God; they get distracted by their pain, forgetting to lament to God.

In one of his sermons, my teacher John Stek remarked that God has a big building project. God is building a kingdom of peace and justice, and, in so doing, has entrusted people like us with some of the jobs in this project. The problem is that we keep getting distracted by our own interests. We keep wanting to borrow God's tools to attempt side projects of our own, and then we complain that God doesn't bless these side projects as much as we would like.

As this last example suggests, some of our forgetfulness is owed to sin. We neglect God because we find ourselves more interesting. We avoid God because the knowledge of God makes us feel guilty or small by comparison. Above all, we ignore God because we prefer to lead our lives without divine interference. This forgetfulness is usual, but it is not normal and it is not trivial. As George MacDonald somewhere remarks, "the one principle of hell is 'I am my own.'"

According to Psalm 14 "fools say in their hearts, 'There is no God.'" Most believers who read these words think of classic theoretical atheists. They think of Marx, Nietzsche, and Freud. Or nowadays they think of scientific naturalists who insist that the great engine of life is ungoverned randomness. *That's* atheism – complete with gross inhospitality to God and a stubborn insistence that plain, dumb luck must be the ultimate source of life. To Christian believers such naturalistic atheism sounds narrow-minded. It sounds absurd. In a world of staggering complexity inside a single cell, what could be more provincial than refusing to make room for God? Only fools say in their hearts, "There is no God."

How awkward it is that when Christian believers take these words upon their lips they discover that the words are a boomerang. The psalmist is not talking about scientific naturalists. He is not talking about those who scorn the very idea of purposeful design in the world. Of course the psalmist would have found such naturalists foolish too, but he is not talking about them. He is talking about believers – people who say they believe in God and claim they believe in God, but who live as if heaven has closed its doors.

These are practical atheists and every church has them. They are theists in their heads, but atheists in their hearts and therefore in their practice. Practical atheism of the sort that we find in Psalm 14 has almost nothing to do with sheer disbelief. It has almost everything to do with sheer disobedience. Practical atheists discount God because they presume that God is "shut up idle in heaven" and that we are free to do what we want.[13] To be a practical atheist is to say with our lips, "There is a God" and to say with our hearts, "but he's out to lunch."

It is important to emphasize that practical atheism is a disease of the religious. In fact, when we are most religious we may be most at risk of contracting this disease. It is true that the spiritual exercises of religion may make God real for us in some of the ways that I have described. Reading scripture, preaching and listening to sermons, singing hymns of praise and thanksgiving, answering the call to fight for social justice – all such things tie us to the living God in such a way that by repeating them we may come to know God more keenly and to serve God more fruitfully. Honest religious practice builds spiritual momentum. "To those who have, more will be given" (Mark 4:25).

Needless to say, not nearly all religious practice is honest. Some of it gets diverted from the kingdom of God to side projects of our own, as John Stek said. For example, people use religion to get rich or to get happy or to feel good about themselves. They use it to build a power base and to bend other people to their will. Believers are entirely capable of using religion to *conceal* the character of God, as in those cases where they turn God into a white supremacist or a liberal Democrat. It is not only secularists who "suppress the truth" about God. This famous Pauline characterization of sinners in Romans 1:18 indicts believers as well. Believers, not just secularists, exchange "the glory of the immortal God for images resembling a mortal human being" (Rom. 1:23).

Why else do new revised versions of God keep appearing? Why else does God emerge in believing communities as a capitalist, and then an anti-capitalist for a few decades, and then a capitalist again? If we are intellectuals, God is our tenured professor in heaven; if we are anti-intellectuals, God is a small-group leader who hates theology; if we are poor, God is a revolutionary; if we are propertied, God is a night watchman over our goods. If we are theologians of a certain sort, God is the essential and existential dynamic of our ultimate horizon situation. The gods of the Persians always look like Persians. "Unbelief is not the only way of suppressing the truth about God," writes Merold Westphal, "it is only the most honest."[14]

The preacher's job is to bring *God* home to us – not some blown up portrait of ourselves.

Preaching God

What this means in the pulpit is that the preacher must be willing to practice not only faith, but also suspicion. He must suspect us all, including himself, of a tendency toward idolatry, and he must suspect us all, including himself, of a tendency to mix some hypocrisy in with our idolatry.

These religious sins are triply dangerous. In the first place, they make God's actual character and will obscure to us. In the second place, these sins typically hide under a cloak of innocence, or even of holiness, with the result that they are hard for others to detect. (If you say Jesus' name often enough and piously enough, people might not notice that you are a fraud.) In the third place, particularly where hypocrisy is concerned, these religious sins corrupt our own consciousness so that they are hard for *us* to detect too. There is no more fertile field for self-deception than the presumption that we are sincere in our faith, and there is no scarier figure than a sincere hypocrite – a person who is false to the core, but who really believes in his integrity.

In order to bring God home to us, the faithful preacher will try to counter our tendency toward idolatry and hypocrisy. He will adopt a healthy self-suspicion and encourage the rest of us to follow suit.

One way in which preachers may express both faith and self-suspicion is by asking questions about God. Psalm 14 says that fools turn their backs on God but that the wise "seek after God" (v. 2). So in the spirit of Psalm 14 wise preachers adopt the posture of a seeker. They know that God is not only intimately present, but also hidden. They know as well that seekers are not limited to the ecclesiastically homeless folk who visit a mission-minded mega-church. A seeker is anybody in search of God. This means that many long-term believers qualify for seeker status. Many ministers qualify. Also some theologians and theology students, for in its most famous definition theology is "faith seeking understanding," and the main object of our understanding in theology is God.[15]

The wise seek after God in their preaching and in their listening to preaching. What makes them wise is that they have discovered something about God and the world, and they have discovered a knack for fitting themselves into God's world. At the same time, they have also discovered how little they know of God and of the divine purposes, and how clumsy are some of their attempts to fit themselves into God's project in the world.

How do the wise make such discoveries? By taking an alert and receptive attitude toward reality. By assuming that reality is a lot bigger than what happens within the confines of their own skull. By letting scripture teach them and the Holy Spirit lead them. By apprenticing themselves to saints. And, all along, by spending time in the interrogative mood.

The wise seek after God by asking questions. They ask questions and then they wait. How simple it sounds, and how seldom it happens. The wise ask questions and then they wait for a response. Fools, on the other hand, do not ask anything. They just make statements. As the saying goes, fools are often in error, but never in doubt. They do not *wonder* about anything.

But the wise, including wise preachers, ask a lot of questions. They know that we have not created our own natural riches – beauty, memory, will – and this thought leads them to wonder who did. They know that we human beings are finite and corruptible, and they wonder who might be infinite and incorruptible. They know that if we human beings try to put the weight of our longing and adoration on other human beings, those other human beings will break and so will we – as when a celebrity breaks under the weight of our worship and leaves disillusioned fans to sift through the wreckage. The wise person wonders if anyone in the universe can actually satisfy our longing, forgive our folly, and bear the weight of our worship. In short, the wise and restless heart seeks a supreme good to bring it to rest.[16]

Wise persons keep seeking God. They wonder about things and they wonder about persons and so, like Augustine, they wonder about God. How does God speak? Is God inside or outside? How can God be immense without a body? Is God more like a single complex person or more like a close society of three persons? Is Jesus the same as God or different? Can a person under the wings of God get brain cancer there? Where is God's home? How masculine or feminine is God? Can we cause God to suffer? If so, is God at our disposal? If not, can God have compassion? When human beings lobby God in group prayer, does this really make any difference to God's plans?

The wise seek God by wondering, and by asking questions that arise from their wondering, and often they do these things by preaching and listening to sermons.

"Most persons," wrote Rufus Jones, "would listen on their knees to anyone who would make God absolutely real to them."[17] Maybe so and maybe not, but nobody should underestimate the challenge of making absolutely real to us the God who is both hidden and intimately present. The challenge is large in those liberal, cerebral churches where God is unspeakable and remote, less a person than an idea. Here the portrait of God seems to have been drawn by an abstract impressionist, and the pious hesitancy of the faithful is hard to tell from agnosticism. To rebalance Augustine's equation in such settings the wise preacher will lean hard on the truth of God's intimate presence with us. She will speak of hearts that have been strangely warmed by God. She will testify of lives that have been renewed by the Spirit of God, and she will share the words "born again" when she testifies. She will tell of "a personal relationship with Jesus Christ," and she will have something thoughtful to say when people ask her the meaning of this phrase. Most important, to Christians whose God seems remote, the wise preacher will bring good news of great joy: God has come to us. A child, Immanuel, has been born to us, and even the wise men from the East – those from Harvard, Yale, and Princeton – belong on their knees before him.

The challenge of making God real to believers is big enough in cerebral churches where the knowledge of God "merely flits in the brain."[18] Surprisingly, the challenge is just as big in those evangelical churches where a sermon about God has to get through layers of old bumper sticker piety. Here the sermon must reach people whose God does not seem to them hidden at all. Are not their lives filled with signs and wonders? Does not God speak to them in plain English? Did not they just talk with God face to face this very morning – the way a man talks to his friend?

To rebalance Augustine's equation in such settings the preacher must lean hard on the hiddenness side of the equation. Here the wise preacher will offer a tart and astringent God for people with too much spiritual fat in their diet. She will preach a strange and elusive God for people who have become too familiar with God. She will preach an austere God to straighten the spines of evangelical Christians whose lyrics have already slumped into sentimentality by ten o'clock on the first morning of the week ("I felt every teardrop when in darkness you cried; and I came to remind you that for those tears I died").

Sentimental Christians sometimes suppose that a meeting with God would be like a walk in a garden or a coffee date with a friend. The truth is that it might be more like getting electrocuted. Calvin comments that the saints in scripture who feel the presence of God are "stricken and overcome." In fact, they are "so shaken" as to be "almost annihilated."[19]

Conclusion

In this fact lies a sobering truth, namely that no matter what our religious style, we probably want God less than we think. We human beings do seek God in prayer and in sacraments and in the push toward justice. We do seek God in preaching sermons and in listening to them. We seek God and we should. It is natural for creatures to want their creator, and it is wise for sinners to want their savior.

But the people who really want God – the ones who thirst for God the way a parched creature thirsts for water in a desert – are typically people who are in deep trouble. It is the lepers and the lame and the besieged who want God in their lives. It is people who have been deprived and diminished who cry out for God their savior. The rest of us have reason to keep the search going as long as we can. Comfortable people have reason to hear sermons about God with half a mind, and to launch prayers toward God with half a heart, and to sing hymns to God with words they cannot recount five minutes later.

The reason is that God slays in order to save, and the search for God is therefore a death wish.[20] Our interest in God is often mild; God's interest in us is fierce. That is why the heavens get ripped open in Mark 1. It is not as if we keep "bumping our heads against the glass ceiling" as we try to get at God. Just the opposite. God rips open the heavens to get at *us*. Mark's gospel says that God is on the loose in Jesus Christ and that nobody is safe.[21] None of our favorite sins is safe. Everything in us that is smug or envious has to die. Everything grudging or greedy has to die. All our self-indulgence has to die. Because these sins have grown into our hearts (the place where we say there is no God), we cannot be rid of them unless we ourselves die and rise with Christ.

The upshot is that when we think of meeting God we ought to do so with a sense not only of joy, but also of horror. According to C. S. Lewis, who was an accomplished seeker, when we talk of searching for God, we "might as well talk about the mouse's search for the cat."[22]

We are divided creatures who want God but also flee from God. We are like Cain in Genesis 4. He wants neither to obey God ("Am I my brother's keeper?"), nor to lose God. And so when God banishes him, the desolate Cain first protests ("My punishment is greater than I can bear") and then grieves ("I shall be hidden from your face!").

That is who we are, and the preacher must say so. She must speak the truth not only about God but also about us – people who look so much like God, have wandered so far from God, and so urgently need the grace of God.

255

Notes

1 Elam Davies, "The God with Whom We Can be Confident," a sermon preached in the Fourth Presbyterian Church, Chicago, 6 May 1984 (cassette tape).

2 Augustine, cited in Mary Catherine Hilkert, "Preaching, Theology Of," *The New Dictionary of Sacramental Worship*, ed. Peter E. Fink, SJ (Collegeville, MN: Liturgical Press, 1990), p. 998.

3 Roger E. Van Harn, *Pew Rights: For People Who Listen to Sermons* (Grand Rapids: Eerdmans, 1992), p. 18.

4 Martin Luther King, Jr., cited in Stephen L. Carter, *The Culture of Disbelief: How American Law and Politics Trivialize Religious Devotion* (New York: Basic Books, 1993), p. 48.

5 Jonathan Edwards, *Religious Affections*, ed. John E. Smith, *The Works of Jonathan Edwards*, ed. Perry Miller, vol. 2 (New Haven: Yale University Press, 1959), p. 99.

6 Ibid., p. 115.

7 Ibid., p. 95.

8 Karl Barth, *Church Dogmatics*, ed. G. W. Bromiley and T. F. Torrance, trans. G. W. Bromiley (Edinburgh: T. & T. Clark, 2nd edn, 1975), I/1, p. 165.

9 Augustine, *Confessions*, trans. Henry Chadwick (Oxford: Oxford University Press, 1992), 4, I:iv(4).

10 Ibid., 3, I:i (1).

11 C. S. Lewis, *Mere Christianity* (New York: Macmillan, 1960), p. 109.

12 Increase Mather, cited in Michael G. Hall, *The Last American Puritan: The Life of Increase Mather, 1639–1723* (Middletown, CT: Wesleyan University Press, 1988), p. 65.

13 John Calvin, *Institutes of the Christian Religion*, ed. John T. McNeill, trans. Ford Lewis Battles, The Library of Christian Classics (Philadelphia: Westminster, 1960), 48, I.4.2.

14 Merold Westphal, "Taking St. Paul Seriously: Sin as an Epistemological Category," in Thomas P. Flint (ed.), *Christian Philosophy* (Notre Dame: University of Notre Dame Press, 1990), p. 214.

15 St. Anselm, *An Address (Proslogion)*, in *A Scholastic Miscellany: Anselm to Ockham*, ed. and trans. Eugene R. Fairweather (Philadelphia: Westminster, 1961), p. 70.

16 Augustine, *Confessions*, 3, I:1(1).

17 Rufus Jones, *Social Law in the Spiritual World: Studies in Human and Divine Inter-Relationship* (Philadelphia: John C. Winston, 1904), p. 33.

18 Calvin, *Institutes*, 61, I.5.9.

19 Ibid., 39, I.1.3.

20 Stanley Sturing, "To See God," an unpublished course paper at Calvin Theological Seminary, Grand Rapids, MI (20 November 1997), p. 3. Cf. Augustine, *Confessions*, 5, I:v(5): "Lest I die, let me die. . . ."

21 Donald Juel, "What Makes for 'Engagement?' Interpreting at the Beginning (Mark 1:1–15)," a lecture at the St. Olaf Conference on Theology & Music, St. Olaf College, Northfield, MN (15 July 1997).

22 C. S. Lewis, *Surprised by Joy: The Shape of My Early Life* (New York: Harcourt, Brace & World, 1955), p. 227.

Inquiring after God around the Lord's Table

Most Christians practice liturgical rites or sacraments either directly commanded by Jesus, suggested by the New Testament, or developed by the Church. In the medieval Church in the west there were seven sacraments: baptism, confirmation, penance, eucharist, marriage, holy orders, and anointing of the dying. Most Protestant churches retained two of these, baptism and eucharist, although some eliminated sacraments altogether.

In the Augustinian tradition a sacrament is the visible sign of the sacred that conveys God's grace to or sanctifies those who receive it properly. The visible sign of a sacrament is a ritual action using water, food, or, when more than two liturgical rites are acknowledged, oil, or a liturgical gesture like the laying on of hands and signing with the cross. The grace or sanctity of God that the liturgical action conveys nonverbally is explained to those receiving the sacrament through its accompanying liturgy and perhaps preaching. The meaning of both the verbal and the nonverbal parts of the sacrament must be accepted by the recipient in order for the rite to achieve its purpose: initiation into the Body of Christ, encouragement in the Christian life, ordination to special ministries, repentance and forgiveness, healing, or preparation for death in the catholic traditions. The sacraments symbolize God's grace both verbally and nonverbally to guide Christian life and ministry.

While Christian churches no longer agree about sacraments most honor in some way Jesus' command to his disciples to eat together in his name at the last meal (a Passover celebration) he had with his disciples before he died, as recorded in all four Gospels. Jesus distributed bread and wine to his friends, instructing them that these elements were his body and blood that were soon to be given over to death on their behalf and enjoining them that whenever they shared such a meal they remember him.

The celebration of this event is variously known as the Lord's Supper, Communion, the sacrament of the altar, or the Holy Eucharist, the Greek word for thanksgiving. Specifically, eucharist refers to the liturgical aspect of the rite. It gives thanks for the gracious work of the Trinity from the creation of the world through Christ's sacrifice for humanity, anticipates his final return in victory, includes the biblical testimony to Jesus' institution of the sacrament in 1 Corinthians 11:23–6, and prays for the Holy Spirit to sanctify the bread and wine for the people. Communion refers to the distribution and eating of the elements in the gathered community that follows the Eucharistic Prayer.

There has long been controversy on just what happens in the Lord's Supper and therefore about the liturgy that describes it. In the early Christian centuries eucharistic celebration was the center of ecclesial life. In fact, it constituted or defined the Church as those who gather weekly to recall Jesus' life and death and to celebrate his resurrection. In the Middle Ages the western Church focused on Christ's death, and the sacrament of the altar was understood as a re-enactment not so much of the last supper as of the mystery of salvation, Christ's death itself as sacrifice for human sin. This sacrifice of the Mass constituted the Church as the instrument of the renewal of the world. Christ became truly present in the world again in the sacrament. This theology was central to St. Catherine as we saw earlier. The Church, on this view, is not a building or bureaucratic institution but an act: the communion of believers with God and one another through God.

During the Protestant Reformation, the leaders of the Reform understood the faith of the believer rather than the celebration of the Mass to constitute the Church, creating a major rift with Rome. All the sacraments had to be completely rethought. The Reformers were unable to agree on what sacraments were generally, nor could they agree about the Lord's Supper. Ulrich Zwingli understood the rite as a memorial only, while Martin Luther and John Calvin held mediating positions between Zwingli and Rome. Thus, the Protestant churches divided from one another as well as from Rome, which taught that the elements actually become the body and blood of Christ even though they look and taste like bread and wine. In the late twentieth century the member churches of the World Council of Churches prepared a broadly catholic eucharistic liturgy as a step toward reuniting the divided churches of the west.*

The two pieces we have in this chapter represent two of the traditions that retain the real presence of Christ: Lutheran and Roman Catholic. Calvinist sacramentology and the nonsacramental position of the Radical Reformation are not represented here, although they would have to be included in any full discussion of sacraments. Although separated by 450 years, the two offerings we have here are strikingly similar in their understanding of the Lord's Supper, indicating how thinking has changed over this span of time. Martin Luther's treatise was written in 1519, at the beginning of the

---

* *Baptism, Eucharist, Ministry.* Geneva: Secretariat on Faith and Order, World Council of Churches (1982).

Protestant Reformation. He had a fresh sacramental theology. The Lord's Supper, he argued, is not a sacrifice that the priest re-enacts on behalf of the people to placate God's anger. The direction of the action is the reverse. The salvation wrought by the once-for-all sacrifice of Christ is conveyed to the people by the minister who is ordained by the Church to administer the sacrament as the gift of God to the whole Church. By partaking of the food of God, believers are both reassured of God's love for them and gain strength from that assurance. They regularly recall that they are one with God in Christ in the power of the Holy Spirit and with the entire Church.

Luther held that the consecrated elements are the real presence of Christ. By eating his body people participate in the Incarnate Christ, and by drinking his blood they participate in his atoning death. They take comfort for their sins and remember God's forgiveness in Christ so that their fear of death and punishment subsides. But even those who are not afraid on account of their own sins need the sacrament. Christians are no longer individuals concerned only for themselves. As members incorporate in the mystical body of Christ by the work of the Holy Spirit in baptism, they themselves bear the sins as well as the strengths and virtues of all the other members of the Church past and present. This responsibility and power is symbolized by the bread that is one loaf made of many grains of wheat, and the wine that is pressed from many grapes. All take on this new identity in communion with God and one another.

Union with Christ and the saints means both that they lend the believer their strength and virtue and that each member of the Church is called to carry the sins and burdens of all other members, especially the sick, the poor, and other sinners. The sacrament of the table then unites the mystery of the Incarnation (that God became human in Jesus Christ), baptism (that individuals are taken into Christ's death and resurrection by the power of the Holy Spirit and made a member of his mystical body, the Church), the doctrine of the Church, sin and repentance, and love of neighbor as the foundation of Christian life. Communion symbolizes and actualizes mutual love and support in which the believer is strengthened for godly living and in turn offers him or herself to assist others to do the same.

The liturgical rite is a regular reminder that the Christian life is mutual burden-bearing (Gal. 6:2) and growth in mutual caring in a community that is made up of both the church militant (on earth) and the church triumphant (the communion of saints). The sacrament, Luther is clear, is a means for gradual transformation in love so that one makes others' concerns and burdens one's own and can rely on others to do so for oneself. Mutual encouragement and comfort, as well as mutual admonition and correction, are community responsibilities.

The contemporary Roman Catholic commentator Raymond Moloney is in striking agreement with Luther that the benefit of this sacrament is in its offer of the Christian life. This foretaste of the heavenly banquet is the foundation of the Church's life because it offers everyone the equal opportunity to join together in living an unselfish life following Jesus. The paschal mystery is that just as Jesus gave his life in the crucifixion and was raised up again to new life on the third day, the Christian who follows his example affirms this way of life in the eucharist. The mystery is that one loses one's life to gain it. Communion celebrates and orders Christian life in the Church and inaugurates eternal life with God.

Martin Luther, *The Blessed Sacrament of the Holy and True Body of Christ*

The holy sacrament of the altar, or of the holy and true body of Christ, also has three parts which it is necessary for us to know. The first is the sacrament, or sign. The second is the significance of this sacrament. The third is the faith required with each of the first two. These three parts must be found in every sacrament. The sacrament must be external and visible, having some material form or appearance. The significance must be internal and spiritual, within the spirit of the person. Faith must make both of them together operative and useful.

The sacrament, or external *sign*, consists in the form or appearance of bread and wine, just as baptism has water as its sign; only the bread and wine must be used in eating and drinking, just as the water of baptism is used by immersion or pouring. For the sacrament, or sign, must be received, or at least desired, if it is to work a blessing. Of course at present both kinds are not given to the people daily, as in former times. But this is not necessary since the priesthood partakes of it daily in sight of the people. It is enough that the people desire it daily and at present receive one kind, as the Christian Church ordains and provides.

For my part, however, I would consider it a good thing if the church should again decree in a general council that all persons be given both kinds, like the priests. Not because one kind is insufficient, since indeed the desire of faith is alone sufficient, as St. Augustine says, "Why do you prepare stomach and teeth? Only believe, and you have already partaken of the sacrament."* But it would be fitting and fine that the form, or sign, of the sacrament be given not in part only, but in its entirety, just as I said of

---

* St. Augustine, *Sermon* 112.5, in Migne 38, 645.

baptism: it would be more fitting to immerse in the water than to pour with it, for the sake of the completeness and perfection of the sign. For this sacrament [of the Body of Christ], as we shall see, signifies the complete union and the undivided fellowship of the saints; and this is poorly and unfittingly indicated by [distributing] only one part of the sacrament. Nor is there as great a danger in the use of the cup as is supposed, since the people seldom go to this sacrament. Besides Christ was well aware of all future dangers, and yet he saw fit to institute both kinds for the use of all his Christians.

The *significance* or effect of this sacrament is fellowship of all the saints. From this it derives its common name *synaxis* [Greek] or *communio* [Latin], that is, fellowship. And the Latin *communicare* [commune or communicate], or as we say in German, *zum sacrament gehen* [go to the sacrament], means to take part in this fellowship. Hence it is that Christ and all saints are one spiritual body, just as the inhabitants of a city are one community and body, each citizen being a member of the other and of the entire city. All the saints, therefore, are members of Christ and of the church, which is a spiritual and eternal city of God. And whoever is taken into this city is said to be received into the community of saints and to be incorporated into Christ's spiritual body and made a member of him. On the other hand *excommunicare* [excommunicate] means to put out of the community and to sever a member from this body; and that is called in our language "putting one under the ban" – though a distinction [is to be made in this regard] as I shall show in the following treatise, concerning the ban.

To receive this sacrament in bread and wine, then, is nothing else than to receive a sure sign of this fellowship and incorporation with Christ and all saints. It is as if a citizen were given a sign, a document, or some other token to assure him that he is a citizen of the city, a member of that particular community. St. Paul says this very thing in 1 Corinthians 10[:17], "We are all one bread and one body, for we all partake of one bread and of one cup."

This fellowship consists in this, that all the spiritual possessions of Christ and his saints are shared with and become the common property of him who receives this sacrament. Again all sufferings and sins also become common property; and thus love engenders love in return and [mutual love] unites. To carry out our homely figure, it is like a city where every citizen shares with all the others the city's name, honor, freedom, trade, customs, usages, help, support, protection, and the like, while at the same time he shares all the dangers of fire and flood, enemies and death, losses, taxes, and the like. For he who would share in the profits must also share in the costs, and ever recompense love with love. Here we see that whoever injures one citizen injures an entire city and all its citizens; whoever benefits one [citizen] deserves favor and thanks from all the others. So also in our natural body, as St. Paul says in 1 Corinthians 12[:25–26], where he gives this sacrament a spiritual explanation, "The members have [the same] care for one another; if one member suffers, all suffer together; if one member is honored, all rejoice together." This is obvious: if anyone's foot hurts him, yes, even the little toe, the eye at once looks at it, the fingers grasp it, the face puckers, the whole body bends over to it, and all are concerned with this small member; again, once it is cared for all the other members are benefited. This comparison must be noted well if one wishes to understand this sacrament, for Scripture uses it for the sake of the unlearned.

In this sacrament, therefore, man is given through the priest a sure sign from God himself that he is thus united with Christ and his saints and has all things in common [with them], that Christ's sufferings and life are his own, together with the lives and sufferings of all the saints. Therefore whoever does injury to [the believer], does injury to Christ and all the saints, as he says through the prophet [Zech. 2:8], "He who touches you touches the apple of my eye." On the other hand whoever does him a kindness does it to Christ and all his saints; as he says in Matthew 25[:40], "As you did it to one of the least of these my brethren, you did it to me." Again, man must be willing to share all the burdens and misfortunes of Christ and his saints, the cost as well as the profit. Let us consider more fully these two [sides of the fellowship].

Now adversity assails us in more than one form. There is, in the first place, the sin that remains in our flesh after baptism: the inclination to anger, hatred, pride, unchastity, and so forth. This sin assails us as long as we live. Here we not only need the help of the community [of saints] and of Christ, in order that they might with us fight this sin, but it is also necessary that Christ and his saints intercede for us before God, so that this sin may not be charged to our account by God's strict judgment. Therefore in order to strengthen and encourage us against this same sin, God gives us this sacrament, as much as to say, "Look, many kinds of sin are assailing you; take this sign by which I give you my pledge that this sin is assailing not only you but also my Son, Christ, and all his saints in heaven and on earth. Therefore take heart and be bold. You are not fighting alone. Great help and support are all around you." King David speaks thus of this bread, "The bread strengthens a man's heart" [Ps. 104:15]. And the Scriptures in numerous places ascribe to this sacrament the property of strengthening, as in Acts 9[:18–19] [where it is written] of St. Paul, "He was baptized, and when he had received the food, he was strengthened."

In the second place the evil spirit assails us unceasingly with many sins and afflictions. In the third place the world, full of wickedness, entices and persecutes us and is altogether bad. Finally our own guilty conscience assails us with our past sins; and there is the fear of death and the pains of hell.

All of these afflictions make us weary and weak, unless we seek strength in this fellowship, where strength is to be found.

Whoever is in despair, distressed by a sin-stricken conscience or terrified by death or carrying some other burden upon his heart, if he would be rid of them all, let him go joyfully to the sacrament of the altar and lay down his woe in the midst of the community [of saints] and seek help from the entire company of the spiritual body – just as a citizen whose property has suffered damage or misfortune at the hands of his enemies makes complaint to his town council and fellow citizens and asks them for help. The immeasurable grace and mercy of God are given us in this sacrament to the end that we might put from us all misery and tribulation [*Anfechtung*] and lay it upon the community [of saints], and especially on Christ. Then we may with joy find strength and comfort, and say, "Though I am a sinner and have fallen, though this or that misfortune has befallen me, nevertheless I will go to the sacrament to receive a sign from God that I have on my side Christ's righteousness, life, and sufferings, with all holy angels and the blessed in heaven and all pious men on earth. If I die, I am not alone in death; if I suffer, they suffer with me. [I know that] all my misfortune is shared with Christ and the saints, because I have a sure sign of their love toward me." See, this is the benefit to be derived from this sacrament; this is the use we should make of it. Then the heart cannot but rejoice and be strengthened.

When you have partaken of this sacrament, therefore, or desire to partake of it, you must in turn share the misfortunes of the fellowship, as has been said. But what are these? Christ in heaven and the angels, together with the saints, have no misfortunes, except when injury is done to the truth and to the Word of God. Indeed, as we have said, every bane and blessing of all the saints on earth affects them. Here your heart must go out in love and learn that this is a sacrament of love. As love and support are given you, you in turn must render love and support to Christ in his needy ones. You must feel with sorrow all the dishonor done to Christ in his holy Word, all the misery of Christendom, all the unjust suffering of the innocent, with which the world is everywhere filled to overflowing. You must fight, work, pray, and – if you cannot do more – have heartfelt sympathy. See, this is what it means to bear in your turn the misfortune and adversity of Christ and his saints. Here the saying of Paul is fulfilled, "Bear one another's burdens, and so fulfill the law of Christ" [Gal. 6:2]. See, as you uphold all of them, so they all in turn uphold you; and all things are in common, both good and evil. Then all things become easy, and the evil spirit cannot stand up against this fellowship.

When Christ instituted the sacrament, he said, "This is my body which is given for you, this is my blood which is poured out for you. As often as you do this, remember me" [see 1 Cor. 11:25–26]. It is as if he were saying,

"I am the Head, I will be the first to give himself for you. I will make your suffering and misfortune my own and will bear it for you, so that you in your turn may do the same for me and for one another, allowing all things to be common property, in me, and with me. And I leave you this sacrament as a sure token of all this, in order that you may not forget me, but daily call to mind and admonish one another by means of what I did and am still doing for you, in order that you may be strengthened, and also bear one another in the same way."

This is also a reason, indeed the chief reason, why this sacrament is received many times, while baptism is received but once. Baptism is the taking up or entering upon a new life, in the course of which boundless adversities assail us, with sins and sufferings, both our own and those of others. There is the devil, the world, and our own flesh and conscience, as I have said. They never cease to hound us and oppress us. Therefore we need the strength, support, and help of Christ and of his saints. These are pledged to us here, as in a sure sign, by which we are made one with them – incorporated into them – and all our woe is laid down in the midst of the community [of saints].

For this reason it even happens that this holy sacrament is of little or no benefit to those who have no misfortune or anxiety, or who do not sense their adversity. For it is given only to those who need strength and comfort, who have timid hearts and terrified consciences, and who are assailed by sin, or have even fallen into sin. How could it do anything for untroubled and secure spirits, who neither need nor desire it? For [Mary] the Mother of God says, "He fills only the hungry [Luke 1:53], and comforts them that are distressed."

In order that the disciples, therefore, might by all means be worthy and well prepared for this sacrament, Christ first made them sorrowful, held before them his departure and death, by which they became exceedingly troubled. And then he greatly terrified them when he said that one of them would betray him. When they were thus full of sorrow and anxiety, disturbed by sorrow and the sin of betrayal, then they were worthy, and he gave them his holy body to strengthen them. By which he teaches us that this sacrament is strength and comfort for those who are troubled and distressed by sin and evil. St. Augustine says the same thing, "This food demands only hungry souls, and is shunned by none so greatly as by a sated soul which does not need it."* Thus the Jews were required to eat the Passover with bitter herbs, standing and in haste [Exod. 12:8, 11]; this too signifies that this sacrament demands souls that are desirous, needy, and sorrowful. Now if one will make the afflictions of Christ and of all Christians his own, defend the truth,

---

* See Augustine's commentary on Psalm 22:26, in Migne 36, 178.

oppose unrighteousness, and help bear the needs of the innocent and the sufferings of all Christians, then he will find affliction and adversity enough, over and above that which his evil nature, the world, the devil, and sin daily inflict upon him. And it is even God's will and purpose to set so many hounds upon us and oppress us, and everywhere to prepare bitter herbs for us, so that we may long for this strength and take delight in the holy sacrament, and thus be worthy (that is, desirous) of it. . . .

There are those, indeed, who would gladly share in the profits but not in the costs. That is, they like to hear that in this sacrament the help, fellowship, and support of all the saints are promised and given to them. But they are unwilling in their turn to belong also to this fellowship. They will not help the poor, put up with sinners, care for the sorrowing, suffer with the suffering, intercede for others, defend the truth, and at the risk of [their own] life, property, and honor seek the betterment of the church and of all Christians. They are unwilling because they fear the world. They do not want to have to suffer disfavor, harm, shame, or death, although it is God's will that they be thus driven – for the sake of the truth and of their neighbors – to desire the great grace and strength of this sacrament. They are self-seeking persons, whom this sacrament does not benefit. Just as we could not put up with a citizen who wanted to be helped, protected, and made free by the community, and yet in his turn would do nothing for it nor serve it. No, we on our part must make the evil of others our own, if we desire Christ and his saints to make our evil their own. Then will the fellowship be complete, and justice be done to the sacrament. For the sacrament has no blessing and significance unless love grows daily and so changes a person that he is made one with all others.

To signify this fellowship, God has appointed such signs of this sacrament as in every way serve this purpose and by their very form stimulate and motivate us to this fellowship. For just as the bread is made out of many grains ground and mixed together, and out of the bodies of many grains there comes the body of one bread, in which each grain loses its form and body and takes upon itself the common body of the bread; and just as the drops of wine, in losing their own form, become the body of one common wine and drink – so it is and should be with us, if we use this sacrament properly. Christ with all saints, by his love, takes upon himself our form [Phil. 2:7], fights with us against sin, death, and all evil. This enkindles in us such love that we take on his form, rely upon his righteousness, life, and blessedness. And through the interchange of his blessings and our misfortunes, we become one loaf, one bread, one body, one drink, and have all things in common. O this is a great sacrament, says St. Paul, that Christ and the church are one flesh and bone. Again through this same love, we are to be changed and to make the infirmities of all other Christians our own; we are to take upon ourselves their form and their necessity, and all the good that is within our power we are to make theirs, that they may profit from it. That is real fellowship, and that is the true significance of this sacrament. In this way we are changed into one another and are made into a community of love. Without love there can be no such change.

Christ appointed these two forms of bread and wine, rather than any other, as a further indication of the very union and fellowship which is in this sacrament. For there is no more intimate, deep, and indivisible union than the union of the food with him who is fed. For the food enters into and is assimilated by his very nature, and becomes one substance with the person who is fed. Other unions, achieved by such things as nails, glue, cords, and the like, do not make one indivisible substance of the objects joined together. Thus in the sacrament we too become united with Christ, and are made one body with all the saints, so that Christ cares for us and acts in our behalf. As if he were what we are, he makes whatever concerns us to concern him as well, and even more than it does us. In turn we so care for Christ, as if we were what he is, which indeed we shall finally be – we shall be conformed to his likeness. As St. John says, "We know that when he shall be revealed we shall be like him" [1 John 3:2]. So deep and complete is the fellowship of Christ and all the saints with us. Thus our sins assail him, while his righteousness protects us. For the union makes all things common, until at last Christ completely destroys sin in us and makes us like himself, at the Last Day. Likewise by the same love we are to be united with our neighbors, we in them and they in us.

Besides all this, Christ did not institute these two forms solitary and alone, but he gave his true natural flesh in the bread, and his natural true blood in the wine, that he might give a really perfect sacrament or sign. For just as the bread is changed into his true natural body and the wine into his natural true blood, so truly are we also drawn and changed into the spiritual body, that is, into the fellowship of Christ and all saints and by this sacrament put into possession of all the virtues and mercies of Christ and his saints, as was said above of a citizen who is taken and incorporated into the protection and freedom of the city and the entire community. For this reason he instituted not simply the one form, but two separate forms – his flesh under the bread, his blood under the wine – to indicate that not only his life and good works, which are indicated by his flesh and which he accomplished in his flesh, but also his passion and martyrdom, which are indicated by his blood and in which he poured out his blood, are all our own. And we, being drawn into them, may use and profit from them.

So it is clear from all this that this holy sacrament is nothing else than a divine sign, in which are pledged, granted, and imparted Christ and all saints together with all their works, sufferings, merits, mercies, and possessions, for the comfort and strengthening of all who are in anxiety and sorrow, persecuted by the devil, sins, the world, the flesh, and every evil. And to receive the sacrament is nothing else than to desire all this and firmly to believe that it is done.

Here, now, follows the third part of the sacrament, that is, the *faith* on which everything depends. For it is not enough to know what the sacrament is and signifies. It is not enough that you know it is a fellowship and a gracious exchange or blending of our sin and suffering with the righteousness of Christ and his saints. You must also desire it and firmly believe that you have received it. Here the devil and our own nature wage their fiercest fight, so that faith may by no means stand firm. There are those who practice their arts and subtleties by trying [to fathom] what becomes of the bread when it is changed into Christ's flesh and of the wine when it is changed into his blood and how the whole Christ, his flesh and blood, can be encompassed in so small a portion of bread and wine. It does not matter if you do not see it. It is enough to know that it is a divine sign in which Christ's flesh and blood are truly present. The how and the where, we leave to him.

See to it that here you exercise and strengthen your faith, so that when you are sorrowful or when your sins press you and you go to the sacrament or hear mass, you do so with a hearty desire for this sacrament and for what it signifies. Then do not doubt that you have what the sacrament signifies, that is, be certain that Christ and all his saints are coming to you with all their virtues, sufferings, and mercies, to live, work, suffer, and die with you, and that they desire to be wholly yours, having all things in common with you. If you will exercise and strengthen this faith, then you will experience what a rich, joyous, and bountiful wedding feast your God has prepared for you upon the altar. Then you will understand what the great feast of King Ahasuerus signifies [Esther 1:5]; and you will see what that wedding feast is for which God slew his oxen and fat calves, as it is written in the gospel [Matt. 22:2–4]. Then your heart will become truly free and confident, strong and courageous against all enemies [Ps. 23:5]. For who will fear any calamity if he is sure that Christ and all his saints are with him and have all things, evil or good, in common with him? So we read in Acts 2[:46] that the disciples of Christ broke this bread and ate with great gladness of heart. Since, then, this work is so great that the smallness of our souls would not dare to desire it, to say nothing of hoping for it or expecting it, therefore it is necessary and profitable to go often to the sacrament, or at least in the daily mass to exercise and strengthen this faith on which the whole thing depends and for the sake of which it was instituted. For if you doubt, you do God the greatest dishonor and make him out to be a faithless liar; if you cannot believe, then pray for faith. . . .

See to it also that you give yourself to everyone in fellowship and by no means exclude anyone in hatred or anger. For this sacrament of fellowship, love, and unity cannot tolerate discord and disunity. You must take to heart the infirmities and needs of others, as if they were your own. Then offer to others your strength, as if it were their own, just as Christ does for you in the sacrament. This is what it means to be changed into one another through love, out of many particles to become one bread and drink, to lose one's own form and take on that which is common to all.

For this reason slanderers and those who wickedly judge and despise others cannot but receive death in the sacrament, as St. Paul writes in 1 Corinthians 11[:29]. For they do not do unto their neighbor what they seek from Christ, and what the sacrament indicates. They begrudge others anything good; they have no sympathy for them; they do not care for others as they themselves desire to be cared for by Christ. And then they fall into such blindness that they do not know what else to do in this sacrament except to fear and honor Christ there present with their own prayers and devotion. When they have done this, they think they have done their whole duty. But Christ has given his holy body for this purpose, that the thing signified by the sacrament – the fellowship, the change wrought by love – may be put into practice. And Christ values his spiritual body, which is the fellowship of his saints, more than his own natural body. To him it is more important, especially in this sacrament, that faith in the fellowship with him and with his saints may be properly exercised and become strong in us; and that we, in keeping with it, may properly exercise our fellowship with one another. This purpose of Christ the blind worshippers do not perceive. In their devoutness they go on daily saying and hearing mass, but they remain every day the same; indeed every day they become worse but do not perceive it.

Therefore take heed. It is more needful that you discern the spiritual than the natural body of Christ; and faith in the spiritual body is more necessary than faith in the natural body. For the natural without the spiritual profits us nothing in this sacrament; a change must occur [in the communicant] and be exercised through love. . . .

We see now how necessary this sacrament is for those who must face death, or other dangers of body and soul, that they not be left in them alone but be strengthened in the fellowship of Christ and all saints. This is why Christ instituted it and gave it to his disciples in the hour of their extreme need and peril. Since we then are all daily surrounded by all kinds of danger, and must at last die, we should humbly and heartily give thanks with all our powers to the God of all mercy for giving us such a gracious sign, by which – if we hold fast to it in faith – he leads and draws us through death and every danger unto himself, unto Christ and all saints.

Therefore it is also profitable and necessary that the love and fellowship of Christ and all saints be hidden, invisible, and spiritual, and that only a bodily, visible, and outward sign of it be given to us. For if this love, fellowship, and support were apparent to all, like the transient fellowship of men, we would not be strengthened or trained by it to desire or put our trust in the things that are unseen and eternal [2 Cor. 4:18]. Instead we would be trained to put our trust only in things that are transient and seen, and would become so accustomed to them as to be unwilling to let them go; we would not follow God, except so far as visible and tangible things led us. We would thereby be prevented from ever coming to God. For everything that is bound to time and sense must fall away, and we must learn to do without them, if we are to come to God.

For this reason the mass and this sacrament are a sign by which we train and accustom ourselves to let go of all visible love, help, and comfort, and to trust in the invisible love, help, and support of Christ and his saints. For death takes away all the things that are seen and separates us from men and transient things. To meet it, we must, therefore, have the help of the things that are unseen and eternal. And these are indicated to us in the sacrament and sign, to which we cling by faith until we finally attain to them also with sight and senses.

Thus the sacrament is for us a ford, a bridge, a door, a ship, and a stretcher, by which and in which we pass from this world into eternal life. Therefore everything depends on faith. He who does not believe is like the man who is supposed to cross the sea, but who is so timid that he does not trust the ship; and so he must remain and never be saved, because he will not embark and cross over. This is the fruit of our dependence on the senses and of our untrained faith, which shrinks from the passage across the Jordan of death; and the devil too has a gruesome hand in it.

This was signified long ago in Joshua 3[:14–17]. After the children of Israel had gone dry-shod through the Red Sea [Exod. 14:21–2] – in which [event] baptism was typified – they went through the Jordan also in like manner. But the priests stood with the ark in the Jordan, and the water below them was cut off, while the water above them rose up like a mountain – in which [event] this sacrament is typified. The priests hold and carry the ark in the Jordan when, in the hour of our death or peril, they preach and administer to us this sacrament, the fellowship of Christ and all saints. If we then believe, the waters below us depart; that is, the things that are seen and transient do nothing but flee from us. The waters above us, however, well up high; that is, the horrible torments of the other world, which we envision at the hour of death, terrify us as if they would overwhelm us. If, however, we pay no attention to them, and walk over with a firm faith, then we shall enter dry-shod and unharmed into eternal life.

We have, therefore, two principal sacraments in the church, baptism and the bread. Baptism leads us into a new life on earth; the bread guides us through death into eternal life. And the two are signified by the Red Sea and the Jordan, and by the two lands, one beyond and one on this side of the Jordan. This is why our Lord said at the Last Supper, "I shall not drink again of this wine until I drink it new with you in my Father's kingdom" [Matt. 26:29]. So entirely is this sacrament intended and instituted for a strengthening against death and an entrance into eternal life.

In conclusion, the blessing of this sacrament is fellowship and love, by which we are strengthened against death and all evil. This fellowship is twofold: on the one hand we partake of Christ and all saints; on the other hand we permit all Christians to be partakers of us, in whatever way they and we are able. Thus by means of this sacrament, all self-seeking love is rooted out and gives place to that which seeks the common good of all; and through the change wrought by love there is one bread, one drink, one body, one community. This is the true unity of Christian brethren. . . .

CONTEMPORARY REFLECTION

from *The Eucharist*, Chapter 12

Raymond Moloney, SJ

For every house there is a key, and, ideally, for every treatise there is an opening chapter which sets the stage for all that is to follow. Here, at the beginning of these personal reflections on the Eucharist, one looks for some concept which will provide a point of entry into the mystery, some commanding idea which, in a sense, will contain within itself all that is to follow.

For such an idea I would like to go back to one of the most ancient terms in our Eucharistic vocabulary. We find it first in St. Paul's Greek: *koinonia*, sharing. Now we break bread in order to share it, so that the notion already contains two aspects within itself, that of giving and that of receiving. In this chapter we will trace this duality through various levels of meaning in the sacrament.

The Banquet of Life

When people today begin to ask themselves about the Eucharist, inevitably their minds turn to the night before Our Lord died and to the accounts we have of the institution of the sacrament at the Last Supper. Joachim Jeremias however liked to make the point that we should really begin further back with the meals Our Lord frequently held during his public life with outcasts and sinners.[1] Here I would like to extend the line further still, back into the Old Testament on the one hand, and forward towards the future of the kingdom on the other.

In establishing his worship in a table context, Our Lord was setting it within an ancient biblical tradition, which understood the goal of salvation history under the image of a meal. This thought is suggested already by the gift of manna with which God fed the people in the desert. The prophet Isaiah speaks of the coming of the kingdom under the image of a great banquet. Our Lord himself takes up the image with his many parables about the wedding feast or the festival at the end of time. His own meals with sinners were a way of announcing the same message of the divine offer of universal salvation. He gave the message further emphasis when he fed the multitude at the multiplication of the loaves. Again, after the resurrection, his meals with his disciples have something of the quality of that final banquet.

However we must not think of these meals as referring exclusively to the next life. The plan of salvation which they reveal is saying something about this life also. As an image of God's providence, they remind us of how the Creator wants the whole of creation to participate in the great banquet of life, "to which all are equally invited by God"[2] – for "your heavenly Father knows that you have need of all these things" (Matt. 6:32).

Seeing this background, it becomes more understandable why Our Lord should turn to the notion of a banquet when he wanted to give shape and form to the central act of worship of Christians. But the reality is not as straightforward as one might at first have supposed. All we have said about the banquet of life is optimistic, positive and consoling, but it leaves something out of account. So far we have been speaking of God's plan for the world and of what it would have been if it depended on him alone. But one of the key points in that plan is that we human beings should play an active part within it. Our co-operation is to be intrinsic to it all, and that is where things begin to fall apart. In the actual course of human history there is the great dislocation of sin. Just as the main cause of famine in today's world is human wars and mismanagement, so the main cause of the imperfections of this world is human selfishness and sin.

Christ's vision of the world, where all human beings are to have their share of the banquet of life, does not come about automatically. There is not only the fact of real hunger and famine, but there is all the injustice and deprivation which manifest the reality of sin. If human beings are to overcome sin and selfishness, a painful process of withdrawal is necessary, withdrawing ourselves from the morass into which human sin has plunged the world. It is precisely because of the pain in such a process that Christ came to lead the way with his sacrifice on the cross. The answer to sin is found on Calvary. Just as Christ's heart was possessed by this vision of the banquet, he realized that it could be purchased only at a price. It is only through self-sacrifice that a new world can be born. It is only in dying to self that we can begin to give reality to the banquet of which Christ dreamed. Not only is there the pain involved in withdrawing ourselves from our personal sinfulness, there is also the necessary struggle against physical and spiritual hunger in the world, so that more and more people can have their share in the banquet of life.

The more we think about it, the clearer it becomes why the celebration of Christian life which Our Lord has left us in the Eucharist comes to us, not in one image, but in two. The Eucharist is not sacrifice alone, nor is it banquet alone. It is both sacrifice and banquet. The Last Supper formed the center of the great series of salvific meals, in which God's plan for the world was revealed. At that moment, when the events leading to his death were already in train, Our Lord introduced into this line of revelation the element of sacrifice, as the disciples recalled the Passover sacrifice of their ancestors. There is no community without self-denial. There is no resurrection without the cross. There is no banquet without sacrifice. The bread of life is a bread broken for a broken world.

Celebrating a way of life

This duality at the heart of the Eucharist can be approached from another angle. Our Lord had a certain view of how life was to be lived by his followers. One of the most fundamental things he ever said about it was that those who would save their lives must lose them, and that those who lose their lives for Christ's sake will find them (Matt. 16:25). This losing of life to find it lies at the heart of what we mean by the Christian way of life. To love is to be unselfish and to give oneself to others. But it is in giving that we receive. The true democracy of Christianity lies here. All that Christianity has to bestow on its followers comes not to those of any particular class or rank in society, nor to those with superior education or large bank accounts, but simply to those who are prepared to be unselfish. For such souls there is a joy and peace in life, a peace which the world cannot give.

There are, therefore, what we might call the two movements of Christian love, a giving and a receiving. They are found in any act of love and unselfishness, and they are the key to the way of life which Our Lord wished his disciples to follow. He himself not only preached this way but practiced it, not only throughout his life of love and service, but above all in the events with which his life reached its climax. Christ's death and resurrection are the supreme instance of that losing of life to find life. They are the ultimate model of his way of life.

But these events also constitute "the paschal mystery." By this phrase we wish to indicate that they are not simply an heroic paradigm from two thousand years ago. There is a power in these events, which can change our lives here and now, if we let it. These two events together constitute a kind of power-house, a source of energy, flowing into our lives, to enable us to live according to the same pattern. Whenever we Christians love one another, there is present to us something of Our Lord's dying on the cross, helping us to take up the cross of unselfishness. By the same token there is also present something of Our Lord's rising, enabling us to share in the peace and joy which only Christ can give. As a result, the life of a Christian is not only a succession of crosses, which we take up every day; it is also a series of little Easters, as we win through to the graces and benefits of the risen Christ.

It now remains to us to apply this reflection to the Eucharist, since this sacrament is our principal celebration of the Christian way of life. First we might reflect on what it means to celebrate a way of life by considering some examples. Once a year, for instance, during the 70 years of its existence, the Communist state in Russia celebrated a way of life based on force and centralized control, and it did this with a display of military might in Red Square in Moscow. Every so often in Britain the monarch opens Parliament by reading the speech from the throne in the House of Lords. This too is a celebration of a way of life, but in a different key. Here the will of the people and the power of inherited tradition are given expression as central values in that society. In a somewhat similar way the Christian community has been given rituals by Christ and the Church which embody the rather different values on which his community is based. Every week, therefore, our congregations gather together to express and deepen the way of life which we have from Christ. That is one way of explaining what the Eucharist is; but of course it is much more than this, since in our case the founder of the community is part of the celebration, uniting our rituals with those events in his life which are at once the paradigm and the power behind all our living out of his way.

Given the twofold movement of Christian love, it is not surprising that this duality is reflected in the Eucharist itself. First of all it comes out in the very words of the Lord in the Institution Narrative. While these refer predominantly to the death of Christ, they also refer to his resurrection in so far as that death is seen as victorious and issuing in the new covenant and the forgiveness of sins. Then there is the very structure of the rituals Our

Lord has left us. Commonly they are broken up into four main parts, reflecting the four original actions of Christ in instituting this sacrament: he took, he blessed, he broke, he gave.[3] This gives us the four parts of the sacrament: the presentation of the gifts, the Eucharistic Prayer, the breaking of the bread, holy communion. Of these the first and the third parts are preparatory to the second and fourth, which thus form the two main sections of the liturgy.

While the death and resurrection of the Lord are present and operative throughout the entire celebration, there is a particular kinship between the offering of Christ's sacrifice and the Eucharistic Prayer on the one hand, and between the resurrection and holy communion on the other. The Eucharist as the actuality of Christ's death and resurrection embodies in this dramatic way not only the two movements of Christian love as they are lived by Christians in their daily lives, but also those two movements as they are found at their zenith in the death and resurrection of the Lord.

The Trinitarian background

It might be thought that, in uncovering the levels of meaning in the Eucharist, one could hardly go deeper than the Lord's paschal mystery. But in fact there is a further level to be explored, without which the picture would not be complete. Our Lord's own life on earth does not contain its full meaning within itself. In coming to understand that life, the early Christians soon found that they had to think in terms of Our Lord's pre-existence and of a life that he led before his Father of which we know next to nothing (John 4:32). From this point of view, Our Lord's earthly existence was but the transposition into time of relationships between Father, Son and Holy Spirit within the Trinity. Edward Schillebeeckx put it well when he wrote: "The absolute generosity, which the Trinity simply *is*, remains the universally dominant background of the mystery of saving worship in Christ."[4]

The ancient Eucharistic term "communion" serves as a useful link between the various levels. The Eucharist is about sharing and communion, not only our communion in the sacrament, but our communion with God and one another in our daily lives. This communion looks back to that communion which Christ shared with his disciples when he was on earth and which he consummated in the events of the paschal mystery; but this in turn has its background and source in the mysterious communion between Father, Son and Holy Spirit, which is part of the very definition of Trinitarian life.

The Father loves the Son and shares his being with him. The Son loves the Father and exists before him in "perfect active receptivity."[5] It is in these relationships between the persons of the Trinity that the giving and receiving of created love have their origin. When creation comes out from God and when incarnation and redemption are added to God's gifts, all these are but the overflowing into our world of a Trinitarian love which transcends our understanding and imagination. But in so far as we can discern, all along the line, something of that one pattern of giving and receiving, we can come to regard the Eucharist as the final outreach into our lives of what is the mystery behind the universe. The love, of which the Eucharist is the sacrament, is ultimately the love which God himself is in the mystery of the Trinity.

The Church

The eternal communion with God, which we have just been considering, is another name for the kingdom of God in its fullness. Oscar Cullmann once remarked that Baptism and Eucharist are for the life of the Church what the miracles were in Our Lord's public life; they are the signs of the presence of that kingdom.[6] For many theologians today the Eucharist is essentially an eschatological sign in the way Cullmann suggested, but to approach it in this way can be done only through another truth, namely that of the Church, since the Church itself is the primary sacrament of the kingdom here below.

Eucharist and Church belong together. There are a number of reasons for this. For one thing, all ritual implies community. A sacrament of love necessarily implies other people. But the basic reason comes out of the way that both mysteries converge on the one goal, that eternal communion with God, which we have just been considering in the previous section. The kingdom of heaven is not only communion with God but communion with one another in God. It is the communion of saints in its fullness, which is another name for the fullness of the Church. Eucharist and Church here below are consequently two different anticipations of the one ultimate reality, and so each in different ways finds its truth in the other. The Eucharist, said Henri de Lubac, is "the heart of the Church."[7]

The notion of the coming of God's kingdom is not a straightforward one. Linking kingdom, Church and Eucharist, in the way which has just been indicated, suggests that some of the paradoxes and difficulties associated with the Eucharist have their origin in the tensions and difficulties which attend the Church as the sign of God's kingdom. In one way the kingdom has come about *already* in all the graces of the Christian Church, but in another sense the kingdom has *not yet* come, at least not yet in its fullness. This will happen only at the end of time. In this intermediary period we live in a state of tension between that "already" and that "not yet." On the one hand, therefore, theologians cannot be surprised at the constraints and tensions which seem inseparable from the experience of grace in an imperfect world. On the other hand we must not let this awareness of limitation lead us into underestimating the very real wonders of divine grace which God has put before us in the Church and in the sacraments.

This familiar piece of biblical theology[8] serves as a useful introduction to the section of this chapter in which we broach the ecclesial aspect of the sacrament. The Church really enters into reflection on the Eucharist at two points in particular, as first-fruit of the sacrament and as its presupposition. The Eucharist, as is commonly said today, "makes the Church," but only if the Church "makes the Eucharist."[9] In this section it is the second of these aspects which will be treated, and, as will soon become plain, it is a subject where all that has just been said about tension and constraint will be found to have a special relevance.

Behind what we wish to say in this section lies a particular vision of the Eucharist and of the Church, which I take from one of its earliest exponents, St. Ignatius of Antioch.* At the heart of this martyr's view of things is the Johannine doctrine that God is *agape*, love. In the light of this Ignatius sees that the Church is *agape*.[10] The one reality unites them all. That is the basic insight, and without it much that follows will seem like mere juridicism.

Ignatius is blunt. For him there is no genuine Eucharist apart from the Church, just as there is no genuine Church apart from the hierarchy.[11] It is not so much a matter of law as of the very meaning of what we do. It is of the very essence of the Eucharist as sacrament of love, union and community.

Since the implications of what we are saying in this chapter are practical and often painful, it is good to be clear from the outset about the spiritual values involved in assigning such a primacy to the Church in the reality of our celebration. One of the main values for us here is the sovereignty of grace and our dependence on the divine initiative in all things. The Eucharist is not the creation of the human search for the divine. It is a work of God's initiative in coming to the rescue of a fallen race.

Our dependence on the Church and on its structures, as manifested in the Eucharist, is a way of saying that we cannot go to God on our own. Of ourselves we are nothing. This was one of the issues involved when Luther identified the Mass as a human work. It is ironic that in rejecting the divine aspect of the Church, Luther was rejecting the very aspect which would answer his difficulties about the Mass as a human work. Behind the primacy assigned to the Church in our celebration lies a profound belief in the Church as something more than just an organization. It is not just "the institutional Church" of so much popular writing, but the Church as seen by the great saints and mystics, the Church as a mystery of faith, "our Catholic Mother,"

---

* Ignatius, Bishop of Antioch (*c.* 35–*c.* 107).

Bride of Christ, Body of Christ. In the last analysis the Church is Christ for us – the one Christ, the full Christ, the total Christ, as Augustine[12] put it – and the true celebrant of the Eucharist is the Church in this plenary and ultimately mystical sense. . . .

Notes

1 Joachim Jeremias, *New Testament Theology*, vol. 1 (London: SCM, 1971), pp. 289–90.

2 John Paul II, ". . . in the banquet of life, to which all are equally invited by God, we should make 'the other' a sharer on a par with ourselves": *Sollicitudo rei socialis* 39: AAS 80 (1988), p. 567.

3 This "four-action" view of the Eucharist goes back to Gregory Dix, *The Shape of the Liturgy* (Westminster: Dacre Press, 1945), pp. 48–50.

4 Edward Schillebeeckx, *Christ the Sacrament of the Encounter with God* (London: Sheed & Ward, 1963), p. 46.

5 Ibid., p. 33.

6 Oscar Cullmann, *Early Christian Worship* (London: SCM, 1953), p. 118.

7 Henri de Lubac, *The Splendour of the Church* (London: Sheed & Ward, 1956), p. 87.

8 This goes back to Oscar Cullmann, *Christ and Time* (London: SCM, 1965), part I, ch. 5.

9 These expressions are de Lubac's way of summing up his researches into the ancient sources on the point: *The Splendour of the Church*, pp. 92 and 106; also *Corpus mysticum* (Paris: Aubier, 1944), pp. 103, 299.

10 That God is love is stated in 1 John 4:8, 16; for the Church as *agape*, see Ignatius, Inscription of his *Letter to the Romans* (RJ 52); for the Eucharist as *agape*, see his *Letter to the Romans* 7 (PG 5, 693B).

11 Ignatius, *Letter to the Smyrnaeans* 8 (PG 5, 713; RJ 65).

12 Ignatius, *On the Merits of Sinners* I, 1, 36, 60 (PL 44, 145). The phrase "Our Catholic Mother" is also from Augustine. *Sermon* 46, 18 (PL 38, 280).

Inquiring after God through Art

Art, like sacraments, has recurrently been a controversial issue in the Christian tradition. Exodus 20:4–5 (Deut. 5:8–9) specifically prohibits the making of images. The prohibition of images is not a prohibition of art, however. Throughout history Christians have used art, including image-filled art, to teach the faith to people who cannot read or who are visual rather than aural, to enliven the devotion of believers, and to honor God by beautifying their houses of worship and worship services. Painting, sculpture, mosaics, architecture, stained-glass windows, poetry, and music would not be what they are without their Christian applications.

Despite a rich artistic tradition the commandment against image-making has a strong testimony of its own. A fierce controversy broke out in the eighth century in Constantinople about the appropriateness of venerating icons – paintings of the central figures of the Christian story. Iconoclasts considered icon veneration idolatrous while iconodules or iconophiles supported the practice. At first the inconoclasts' denunciation of icon painting (presented here) triumphed at the Synod of Hieria in 754. Eventually, however, at the Seventh Ecumenical Council at Nicaea (Nicaea II) in 787 the iconoclasts were defeated and icons were vindicated.

Like most ecclesiastical controversies ended by councils the issue was not really settled. Conflict broke out again during the Protestant Reformation. The earlier debate about the biblical commandment became a struggle about religious art altogether. Churches were looted, whitewashed, and stripped of all paintings in Protestant areas. Sculptures were broken or defaced, stained-glass windows smashed, and vestments and carved choir stalls burned by zealous reformers. In some traditions music was eliminated or severely curtailed in the name of Christian simplicity or austerity. As with most controversial topics this one is many layered.

Art is a luxury. It is usually expensive. Precious materials have to be obtained and artists and artisans trained and employed. So the art controversy that poses decoration against simplicity is also about the proper Christian use of money as well as about style. These enduring issues are worthy of revisiting generation after generation.

This chapter includes classic texts on both sides of the Christian art debate, beginning with the Iconoclastic Controversy from 725 to 842. In addition there is a selection advocating decoration in church architecture and a countervailing argument for simplicity made regarding poetry. The themes and issues carry over regardless of the artistic medium. The question of whether art should be used to teach the faith to people, glorify God, and enhance Christian worship, or whether art detracts from piety, God's glory, and worship, and that Christians are called to a life of strict aesthetic and economic simplicity remains.

The debate on Christian art, like all theological topics, cannot be easily separated off from central doctrines of the faith. Like so many other issues, as we saw with sacraments, the doctrines of the faith imply one another and so converge at every point. And so it was in the Iconoclastic Controversy. In a sense it was not only, perhaps not even really, about art but about christology, the doctrine of the Incarnation, one of the two basic mysteries of the Christian faith adjudicated by conciliar definition (the other being the doctrine of the Trinity). Christology is central to the teaching on the Eucharist as well as to the teaching on prayer presented in the following chapter.

To appreciate the urgency of the Iconoclastic Controversy it is necessary to consider the definitive Christian teaching on the mystery of the Incarnation formulated by the Council of Bishops held at Chalcedon in 451 known as the Chalcedonian Definition. The Council articulated the paradox that Christ was thoroughly God and thoroughly human in the following formula:

> We . . . teach . . . one and the same Son, our Lord Jesus Christ, at once complete in Godhead and complete in manhood, truly God and truly man, consisting also of a reasonable soul and body; of one substance (*homoousios*) with the Father as regards his Godhead, and at the same time of one substance with us as regards his manhood; . . . one and the same Christ, Son, Lord, Only-begotten, recognized in two natures, without confusion, without change, without division, without separation; the distinction of natures being in no way annulled by the union, but rather the characteristics of each nature being preserved and coming together to form one person and subsistence (*hypostasis*) not as parted or separated into two persons, but one and the same Son and Only-begotten God the Word, Lord Jesus Christ. . . .

The Definition does not explain how Jesus Christ is simultaneously divine and human without confusing these two aspects of his identity. It merely asserts that this is the case. This language hopes to preserve Christ's completeness as God so that it is clear that it is truly God who becomes a human being, and to preserve his completeness as human (except for sin) in order to be clear that humanity in its fullness is truly the object of God's presence. To say that Christ was really divine yet really a person with a human soul and body (and not just divine *logos* poured into a human body) suggests that Christ has a dual identity. A major debate raged about how best to express this divine–human identity. The decision is the doctrine known as the *hypostatic* union: Christ has two "natures" that are united but not fused in one God-man. (The word "person" often used in the west is misleading since it fails to convey the presence of divinity.) Yet, because it was important to insist that divinity and humanity are not blended, since that was deemed unseemly for God, the Fathers insisted that Christ had two wills or energies, one human and one divine, since scripture suggests that sometimes he acted out of human motivations and at other times as God.

Despite the Definition some regional churches held to the doctrine that Christ had only one single divine nature, will, and energy, thus denying the *hypostatic* union and Christ's complete humanity. This was the position of the Monophysites (one nature party) who contrasted their position with the orthodox whom they termed Dyophysites. The Iconoclastic Controversy arose in this context.

The iconoclasts argued that because a painting of Christ is made from and by purely human artifice it suggests that Christ is contained or circumscribed in the art work. This denies the hypostatic union. Divinity cannot be contained anywhere, let alone in a painting. Only the humanity can be captured there and so adoring an icon of Christ was thought to amount to worshiping a person. This is idolatrous. Christians do not worship Jesus; they worship God. Their position is represented here by their condemnation of iconography issued at the Synod of Hieria of 753–4.

The iconodules on the other hand, represented here by their two most famous apologists, John of Damascus and Theodore of Studios, argued that icons teach the faith to the unlettered. The Incarnation itself, the presence of God in flesh and blood, permits the depiction of God with paint and wood. This does not exhaust or contain God himself, but only points to him. Eventually the iconophiles won the day when the Seventh General Council, which met at Nicaea, decreed the restoration of icons in A.D. 787.

Until the sixteenth century it was assumed that Christian worship and houses of worship were appropriate objects of beautification as a way of honoring God. Abbot Suger's account of the building of the church of St. Denis near Paris that he was supervising represents the view that nothing could be too lavish to honor God's house. The cathedrals of the Middle Ages were great outpourings of wealth, skill, and effort at constructing and decorating monumental buildings.

The Protestant Reformation was in part a criticism of the wealth, power, and ostentation of the medieval church. Again, as we noted in the eucharistic controversy of the sixteenth century, there was no consensus among Protestants themselves. Calvin preferred simplicity, even austerity in this matters, while Luther took a more moderate view, and was especially supportive of music to enrich Christian worship.

(J. S. Bach was a Lutheran and Mozart was a Roman Catholic.) Luther became alarmed because Protestants were destroying church property. The Protestant world continues to be divided about the place of art and music in Christian worship.

The last text represents the teaching on simplicity applied to hymns through a lecture on the hymnody of Isaac Watt, an English dissenter of Calvinist views. Ironically, he argues for the "dumbing down" or "sinking" of language for hymns in order to carry simple people along with the theology being sung, precisely the argument made by the iconodules in favor of venerating icons! So we see that the argument about art can be made both in favor of and against the very same concern for Christian piety.

While art and music were primarily used to enhance Christian devotion until the Renaissance, at that time art began to have a life of its own. Eventually, the idea that the artist is a theologian whose job it is to assist other believers in their spiritual life gave way to the idea that art is for its own sake. An artist is the master of certain artistic media, and the modern purpose of art is either an expression of the artist's ideas or creativity or the artist's depiction of the everyday world. The theological function of art has been put on the defensive. Art has ceased to connect the viewer or listener with the spiritual world. Art for art's sake overwhelmed the older notion that art appropriately leads people to God and righteousness. Art came to be focused on forms and techniques of light, color, and line. And the finished product was to evoke the skill of the artist rather than to point to something beyond itself that would enhance the viewer's understanding of God.

The contemporary reflection in this collection protests the modern loss of the theological function of art. Professor Nicholas Wolterstorff supports what he calls contemplative art, but here he argues for the theological calling of the artist. Theologically sensitive art (might one go so far as to say godly art?) is art that understands itself to be socially and morally responsible to the public it serves. This is a legitimate use of art, he argues, because God holds us accountable for the world he has placed us in and that vocation applies to one no matter what one is doing or what one's particular gifts may be. In this regard Wolterstorff offers a Calvinist criticism of modern art that rejects its theological vocation.

The larger point Calvinism makes is that Christian ministry is not confined to the Church or the clergy. Every person is called by God to promote the welfare of the common good no matter what walk of life they pursue. Perhaps part of the challenge is to find that ministry and to discern how it may best flourish to serve God's creatures. Still, Wolterstorff is careful to point out that pursuing one's vocation with rigor need not be at the expense of joy and delight in beauty for its own sake. Perhaps here the "without confusion" of the Chalcedonian Definition fails. Service to God and creaturely enjoyment and delight are finally not separable. When enjoyment of God's bounty and beauty serves the upbuilding of his creatures is this not truly a joyous event in which one finds oneself at peace, and made whole?

Icon Painting

The Position of the Byzantine Iconoclasts Issued by the Synod of Hieria in 754 A.D.

[The six preceding] holy and ecumenical councils* piously and in a manner pleasing to God expounding the doctrine of our undefiled Christian faith, having received instruction from the God-given gospels, taught that there is one hypostasis in two natures and wills and energies in the one Christ, our Lord and God, and taught that the miracles and the sufferings were of one and the same [person].

With much care and consideration we have examined and have come to know these things by the inspiration of the all-holy Spirit, and we found that the unlawful craft of painters blasphemes against the crucial doctrine of our salvation, that is, the dispensation of Christ, and subverts the same holy six ecumenical and divinely-gathered councils. . . .

For which reason we have deemed it right to demonstrate in detail by our present *horos* [definition] the error of those who make and worship [images]. Since all the inspired fathers and the holy and ecumenical councils have thus delivered [to us] our pure, undefiled and divinely approved creed and confession, no one should imagine in any manner a division or confusion in the hypostatic union of the two natures of the individually manifested one person, [a union] which surpasses understanding and which is ineffable and unknowable. Therefore, what is the senseless conceit of the painter of foolishness, who, for the sake of miserable sordid greediness, for profit, practices that which should not be practiced, namely the depicting, with profane hands, of those things which are believed with the heart and confessed with the mouth?

Such a person made an image and called it "Christ." The name "Christ" refers to both God and man. Then it is an image of Christ as well as of man. Then [the painter] either circumscribed, according to his vain opinion, the uncircumscribability of the divinity by means of the circumscription of

---

* These general councils of bishops held between 325 and 681 attempted to settle major doctrinal disputes among Christian traditions.

created flesh, or else he confused the unconfused union, falling into the transgression or the confusion; he commits in this way two blasphemies against the Godhead, by the circumscription and the confusion. . . .

Being condemned by those who think rightly [–] in this matter of their attempt to describe the incomprehensible and uncircumscribed divine nature of Christ [–] they surely, we presume, must flee to another defense devised in an evil manner, namely that "We depict the image only of the flesh, which 'we have seen and have handled,' and with which we have associated" – this is impious. . . .

It should . . . be considered concerning this matter that if, according to the orthodox fathers, where the flesh is there is also the flesh of God the Word [John 1:1], since [the flesh] does not admit the notion of division but the whole [flesh] is entirely assumed into the divine nature and is completely deified,* how can [the Person of Christ] be divided into two or made to subsist separately by those who impiously undertake to [paint icons]? Such is the case also concerning the holy soul. . . . Just as where the flesh is, there is the flesh of God the Logos[;] thus where the soul is, there is the soul of God the Logos. Both, namely the body and the soul were deified, and not separated from the divinity even in the parting of the soul from the body during His voluntary passion. Where the soul of Christ is, there is also the divinity, and where the body of Christ is there is also the divinity.

If therefore[,] in the passion[,] the divinity remained unseparated from these, how can these men, senseless and filled with irrationality, separate the flesh entwined with the divinity and deified, and try to depict, as it were, the image of a mere man? . . . It will . . . be inferred by those who suppose that they can depict Christ, either that the divine is circumscribable and mingled with the flesh, or that the body of Christ is without God and separated from it, giving to the flesh a self-existent *prosopon* [person]. . . .

We will also say something about . . . [the images of saints]. Our Catholic church of Christians is the mean between Judaism and paganism, and does not share the customary rites of either. It travels on a new path of divinely-bestowed piety and revelation, not accepting the bloody sacrifices and holocausts of Judaism, and abominating paganism, in addition to sacrifices, also with respect to idol-making and idol-worship, which [i.e. paganism] is the originator and inventor of this abominable craft [of idol-making]. It looked for a plaything worthy of itself, so that what is not present it may make appear as an illusion . . .

May then every mouth stop uttering unrighteous and insulting things against this judgment and decision of ours, which was accepted by God. The saints, having been found pleasing by God, were honored by Him with the

---

* That is, taken up into the divine life.

dignity of holiness, and they live forever with God, even though they have been taken away from here. He who intends to raise up a memorial to them, by means of a craft which is dead and hateful, not one which vivifies, but one vainly invented by the pagan adversaries, is shown to be a blasphemer.

How do they dare to depict, by means of vulgar pagan art, the Mother of God, worthy of all praise, whom the fullness of the Godhead overshadowed [Luke 1:35], through whom the unapproachable light shone upon us, who is higher than the heavens and is more holy than the Cherubim? Or, are they not ashamed to depict with pagan art those who will reign together with Christ, and will judge the world and will become of like form with His glory, of whom, as the oracles say, the world was not worthy? It is not lawful for Christians who have the hope of the resurrection to have recourse to the customs of the demon-worshiping gentiles, and to insult, with dishonorable and dead matter, saints who will shine forth in such glory. . . .

May no one any longer dare to pursue this impious and unholy occupation. He who, from now on, dares to make an image, or to worship it, or to erect it in a church or private dwelling or conceal it – if he is a bishop, priest, or deacon, let him be deposed, if a monk or lay person, let him be anathematized. . . .

[The Anathemas]

[8] If anyone endeavors to perceive the divine form of God the Logos in His Incarnation by means of material colors and not to worship Him with the whole heart, with the eyes of the intellect, as sitting on the throne of glory at the right hand of God. . . . – anathema.

[9] If anyone endeavors to circumscribe in images by means of material colors, in a human form, the uncircumscribable essence and hypostasis of God the Logos, alleging as the reason the Incarnation, rather than acknowledging Him as nothing less than divine, and as being uncircumscribable after the Incarnation – anathema.

[10] If anyone attempts to describe by means of an image the unseparable hypostatic union of the nature of God the Logos with the flesh, that is of the one unconfused and undivided product from two [natures], calling it "Christ" – whereas "Christ" signifies both God and man – and thus makes a monstrosity, a confusion of the two natures – anathema.

[13] If anyone depicts the flesh, deified by means of the union to the divine Logos, thus separating it from the Godhead which assumed [the flesh] and divinized [it], and therefore attempts to depict it as being without God – anathema.

[14] If anyone attempts, by means of material colors, to depict God the

Logos, who is in the form of God [but] who took on the form of a slave in His own hypostasis and became like unto us [Phil. 2:7] in all things except sin, as being a mere man, and to separate Him from the unseparated and unchangeable God, and thus, as it were, introduces a quaternity into the holy and life-giving Trinity – anathema.

[15] If anyone does not confess that the ever-virgin Mary is properly and truly the Theotokos [i.e. Mother of God], higher than all visible and invisible creation, and does not, with pure faith, ask for her intercession as having free access to our God, the one begotten by her – anathema.

[16] If anyone undertakes to set up the forms of all the saints in lifeless and dumb icons, made of material colors, something which is without profit – for this aim is vain and the invention of demonic craft – rather than [to depict] their virtues, manifested in the writings about them, painting as it were, living images for himself, exciting his zeal to be like unto them, as our inspired fathers said – anathema.

[17] If anyone does not confess that all the saints from the beginning until now, before the Law, or under the Law, or under grace were found to be pleasing to God and are honored in His presence in soul and body, and does not ask for their prayers, as of those who have liberty of interceding on behalf of the world, according to the ecclesiastical tradition – anathema. . . .

The Position of the Byzantine Iconophiles

John of Damascus

First Apology Against those who Attack the Divine Images

7. You see that [God, when speaking to Moses], forbids the making of images because of idolatry, and that it is impossible to make an image of the immeasurable, uncircumscribed, invisible God. For "You heard the sound of words, but saw no form; there was only a voice" [Deut. 4:12]. This was Paul's testimony as he stood in the midst of the Areopagus. "Being then God's offspring, we ought not to think that the Deity is like gold, or silver, or stone, a representation by the art and imagination of man" [Acts 17:29].

8. These commandments were given to . . . avoid superstitious error and to come to God in the knowledge of the truth; to adore God alone, to enjoy the fullness of divine knowledge, to attain to mature manhood, that we may no longer be children, tossed to and fro and carried about with every wind of doctrine [Eph. 4:14]. We are no longer under custodians [Gal. 3:25], but we have received from God the ability to discern what may be represented and what is uncircumscript. . . .

16. In former times God, who is without form or body, could never be depicted. But now when God is seen in the flesh conversing with men, I make

an image of the God whom I see. I do not worship matter; I worship the Creator of matter who became matter for my sake, who willed to take His abode in matter; who worked out my salvation through matter. Never will I cease honoring the matter which wrought my salvation! I honor it, but not as God. How could God be born out of things which have no existence in themselves? God's body is God because it is joined to His person by a union which shall never pass away. The divine nature remains the same; the flesh created in time is quickened by a reason-endowed soul. Because of this I salute all remaining matter with reverence, because God has filled it with His grace and power. Through it my salvation has come to me. Was not the thrice-happy and the thrice-blessed wood of the cross matter? What of the life-bearing rock, the holy and life-giving tomb, the fountain of our resurrection, was it not matter? Is not the ink in the most holy Gospel-book matter? Is not the life-giving altar made of matter? From it we receive the bread of life! Are not gold and silver matter? From them we make crosses, patens, chalices! And over and above all these things, is not the Body and Blood of our Lord matter? Either do away with the honor and veneration these things deserve, or accept the tradition of the Church and the veneration of images. Reverence God and His friends; follow the inspiration of the Holy Spirit. Do not despise matter, for it is not despicable. God has made nothing despicable. . . .

[Images] are the books of the illiterate, the never silent heralds of the honor due the saints, teaching without the use of words those who gaze upon them, and sanctifying the sense of sight. Suppose I have few books, or little leisure for reading, but walk into the spiritual hospital – that is to say, a church – with my soul choking from the prickles of thorny thoughts, and thus afflicted I see before me the brilliance of the icon. I am refreshed as if in a verdant meadow, and thus my soul is led to glorify God. I marvel at the martyr's endurance, at the crown he won, and inflamed with burning zeal I fall down to worship God through His martyr, and so receive salvation.

Concerning this business of images, we must search for . . . the intention of those who make them. If it is really and truly for the glory of God and His saints, to promote virtue, the avoidance of evil, and the salvation of souls, then accept them with due honor, as images, remembrances, likenesses and books for the illiterate. Embrace them with the eyes, the lips, the heart; bow before them; love them, for they are likenesses of God incarnate, of His Mother, and of the communion of saints. . . .

Second Apology Against those who Attack the Divine Images
11. If anyone should dare to make an image of the immaterial, bodiless, invisible, formless, and colorless Godhead, we reject it as a falsehood. If

anyone should make images to give glory, honor, and worship to the devil and his demons, we abhor them and deliver them to the flames. Or if anyone makes idols of men, birds, reptiles, or any creature, we anathematize him. . . . But since divine nature has assumed our nature, we have been given a life-bearing and saving remedy, which has glorified our nature and led it to incorruption. Therefore we celebrate the death of the saints; churches are built in their honor, and their icons are painted. But be assured that if any man sets his hand to throw down an image set up as a memorial to glorify Christ, His Mother the holy Theotokos, or any of the saints, an image which shames the devil and his consorts, an image which was made with godly desire and zeal, and will not bow down to honor and embrace the image as he should (but not as God), that man is an enemy of Christ, the holy Theotokos, and the saints, and an advocate of the devil and his crew, for by his actions he reveals his vexation that God and His saints are honored and glorified and the devil put to shame. The icon is a hymn of triumph, a manifestation, a memorial inscribed for those who have fought and conquered, humbling the demons and putting them to flight.

Theodore of Studios

First Refutation of the Iconoclasts
7. "It is a degradation," the heretics [i.e. the iconoclasts] say, "and a humiliation, to depict Christ in material representations. It is better that He should remain in mental contemplation, as He is formed in us by the Holy Spirit, who sends into us a kind of divine formation through sanctification and righteousness. . . ."

If merely mental contemplation were sufficient, it would have been sufficient for Him to come to us in a merely mental way; and consequently we would have been cheated by the appearance both of His deeds, if He did not come in the body, and of His sufferings which were undeniably like ours. . . .

Third Refutation of the Iconoclasts
34. [The iconoclasts say]: "If Christ is of two natures, when you claim to portray Him why do you not portray both natures from which and in which He is, if you are speaking the truth? But since one of the two is falsified, because the human circumscription does not contain the uncircumscribability of the divine nature, it is heretical to circumscribe Christ."

When anyone is portrayed, it is not the nature but the hypostasis [substance] which is portrayed. For how could a nature be portrayed unless it were contemplated in a hypostasis? For example, Peter is not portrayed insofar as he is animate, rational, mortal, and capable of thought and understanding; for this does not define Peter only, but also Paul and John, and all those of the same species. But insofar as he adds along with the common definition certain properties, such as a long or short nose, curly hair, a good complexion, bright eyes, or whatever else characterizes his particular appearance, he is distinguished from the other individuals of the same species. Moreover, although he consists of body and soul, he does not show the property of soul in the appearance of his form: how could he, since the soul is invisible? The same applies to the case of Christ. It is not because He is man simply (along with being God) that He is able to be portrayed; but because He is differentiated from all others of the same species by His hypostatic properties. He is crucified and has a certain appearance. Therefore Christ is circumscribed in respect to His hypostasis, though uncircumscribable in His divinity; but the natures of which He is composed are not circumscribed.

Architecture

Magnificence in Liturgical Fittings and Architecture: Abbot Suger of St. Denis, *On What was Done under his Administration*

27. *Of the Cast and Guilded Doors.* Bronze casters having been summoned and sculptors chosen, we set up the main doors on which are represented the Passion of the Saviour and His Resurrection, or rather Ascension, with great cost and much expenditure for their gilding as was fitting for the noble porch. Also [we set up] others, new ones on the right side and the old one on the left beneath the mosaic which, though contrary to modern custom, we ordered to be executed there and to be affixed to the tympanum of the portal. We also committed ourselves richly to elaborate the tower[s] and the upper crenelations of the front, both for the beauty of the church and, should circumstances require it, for practical purposes. Further we ordered the year of the consecration, lest it be forgotten, to be inscribed in copper-gilt letters in the following manner:

> For the splendor of the church that has fostered and exalted him,
> Suger has labored for the splendor of the church,
> Giving thee a share of what is thine, O Martyr Denis,
> He prays to thee to pray that he may obtain a share of Paradise.

The year was the One Thousand, One Hundred, and Fortieth
Year of the Word when [this structure] was consecrated.

The verses on the door, further are these:

Whoever thou art, if thou seekest to extol the glory of these doors,
Marvel not at the gold and the expense but at the craftsmanship of the work.
Bright is the noble work; but, being nobly bright, the work
Should brighten the minds, so that they may travel, through the true lights
To the True Light where Christ is the true door.
In what manner it be inherent in this world the golden door defines:
The dull mind rises to truth through that which is material
And, in seeing this light, is resurrected from its former submersion. . . .

30. *Of the Church's Ornaments.* We have thought it proper to place on record
the description of the ornaments of the church by which the Hand of God,
during our administration, has adorned His church, His Chosen Bride; lest
Oblivion, the jealous rival of Truth, sneak in and take away the example for
further action. Our Patron, the thrice blessed Denis, is, we confess and
proclaim, so generous and benevolent that we believe him to have prevailed
upon God to such an extent and to have obtained from Him so many and
so great things, that we might have been able to do for his church a hundred
times more than we have done, had not human frailty, the mutability of the
times, and the instability of manners prevented it. What we, nevertheless,
have saved for him by the grace of God is the following.

31. *Of the Golden Altar Frontal in the Upper Choir.* Into this panel, which
stands in front of his most sacred body, we have put, according to our
estimate, about forty-two marks of gold; [further] a multifarious wealth of
precious gems, hyacinths, rubies, sapphires, emeralds and topazes, and also
an array of different large pearls – [a wealth] as great as we had never
anticipated to find. You could see how kings, princes, and many
outstanding men, following our example, took the rings off the fingers of
their hands and ordered, out of love for the Holy Martyrs, that the gold,
stones, and precious pearls of the rings be put into that panel. Similarly
archbishops and bishops deposited there the very rings of their investiture
as though in a place of safety, and offered them devoutly to God and His
Saints. And such a crowd of dealers in precious gems flocked in on us from
diverse dominions and regions that we did not wish to buy any more than
they hastened to sell, with everyone contributing donations. And the verses
on this panel are these:

Great Denis, open the door of Paradise
And protect Suger through thy pious guardianship.

289

> Mayest thou, who has built a new dwelling for thyself through us,
> Cause us to be received in the dwelling of Heaven,
> And to be seated at the heavenly table instead of at the present one.
> That which is signified pleases more than that which signifies. . . .

We should have insisted with all the devotion of our mind – had we but had the power – that the adorable, life-giving cross, the health-bringing banner of the eternal victory of Our Saviour (of which the Apostle says: "But God forbid that I should glory, save in the cross of our Lord Jesus Christ" [Gal. 6:14]), should be adorned all the more gloriously as the sign of the Son of Man, which will appear in Heaven at the end of the world, will be glorious not only to men but also to the very angels; and we should have perpetually greeted it with the Apostle Andrew: "Hail Cross, which art dedicated in the body of Christ and adorned with His members even as with pearls." But since we could not do as we wished, we wished to do as best we could, and strove to bring it about by the grace of God. Therefore we searched around everywhere by ourselves and by our agents for an abundance of precious pearls and gems, preparing as precious a supply of gold and gems for so important an embellishment as we could find and convoked the most experienced artists from diverse parts. They would with diligent and patient labor glorify the venerable cross on its reverse side by the admirable beauty of those gems; and on its front – that is to say in the sight of the sacrificing priest – they would show the adorable image of our Lord the Saviour, suffering, as it were, even now in remembrance of His Passion. . . . One merry but notable miracle which the Lord granted us in this connection we do not wish to pass over in silence. For when I was in difficulty for want of gems and could not sufficiently provide myself with more (for their scarcity makes them very expensive): then, lo and hold, [monks] from three abbeys of two Orders . . . entered our little chamber adjacent to the church and offered us for sale an abundance of gems such as we had not hoped to find in ten years, hyacinths, sapphires, rubies, emeralds, topazes. . . . We, however, freed from the worry of searching for gems, thanked God and gave four hundred pounds for the lot though they were worth much more.

33. . . . Often we contemplate, out of sheer affection for the church our mother, these different ornaments both new and old; and when we behold how that wonderful cross of St. Eloy* – together with the smaller ones – and that incomparable ornament commonly called "the Crest" are placed upon the golden altar, then I say, sighing deeply in my heart: "Every precious stone was thy covering, the sardius, the topaz, and the jasper, the

---

* St. Eloy (590–660) was Bishop of Noyon and patron saint of metalworkers.

chrysolite, and the onyx, and the beryl, the sapphire, and the carbuncle, and the emerald" [Ezek. 28:13]. To those who know the properties of precious stones it becomes evident, to their utter astonishment, that none is absent from the number of these (with the only exception of the carbuncle), but that they abound most copiously. Thus, when – out of my delight in the beauty of the house of God – the loveliness of the many-colored gems has called me away from external cares, and worthy meditation has induced me to reflect, transferring that which is material to that which is immaterial, on the diversity of the sacred virtues: then it seems to me that I see myself dwelling, as it were, in some strange region of the universe which neither exists entirely in the slime of the earth nor entirely in the purity of Heaven; and that, by the grace of God, I can be transported from this inferior to that higher world in an anagogical manner. . . . To me, I confess, one thing has always seemed preeminently fitting: that every costlier or costliest thing should serve, first and foremost, for the administration of the Holy Eucharist. *If* golden pouring vessels, golden vials, golden little mortars used to serve, by the word of God or the command of the Prophet, to collect the blood of goats or calves or the red heifer; how much more must golden vessels, precious stones, and whatever is most valued among all created things, be laid out, with continual reverence and full devotion, for the reception of the blood of Christ! [See Heb. 9:12–14.] Surely neither we nor our possessions suffice for this service. . . . The detractors also object that a saintly mind, a pure heart, and faithful intention ought to suffice for this sacred function; and we, too, explicitly and especially affirm that it is these that principally matter. [But] we profess that we must do homage also through the outward ornaments of sacred vessels, and to nothing in the world in an equal degree as to the service of the Holy Sacrifice, with all inner purity and with all outward splendor. For it behooves us most becomingly to serve our Saviour in all things in a universal way – Him Who has not refused to provide for us in all things in a universal way and without any exception. . . .

Poetry

Simplicity in Hymnody: Isaac Watts

Donald Davie

I want to begin by reading a poem. And since I shall rather seldom in these lectures be able to do this, let us enjoy together while we may the *presence* of poetry, as distinct from more or less impertinent prattle about it. The poem is called "Man frail, and God eternal", and it will be familiar to most of you, though probably not under that title.

> O God, our help in ages past,
> Our hope for years to come,
> Our shelter from the stormy blast,
> And our eternal home.
>
> Under the shadow of the throne
> Thy saints have dwelt secure;
> Sufficient is thine arm alone,
> And our defense is sure.
>
> Before the hills in order stood,
> Or earth receiv'd her frame,
> From everlasting thou art God,
> To endless years the same.
>
> Thy word commands our flesh to dust,
> "Return, ye sons of men";
> All nations rose from earth at first,
> And turn to earth again.
>
> A thousand ages in thy sight
> Are like an evening gone;
> Short as the watch that ends the night
> Before the rising sun.
>
> The busy tribes of flesh and blood,
> With all their lives and cares,
> Are carry'd downwards by thy flood,
> And lost in following years.
>
> Time like an ever-rolling stream
> Bears all its sons away;
> They fly forgotten as a dream
> Dies at the opening day.
>
> Like flowering fields the nations stand
> Pleas'd with the morning light;
> The flowers beneath the mower's hand
> Lie withering ere 'tis night.
>
> Our God, our help in ages past,
> Our hope for years to come,

> Be thou our guard while troubles last,
> And our eternal home.

We think of this poem as a hymn. And that sounds right, for "hymn" is indeed the traditionally appropriate title for one sub-category of the sort of tribal lyric that we seem to have to do with. More precisely, however, our poem is not a hymn but a *psalm*. In fact it is specifically and deliberately a version of one of the Psalms of David, or rather of the first six verses of that psalm, Ps. 90. . . . Need it be said that just such dependence on a sacred or canonical text, and in consequence just such total disregard for "originality" or "self-expression," is entirely typical of the poet of the tribal lay? Nevertheless it is clear that our poet has intended more than a metrical translation of the verses of Scripture. . . . Our poem is working in [the] Calvinist tradition but at the same time transforming it, administering to it a shock which in fact provoked many guardians of that tradition to rise up in arms against him. What he gives us is a psalm, not translated, but paraphrased and modernized, and yet in no sense "freely adapted," but modernized according to a very strict method. He said himself of these compositions of his that they were "The Psalms of David Imitated in the Language of the New Testament." And what this means in effect, schematically, is that every time the ancient Hebrew poet looks back ("Lord, thou hast been our dwelling place in all generations"), our English poet looks back with him, but then immediately forward; thus, "Our hope for years to come". . . .

Yet, all of this is of no account at all if, when we hear or read or sing "O God, our help in ages past", it strikes us as a merely *dull*. . . . About such matters there can be no argument – at least in this sense, that no one should allow himself to be browbeaten into pretending that what he registers as "dull" somehow isn't. All that a lecturer can do is to avow quite sincerely that "dull" isn't how such verses register for him now, though it's true that once they did; to quote from his author to show that dullness was one risk the author foresaw yet decided to take; and finally to offer what he has found for his own part to be an instructive comparison. This I now proceed to. . . .

In the first place Isaac Watts (for he, of course, is the poet we are dealing with), speaking of such compositions as this one, declared:

> In many of these composures, I have just permitted my verse to rise above a flat and indolent style; yet I hope it is everywhere supported above the just contempt of the critics: though I am sensible that I have often subdued it below their esteem; because I would neither indulge any bold metaphors, nor admit of hard words, nor tempt the ignorant worshiper to sing without his understanding.

and in "A Short Essay toward the improvement of Psalmody," he made the same point more vehemently: "It was hard to restrain my verse always within the bounds of my design; it was hard to sink every line to the level of a whole congregation, and yet to keep it above contempt." This was a poet who, if he practiced what Pope and the Scriblerus Club called "the art of sinking," did so deliberately, after counting the cost, his eyes open to the risk he was running. . . .

Well, but (it may be said) we ask of a poetic style – of a style in any art, and indeed of a style of life – that it possess more than negative virtues. It is a weighty point, and one indeed that takes us at once to the heart of the Calvinist aesthetic. For that is what we are now concerned with. And in the first place a Calvinist aesthetic exists: "In nothing perhaps has Calvin been more misjudged than in the view that he lacked an aesthetic sense. . . ." It was after all John Calvin who clothed Protestant worship with the sensuous grace, and necessarily the aesthetic ambiguity, of song; and who that has attended worship in a French Calvinist church can deny that – over and above whatever religious experience he may or may not have had – he has had an aesthetic experience, and of a peculiarly intense kind? From the architecture, from church furnishings, from the congregational music, from the Geneva gown of the pastor himself, everything breathes *simplicity, sobriety, and measure* – which are precisely the qualities that Calvinist aesthetics demands of the art object. Just here, in fact, is where negative virtues become positive ones. And this is true not just of Calvinist art but of all art, not just of Calvinist ethics but of all ethics. The aesthetic *and* the more perceptions have, built into them and near to the heart of them, the perception of license, of abandonment, of superfluity, foreseen, even invited, and yet in the end denied, fended off.

Art *is* measure, *is* exclusion; is therefore simplicity (hard-earned), is sobriety, tense with all the extravagances that it has been tempted by and has denied itself. I appeal to you, and to your experience, whether in making art or in responding to it: Isn't this the way it is? And so, even if we admit for the sake of argument that Calvinism denies sensuous pleasure, we encounter time and again the question, when faced with a Calvinistic occasion: Do we have here a denial of sensuous pleasure, or do we not rather have sensuous pleasure deployed with an unusually frugal, and therefore exquisite, fastidiousness. It is peculiarly of the nature of Puritan art to pose just this question, though that is by no means the account of it that is usually given. . . .

CONTEMPORARY REFLECTION

Theology in Art

Nicholas Wolterstorff, adapted from Art in Action, *Chapter 1*

Christians, along with all other human beings, are engaged with art: with music, poetry, fiction, drama, visual design and representation, architecture. Many Christians join their fellow citizens in going to concerts, attending plays, visiting museums, reading novels; all are nowadays united with their fellow citizens in being subjected to advertising art in all its many forms. Most Christians, in addition, interact with Christian liturgical art: they worship inside churches, they sing hymns. Virtually all of them interact with Christian memorial art: with paintings, sculptures, works of music, in which persons and events from the Bible and Christian tradition are recalled and honored. Our focus in this essay is on the theological reflections which emerge from these engagements of Christians with art.

The body of such reflections is rich. In our century, the great bulk of these reflections have focussed on the engagement of Christians with art intended for disinterested contemplation: concert hall music, museum paintings, reading room poetry, and so forth. In the modern western world, such art is of course extraordinarily prominent, so much so that many authors write as if there were no other than such art. Among such authors have to be numbered many of those who have contributed most significantly to Christian reflections on the arts, and on the Christian's engagement with the arts. I have in mind, among others, Gerardus vander Leeuw, Paul Tillich, and Dorothy Sayers. But while Christians have always been engaged with the arts, not until the eighteenth century did art for disinterested contemplation acquire the prominence which it now has; and even in the modern world, the engagement of Christians with art extends well beyond their engagement with such art. There has always been, and there is yet today, Christian liturgical art, just as there has always been, and there is yet today, Christian memorial art.

The selections which accompany this essay offer reflections on memorial and liturgical art. Slowly in the ancient Christian world there arose the practice of composing representations of Christ, the Virgin, and the saints, and the accompanying practice of venerating these icons – that is, of kneeling and bowing before them, lighting candles before them, kissing them, parading them through the streets, and so forth. Then, around 725, there arose enormous controversies in Eastern Christianity concerning this very striking form of memorial art. This so-called "iconoclast controversy" raged for about a century and a quarter. It is regularly said nowadays that the iconoclasts, that is, "icon-destroyers," held a negative view of the material world, and that, accordingly, the eventual victory of the iconodules, the "icon-servants" (also called "iconophiles," icon-lovers), represents the victory of the orthodox Christian affirmation of the goodness of the material creation. There is no evidence that that was in fact the point of controversy. Instead, the iconoclasts questioned, for one thing, the propriety of making icons. It was heretical, so they claimed, to make an icon of Christ. The painter was limited to representing Christ's humanity; representing his divinity was impossible. But does this not heretically presuppose, so they asked, that his humanity and divinity are separable? As to icons of the saints and the Virgin, though no heresy is involved in the making of such icons, is it not better, they asked, to imitate the saints in our lives than in "dead matter"? Those were the main issues raised concerning the practice of making icons. And as to the practice of veneration, the iconoclasts claimed that though it was right to venerate the saints – especially by imitating their holiness in our own lives – it was wrong to venerate the icons, which were but pieces of wood. To give a glimpse – no more than that – of the complex theological issues raised by the practice of icon-veneration, our selections include some passages from the *horos*, that is, the "pronouncement," of the iconoclast church council of 757, and from John of Damascus and Theodore of Studios, who undertook to answer the iconoclasts.

The theological reflections stimulated by *liturgical* art have been, if anything, even richer than those stimulated by memorial art. Here too, nothing more than a glimpse is possible. Statements of two contrasting positions have again been chosen. Abbot Suger, responsible for building the church of St. Denis in the early thirteenth century in Paris, was convinced that, in materials and workmanship, the church had to be *magnificent*. In Suger's praise of magnificence it is difficult for us not to hear his own personal love for jewels and gems; but the reason he offers, and assumes, is theological: the church building is to symbolize the magnificence of God, and only if the building is itself magnificent can it symbolize divine magnificence.

One finds, in the Christian tradition, several distinct lines of reflection in opposition to Suger. Calvin, for example, argued that light, pure natural light, is, of all natural phenomena, the best symbol that we have of God: light, alone, is uncircumscribed. One can see, says Calvin, why God uses this as a symbol of himself in Scripture. Above everything else, then, our church buildings must be full of light: symbolic of God. Other writers, following out a different line of opposition to Suger, have argued that the Church, instead of attempting to reflect the magnificence of the Godhead, must reflect the evangelical poverty and simplicity of Christ among us. Not the magnificence of the costly, but the dignity of the ordinary, is what the Church must exhibit in its architecture – and in its liturgical art generally. From among many possibilities, a selection from the contemporary English poet, Donald Davie, reflecting on the hymnody of Isaac Watts, has been chosen to express the point of view.

Liturgical and Contemplative Art

The accompanying selections give a glimpse, then, of the rich theological reflections that have been stimulated by debates which have arisen concerning the mode and manner in which Christians should be engaged with the arts: debates concerning what sort of art Christians should be producing in their churches and elsewhere, debates concerning how Christians should interact with the art produced by themselves and others. But rather than pursue any such issues of mode and manner, profoundly important though many of them are and have been, I propose in this present essay to offer some theological reflections on the arts themselves, and on the propriety and importance of our interaction with them.

One issue to be addressed before we can ever get underway is whether we will accept the dictum, common among writers on the arts since the eighteenth century, that art for disinterested contemplation represents the arts come into their own, and correspondingly, that the action of disinterested contemplation represents the highest and noblest use to which works of art can be put. Elsewhere I have discussed these issues in detail;[1] on this occasion, I must confine myself to a brisk indication of my most fundamental reason for rejecting the dictum.

Many examples of the arts are indeed made for the sort of contemplation typical of the concert hall, the museum, the library; but neither now nor in the past are all of them made for that purpose. And it is my contention that there is nothing about the arts themselves which implies that contemplation of that sort is somehow the "true" function of the arts. Chairs are clearly for sitting on. They can be put to other uses – holding doors open, for example – but they are made and distributed for sitting on. When put to other uses, one might say that they "aren't in their own." The relation of the arts to contemplation is different. The situation is not that examples of the arts are made and distributed for contemplation, but that they can be put to other uses as well. The situation is rather that they are *also* made and distributed for other uses: for employment in the liturgy, for honoring events and persons from our past, for getting us to buy merchandise, and so forth. They too can be put to uses other than those for which they are made and distributed; sculptures, like chairs, can be used to hold doors open. But the point is that, unlike chairs, the uses for which they are made and distributed are multiple. Liturgical art is just as much "art come into its own" as is art for contemplation.

May it be, though, that serving as object of contemplation is the highest and noblest use to which examples of the arts an be put? Why so? Why, for example, is that a higher and nobler use than functioning in the liturgy? Of course, if one held that the activity of disinterested perceptual contemplation is inherently higher and nobler than the activity of participating in the liturgy, then one would have a reason for regarding the use of art in the liturgy as inferior. But would a *Christian* accept that estimate of those two activities?

I propose, then, that we recognize the diversity of intended uses for the arts, and further, that we impose no hierarchy. Composing and employing works of art to recall and honor persons and events from our past is, as such, no worse, though also no better, than composing and employing works of art as objects of perceptual contemplation. Both are indispensable for our flourishing. Of course there are bad works of memorial art; but let us not forget that there are also bad works of museum art. And let us recognize that what makes something good or bad as a work of memorial art is not identical with what makes it good or bad as a work of contemplation art. Works of art are instruments and objects of action; and the actions are legion.

Creation as God's Art

Art invites us, first of all, to reflect on the fact and significance of our embeddedness in the physical creation. The world in which we live is an artifact brought into being by God. It represents a success on the part of God – God who is love – not a failure. In contemplation of what God had made, God found delight. But God knew that it would also serve well God's human creatures. So God pronounced a "Yes" upon it all, a "Yes" of delight and of love. You and I must do no less. Of course, nothing in this created world is worthy of worship – neither sun nor moon, neither trees nor hills. Its maker alone is worthy of that, and its maker is distinct from the world. But God the Creator is worthy of worship in part *because* of the magnificence and benefit of this which God has made. "The heavens tell out the glory of God, the vault of heaven reveals God's handiwork," says the Psalmist (Ps. 19:1).

We fit into the *spatial* structure of physical reality. I am at such-and-such a distance and direction from this desk, and at such-and-such a distance and direction from that plant. In addition we fit into the *causal* structure of physical reality. We interact causally with the things around us. To express the intimacy and also the fragility of this interaction, Pascal once remarked that a drop of water can kill a person. But thirdly, and more importantly, we in our bodily composition are made of the same stuff as the rest of the physical creation. There is in us no peculiar element, no quintessence. We are made of dust – that is how Genesis puts it. Having said that, Genesis goes on to say that we are *ensouled* bodies. But that does not point to some peculiar composition we have. It points rather to the fact that we are biologically alive (see Gen. 7:21–2).

So when you and I carve wood, apply paint to canvas, pile stone on stone, or inscribe marks on paper, we are dealing with things which bear to us the most intimate of relations. To an angel art must seem a very foreign thing indeed. With us, it shares its substance.

Earthly existence is one of God's favors to us. When Christians affirm the goodness of the physical creation, they are not just praising its magnificence. They are saying that the physical creation is good *for human beings*. It serves human fulfillment. Earth is our home, the world our dwelling place.

Human Answerability

Deeply embedded in the Christian confession concerning creation is the conviction that we are indeed uniquely unique among our fellow earthlings. "What is man that thou art mindful of him," asks the songwriter of ancient Israel (Ps. 8:4, RSV), "and the son of man, that thou dost care for him?" He finds it astonishing that from the vast cosmic array God should have singled out human beings for special attention. But his astonishment does not shake his conviction that this is exactly what has happened. For at once he goes on to say, "Thou hast made him little less than God, and dost crown him with glory and honor."

In what way have we been singled out by God? In a variety of ways; the question has no one answer. But surely part of the biblical vision is this: we have been singled out *to be answerable*. We alone are responsible, accountable. The dignity of the human being calls for recognizing that we are answerable, and so for recognizing guilt, which is the dark side of answerability.

We do not, however, *just come* as answerable creatures. Our being such inheres in God's *holding us* answerable. What we are answerable for doing is what God *holds us* answerable for doing. Thus all human responsibilities are ultimately responsibilities to God. To fail in one's responsibilities is to let God down. It is in holding us answerable to himself that, above all, God dignifies us. Our uniqueness lies in being bound to God by cords of answerability.

We are answerable, in the first place, with respect to the natural world surrounding us. We are to *subdue* it – that is, to tame it, to eliminate its unruliness, to order it, to place our imprint upon it.

There is no point in circling delicately round the fact that to many of us, in the latter part of the twentieth century, it sounds deeply offensive to speak of human beings as called to subdue and dominate the earth and all that dwells therein.

What is even clearer, though, is a second point: that we are not to impose form out of infatuation with seeing the imprint of our own selves on the world around, but to do so *for human benefit*. Our imposition of order is to be for the sake of human livelihood and delight. For after the injunction to subdue the earth, God says, "Behold, I have given you every plant yielding seed which is upon the face of all the earth, and every tree with seed in its fruit, you shall have them for food" (Gen. 1:29). And then, in the second chapter of Genesis, we find it said, about the garden of Eden, that "The Lord God made to grow every tree that is pleasant to the sight and good for food" (2.9). Subduing, then, is the imposition of order for the purpose of serving human livelihood and delight. (No doubt also for the purpose of rendering honor to God, though that happens not to be mentioned in the texts before us.) When the imposition of order goes beyond what serves human benefit and God's honor, then it goes beyond our authorization. Today we in the west are beginning to realize just how far we have gone beyond.

It is not difficult to see how our vocation of master, of subduer, of humanizer of the world, of one who imposes order for the sake of benefiting humankind or honoring God, applies to the artist. The artist takes an amorphous pile of bits of colored glass and orders them upon the wall of the basilica so that the liturgy can take place in the splendor of flickering colored light and in the presence of the invoked saints. She takes a blob of clay and orders it into a pot of benefit and delight. He takes a disorderly array of pigments and a piece of canvas and orders them into a painting richly intense in color and evocative of the South Seas. He takes a piece of stone rough from the quarry and by slowly chipping away orders it into a representation of Virgin and son. He makes from our huge store of words – of sounds with meanings – a selection and puts them into an order so as thereby to inspire his fellow human beings to "not go gentle into that good night" (Dylan Thomas). The artist, when he brings forth order for human benefit or divine honor, shares in our human vocation to garden the earth.

But there is more to human answerability than answerability with respect to nature. That more can be treated more briefly, not because it is less important, nor because it is easier to carry out, but rather because it is easier for us to comprehend. We are answerable with respect to each other. We are to love our neighbors as ourselves. This presupposes that each is to love himself or herself. To despise oneself, to hate oneself, to long to be what one cannot be and so to neglect becoming what one can become, to squander one's life instead of nourishing one's potential – that is to fail in one's answerability to God. Each is to seek his or her fulfillment. But equally, each is to exhibit solidarity with the other, to stand in her stead, to love the other as one loves oneself, to seek the other's fulfillment as one seeks one's own. Indeed, in seeking the other's, we find our own.

Need it be emphasized that the artist shares in this human vocation to love one's neighbor? Without the artist, human life would be impoverished, almost impossible. Much of what we find worth doing could not be done at all; much else, only limpingly. The artist, like all of us, is answerable not only to nature, but to his or her fellow human beings.

There is yet one more phase of human answerability. Not only are we answerable to God for subduing the earth and for loving our neighbors as ourselves. We are also answerable to God for actions with respect to God, our Creator. We are answerable to God for acknowledging God – praising God for the magnificence and goodness of God's deeds, trusting God that he will lead his creatures into green pastures.

Undoubtedly it is on this point of art and answerability that the Christian image of the artist diverges most sharply from the heaven-storming image of post-Enlightenment western humanity. For where the Christian sees the artist as an answerable agent before God, sharing in our human vocation, modern writers have regularly seen the artist as freed from all answerability, struggling simply to express himself in untrammelled freedom. Though often it is assumed that the public is answerable to the artist, even more often it is assumed that the artist has no answerability to the public. It is often suggested, indeed, that if the artist so much as thinks in terms of responsibility, her flow of creativity will be stanched. One might ask why, then, the architect remains creative? But more profoundly, our discussion enables us now to put this question: why should the artist, an earthling with the rest of us, be seen as deprived of that human dignity which resides in the fact that the human being, and the human being alone among earthlings, is answerable?

Aesthetic Delight

Some readers may feel that my discussion in the preceding section has a "Calvinistic" sternness about it. If art is the instrument and object of actions of a wide range, and if we human beings, in our actions, are answerable to God for how we treat God, each other, and nature, then art will indeed occur within, and should accordingly be seen within, the context of human answerability. All true. Nonetheless one wants to shout, "What about delight? Isn't there more to life than answerability? Is answerability everything? Isn't there also the delight that we experience in contemplating works of art – listening to music, reading poetry, looking at paintings and sculptures?"

The supplement needed is the introduction of another theme concerning humanity in creation, a theme as prominent in the biblical writers as the theme of humanity as answerable, yet a theme seldom noticed in the Christian tradition. It is the theme of *shalom, eirené* – usually translated as "peace," but better translated as "flourishing." Shalom is human beings flourishing in all their relationships: with God, with themselves, with their fellows, with nature. Shalom is not merely the absence of hostility, though certainly it is that. Shalom is justice. And more yet than that; shalom, at its highest, is *enjoyment*. To dwell in shalom is to *enjoy* living before God, to *enjoy* living in nature, to *enjoy* living with one's fellows, to *enjoy* life with oneself.

Responsible action is our vocation; shalom, our end and goal. And in this end lies our uniqueness as much as in our vocation. Responsible action is a condition of shalom; where righteousness is missing, there shalom is grievously wounded. Yet responsible action, though a condition of shalom, is not a guarantee thereof. All too often, flourishing eludes us as we pursue our duty.

Just two matters call for brief additional comment. Joy comes in a multiplicity of forms, among them the joy of aesthetic satisfaction. Such joy is not the sole form worthy of our pursuit and acceptance. Neither is it the ultimate form. Certainly, though, it is one among others.

The practice, in one's contemplation of a work of art, of looking only for the message and of fixing only on the world projected, of taking no delight in the artifact which bears the message and presents the world, might be called a "docetic" approach to the arts – on analogy to an early Christian heresy that denied the genuine bodily nature of Christ. All such docetism must be rooted out of our commerce with the arts. The person who in looking at the paintings of Paul Klee looks only for the threateningly mystical message and never notices the wondrousness of the colors is practicing an heretical approach to the arts. Equally, the person who only revels in the colors and never discerns what it is that Klee is using his art to express is practicing an heretical approach.

It is true that sensory delight can be a threat to one's obedience to God. It can function as a distraction from one's other responsibilities. Worse, it can function as a surrogate for God. But a Christian's repudiation of this must not obscure from her the fact that the structure of this idolatry, as of every other, is that of a limited good being treated as an ultimate good. Its structure is not that of something evil being treated as good.

One other matter pertaining to joy and art merits brief comment. Not only does the joy of aesthetic delight have its legitimate place in human life. So too does the joy which the artist experiences in creating her work, and the performer in performing. We must, it is true, keep in mind a point vividly made by Karl Barth when he once said that we are allowed to "have joy, and therefore will it, only as we give it to others." And it must be acknowledged that the contemporary artist's intense concern with solving artistic problems set by himself and his fellow artists sometimes excludes the note of "rejoice along with me." When that happens, the artist has fallen into irresponsible self-indulgence. Yet in posing and solving artistic problems because one *enjoys* doing so, there is nothing wrong. Life was not meant to be grim.

In conclusion we must come back to insist on the opposite point, so often denied in the contemporary arts – namely, that joy is to be found in acknowledging one's answerability to one's fellows. Indeed, is it not true here too that the one who loses herself will find herself? Is it not precisely the artist narcissistically concerned to find herself who will at last discover that she has irretrievably lost herself? The Byzantine artist placed himself humbly at the service of the Church, invoking the presence of the departed saints by depicting them, so that the liturgy could take place in their presence as well as in the presence of us on earth. Is it likely that he found less joy in his work than does the contemporary artist who sets himself his own problems in the hope that in solving them he will find joy? And is it not a specious concept of *integrity* that is being used, when it is said that for the artist to bend his talents to the service of others is to sacrifice his personal integrity?

Responsible Art

Lastly, the Christian speaks of more than creation. He speaks also of our rejection of God's rule, with its attendant defection from answerability and its consequent evils. And he sees that art, over and over, has served the cause of that rejection and defection. To read, for example, Lewis Mumford's *The City in History* is to read the long tale of the ever novel ways in which human beings, in building their cities, have used art to mutilate nature, to oppress their fellows, to serve idols, and even to thwart their own fulfillment. The art you and I now admire in the scrubbed stillness of the museum once dripped with blood, reeked of idolatry, or caused its makers suicidal depression and anguish. Contrary to the classic Romantic picture, art is not isolated from the radical fallenness of our nature and condition. Art is an instrument thereof. Rather than lifting us out of the radical evil of our history, art plunges us into it. Art is not our savior, but a willing accomplice in our crimes.

But the Christian speaks also of redemption. He dares to say that the ultimate drift of history is toward the attainment of justice in shalom; for he believes that God, not being willing to abandon God's favored creatures with justice never won and flourishing never attained, is working toward that goal. The Christian hopes for the full coming of "the Reign of God," where God is universally acknowledged as Lord.

Admittedly there are those who perceive the message of the Christian gospel as the message of escape from our creaturely, earthly existence. In such a view art will appear in a radically different light from that in which I have placed it. But such a view can make no sense of those factors in the Christian confession to which I have been calling attention. The Reign of God is not escape from our earthly condition; it is that state in which human beings acknowledge God's rule and carry out their creaturely responsibilities. Such a state is not merely the *restoration* of Eden; what has taken place in history will play its constructive role in the character of life in the Reign of God. Rather it is the *renewal* of human existence, so that our creaturely vocation and fulfillment may be attained, already now and in the future.

This acknowledging of God at work in human redemption does not compromise our contention that art is an indispensable instrument in the fulfillment of our responsibilities and a crucial component in the shalom for which men and women were made. Rather, since we are now called to be God's agents in God's cause of renewal, of whose ultimate success God has assured us, art now gains new significance. Art, in addition to everything else, can serve as instrument in our struggle to overcome the fallenness of our existence, while also, in the delight it affords, anticipating the shalom which awaits us. Paradise is forever behind us. But the City of God, full of song and image, remains to be built.

Christian Art

I have cast a wide net in these reflections. The accompanying texts will have made obvious how fundamental is the role that liturgical and memorial art play in shaping our knowledge and love of God. Byzantine icons, Rembrandt's biblical portraits; Gregorian chant, Genevan psalm tunes; St. Peter's in Rome, a New England meeting house; the biblical psalms, "Amazing Grace": these works of art, along with hundreds of thousands more, have formed our Christian lives, including, then, our knowledge and love of God. One cannot imagine Christian existence without art. Rather than dwelling on that point, however, I have looked beyond liturgical and memorial art, to art in general. The upshot of my reflections is that to do so is to have one's existential knowledge of God profoundly enhanced. In art we discern in what high esteem God holds us, and with what love God showers us. God has dignified us with answerability – plus intelligence, imagination, and much more. Art is the embodiment of those. God's love has as its goal that we live in shalom. Art gives us a taste of that.

Note

1   See especially Parts One and Two of my *Art in Action* (Grand Rapids: Eerdmans, 1980).

Inquiring after God when at Prayer

Prayer is often thought of as asking for things, but there is really more to it. Even petitionary prayer requires thought. What is it appropriate to pray for and what not? If one prays for one's enemies, what should one seek? If one realizes that one's own desires may be distorted rather than pure, how can one be sure what to pray for?

Yet beyond asking for things prayer is a gateway to understanding God. The two selections included here, both from the Eastern Orthodox tradition, treat contemplative rather than either liturgical prayer or spontaneous vocal prayer. It requires silence and a quiet mind in which the truth of God may emerge. The classic text comes from the pen of St. Maximus the Confessor (580–662). Although Maximus lived before the official schism between east and west in the eleventh century, and so is equally venerated in both theological traditions, theologically and spiritually he belongs to the east. Maximus started his professional life in Constantinople, the capital of Byzantium, with a high ranking position at court. But after three years on the career ladder he resigned to become a monk. In 626 foreign invaders were seeking to take over the Byzantine Empire. Maximus went into exile and made his way to North Africa, part of the western church centered at Rome.

As a thinker, Maximus participated in the theological controversies of his day, notably the christological controversy that continued after the Council of Chalcedon, especially in the east. Maximus' support for the Chalcedonian position put him at odds with the Church at Constantinople that took the Monophysite side in the argument, holding that Christ had but one (divine) will in order to be clear about the singularity of Christ. This position minimized the human aspect of the Incarnation, however. Although Maximus was mutilated as punishment, he refused to recant. This earned him the title "the Confessor." He was tried for treason and banished. He died soon thereafter.

Maximus' treatise on prayer is a commentary on the "Our Father," the Lord's Prayer of Matthew 6. In the Gospel Jesus is instructing his followers how to pray, for prayer is difficult and often embarrassing. It can be misused to show off one's piety, for example, and so Jesus counsels his followers to pray alone. And the prayer itself acknowledges that those who pray are often too confused to know what is best for them. And so Jesus tells them what to do. The fact that the Lord's Prayer is recited so commonly may lead to its losing its meaning. Maximus uses the text to take his reader deep into God. He is not interested in the historical-critical interpretation of the text, or the reception history of the Prayer. Rather, like Augustine's homilies, the commentary seeks the knowledge of God that can help seekers.

Maximus argues, in part, that prayer is a way to gain control of oneself. Those who pray deeply enjoy the benefits of Christ's Incarnation and passion to the goal of deification, fulfillment in the mystery of God. To this end Maximus parses each petition of the Prayer, leading the reader ever further into the reality of the triune God as taught by scripture and the Church. The benefits of Christ, made translucent through the Lord's Prayer, derive mostly from the Incarnation, the physical presence of God in a human being. The person who prays comes to know God as the Holy Trinity, the source of our creation and as Father through adoption by grace.

The Incarnation holds divinity and humanity in paradoxical unity. It concretizes the overcoming of human alienation from God. Christ thereby reconciles opposites, even though the Chalcedonian teaching on the identity of Christ does not specify exactly how this happens. The purity of Christ, symbolized by his virginal conception, purifies human nature from the power of lust and anger. Christ's death on a cross brings many types of people, even enemies, together in the worship of God, abolishing enmity on earth. His becoming food in communion enables believers to know God's goodness in providing for them. These works of God which are with and in human nature are themselves redemptive. In short, Christ's person works salvation.

An important theme of this treatise is Maximus' analysis of forgiveness. He points out that the saving power of God lies in "his" restraining "his" justifiable anger at us in order to forgive our sins in the death of Christ. Applying this insight into God's nature to ourselves, without the ability to let go of or at least control hurt and lust, we readily sink to nothing. Forgiving requires stilling the hurt, resentment, and anger that naturally accompany pain and suffering. The idea that self-control that enables one to "see" the other is made possible by prayer is perhaps hard for our age to appreciate. American society especially is given to self-assertiveness and acting on one's feelings rather than careful discernment prior to action. Yet forgiveness must be grounded in self-restraint, if it is to be genuine. Maximus particularly commends controlling lust and anger. Prayer that enables one to gain wisdom from contemplating the goodness of God is genuine theological inquiry.

Maximus' insistence on human ability to cooperate with God's grace is another controversial theme in Christian theology. He depicts sanctification as struggle and hard work; it is not automatic. Desisting from impulsive behavior in order to forgive others and protect them from our worst self is an arduous, sometimes uphill battle. Maximus' point is that prayer, the way to know God better, is the instrument of choice for successful combat against one's own personal demons. The contemplative life that Maximus adopted when he dropped out of the corporate rat-race countenances no withdrawal. It is an activist life in which the believer partakes of the divine energy to become as like to God as possible. The common contrast between the contemplative life of prayer and active life in the world is based on a fundamental misunderstanding of both.

Although their writing spans a thousand years, there are deep resonances among Bonaventure's treatment of the Trinity, Chrysostom's spiritual approach to affliction, Catherine's teaching on repentance and forgiveness, and Maximus' treatise on prayer. All these treatises point to the need for the inner life to guide action. This is made possible through the discipline of prayer. Those unaccustomed to reading spiritual texts may find Maximus difficult to read and may prefer to read the contemporary text first.

The contemporary essay on prayer follows and interprets the path carved by Maximus and other Byzantine theologians. Bishop Kallistos Ware explains three aspects of the spiritual life of prayer that develop and form one's spiritual intellect: preparation through repentance, knowing God through created things (including other persons), and direct experience of and union with God through prayer. There are in addition three elements of the context one must put oneself into in order to practice the spiritual life effectively: active participation in the Church, the sacramental setting of Christian worship, and dwelling in the scriptural heritage of the tradition.

In the process of explaining and integrating these six requirements of the Christian spiritual life, Bishop Ware, like Maximus, confutes the incorrect, but widely held view that an active life of work in the world is different from the contemplative life of people who seek refuge in monasteries. The bishop explains that the spiritual life is both active and contemplative both in the monastery and in a corporate office. The activity of the spiritual life is purification from selfishness and uncontrolled desires. The contemplation of the spiritual life is union with God in love, inner peace, and calm. Both facilitate daily life.

The Lord's Prayer: Matthew 6:9–13

Our Father who art in heaven
Hallowed be thy name.
Thy kingdom come,
Thy will be done,
On earth as it is in heaven.
Give us this day our daily bread.
And forgive us our trespasses
As we forgive those who trespass against us.
Lead us not into temptation,
But deliver us from evil.

St. Maximus Confessor, *Commentary on the Our Father**

Prologue

My Lord, in divine keeping, it is yourself that I received, you who come to me through your very praiseworthy letters. Indeed, you are always present and totally incapable of being absent in spirit, and likewise you do not refuse to converse in imitation of God with your servants by the abundance of your virtue and the utterance which God has given to your nature.

For this reason, admiring the greatness of your condescension, I blended my fear with affection, and from these two, fear and affection, I created a single thing, love, made up of modesty and benevolence, in such manner that

---

* Punctuation in this text has been silently corrected.

a fear devoid of affection did not become hatred, nor did an affection not joined to a prudent fear become presumption; but on the contrary, that love be shown to be an immanent law of devotedness which harmonizes whatever is related by nature. By benevolence it masters hatred, and by reverence it pushes away presumption. Realizing that it (that is, fear) confirms divine love more than anything else, the blessed David has said, "The fear of the Lord is chaste and remains from age to age" (Ps. 19:9). He well knew that this fear is different from the fear which consists of being afraid of punishments for faults of which we are accused, since for one thing this (fear of punishment) disappears completely in the presence of love, as the great evangelist John shows somewhere in his words, "Love drives out fear" (1 John 4:18). For another thing, the former (fear of the Lord) naturally characterizes the law of true concern; it is through reverence that the saints keep forever completely uncorrupted the law and mode of life of love toward God and toward each other.

Thus, as I was saying, having myself joined to affection the fear I have toward you, my Lord, I established the present day this law of love. By reverence I refrained from writing lest I open myself to presumption, while by kindness I was driven to write lest the complete refusal to write be not interpreted as hatred. I write then because I must, not what I think, "since the thoughts of men are vile" (Wis. 9:14), as Scripture says, but what God wants and grants through grace to begin this undertaking. Indeed, "the counsel of God," says David, "remains forever, the thoughts of his heart from generation to generation" (Ps. 33:11). Undoubtedly he calls "counsel" of God the Father the mysterious self-abasement of the only-begotten Son, with a view to the deification of our nature, a self-abasement in which he holds enclosed the limits of all history; while by "thoughts of his heart" he means the principles of Providence and judgment according to which he directs with wisdom – as different generations – our present life and the life to come, imparting differently to each the mode of activity which is proper to it.

1.   If, then, the realization of the divine counsel is the deification of our nature, and if the aim of the divine thoughts is the successful accomplishment of what we ask for in our life, then it is profitable to recognize the full import of the Lord's prayer, to put it into practice and to write about it properly. And since you, my Lord, in writing to me your servant, have mentioned this prayer under God's influence, I thus make it of necessity the theme of my words, and I ask the Lord who taught us this prayer to open my mind to understand the mysteries it contains and to give me a power of expression in proportion to the meaning of the mysteries apprehended. Indeed, this prayer contains in outline – mysteriously hidden, or to speak

more properly, openly proclaimed – for those whose understanding is strong enough, the whole scope of what the words deal with. For the words of the prayer make request for whatever the Word of God himself wrought through the flesh in his self-abasement. It teaches us to strive for those goods of which only God the Father, through the natural mediation of the Son in the Holy Spirit, is in all truth the bestower, since, according to the divine Apostle, the Lord Jesus is "mediator between God and men" (1 Tim. 2:5). Through his flesh he made manifest to men the Father whom they did not know, and through the Spirit he leads the men whom he reconciled in himself to the Father.

For them and on their account, he became man without any change, and he himself worked and taught many new mysteries whose number and dimension the mind can in no way grasp or measure. There are seven in number which are more general than the others which he appears to have given to men in his extraordinary generosity. The scope of the prayer, as I have said, mysteriously contains their meaning: theology, adoption in grace, equality of honor with the angels, participation in eternal life, the restoration of nature inclining toward itself to a tranquil state, the abolition of the law of sin, and the overthrowing of the tyranny of evil which has dominated us by trickery. Let us now examine the truth of what has just been said.

2. In becoming incarnate, the Word of God teaches us the mystical knowledge of God, because he shows us in himself the Father and the Holy Spirit. For the full Father and the full Holy Spirit are essentially and completely in the full Son, even the incarnate Son, without being themselves incarnate. Rather, the Father gives approval and the Spirit cooperates in the incarnation with the Son who effected it, since the Word remained in possession of his own mind and life – contained in essence by no other than the Father and the Spirit – while hypostatically realizing out of love for man the union with the flesh.

He gives adoption by giving through the Spirit a supernatural birth from on high in grace, of which divine birth, the guardian and preserver is the free will of those who are thus born. By a sincere disposition [the soul] cherishes the grace bestowed and by a careful observance of the commandments it adorns the beauty given by grace. By the humbling of the passions it takes on divinity in the same measure that the Word of God willed to empty himself in the incarnation of his own unmixed glory in becoming genuinely human.

He rendered men equal in honor to the angels not only in "reconciling through the blood of his cross what is in heaven and what is on earth" (Col. 1:20) and destroying the hostile forces which fill up the middle space between heaven and earth, he showed [that] there was only one gathering

of earthly and heavenly powers for the distribution of divine gifts which sings
with joy the glory of God with one and the same will with the powers on
high. But even more than this, after the fulfillment of the dispensation
toward us, and after having ascended with the body he had assumed, he
united through himself heaven and earth, joined sensible to intelligible
things, and showed the unity of created nature, internally coherent in its
furthest parts, by virtue and exact knowledge of the first cause. . . .

He gives a sharing in the divine life by making himself food for those
whom he knows and who have received from him the same sensibility and
intelligence. Thus in tasting this food they know with a true knowledge that
the Lord is good, he who mixes in a divine quality to deify those who eat,
since he is and is clearly called bread of life and of strength.

He restores nature to itself not only in that, having become man he kept
a free will tranquil and undisturbed in the face of nature and did not allow
it to become unsettled in its own movement in a way contrary to nature, even
in the face of those who were crucifying him; he even chose death at their
hands rather than life, as the voluntary character of the passion shows, which
was accomplished by the disposition of love for men by the one who
underwent this passion. But even more than this, he abolished enmity in
nailing to the cross the bond by which nature waged implacable war against
itself; and, having called those who are far and those who are near (that is,
of course, those who are under the Law and those who are outside the Law),
"and having broken down the dividing wall of hostility – by abolishing in
his flesh the law of commandments and ordinances – [he created] in himself
one new man in place of the two, so making peace, and reconciling" (Eph.
2:14–16) us through himself to the Father and with each other – in such a
way that we no longer have a will opposed to the principle of nature and that
thus we be as changeless in our free decisions as we are in our nature.

He purified nature from the law of sin in not having permitted pleasure
to precede his incarnation on our behalf. Indeed, his conception wondrously
came about without seed, and his birth took place supernaturally without
corruption: with God being begotten of a mother and tightening much more
than nature can, the bonds of virginity by his birth. He frees the whole of
nature from the tyranny of the law which dominated it in those who desire
it and who, by mortification of the sensuality of the earthly members, imitate
his freely chosen death. For the mystery of salvation belongs to those who
desire it, not to those who are forced to submit to it.

He effects the destruction of the tyranny of evil which has lorded over
us by trickery. He conquers the flesh which had been overcome in Adam
by brandishing it as an instrument against evil. Thus does he show how the
flesh, which had been bruised first by death, captures its captor and destroys
its life by natural death. The flesh has become both a poison strong enough

to make him vomit out all those whom he had swallowed by confining them in death's dominion, and also a life for the human race, which causes the whole nature to rise like a loaf for a resurrection of life. It is wholly on account of this life that the Word who is God has become man (certainly an incredible fact and story) and willingly accepts the death of the flesh. All of this, as I have said, the words of the Prayer are found to request.

3. It speaks, in fact, of the Father, of the Father's name, and of his kingdom. Moreover, it sets before the one who prays in grace the Son of this Father. It asks that those in heaven and on earth come to be of a single will. It enjoins the request for daily bread. It establishes reconciliation as a law for men, and by the fact of forgiving and being forgiven it binds the nature to itself to be no longer mutilated by the difference of will. It teaches us to beg not to be led into temptation, which is the law of sin, and it exhorts us to be protected from evil. It was necessary, indeed, that he who effects and gives the benefits to those who believe in him and imitate his conduct in the flesh give and teach them as well as his disciples the words of the prayer as precepts of this life. By these words he pointed out the hidden treasures of wisdom and knowledge which exist as such in himself, in furthering the desire of those who pray it toward the enjoyment of these treasures.

This is why, I think, Scripture calls this teaching a prayer because it makes a request for the gifts which God gives to men by grace. Indeed, just as our fathers, inspired by God, explained and defined prayer by saying that it is a request of what God gives to men in a way which is fitting to himself, so they defined that the vow is a profession or promise of what men offer to God in genuine and worshipful service. They have often explained that Scripture witnesses to this by its own language; thus, "Make vows to the Lord our God and fulfill them" (Ps. 76:12), and, "What I have vowed I will offer you, Lord our God" (Jonah 2:9). This is what is said for vow; and for prayer, "Hannah prayed to the Lord and said, 'Lord Adonai, Eloi Sabaoth, if you deign to hear your servant and give fruit to my womb!'" (1 Sam. 1:11) and "Hezechiah, king of Judah, as well as Isaiah, son of Amos, prayed to the Lord" (2 Chr. 32:20), and also what the Lord says to his disciples, "When you pray, say, 'Our Father who art in heaven'" (Matt. 6:9). Thus the vow can be a keeping of the commandments ratified by the will of the one who makes the vow; and prayer is the petition that the one who observes them be brought to the enjoyment of what they contain. Or else, vow is the combat of virtue, an offering that God accepts with the greatest pleasure, and prayer is the reward of virtue, that God gives back with the greatest joy.

Thus, since it has been shown that prayer is a petition for blessings which come from the Word incarnate, let us, by setting at the head the very one who taught us the words of the prayer, advance with confidence, carefully

313

unraveling by contemplation the meaning of each word, as far as possible, as the Word himself is accustomed to furnish profitably and to give the power to understand the meaning of what is said.

Our Father Who Art in Heaven, Hallowed Be Thy Name: Thy Kingdom Come

4. First of all the Lord, by these words, teaches those who say this prayer to begin, as is fitting, by "theology,"* and he initiates them into the mystery of the mode of existence of the creative Cause of things, since he himself is, by essence, the Cause of things. Indeed, the words of the prayer point out the Father, the Father's name, and the Father's kingdom to help us learn from the source himself to honor, to invoke, and to adore the one Trinity. For the name of God the Father who subsists essentially is the only-begotten Son, and the kingdom of God the Father who subsists essentially is the Holy Spirit. Indeed, what Matthew here calls kingdom another evangelist elsewhere calls Holy Spirit: "May your Holy Spirit come and purify us."† The Father indeed has no acquired name and we should not think of the kingdom as a dignity considered after him. For he did not begin to be – as if he had a beginning as Father and King – but he always is, and is always both Father and King, not having in any way begun to exist or to be Father or King. And if he who always is, is always Father and King as well, then also the Son and Spirit always coexisted in essence with the Father. They are by nature from him and in him beyond cause and understanding, but they are not after him as if they had come about subsequently as being caused by him. For relation has the capacity of joint indications without, at the same time, allowing the terms of the relationship to be thought of as coming one after the other.

Our Father. Thus, at the beginning of this prayer we are directed to honor the consubstantial and superessential Trinity as the creative Cause of our coming into existence. Further, we are also taught to speak to ourselves of the grace of adoption, since we are worthy to call Father by grace the one who is our Creator by nature. Thus, by respecting the designation of our Begetter in grace, we are eager to set on our life the features of the one who gave us life: We sanctify his name on earth in taking after him as a Father, in showing ourselves by our actions to be his children, and in extolling by our thoughts and our acts the Father's Son by nature, who is the one who brings about this adoption.

Hallowed Be Thy Name. We sanctify the name of the Father in grace who

---

* The doctrine of God, that is, the Trinity.

† From a textual variant of Luke 11:2.

is in heaven by mortifying earthly lust, of course, and by purifying ourselves from corrupting passions, since sanctification is the total immobility and mortification of sensual lust. Arrived at that point, we quiet the indecent howling of anger which no longer has – to excite it and persuade it to be carried over to familiar pleasures – the lust which is already mortified by a holiness conformed to reason. Indeed, anger, as a natural ally of lust, ceases to rage once it sees that lust is mortified.

Thy Kingdom Come. It is right, then, that after the elimination of anger and lust there comes, according to the prayer, the victory of the kingdom of God the Father for those who, having rejected them, are worthy to say, "thy kingdom come," that is to say, the Holy Spirit, for, by the principle and path of meekness, they have already become temples of God by the Spirit. For it is said, "On whom shall I rest if not on the one who is meek, on the one who is humble and who fears my words?" (Isa. 66:2, LXX). From this it is obvious that the kingdom of God the Father belongs to the humble and the meek. For it is said, "Blessed are the meek, for they shall inherit the earth" (Matt. 5:4). It is not this earth which by nature occupies the middle place of the universe which God promised as an inheritance to those who love him, since he speaks the truth in saying, "When they rise from the dead they neither marry nor are given in marriage but are like the angels in heaven" (Matt. 22:30), and, "Come, blessed of my Father, inherit the kingdom prepared for you since the foundation of the world" (Matt. 25:34). And again elsewhere to another who served with devotion, "Enter into the joy of your Lord" (Matt. 25:21). And after him the divine Apostle says, "For the trumpet will sound, and those who have died in Christ will rise first, incorruptible; then we the living who remain here will be taken up together with them into the clouds to meet the Lord in the air, and thus we shall always be with the Lord" (1 Thess. 4:15, 16; 1 Cor. 15:52).

. . . the holiness of the divine image has been naturally included [within human reason] to persuade the soul to transform itself by its free will to the likeness of God and to belong to the great kingdom which subsists substantially with God, the Father of all. It becomes a radiant abode of the Holy Spirit and receives, if one can say it, the full power of knowing the divine nature insofar as this is possible. By this power there is discarded the origin of what is inferior, to be replaced by that of what is superior, while the soul, like God, keeps inviolable in itself, by the grace of its calling, the realization of the gifts which it has received. By this power, Christ is always born mysteriously and willingly, becoming incarnate through those who are saved. He causes the soul which begets him to be a virgin-mother who, to speak briefly, does not bear the marks of nature subject to corruption and generation in the relationship of male and female.

No one should be astonished to hear corruption placed before generation.

For the one who examines without passion and with a correct reason the nature of things which come to be and which pass away will clearly discover that generation takes its beginning from corruption and ends up in corruption. The passions associated with this generation and corruption, as I was saying, do not belong to Christ, that is, to the life and logic of Christ and according to Christ, if we can believe the one who says, "For in Christ there is neither male nor female" [see Gal. 3:28], thus clearly indicating the characteristics and the passions of a nature subject to corruption and generation. Instead, there is only a deiform principle created by divine knowledge and one single movement of free will which chooses only virtue.

. . . "But Christ is in all" [Col. 3:11], creating – by what surpasses nature and the Law – the spiritual configuration of the kingdom which has no beginning, a configuration characterized, as has been shown, by humility and meekness of heart. Their concurrence shows forth the perfect man created according to Christ. For every humble man is also thoroughly meek, and every meek man is also thoroughly humble: humble because he knows that his being has come to him as a loan, meek because he knows how to use the natural powers which have been given to him, since he gives them over to the service of reason to give rise to virtue and because he restrains in a perfect way their sense activity. That is why this man is always in movement toward God by his mind. Even if he experiences at one time everything that can afflict the body, he is not at all moved according to the senses, nor does he mark his soul with any trace of affliction as a substitute for a joyful attitude, for he does not think that physical suffering means a loss of happiness. Indeed there exists but one happiness, a communion of life with the Word, the loss of which is an endless punishment which goes on for all eternity. And that is why by abandoning his body and whatever is the body's he strives intensely toward that communion of life with God, thinking that the only loss – even if he were master of everything on earth – would be in the failure of the deification by grace which he pursues.

Let us therefore purify ourselves from all defilements of the flesh and of the spirit so that we may sanctify God's name by extinguishing lust which indecently flirts with the passions, and let us by reason rein in anger which pleasures incite to a reckless fury. Thus will we welcome the kingdom of God the Father which comes through meekness. And to these opening words let us join the following words of the prayer in saying,

Thy Will Be Done on Earth as it is in Heaven

The one who mystically offers God worship through the spiritual power alone, separated from concupiscence and anger, has accomplished the will of God on earth as the angelic orders do in heaven. He has become in every way the companion of the angels in their worship and in their life, as the great Apostle somewhere says, "Our citizenship is in heaven" (Phil. 3:20), where there is no concupiscence to relax the mind's reach by pleasures, nor raging anger to bark indecently against one's kinsmen, but where there will be reason all by itself to lead naturally rational beings to the first Principle. It is this alone which gladdens God and which God requests of us his servants. It is what he shows in saying through the great David, "What exists for me in heaven, and besides you what did I wish for on earth?" (Ps. 73:25). There is nothing which is offered to God in heaven by the holy angels except the spiritual worship he expects of us when he teaches us to pray in saying, "Thy will be done on earth as it is in heaven."

Our reason also should therefore be moved to seek God; the force of desire should struggle to possess him and that of anger to hold on to him, or rather, to speak more properly, the whole mind should tend to God, stretched out as a sinew by the temper of anger, and burning with longing for the highest reaches of desire. Thus, indeed, we will be found to be giving God worship in every way in imitation of the angels in heaven, and we shall exhibit on earth the same manner of life as the angels in having – as they do – the mind totally moved in the direction of nothing less than God. For by such a manner of life according to our vows, we shall receive – as a supersubstantial and life-giving bread to nourish our souls and to keep in good condition the goods with which we have been favored – the Word who said, "I am the bread which has come down from heaven and which gives life to the world" (John 6:33). He becomes everything for us in proportion to the virtue and wisdom with which we have been nourished, taking a body in a variety of ways, as only he knows, in each of the saved, while we are yet in this age according to the force of the text of the prayer which says,

Give Us This Day Our Daily Bread

I think, in fact, that "this day" means in present history. Thus, to understand this passage of the prayer in its clearest meaning we should say: "Our bread," which you prepared in the beginning for the immortality of nature; "give us this day," to us who belong to the mortal condition of the present life, so that nourishment – by the bread of life – and knowledge triumph over the death of sin. The transgression of the divine commandment did not allow the first man to become a sharer in this bread. For if he had satisfied himself with this heavenly food, he would not have fallen prey to the death brought in by sin.

But, in fact, the one who prays to receive this supersubstantial bread does not receive it altogether as this bread is in itself, but as he is able to receive it. For the Bread of Life, out of his love for men, gives himself to all who ask him, but not in the same manner to everyone: to those who have done great works, he gives himself more fully, to those who have done smaller ones, less; to each, then, according to the spiritual dignity enabling him to receive it.

The Savior has led me to this understanding of the present word when he expressly enjoins his disciples not to be overly concerned with sensible food. "Do not worry," he says, "about your life, what you will eat or what you will drink; nor for your bodies, what you will wear. For all these things the people of the world worry about. But seek first the kingdom of God and his justice [righteousness], and all of this will be given to you in abundance" (Matt. 6:25, 31, 33). How then does he teach us to pray for what he had previously ordered us not to seek after? It is obvious that he did not enjoin us to ask in the prayer what he had exhorted us not to seek in his commandment. For we should ask in the prayer only what should be sought after according to the commandment. Therefore it happens that what he did not by commandment allow us to seek, he did not set up as lawful to ask for in the prayer. And if the Savior has commanded us to seek only the kingdom of God and his justice, then it is evidently this that he suggested, that those who desire the divine gifts should ask for in prayer. Thus, by confirming through prayer the grace of what is natural to seek after, he will join to the will of the one who supplies the grace the free will of those who request it, by rendering it identical to it in a union of relation. If we are also charged in the prayer to ask for this day's bread which sustains the present life, let us not go beyond the borders of the prayer in greedily speculating on periods of many years. And let us not forget that we are mortal and possess a life as fleeting as a shadow. On the contrary, let us without anxiety ask in prayer for one day's bread and let us show that in the Christian way of life we make life a preparation for death, by letting our free will overtake nature, and before death comes, by cutting the soul off from the concerns for bodily things. In this way it will not be nailed down to corruptible things, nor pass on to matter the use of the natural desire, nor learn the greediness which deprives one of the abundance of divine gifts. . . .

Forgive Us Our Trespasses As We Forgive Those Who Trespass Against Us

The one who, according to the first contemplative reading of the preceding words, seeks in the prayer – according to the present history of which we said that "this day" is the symbol – the incorruptible bread of wisdom of which the transgression in the beginning deprived us . . ., that person does not at all incline his free choice toward anything visible, and because of this he is not subject to painful things befalling his body. In truth he forgives, in spiritual detachment, those who sin against him because no one at all can lay his hand on the good he zealously seeks with all his desire and which we believe is by nature unattainable. And for God he makes himself an example of virtue, if one can say this, and invites the inimitable to imitate him by saying, "Forgive us our trespasses as we forgive those who trespass against us." He summons God to be to him as he is to his neighbors. For if he wishes that, as he forgave the debts of those who have sinned against him, he also be forgiven by God, and it is obviously in detachment from passion that God forgives those who forgive, then also the one who remains in detachment in what befalls him forgives those who have offended him, without allowing the memory of whatever painful that has happened to him to be imprinted in his mind, so as not to be accused of dividing nature by his free will by separating himself as man from any other man. For, since free will has been thus united to the principle of nature, the reconciliation of God with nature comes about naturally, for otherwise it is not possible for nature, in rebellion against itself by free will, to receive the inexpressible divine condescension. And it is perhaps for this reason that God wants us first to be reconciled with each other, not to learn from us how to be reconciled with sinners and to agree to wipe away the penalty of their numerous and ugly crimes, but to purify us from the passions and to show that the disposition of those who are forgiven accords with the state of grace. . . .

Such, then, is the disposition of the one who asks in prayer for spiritual bread, and the one who out of natural need seeks only the bread of today is disposed in the same fashion. Forgiving the debtors their debts inasmuch as knowing himself mortal by nature, and waiting each day with uncertainty for what makes him live by nature, he outstrips nature by his intention and voluntarily he dies to the world according to the passage which says, "For your sake we are put to death the whole day, we are considered as sheep of the slaughterhouse" (Ps. 44:23; Rom. 8:36). That is why he pours himself out in libation for everyone so as not to bring away with him the mark of the wretchedness of the present life, in passing into the life which does not grow old and to receive from the Judge and Savior of all the reward equal to what he had undergone here below. For a pure disposition in regard to those who have caused pain is necessary for the mutual advantage of both, because of all that precedes and not least because of the force of the words which remain to be said and which present themselves in this manner:

Lead Us Not Into Temptation, But Deliver Us From Evil

In these words Scripture makes us see how the one who does not perfectly forgive those who offend him and who does not present to God a heart purified of rancor and shining with the light of reconciliation with one's neighbor will lose the grace of the blessings for which he prays. Moreover, by a just judgment, he will be delivered over to temptation and to evil in order to learn how to cleanse himself of his faults by canceling his complaints against another. He here calls "temptation" the law of sin which the first man did not bear when he came into existence, and "evil" the devil, who mingled this law of sin with human nature and who by trickery persuaded man to transfer his soul's desire from what was permitted to what was forbidden, and to be turned around to transgress the divine commandment. And the result of this transgression was the loss of incorruptibility given by grace. . . .

5.   This is why, to step back and review briefly the import of what has been said, if we wish to be rescued from evil and not enter into temptation, we also should have faith in God and forgive the trespasses of those who trespass against us, "for," it is said, "if you do not forgive men their sins, neither will your heavenly Father forgive you yours" (Matt. 6:15). In this way not only shall we acquire forgiveness for our sins but we shall also be victors over the law of sin without being left behind to undergo the experience of it. We shall trample underfoot the evil serpent which gave rise to this law from whom we beg to be delivered. When Christ who has overcome the world has become our leader, he will fully arm us with the law of the commandments by which he makes us reject the passions and thus binds the nature back to itself by love. He sets in movement in us an insatiable desire for himself who is the Bread of Life, wisdom, knowledge, and justice. When we fulfill the Father's will he renders us similar to the angels in their adoration, as we imitate them by reflecting the heavenly blessedness in the conduct of our life. From there he leads us finally in the supreme ascent in divine realities to the Father of lights wherein he makes us sharers in the divine nature by participating in the grace of the Spirit, through which we receive the title of God's children and become clothed entirely with the complete person who is the author of this grace, without limiting or defiling him who is Son of God by nature, from whom, by whom, and in whom we have and shall have being, movement, and life.

6.   The aim of the prayer should direct us to the mystery of deification so that we might know from what things the condescension through the flesh

of the Only Son kept us away and whence and where he brought up by the strength of his gracious hand, those of us who had reached the lowest point of the universe where the weight of sin had confined us. Let us love more intensely the one who so wisely prepared for us such a salvation. By what we do let us show that the prayer is fulfilled, and manifest and proclaim that God is truly a Father through grace. Let us show clearly that we do not at all have as a father of our life the Evil One who, by the dishonorable passions, always tries to impose tyrannically his domination over nature. Let us not unwittingly exchange death for life, since each of the adversaries (God and the devil) agrees to make an exchange with his associates, one bestowing eternal life on those who love him and the other causing death in those who come near him through the stratagem of voluntary temptations.

For according to Scripture there are two kinds of temptation, one pleasurable and the other painful, the first being intentional and the other unintentional. The former begets sin, and the Lord's teaching instructs us to pray not to enter into this when he tells us, "And lead us not into temptation," and "Watch and pray that you do not enter into temptation" (Matt. 26:41). The latter, a penalty for sin, chastises the disposition of loving sin by involuntary recurrences of troubles. If we endure them and especially if we are not attached to them by the nails of wickedness, we shall hear the great Apostle James who clearly proclaims, "Count it all joy, my brethren, when you meet various trials, for the testing endured by your faith produces constancy, constancy produces fidelity, and fidelity accompanies a perfect work" (Jas. 1:2–4). The Evil One mischievously uses both types of temptations, voluntary and involuntary, the first by sowing and greatly provoking the soul with bodily pleasures and scheming first to take away the desire of divine love. Then he cunningly works on the other type, hoping to corrupt the nature by pain so as to constrain the soul, struck down by the weakness of sufferings, to set in motion the attitudes of hatred of the Creator.

But we who know well the designs of the Evil One pray to avoid voluntary temptation so that we will not turn aside our desire from divine love. As far as involuntary temptation is concerned, let us endure it nobly as coming with God's consent, so that we might show that we prefer the Creator of nature to nature itself. And may it happen that all who call on the name of our Lord Jesus Christ be ransomed from the devil's present delights and be freed from future sufferings by the participation in the formal realization of the blessings to come, which we shall attain in Christ our Lord himself, who alone with the Father and the Holy Spirit is glorified by the whole creation. Amen.

Inquiring into "God as Prayer"[1]

Bishop Kallistos Ware, The Orthodox Way, Chapter 6

Not I, but Christ in me. (Galatians 2:20)

There is no life without prayer. Without prayer there is only madness and horror. The soul of Orthodoxy consists in the gift of prayer.[2]

The brethren asked Abba Agathon: "Amongst all our different activities, father, which is the virtue that requires the greatest effort?" He answered: "Forgive me, but I think there is no labour greater than praying to God. For every time a man wants to pray, his enemies the demons try to prevent him; for they know that nothing obstructs them so much as prayer to God. In everything else that a man undertakes, if he perseveres, he will attain rest. But in order to pray a man must struggle to his last breath."[3]

The Three Stages on the Way

Shortly after being ordained priest, I asked a Greek bishop for advice on the preaching of sermons. His reply was specific and concise. "Every sermon," he said, "should contain three points: neither less nor more."

It is customary likewise to divide the spiritual Way into three stages. For St. Dionysius the Areopagite these are *purification*, *illumination*, and *union* – a scheme often adopted in the west. St. Gregory of Nyssa, taking as his model the life of Moses, speaks of *light*, *cloud*, and *darkness*.* But in this chapter we shall follow the somewhat different threefold scheme devised by Origen, rendered more precise by Evagrius, and fully developed by St. Maximus the Confessor. The first stage here is *praktiki* or the practice of the virtues; the second stage is *physiki* or the contemplation of nature; the

---

* St. Gregory of Nyssa, a fourth–century Cappadocian theologian who made important contributions to the doctrine of the Trinity as well as to ascetical literature.

third and final stage, our journey's end, is *theologia* or "theology" in the strict sense of the word, that is, the contemplation of God himself.

The first stage, the practice of the virtues, begins with repentance. The baptized Christian, by listening to his conscience and by exerting the power of his free will, struggles with God's help to escape from enslavement to passionate impulses. By fulfilling the commandments, by growing in his awareness of right and wrong, and by developing his sense of "ought," gradually he attains purity of heart; and it is this that constitutes the ultimate aim of the first stage. At the second stage, the contemplation of nature, the Christian sharpens his perception of the "isness" of created things, and so discovers the Creator present in everything. This leads him to the third stage, the direct vision of God, who is not only in everything but above and beyond everything. At this third stage, no longer does the Christian experience God solely through the intermediary of his conscience or of created things, but he meets the Creator face to face in an unmediated union of love. The full vision of the divine glory is reserved for the Age to come, yet even in this present life the saints enjoy the sure pledge and first fruits of the coming harvest.

Often the first stage is termed the "active life," while the second and third are grouped together and jointly designated the "contemplative life." When these phrases are used by Orthodox writers, they normally refer to inward spiritual states, not to outward conditions. It is not only the social worker or the missionary who is following the "active life"; the hermit or recluse is likewise doing so, inasmuch as he or she is still struggling to overcome the passions and to grow in virtue. And in the same way the "contemplative life" is not restricted to the desert or the monastic enclosure: a miner, typist, or housewife may also possess inward silence and prayer of the heart, and may therefore be in the true sense a "contemplative." . . .

The image of three stages on a journey, while useful, should not be taken too literally. Prayer is a living relationship between persons, and personal relationships cannot be neatly classified. In particular it should be emphasized that the three stages are not strictly consecutive, the one coming to an end before the next begins. Direct glimpses of the divine glory are sometimes conferred by God on a person as an unexpected gift, before the person has even begun to repent and to commit himself to the struggle of the "active life." Conversely, however deeply a man may be initiated by God into the mysteries of contemplation, so long as he lives on earth he must continue to fight against temptations; up to the very end of his time in this world he is still learning to repent. . . .

No one, then, can ever claim in his life to have passed beyond the first stage. The three stages are not so much successive as simultaneous. We are to think of the spiritual life in terms of three deepening levels, interdependent, coexisting with each other.

Three Presuppositions

Before speaking further about these stages or levels, it will be wise to consider three indispensable elements, presupposed at every point upon the spiritual Way.

First, it is presupposed that the traveler on the Way is a *member of the Church*. The journey is undertaken in fellowship with others, not in isolation. The Orthodox tradition is intensely conscious of the ecclesial character of all true Christianity. . . .

As Fr. Alexander Elchaninov observes: "Ignorance and sin are characteristic of isolated individuals. Only in the unity of the Church do we find these defects overcome. Man finds his true self in the Church alone; not in the helplessness of spiritual isolation but in the strength of his communion with his brothers and his Saviour."[4] . . .

Secondly, the spiritual Way presupposes not only life in the Church but *life in the sacraments*. As Nicolas Cabasilas affirms with great emphasis, it is the sacraments that constitute our life in Christ. Here again there is no place for elitism. We are not to imagine that there is one path for the "ordinary" Christian – the path of corporate worship, centered around the sacraments – and another path for a select few who are called to inner prayer. On the contrary there is only *one* way; the way of the sacraments and the way of inner prayer are not alternatives, but form a single unity. None can be truly a Christian without sharing in the sacraments, just as none can be truly a Christian if he treats the sacraments merely as a mechanical ritual. The hermit in the desert may receive Communion less frequently than the Christian in the city; that does not mean, however, that the sacraments are any the less important to the hermit, but simply that the rhythm of his sacramental life is different. Certainly God is able to save those who have never been baptized. But while God is not bound to the sacraments, we are bound to them.

Earlier we noted, with St. Mark the Monk,* how the whole of the ascetic and mystical life is already contained in the sacrament of Baptism: however far a person advances upon the Way, all that he discovers is nothing else than the revelation or making manifest of baptismal grace. The same can be said of Holy Communion: the whole of the ascetic and mystical life is a deepening and realization of our Eucharistic union with Christ the Saviour. . . .

The spiritual Way is not only ecclesial and sacramental; it is also *evangelical*. This is the third indispensable presupposition for an Orthodox Christian. At each step upon the path, we turn for guidance to the voice of

---

* St. Mark the Monk or Hermit, a fifth-century ascetical writer.

God speaking to us through the Bible. According to *The Sayings of the Desert Fathers*, "The old men used to say: God demands nothing from Christians except that they shall hearken to the Holy Scriptures, and carry into effect the things that are said in them."[5] (But elsewhere *The Sayings* also insist on the importance of having the guidance of a spiritual father, to help us to apply Scripture aright.) When St. Antony of Egypt* was asked, "What rules shall I keep so as to please God?", he replied: "Wherever you go, have God always before your eyes; in whatever you do or say, have an example from the Holy Scriptures; and whatever the place in which you dwell, do not be quick to move elsewhere. Keep these three things, and you will live."[6] "The only pure and all-sufficient source of the doctrines of the faith," writes Metropolitan Philaret of Moscow, "is the revealed word of God, contained in the Holy Scriptures."[7]

To one entering the monastery as a novice, St. Ignatii Brianchaninov gives these instructions, which certainly apply with equal force to lay people:

> From his first entry into the monastery a monk should devote all possible care and attention to the reading of the Holy Gospel. He should study the Gospel so closely that it is always present in his memory. At every moral decision he takes, for every act, for every thought, he should always have ready in his memory the teaching of the Gospel. . . . Keep on studying the Gospel until the end of your life. Never stop. Do not think that you know it enough, even if you know it all by heart. . . .[8]

Church, sacraments, Scripture – such are the presuppositions for our journey. Let us now consider the three stages: the active life or practice of the virtues, the contemplation of nature, the contemplation of God.

The Kingdom of Heaven suffers Violence

As its title implies, the active life requires on our side effort, struggle, the persistent exertion of our free will. "Strait is the gate and narrow is the way that leads to life. . . . Not everyone that says to me, Lord, Lord, shall enter into the kingdom of heaven, but he that does the will of my Father" (Matt. 7:14, 21). We are to hold in balance two complementary truths: without God's grace we *can* do nothing; but without our voluntary co-operation God *will* do nothing. "The will of man is an essential condition, for without God

---

* St. Antony of Egypt, reportedly a third-century desert hermit whose ascetical feats were memorialized in a biography written by St. Athanasius of Alexandria.

does nothing."[9] Our salvation results from the convergence of two factors, unequal in value yet both indispensable: divine initiative and human response. What God does is incomparably the more important, but man's participation is also required.

In an unfallen world man's response to divine love would be altogether spontaneous and joyful. Even in a fallen world the element of spontaneity and joy remains, but there is also the need to fight resolutely against the deeply rooted habits and inclinations that are the result of sin, both original and personal. One of the most important qualities needed by the traveler on the Way is faithful perseverance. The endurance required from one who climbs a mountain physically is required likewise from those who would ascend the mountain of God.

Man must do violence to himself – to his fallen self, that is to say – for the kingdom of heaven suffers violence, and it is the men of violence who take it by force (Matt. 11:12). This we are told repeatedly by our guides upon the Way; and they are speaking, it should be remembered, to married Christians as well as to monks and nuns. "God demands everything from a man – his mind, his reason, all his actions. . . . Do you wish to be saved when you die? Go and exhaust yourself; go and labour; go, seek and you shall find; watch and knock, and it shall be opened to you."[10] "The present age is not a time for rest and sleep, but it is a struggle, a combat, a market, a school, a voyage. Therefore you must exert yourself, and not be downcast and idle, but devote yourself to holy actions."[11] "Nothing comes without effort. The help of God is always ready and always near, but is given only to those who seek and work, and only to those seekers who, after putting all their powers to the test, then cry out with their whole heart: Lord, help us."[12] "Peace is gained through tribulations."[13] "To rest is the same as to retreat."[14] Yet, lest we should be too much downcast by this severity, we are also told: "The whole of a man's life is but a single day, for those who labour with eagerness."[15]

And what do all these words about exertion and suffering signify in practice? They mean that each day we are to renew our relationship with God through living prayer; and to pray, as Abba Agathon reminds us, is the hardest of all tasks. If we do not find prayer difficult, perhaps it is because we have not really started to pray. They mean also that each day we are to renew our relationship with others through imaginative sympathy, through acts of practical compassion, and through cutting off our own self-will. They mean that we are to take up the Cross of Christ, not once for all through a single grandiose gesture, but every day afresh: "If any man will come after me, let him deny himself and take up his cross *daily*" (Luke 9:23). And yet this daily cross-bearing is at the same time a daily sharing in the Lord's Transfiguration and Resurrection: "sorrowful, yet always rejoicing; poor, yet making many rich; having nothing, yet possessing all things . . . dying, and behold, we live" (2 Cor. 6:9, 10).

A Change of Mind

Such is the general character of the active life. It is marked above all by four qualities: repentance, watchfulness, discrimination, and the guarding of the heart. Let us look briefly at each of these.

"The beginning of salvation is to condemn oneself" (Evagrius). *Repentance* marks the starting-point of our journey. The Greek term *metanoia* . . . signifies primarily a "change of mind." Correctly understood, repentance is not negative but positive. It means not self-pity or remorse but conversion, the recentering of our whole life upon the Trinity. It is to look not backward with regret but forward with hope – not downwards at our own shortcomings but upwards at God's love. It is to see, not what we have failed to be, but what by divine grace we can now become; and it is to act upon what we see. To repent is to open our eyes to the light. In this sense, repentance is not just a single act, an initial step, but a continuing state, an attitude of heart and will that needs to be ceaselessly renewed up to the end of life. In the words of St. Isaias of Sketis, "God requires us to go on repenting until our last breath."[16] "This life has been given you for repentance," says St. Isaac the Syrian. "Do not waste it on other things."[17]

To repent is to wake up. Repentance, change of mind, leads to *watchfulness*. The Greek term used here, *nepsis*, means literally sobriety and wakefulness – the opposite to a state of drugged or alcoholic stupor; and so in the context of the spiritual life it signifies attentiveness, vigilance, recollection. When the prodigal son repented, it is said that "he came to himself" (Luke 15:17). The "neptic" man is one who has come to himself, who does not day-dream, drifting aimlessly under the influence of passing impulses, but who possesses a sense of direction and purpose. As *The Gospel of Truth* (mid-second century) expresses it, "He is like one who awakens from drunkenness, returning to himself. . . . He knows where he has come from and where he is going."[18]

Watchfulness means, among other things, to be *present where we are* – at this specific point in space, at this particular moment in time. All too often we are scattered and dispersed; we are living, not with alertness in the present, but with the nostalgia in the past, or with misgiving and wishful thinking in the future. While we are indeed required responsibly to plan for the future – for watchfulness is the opposite of fecklessness – we are to think about the future only as far as it depends upon the present moment. Anxiety over remote possibilities which lie altogether beyond our immediate control is sheer waste of our spiritual energies. . . .

The "neptic" man is the one who understands this "sacrament of the present moment," and who tries to live by it. He says to himself, in the words of Paul Evdokimov: "The hour through which you are at present passing, the man whom you meet here and now, the task on which you are engaged at this very moment – these are always the most important in your whole life."[19] He makes his own the motto written on Ruskin's coat of arms: *Today, today, today.* "There is a voice which cries to a man until his last breath, and it says: Be converted today."[20]

Growing in watchfulness and self-knowledge, the traveler upon the Way begins to acquire the power of *discrimination* or discernment (in Greek, *diakrisis*). This acts as a spiritual sense of taste. Just as the physical sense of taste, if healthy, tells a man at once whether food is mouldy or wholesome, so the spiritual taste, if developed through ascetic effort and prayer, enables a man to distinguish between the varying thoughts and impulses within him. He learns the difference between the evil and the good, between the superfluous and the meaningful, between the fantasies inspired by the devil and the images marked upon his creative imagination by celestial archetypes.

Through discrimination, then, a man begins to take more careful note of what is happening within him, and so he learns to *guard the heart*, shutting the door against the temptations or provocations of the enemy. "Guard your heart with all diligence" (Prov. 4:23). When the heart is mentioned in Orthodox spiritual texts, it is to be understood in the full Biblical sense. The heart signifies not simply the physical organ in the chest, not simply the emotions and affections, but the spiritual center of man's being, the human person as made in God's image – the deepest and truest self, the inner shrine to be entered only through sacrifice and death. The heart is thus closely related to the spiritual intellect . . .; in some contexts the two terms are almost interchangeable. But "heart" has often a more inclusive sense than "intellect." "Prayer of the heart," in the Orthodox tradition, means prayer offered by the whole person, involving intellect, reason, will, affections, and also the physical body.

An essential aspect of guarding the heart is *warfare against the passions*. By "passion" here is meant not just sexual lust, but any disordered appetite or longing that violently takes possession of the soul: anger, jealousy, gluttony, avarice, lust for power, pride, and the rest. Many of the Fathers treat the passions as something intrinsically evil, that is to say, as inward diseases alien to man's true nature. Some of them, however, adopt a more positive standpoint, regarding the passions as dynamic impulses originally placed in man by God, and so fundamentally good, although at present distorted by sin. On this second and more subtle view, our aim is not to eliminate the passions but to redirect their energy. Uncontrolled rage must be turned into righteous indignation, spiteful jealousy into zeal for the truth, sexual lust into an *eros* that is pure in its fervor. The passions, then, are to be purified, not killed; to be educated, not eradicated; to be used positively, not negatively. To ourselves and to others we say, not "Suppress," but "Transfigure."

This effort to purify the passions needs to be carried out on the level of both soul and body. On the level of the soul they are purified through prayer, through the regular use of the sacraments of Confession and Communion, through daily reading of Scripture, through feeding our mind with the thought of what is good, through practical acts of loving service to others. On the level of the body they are purified above all through fasting and abstinence, and through frequent prostrations during the time of prayer. Knowing that man is not an angel but a unity of body and soul, the Orthodox Church insists upon the spiritual value of bodily fasting. We do not fast because there is anything in itself unclean about the act of eating and drinking. Food and drink are, on the contrary, God's gift, from which we are to partake with enjoyment and gratitude. We fast, not because we despise the divine gift, but so as to make ourselves aware that it is indeed a gift – so as to purify our eating and drinking, and to make them, no longer a concession to greed, but a sacrament and means of communion with the Giver. Understood in this way, ascetic fasting is directed not against the body but against the flesh. Its aim is not destructively to weaken the body, but creatively to render the body more spiritual.

Purification of the passions leads eventually, by God's grace, to what Evagrius terms *apatheia* or "dispassion." By this he means, not a negative condition of indifference or insensitivity in which we no longer *feel* temptation, but a positive state of reintegration and spiritual freedom in which we no longer *yield* to temptation. Perhaps *apatheia* can best be translated "purity of heart." It signifies advancing from instability to stability, from duplicity to simplicity or singleness of heart, from the immaturity of fear and suspicion to the maturity of innocence and trust. For Evagrius dispassion and love are integrally connected, as the two sides of a coin. If you lust, you cannot love. Dispassion means that we are no longer dominated by selfishness and uncontrolled desire, and so we become capable of true love.

The "dispassioned" person, so far from being apathetic, is the one whose heart burns with love for God, for other humans, for every living creature, for all that God has made. As St. Isaac the Syrian writes:

> When a man with such a heart as this thinks of the creatures and looks at them, his eyes are filled with tears because of the overwhelming compassion that presses upon his heart. The heart of such a man grows tender, and he cannot

endure to hear of or look upon any injury, even the smallest suffering, inflicted upon anything in creation. Therefore he never ceases to pray with tears even for the dumb animals, for the enemies of truth and for all who do harm to it, asking that they may be guarded and receive God's mercy. And for the reptiles also he prays with a great compassion, which rises up endlessly in his heart, after the example of God.[21]

Through Creation to the Creator

The second stage upon the threefold Way is the contemplation of nature – more exactly, the contemplation of nature in God, or the contemplation of God in and through nature. The second stage is thus a prelude and means of entry to the third: by contemplating the things which God has made, the man of prayer is brought to the contemplation of God himself. This second stage of *physiki* or "natural contemplation," as we have stated, is not necessarily subsequent to *praktiki* but may be simultaneous with it.

No contemplation of any kind is possible without *nepsis* or watchfulness. I cannot contemplate either nature or God without learning to be present where I am, gathered together at this present moment, in this present place. Stop, look, and listen. Such is the first beginning of contemplation. The contemplation of nature commences when I open my eyes, literally and spiritually, and start to notice the world around myself – to notice the *real* world, that is to say, *God's* world. . . .

All things are permeated and maintained in being by the uncreated energies of God, and so all things are a theophany that mediates his presence. At the heart of each thing is its inner principle or *logos*, implanted within it by the Creator Logos; and so through the *logoi* we enter into communion with the Logos. God is above and beyond all things, yet as Creator he is also within all things – "panentheism," not pantheism. To contemplate nature, then, is in Blake's phrase to cleanse the "doors of our perception," both on the physical and on the spiritual level, and thereby to discern the energies or *logoi* of God in everything that he has made. It is to discover, not so much through our discursive reason as through our spiritual intellect, that the whole universe is a cosmic Burning Bush, filled with the divine Fire yet not consumed.

Such is the theological basis; but the contemplation of nature requires also a moral basis. We cannot make progress on the second stage of the Way unless we make progress on the first stage by practicing the virtues and fulfilling the commandments. Our natural contemplation, if it lacks a firm foundation in the "active life," becomes merely aesthetic or romantic, and fails to rise to the level of the genuinely noetic or spiritual. There can be no perception of the world in God without radical repentance, without a continual change of mind.

The contemplation of nature has two correlative aspects. First, it means appreciating the "thusness" or "thisness" of particular things, persons and moments. We are to see each stone, each leaf, each blade of grass, each frog, each human face, for what it truly is, in all the distinctness and intensity of its specific being. As the prophet Zechariah warns us, we are not to "despise the day of small things" (4:10). "True mysticism," says Olivier Clément, "is to discover the extraordinary in the ordinary." . . .

Secondly, the contemplation of nature means that we see all things, persons, and moments as signs and sacraments of God. In our spiritual vision we are not only to see each thing in sharp relief, standing out in all the brilliance of its specific being, but we are also to see each thing as transparent: in and through each created thing we are to discern the Creator. Discovering the uniqueness of each thing, we discover also how each points beyond itself to him who made it. . . .

These two aspects of natural contemplation are exactly indicated in George Herbert's poem "The Elixir":

> Teach me, my God and King,
> In all things thee to see,
> And what I do in any thing,
> To do it as for thee.

> A man that looks on glasse,
> On it may stay his eye;
> Or if he pleaseth, through it passe,
> And then the heav'n espie.

To look *on* the glass is to perceive the "thisness," the intense reality, of each thing; to look *through* the glass and so to "espie" the heaven is to discern God's presence within and yet beyond that thing. These two ways of looking at the world confirm and complement one another. Creation leads us to God, and God sends us back again to creation, enabling us to look at nature with the eyes of Adam in Paradise. For, seeing all things in God, we see them with a vividness that they would never otherwise possess.

. . . All things are indeed sacred in their true being, according to their innermost essence; but our relationship to God's creation has been distorted by sin, original and personal, and we shall not rediscover this intrinsic sacredness unless our heart is purified. Without self-denial, without ascetic discipline, we cannot affirm the true beauty of the world. That is why there can be no genuine contemplation without repentance.

Natural contemplation signifies finding God not only in all *things* but equally in all *persons*. When reverencing the holy ikons in church or at home, we are to reflect that each man and woman is a living ikon of God. "Inasmuch as you did it to one of the least of these my brethren, you did it to me" (Matt. 25:40). In order to find God, we do not have to leave the world, to isolate ourselves from our fellow humans, and to plunge into some kind of mystical void. On the contrary, Christ is looking at us through the eyes of all those whom we meet. Once we recognize his universal presence, all our acts of practical service to others become acts of prayer.

It is common to regard contemplation as a rare and exalted gift, and so no doubt it is in its plenitude. Yet the seeds of a contemplative attitude exist in all of us. From this hour and moment I can start to walk through the world, conscious that it is God's world, that he is near me in everything that I see and touch, in everyone whom I encounter. However spasmodically and incompletely I do this I have already set foot upon the contemplative path. . . .

From Words to Silence

The more a man comes to contemplate God in nature, the more he realizes that God is also above and beyond nature. Finding traces of the divine in all things, he says: "This also is thou; neither is this thou." So the second stage of the spiritual Way leads him, with God's help, to the third stage, when God is no longer known solely through the medium of what he has made but in direct and unmediated union.

The transition from the second to the third level is effected, so we learn from our spiritual masters in the Orthodox tradition, by applying to the life of prayer the way of negation or apophatic approach. In scripture, in the liturgical texts, and in nature, we are presented with innumerable words, images and symbols of God; and we are taught to give full value to these words, images and symbols, dwelling upon them in our prayer. But, since these things can never express the entire truth about the living God, we are encouraged also to balance this affirmative or cataphatic prayer by apophatic prayer. Evagrius puts it, "Prayer is a laying-aside of thoughts."[22] This is not of course to be regarded as a complete definition of prayer, but it does indicate the kind of prayer that leads a man from the second to the third stage of the Way. Reaching out towards the eternal Truth that lies beyond all human words and thoughts, the seeker begins to wait upon God in quietness and silence, no longer talking about or to God but simply listening. "Be still, and know that I am God" (Ps. 46:10).

This stillness or inward silence is known in Greek as *hesychia*, and he who seeks the prayer of stillness is termed a hesychast. *Hesychia* signifies concentration combined with inward tranquility. It is not merely to be understood in a negative sense as the absence of speech and outward activity, but it denotes in a positive way the openness of the human heart towards God's love. Needless to say, for most people if not all, *hesychia* is not a permanent state. The hesychast, as well as entering into the prayer of stillness, uses other forms of prayer as well, sharing in corporate liturgical worship, reading Scripture, receiving the sacraments. Apophatic prayer coexists with cataphatic, and each strengthens the other. The way of negation and the way of affirmation are not alternatives; they are complementary.

But how are we to stop talking and to start listening? Of all the lessons in prayer, this is the hardest to learn. There is little profit in saying to ourselves, "Do not think," for suspension of discursive thought is not something that we can achieve merely through an exertion of will-power. The ever-restless mind demands from us some task, so as to satisfy its constant need to be active. If our spiritual strategy is entirely negative – if we try to eliminate all conscious thinking without offering our mind any alternative activity – we are likely to end up with vague daydreaming. The mind needs some task which will keep it busy, and yet enable it to reach out beyond itself into stillness. In the Orthodox hesychast tradition, the work which is usually assigned to it is the frequent repetition of some short "arrow prayer," most commonly the Jesus Prayer: *Lord Jesus Christ, Son of God, have mercy on me a sinner. . . .*

Normally three levels or degrees are distinguished in the saying of the Jesus Prayer. It starts as "prayer of the lips," oral prayer. Then it grows more inward, becoming "prayer of the intellect," mental prayer. Finally the intellect "descends" into the heart and is united with it, and so the prayer becomes "prayer of the heart" or, more exactly, "prayer of the intellect in the heart." At this level it becomes prayer of the whole person – no longer something that we think or say, but something that we are: for the ultimate purpose of the spiritual Way is not just a person who *says* prayers from time to time, but a person who *is* prayer all the time. The Jesus Prayer, that is to say, begins as a series of specific *acts* of prayer, but its eventual aim is to establish in the one who prays a *state* of prayer that is unceasing, which continues uninterrupted even in the midst of other activities.

So the Jesus Prayer begins as an oral prayer like any other. But the rhythmic repetition of the same short phrase enables the hesychast, by virtue of the very simplicity of the words which he uses, to advance beyond all language and images into the mystery of God. In this way the Jesus Prayer develops, with God's help, into what Western writers call "prayer of loving attention" or "prayer of simple gaze," where the soul rests in God without a constantly varying succession of images, ideas and feelings. Beyond this there is a further stage, when the hesychast's prayer ceases to be the result of his own efforts, and becomes – at any rate from time to time – what Orthodox writers call "self-acting" and Western writers call "infused." It ceases, in other words, to be "my" prayer, and becomes to a greater or lesser extent the prayer of *Christ in me*.

Yet it is not to be imagined that this transition from oral prayer to prayer of silence, or from "active" to "self-acting" prayer, is rapidly and easily made. . . . The best course, when invoking the Holy Name, is to concentrate our full efforts upon the recitation of the words; otherwise, in our premature attempts to attain wordless prayer of the heart, we may find that we end up by not really praying at all, but merely sitting half-asleep. Let us follow the advice of St. John Climacus, "Confine your mind within the words of prayer."[23] God will do the rest, but in his own way and at his own time.

Union with God

The apophatic method, whether in our theological discourse or in our life of prayer, is seemingly negative in character, but in its final aim it is supremely positive. The laying-aside of thoughts and images leads . . . to a plenitude surpassing all that the human mind can conceive or express . . . [like] the sculptor, [who] when chipping away at a block of marble, negates to a positive effect. He does not reduce the block to a heap of random fragments but, through the apparently destructive action of breaking the stone in pieces, he ends up by unveiling an intelligible shape.

So it is on a higher level with our use of apophaticism. We deny in order to affirm. . . . Apophatic theology, in its true and full meaning, leads not to an absence but to a presence, not to agnosticism but to a union of love. Thus apophatic theology is much more than a purely verbal exercise, whereby we balance positive statements with negations. Its aim is to bring us to a direct meeting with a personal God, who infinitely surpasses everything that we can say of him, whether negative or positive.

This union of love which constitutes the true aim of the apophatic approach is a union with God in his energies, not in his essence. Bearing in mind what has been said earlier about the Trinity and the Incarnation, it is possible to distinguish three different kinds of union:

First, there is between the three persons of the Trinity a union *according to essence*: Father, Son and Holy Spirit are "one in essence." But between God and the saints no such union takes place. Although "ingodded" or "deified," the saints do not become additional members of the Trinity. God remains God, and man remains man. Man becomes god by grace, but not God in essence. The distinction between Creator and creature still continues: it is bridged by mutual love but not abolished. God, however near he draws to man, still remains the "Wholly Other."

Secondly, there is between the divine and the human natures of the incarnate Christ a union *according to hypostasis*, a "hypostatic" or personal union: Godhead and manhood in Christ are so joined that they constitute, or belong to, a single person. Once more, the union between God and the saints is not of this kind. In the mystical union between God and the soul, there are two persons, not one (or, more exactly, four persons: one human, and the three divine persons of the undivided Trinity). It is an "I–Thou" relationship: the "Thou" still remains "Thou," however close the "I" may draw near. The saints are plunged into the abyss of divine love, yet not swallowed up. "Christification" does not signify annihilation. In the Age to come God is "all in all" (1 Cor. 15:28); yet "Peter is Peter, Paul is Paul, Philip is Philip. Each one retains his own nature and personal identity, but they are all filled with the spirit."[24]

Since, then, the union between God and the human beings that he has created is a union neither according to essence nor according to *hypostasis*, it remains thirdly that it should be a union *according to energy*. The saints do not become God by essence nor one person with God, but they participate in the energies of God, that is to say, in his life, power, grace and glory. The energies, as we have insisted, are not to be "objectified" or regarded as an intermediary between God and man, a "thing" or gift which God bestows on his creation. The energies are truly *God himself* – yet not God as he exists within himself, in his inner life, but God as he communicates himself in outgoing love. He who participates in God's energies is therefore meeting God himself face to face, through a direct and personal union of love, in so far as a created being is capable of this. To say that man participates in the energies but not in the essence of God is to say that between man and God there is brought to pass union but not confusion. It means that we affirm concerning God, in the most literal and emphatic way, "His life is mine," while at the same time repudiating pantheism. We assert God's nearness, while at the same time proclaiming his otherness. . . .

Notes

1   In this essay the author has adapted translations of the texts cited.
2   Vasilii Rozanov, *Solitaria* (London: Wishart, 1927), pp. 84, 119.
3   *The Sayings of the Desert Fathers*, alphabetical collection, Agathon 9, trans. B. Ward (London: A. R. Mowbray & Co., 1975), pp. 21–2.
4   Alexander Elchaninov, *The Diary of a Russian Priest* (London: Faber & Faber, 1967), p. 87.
5   *The Paradise or Garden of the Holy Fathers*, trans. E. A. W. Budge (Seattle: St. Nectarios Press, 1984), vol. ii, p. 216.

6   *The Sayings of the Desert Fathers*, alphabetical collection, Antony 3, trans. B. Ward, p. 2.

7   Metropolitan Philaret, "Comparison of the Differences in the Doctrines of Faith betwixt the Eastern and Western Churches," in Robert Pinkerton, *Russia* (London: Seeley & Sons, 1833), p. 41.

8   Ignatii Brianchaninov, *The Arena: An Offering to Contemporary Monasticism* (Madras, 1970), pp. 3, 15.

9   *The Homilies of St. Macarius* xxxvii, 10, trans. G. A. Maloney (New York: Paulist Press, 1992), p. 210.

10   *The Sayings of the Desert Fathers*, anonymous collection, p. 122, ed. F. Nau, *Revue de l'Orient chretien*, vol. 12 (1907), p. 403.

11   *Starets* Nazarii of Valamo, in *Little Russian Philokalia*, vol. ii, trans. Fr. Saraphim Rose (Plantina: Saint Herman of Alaska Brotherhood, 1983), p. 28.

12   St. Theophan the Recluse, in Igumen Chariton of Valamo, *The Art of Prayer: An Orthodox Anthology* (London: Faber & Faber, 1966), p. 133.

13   St. Seraphim of Sarov, in Irina Gorainoff, *Séraphim de Sarov* (Abbaye de Bellefontaine: Bégrolles en Mauges, 1973), p. 234.

14   Tito Colliander, *The Way of the Ascetics*, trans. K. Ferré (New York: Harper & Brothers, 1960), p. 55.

15   *The Sayings of the Desert Fathers*, alphabetical collection, Gregory the Theologian 2, trans. B. Ward, p. 45.

16   Isaias of Sketis, *Ascetical Homilies* xvi, 11, ed. Monk Avgoustinos (Jerusalem, 1911), p. 100.

17   Isaac the Syrian, *Ascetical Homilies* 74 (79), trans. Holy Transfiguration Monastery (Boston: Holy Transfigiration Monastery, 1984), p. 364.

18   *The Gospel of Truth*, trans. J. M. Robinson, *The Nag Hammadi Library in English*, 2nd edn (Leiden: E. J. Brill, 1984), p. 40.

19   Paul Evdokimov, *Sacrament de l'amour: Le mystère conjugal à la lumière de la tradition orthodoxe* (Paris: L'Epi, 1962), p. 141.

20   *The Sayings of the Desert Fathers*, anonymous collection, 10, ed. F. Nau, *Revue de l'Orient chrétien*, vol. 12 (1907) p. 52.

21   Isaac the Syrian, *Ascetical Homilies* 71 (74), trans. Holy Transfiguration Monastery, pp. 344–5.

22   Evagrius, *On Prayer* 71, trans. G. Palmer, P. Sherrard, and K. Ware, *Philokalia*, vol. 1 (London: Faber & Faber, 1979), p. 64.

23   St. John Climacus, *The Ladder of Divine Ascent*, Step 28 (*PG* 88:1132C), trans. C. Luibheid and N. Russell (New York: Paulist Press, 1982), p. 276.

24   *The Homilies of St. Macarius* xv, 10, trans. G. A. Maloney, p. 112.

Index

Abel, 163
abstinence, sexual *see* sex
Achtemeier, Elizabeth, 151
action vs. thought, xxviii
Adam, 83, 184
adultery, 137–8, 139, 152
    see also marriage, Christian
Aelred, St., 108–10, 121–3, 209
affliction, 170–8
    effect on Jesus Christ, 172–3
agape, 149, 276
Agathon, Abba, 326
Ahasuerus, King, 267
Allen, Diogenes, 50
Ambrose, St., 118, 120
Anselm of Canterbury, St., 1–2, 19–23, 209
Anthony, St., of Egypt, 325
antichrist, 210, 212
apatheia, 329
apologetics, xxv–xxvi
apophatic theology, 332
Aquinas, St. Thomas
    see Thomas Aquinas, St.
Aristotle, 22–3, 29
art

as blasphemy, 282
contemplative, 297–8
idolatry, 283
intention of artist, 284
irresponsible uses of, 303–4
joy of artistic expression, 303–4
liturgical, 295, 298
memorial, 295
religious purposes of, 278
Renaissance view of, 281
teaching function of, 284
artist, and answerability of, 300–1
asceticism, 99
Athanasius, St., 325
atheism, 251
atheists, practical, 233–4, 250–1
atonement, 184–5
Augustine, St.
    biblical scholar, 225–6
    biblical study, 222–30
    christology, 97
    communion, 264–5
    evil, 33
    friendship, 109, 119
    full communion for laity, 260–1
    intention in human acts, 224

love, 223–5
love of God, 237
marriage, 134–6
preacher required to know God, 250
preparation for baptism, 199–202,
    205n.20, 205n.25
recording of sermons, 226
scripture, 208–9
spiritual life, 181, 232–3
theology and *praxis*, 229
time, 41
authority, household, 134

baptism, 188, 259
apprenticeship of catechumens, 199
catechesis, 198–202, 205n.20
catechumenate, 191–2, 199
delayed, 205n.18
immersion, 201–2
leading to new life, 269
removal of original sin, 185
as ritual drama, 203
sacrament retained by Protestantism,
    257
single occurrence, 264
see also scrutiny, rite of
Barth, Karl, 98, 248, 303
Bauerschmidt, F. C., 66–7
Bernard of Clairvaux, St., 21–2, 181,
    191–2, 195–6, 198
Bernstein, Paul, 96
Bible *see* scripture
Big Bang theory, 40–4
see also cosmology
blind necessity, 174–5
blood of Christ, 184–5, 189–90
Blum, Lawrence, 128
Bonaventure, St., 2–3, 21–5, 308
Bonhoeffer, Dietrich, 126–7
Book of Margery Kempe, 64–5
Book of Showings see Showings
bread of life, 317
Brianchaninov, St. Ignatii, 325
Burton–Christie, Douglas, 230

Cabasilas, Nicolas, 324

Cain, 163, 255
Calvin, John
commentaries, 225
effect of being in presence of God,
    254
good works, 98–9
position in Protestant Reformation,
    258
religious art, 280
self–scrutiny, 232–3
use of light in churches, 296–7
view of religious music, 294
view of work, 81
vocation in the world, 95
Calvinism, 281, 293
caritas see charity
Cassian, John, 22
Catherine of Siena, St., 179–80
fountain of God's love, 197–8
life of prayer, 233
need for spiritual life, 308
relationship of prayerful person to
    God, 191–2
unworthy ministers, 209
Catholic Reformation, 180
Chalcedonian Definition, 279–80, 307
charity, 211–17
see also grace, divine; love, divine
chastity, 144
cherubim, 3, 14
Christian life, 194, 196, 201, 272
active vs contemplative, 308
discipline required, 229
human answerability, 299–303
as journey, 193–5, 198
as preparation for death, 318
responsibility of, 232
spiritual practices of, 195–8, 251,
    205n.25
Christian Theology, 17
Christianity, early, 134
christology, 279
Chrysostom, St. John, 157–8, 205n.18,
    206n.33
need for spiritual life, 308
church

as sacrament, 275
as vineyard, 188–90
church rites *see* rites of the church
Cicero, Marcus Tullius, 109, 111, 121–2, 241
City in History, The, 303
Clement, Olivier, 331
Climacus, St. John *see* John Climacus, St.
communion, 258–60, 334
   benefits to souls most in need, 264, 268
   consequences for unfaithful, 268
   gate to eternal life, 269–70
   gift of God, 307
   Lutheran tradition, 258–9
   origin in Jesus Christ, 263–4, 266
   as sacrifice and banquet, 272
   sharing in divine life, 312
   union with Christ, 324
   worship meal in biblical tradition, 271
   see also eucharist; fellowship of Saints; sacrament of the altar
competentes, 199–201
concupiscence *see* lust
Confessions, 232
connection *see* teaching by connection
contemplation, 22–5
Cooper, Tommy, 43
Copleston, Frederick, 35
corruption in the church, 180, 183–4
cosmology, 39, 50
   causation, 42
   fine–tuning of universe, 39, 44–8
   origin of universe, 39–44
   space–time, concept of, 41–3
   theological implications of, 40–4, 49
   see also Big Bang theory; creation; environmental ethics
Council of Chalcedon, 306
creation, 40, 49–50, 174, 299
   see also Big Bang theory; cosmology; laws of nature
Cressy, Serenus, 65
crucifixion of Christ, 55, 68, 174

bringing people together in worship, 307
example of affliction, 172–3
for Julian of Norwich, 57, 65
reconciling effect, 312
Cullmann, Oscar, 275

Darwin, Charles, 37, 46
David, King of Israel, 198, 262, 310, 317
Davie, Donald, 297
Davies, Elam, 244, 249
Davies, Paul, 43–4, 46–7
De amicitia, 121
De diligendo Deo, 192
Denis, St., church of, 280, 296
Denys the Areopagite, 22–3, 322
Descartes, René, 26
desire for God, 192–3, 195–6, 233
destiny, 122–3, 131
devil, 162, 164, 262, 320–1
   and pride, 212
   renunciation of, 200
Diagoras of Melos, 241
Dialogue of Caterina di Giacomo di Benincasa, 179–80, 192
Dialogues concerning Natural Religion, 36
Dionysius the Areopagite *see* Denys the Areopagite
Dionysius, tyrant of Syracuse, 241
discernment of God, 53, 60, 65–8
discrimination, 328
Disputed Questions on the Mystery of the Trinity, 22, 24–5
divorce, 150
docetism, 302
dogmatic theology, xxiv, xxvi
Donatist controversy, 208
Donatus, 208
dwelling in God, 220
Dyophysites, 280

Edwards, Jonathan, 248
Einstein, Albert, 39
Elchaninov, Fr. Alexander, 324
election, 156

"Elixir, The," 331
Eloy, St., 290
empyrean, 131
enemies
  Christian response to, 219
  see also love, of enemies
Enlightenment, the, 17
environmental ethics, 49–51
eschatology, 135
Eucharist, 180, 199, 202, 258
  ecclesial aspect, 276–7
  embodiment of Christ's death and
    resurrection, 274
  liturgy by World Council of
    Churches, 258
  weekly ritual, 273
  see also communion
Evagrius Pontius, 22, 322, 329, 332
Evdokimov, Paul, 328
evil, 33, 173, 193
excommunicate, 261
Exodus, 203

faith, 61, 69
fasting, 329
fellowship of saints, 259–61, 266, 268–9
feminism, xxvii
feudalism, 54
fidelity
  in the Church, 153
  in marriage, 135, 137–9, 145–7,
    149–53
  for single people, 146–9
Finn, Thomas, 199
five ways
  see Thomas, Aquinas, St.
flourishing *see* shalom
forgiveness, 191, 195–6, 201, 320
  essential to Christian life, 179
  leading to better understanding of
    God, 182
  self–restraint, 307
  teaching God's grace, 191
formation, spiritual *see* spiritual
  formation
fornication, 140, 142

see also sex
foundationalism, 26–7
Francis of Assisi, St., 3
Freud, Sigmund, 251
friendship
  betrayal of, 117
  carnal, 109, 113
  caution in selection, 117
  four steps, 117
  natural to human nature, 136
  origin of, 114
  puerile, 115
  qualities in a friend, 117
  role of imagination in, 124, 128
  spiritual, 109, 111, 113–14
  type to be avoided, 115
  worldly, 109, 113

Galileo, 30
God
  cause of things, 314
  creator, 24, 240, 298, 330–1
  divine purposes, 48
  estrangement from, 5, 54, 100, 193–5,
    307
  experience of, 59–60, 62–4, 67
  father, 311, 313
  in healthy preaching, 247
  instinct for, 233, 241–2
  knowledge of and human self–
    knowledge, 238
  majesty of, 239
  nature of, xviii, 50, 214, 220, 236
  paradoxical nature of, 248–9
  perception by humanity, 240–1, 252
  self–diffusion of, 11–13, 23
  self–limiting creator, 50
  source of all good, 240
  spiritual marriage to, 193–4
  see also love, divine; one–ing; proofs
    for existence of God; revelation,
    divine; Trinity, doctrine of the
God and the New Physics, 44
God of Faith and Reason, The, 20
Golden Legend, The, 62, 66
Gospel of Truth, The, 327

grace, divine
    aid for seeking God, xxiv
    as charity, 193–4
    Christian practices, 197
    forgiving, 191
    and human cooperation, 325
    inability to cure irremediably
        wounded, 174
    power of, 110
    tensions of, 275–6
    and yearning for God, 3
    see also charity
Great Orme, 244–5
Gregory of Nazianzus, St., 205n.18
Gregory of Nyssa, St., 322
guarding the heart, 328

Hartle, James, 42–3
Hauerwas, Stanley, 123
Hawking, Stephen, 42–4
Hegel, Georg Wilhelm Friedrich, 25
Heisenberg's Uncertainty Principle, 43
Herbert, George, 331
hermeneutics of suspicion, 228
hermeneutics of trust, 228
hesychast, 332–3
Hieria, Synod of, 278–80
Hilton, Walter, 64
historical criticism, 221
Holy Spirit
    abiding in the soul, 314
    gift of God, 219
    healing physician, 219–20
    kingdom of God, 314–15
    power to energize preaching, 247
    and spiritual renewal, 194
    Trinity, 311
    unavailable to the unloving, 223–4
    at work in baptism, 259
Homans, Peter, 72
Hosmer, Rachel, OSH, 62–4
Hoyle, Frederick, 40
human answerability, 299–304
Hume, David, 30, 36–7
humility, 84, 190, 229
    see also pride

hypostasis, 287–8
hypostatic union, 279–80, 282

Iconoclastic Controversy, 278–9, 296
icons, 278
Ignatius Loyola, St., 22, 68
Ignatius of Antioch, St., 276
imagination, 22
Imitation of Christ, 94
Incarnation, 180, 259, 279, 306–7
individuation, 72
intimacy, 147
Ironweed, 124–31
Isaac, the Syrian, St., 329

James, St., the Apostle, 321
Jeremias, Joachim, 271
Jesus Christ
    affliction of crucifixion, 172–3
    birth of, 312, 314
    bridge between God and humanity,
        180, 187–8
    Chalcedonian Definition, 279–80
    divine–human identity, 279–80
    fidelity to the church, 153–4
    healing physician, 227–8
    mediator, 240, 244, 311
    redeemer, 240
    significance of death, 246, 274
    son of God, 15, 187–8
    source of all virtues and knowledge,
        193
    symbol of *agape*, 149
    universal submission to, 134
    view by liberation theology, 156
    Word of God, 183–4, 189, 311
    and work, 87, 92–3
    see also blood of Christ; crucifixion of
        Christ
Jesus Prayer, 333
Job, 162, 172
John Climacus, St., 334
John, First Letter of, 208, 222
John of Damascus, St., 280, 296
John Paul II, Pope, 82, 96, 105, 197
John, St., Apostle, 215, 217, 310

Jones, Rufus, 254
Joseph, 162–3
Judaism
   influence on Christian theology, xvii
Judas Iscariot, 169–70
Julian of Norwich, 18, 53, 64, 68–9
   noughting, 68, 70, 72
   one–ing, 65–9
   see also Showings
justice, 201

Kant, Immanuel, 26, 30, 37–9, 40
Kempe, Margery, 64–5
Kennedy, William, 124
Kierkegaard, Søren, 124
King, Martin Luther, Jr., 248, 250
koinonia, 270

laws of nature, 42, 47–8
   see also cosmology; creation
Lent, 199–200
Letters to Karen, 150
Lewis, C. S., 129, 153, 250, 255
liberation theology, 68, 156
Life Together, 126
Lindbeck, George, 27
Locke, John, 26
Lord's Prayer, 200–1, 203, 306, 310
Lord's Supper *see* communion
love
   brotherly, 215, 217–18
   central Christian teaching, 208–11
   divine nature of, 211, 213
   of enemies, 215, 217–18
   gift from God, 225
   and goodwill, 215–16
   and true knowledge, 122
   see also neighbor–love
love, divine, 53–4, 211
   for all of creation, 183
   difficulty of returning love to God, 177
   essence of God, 175, 190, 213
   eternal nature of, 60
   as fountain, 197
   healing nature of, 227–8

Julian of Norwich, 65
   revelation of God, 62
   sacrifice of Christ, 210
   for sinners, 218
   see also charity
love for God, 193, 310
Lubac, Henri de, 275
lust, 137, 139, 142, 314, 316
Luther, Martin, 95, 97–8, 180, 258
   mass, 276
   religious art, 280–1
   religious music, 280–1

MacDonald, George, 251
"Man frail, and God eternal," 291–2
Mark, St., the Monk, 324
marriage, Christian, 133–6
   ancient vs. contemporary, 143–4
   benefits of, 136
   dissolution of, 143–4
   procreation, 136, 139, 142–3, 153
   submission, 135–6, 150–2
   see also adultery; divorce
Marx, Karl, 100, 103, 251
Mary Magdalene, St., 62, 66, 69, 71–2
Maximus, St., "Confessor," 306–7, 322
McClendon, James, 16–17, 19, 21
Meilaender, Gilbert C., 129
method, theological, xxv–xxvi, 52n.9
modernity, xviii–xix, xxi–xxii
monasticism, 108–9
monogamy, 149
Monophysites, 280, 306
Montagu, Ashley, 147
moral integrity, 157
Mumford, Lewis, 303
mutual submission in marriage, 135–6
   see also marriage
mysticism, 54, 66

neighbor–love, 110, 123, 125, 127–8
nepsis, 327, 330
neptic man, 327–8
Nicaea II, Council of, 278
Nicholas of Lyra, 221
Nietzsche, Friedrich Wilhelm, 251

noughting *see* Julian of Norwich
noumena, 37–8, 40
nurture, theological, xxi–iv, xxvi, xxvii

"O God, our help in ages past," 291–2
Octave, 203
one–ing *see* Julian of Norwich
Origen, 322
over–indulgence, 165–6

pain, physical, 171
Paley, William, 36–7, 46
Pascal, Blaise, 131, 299
paschal mystery, 273–4
Passion of Christ *see* crucifixion of
    Christ
passions, 328–9
Paul
    communion, 261–2, 265
    divine love, 178
    God's love spread via holy spirit, 219
    marital sex, 139–40
    mutual fidelity in marriage, 137
    preference for sexual abstinence, 133,
        142–4
    work, 93
Phelan, Francis, 124–31
phenomena, 37, 40
Philaret, Metropolitan, of Moscow, 325
physiki, 322
piety, 181, 239
Plato, 47
Plotinus, 23, 25
postmodernism, xviii–xxi, xxviii
practical atheism
see also atheism
practical atheists, 233–4, 250
praktiki, 322
prayer
    acts of service, 332
    apophatic, 332
    arrow prayer, 333
    contemplative, 68, 306
    dynamic process, 71
    experience of, 62
    for a friend, 120

guide for actions, 308
healing effect of, 187
infused, 333
Jesus Prayer, 333
living relationship, 323
pathway into spiritual comfort, 54
petitionary, 306
purifier of the church, 181
reception by God, 57–8
request of God, 313
self–control, 307
of simple gaze, 333
of stillness, 332–3
support for troubled marriage, 150
union with God, 59, 65-6, 69, 192
way to gain self–control, 307
and work, 85
see also Lord's Prayer
preacher, 249, 252, 255
preaching
    defined, 245
    greater understanding of God, 233
    making God real to listeners, 247,
        254
    preparation of sermons, 245
pride
    barrier to self–knowledge and self–
        love, 123
    and the devil, 212
    expression of human sin, 224
    innate presence in humanity, 239
    resulting in good deeds on occasion,
        216–17
    see also humility
primum mobile, 131
process theology, 25
proofs for existence of God, 20, 35–9
    Anselm, 1, 4, 8–11
    Thomas, Aquinas, St., 29, 31–5
Proslogion, 1, 19
Protestant Reformation, 180, 258–9,
    278, 280

quantum physics, 42–3
Quodvultdeus, 199–200, 203

Rasmussen, Larry, 97
Rauschenbusch, Walter, 156
Raymond of Capua, 187
reconciliation
    among men, 319–20
    of God with nature, 319
redemption, 99–100, 128–9, 180, 304, 307
reformation *see* Catholic Reformation; Protestant Reformation
religion vs. science *see* science vs. religion
religious practices *see* Christian life, spiritual practices of
repentance
    better understanding of God, 182
    and catechumens, 199
    essential to Christian life, 179
    estrangement from God, 194–6
    perception of God, 330–1
    requirement for divine revelation, 18
    in the spiritual life, 323, 327
    teaching God's grace, 191
resurrection, 134, 246, 259
revelation, divine
    dependent upon repentance, 18
    experience of Julian of Norwich, 53–62
    for theologians, 27
Richard of St. Victor, 18
rites of the church, 181
Rolle, Richard, 64-5
Rorty, Richard, 27

sacrament of the altar, 258
    see also communion; Eucharist
sacraments, 257, 324
    see also baptism
Sagan, Carl, 50
salvation, 321, 326
Samaritan, Good, 126
sanctification, 307
Sayers, Dorothy, 295
Sayings of the Desert Fathers, The, 325
Schillebeeckx, Edward, 274
Schleiermacher, Friedrich, 40

science vs. religion, 29–30, 35–7
scriptural interpretation, 207–8
    nurturing function, 226–7
    partner of scriptural meditation, 222
    proper intent required, 228
scripture, 207–8
    healing aspect, 230
    non–sectarian nature of, 229–30
    purpose of writers, 208
    transformative power of, 228
scrutiny, rite of, 200
seraph, 2
sermon
    as audible sacrament, 247–8
    response of listeners, 247–8
sex, 133
    abstinence, 133, 137, 143
    continence, 139–41
    sexual intercourse, 139–40
    sinful outside marriage, 139
    for single people, 146–9
    see also fornication
shalom, 302–4
Shedd, Charlie, 150
Showings, 55–62, 64–72
    chiaroscuro effect, 66, 69–71
    imagery of Christ's blood, 65, 69–70
    use of drama, 66, 71
    see also Julian of Norwich
Shuster, Marguerite, 41
sin
    damaging to human lives, 193
    failure to destroy God's love, 59–60
    forgetting God, 250
    as misdirection, 174
    ongoing struggle with grace, 224
    original, 180, 184–5
    in view of liberation theology, 156
Smedes, Louis, 154
Smith, Adam, 103
Social Gospel Movement, 156
Sokolowski, Robert, 20
Solomon, King of Israel, 83–5, 111
Song of Songs, 71, 181, 192
Soul's Journey into God, The, 22–4
sowing righteousness, 194

space–time, concept of, 42–3
  see also cosmology
Spiritual Exercises, 22
spiritual formation
  Augustine's interpretation of I John, 222
  benefits of, 115
  dissatisfaction with self, 232
  and intellectual inquiry, 17–25
  necessary for discernment of God, 20–1
  process of, 196, 204n.8
  result of facing problems intrinsic to theology, 17–18
Spiritual Friendship, 121
spiritual life
  active vs. contemplative, 323
  contemplation of God through nature, 330–1
  God as means and end of, 181
  as a journey, 322–6
  need for perseverance, 326
  practice of, 308
  qualities of, 327
  repentance and forgiveness, 197
  stages of, 322–3
Stannard, Russell, 46
Steinmetz, David, 230
Stek, John, 250–1
Stoeger, William, 48
suffering, 170, 176
Suger, Abbot of St. Denis, 280, 288–9, 296–7
Summa contra Gentiles, 35–6, 46
Summa Theologiae, 29, 35–6, 42, 46
supernatural charity, 110, 127
systematic theology, xxiv–xxvi

teaching by connection, 151, 155n.7
teleological proofs
  see proofs for existence of God
temptation, 320–1
Theodore of Studios, St., 280, 296
theologia, 323
theology, applied, xxiv
theology, Christian

academic study, 16–17, 19
  as conversation, xvi–xvii
  cultural influences on, 27–8
  definition, xvii
  intellectual and spiritual inquiry, 22
  need for personal involvement, 19–20
  questions extrinsic to theology, 25–6
  as religious practice, xxi, xxii–xxiii, xxvii–xxviii
  religious purpose of, xviii
  secular study of, xix
  and spiritual formation, 17–21
  see also apologetics; dogmatic theology; method, theological; process theology; systematic theology; theology, applied
Thomas Aquinas, St., 29, 41, 46, 95, 98
  "five ways" proof for existence of God, 29, 32–5, 42
thought vs. action, xxviii
Tillich, Paul, 295
Tinder, Glenn, 122
Touching, 147
touching, nonerotic, 135, 147
transformation, spiritual, 198, 203
Trinity, doctrine of the, 2–3, 24–5, 274–5, 311
  for Catherine of Siena, 183
  in *Ironwood*, 130
  for Julian of Norwich, 57, 65
  in Lord's Prayer, 314
  as seen by Bonaventure, 11–15
  as self–diffusion of God, 23

union with God, 65–7, 334
  ecstasy of union, 186–7
  see also God, spiritual marriage to
universe *see* cosmology; creation

Valerius, 222
Vander Leeuw, Gerardus, 295
Vatican Council II, 86, 88, 99
Veritatis Splendor, 197
virtue, human, 160–1, 164
vow, 313

Waite, Arthur Edward, 66
Wallace, Ronald S., 125
watchfulness *see nepsis*
Watts, Isaac, 281, 291, 293–4
wealth, 85, 157, 164–5, 167–8
Weil, Simone, 82, 124–5, 127
Wesley, John, 96
Westphal, Merold, 252
White, Reginald, 95
Wittgenstein, Ludwig, 18
women, status in early church, 179–81
work
  biblical view, 91–3
  Christian duty, 83, 100
  collaboration with God, 97–8

  continuation of crucifixion, 88
  definition, 89–90
  divine support for, 84
  extension of God's work, 82, 87
  in Kingdom of God, 101
  penance for sins, 101
  promotes human virtues, 104–5
  promoting human virtues, 94
  spirituality of, 86
World Council of Churches, 258

yearning for God, 3

Zechariah, 331
Zwingli, Ulrich, 258